Lecture Notes in Computer Science 9229

Commenced Publication in 1973
Founding and Former Series Editors:
Gerhard Goos, Juris Hartmanis, and Jan van Leeuwen

More information about this series at http://www.springer.com/series/7410

Mauro Conti · Matthias Schunter
Ioannis Askoxylakis (Eds.)

Trust and Trustworthy Computing

8th International Conference, TRUST 2015
Heraklion, Greece, August 24–26, 2015
Proceedings

 Springer

Editors
Mauro Conti
University of Padua
Padua
Italy

Matthias Schunter
Intel Labs
Darmstadt
Germany

Ioannis Askoxylakis
Hellas (FORTH), Crete
Institute of Computer Science (ICS),
    Foundation for Research and Technology
Heraklion
Greece

ISSN 0302-9743   ISSN 1611-3349   (electronic)
Lecture Notes in Computer Science
ISBN 978-3-319-22845-7   ISBN 978-3-319-22846-4   (eBook)
DOI 10.1007/978-3-319-22846-4

Library of Congress Control Number: 2015946077

LNCS Sublibrary: SL4 – Security and Cryptology

Printed on acid-free paper

Springer International Publishing AG Switzerland is part of Springer Science+Business Media
(www.springer.com)

Preface

This volume contains the proceedings of the 8th International Conference on Trust and Trustworthy Computing (TRUST), held in Heraklion, Crete, Greece, during August 24–26, 2015. TRUST 2015 is hosted by the Institute of Computer Science of the Foundation for Research and Technology-Hellas (FORTH), Greece, and it is sponsored by Trusted Computing Group, Intel, and Microsoft.

Continuing the tradition of the previous conferences, held in Villach (2008), Oxford (2009), Berlin (2010), Pittsburgh (2011), Vienna (2012), London (2013), and Heraklion (2014), TRUST 2015 provided a unique interdisciplinary forum for researchers, practitioners, and decision makers to explore new ideas and discuss experiences in building, designing, using, and understanding trustworthy computing systems.

The conference program of TRUST 2015 shows that research in trust and trustworthy computing is active, at a high level of competency, and spans a wide range of areas and topics. Papers dealt, for example, with topics such as a largescale security analysis of the Web, trust in cryptocurrency protocols, physically unclonable functions, security aspects of mobile systems, security considerations of TPM 2.0, and privacy aspects of trust.

We received 42 submissions in response to the Call for Papers. All submissions were carefully reviewed by at least three Program Committee members or external experts according to the criteria of scientific novelty, importance to the field, and technical quality. After an online discussion of all reviews, 15 papers were selected for presentation and publication in the conference proceedings. This amounts to an acceptance rate of 35.7 %, for full papers. We also accepted three short papers, and encouraged people to report on work in progress by submitting two-page poster abstracts describing ongoing research. A panel of experts reviewed the submitted abstracts. Seven of these abstracts were selected to be included in these conference proceedings. We hope that these abstracts will convey a sense of the vibrancy and current themes of research in trusted and trustworthy computing. The authors of these abstracts also presented posters of their work at the conference. Furthermore, the conference program contained several keynotes by leaders in academia, industry, and government agencies.

We would like to express our gratitude to those people without whom TRUST 2015 would not have been this successful, and whom we mention now in no particular order: the publicity chair Manolis Stamatogiannakis, the members of the Steering Committee (where Ahmad-Reza Sadeghi deserves a special mention for his continued and valuable advice during the preparation of this conference), the local Organizing Committee, the keynote speakers, and the people that supported the editing of the proceedings (Ann-Kathrin Braun and Ahmad Ibrahim). We also want to thank all Program Committee members and their external reviewers; their hard work made sure that the scientific program was of high quality and reflected both the depth and diversity of research in this area. Our special thanks go to all those who submitted papers, and to all those who presented posters and papers at the conference.

August 2015

Mauro Conti
Matthias Schunter
Ioannis Askoxylakis

Organization

TRUST 2015 was organized by the Institute of Computer Science of the Foundation for Research and Technology-Hellas (FORTH), Greece.

Steering Committee

Alessandro Acquisti	Carnegie Mellon University, USA
Boris Balacheff	Hewlett Packard, UK
Paul England	Microsoft, USA
Michael Huth	Imperial College London, UK
Andrew Martin	University of Oxford, UK
Chris Mitchel	Royal Holloway, University of London, UK
Sean Smith	Dartmouth College, USA
Ahmad-Reza Sadeghi	TU Darmstadt/CASED, Germany
Claire Vishik	Intel, UK

General Chair

Ioannis Askoxylakis	FORTH, Greece

Program Chairs

Mauro Conti	University of Padua, Italy
Matthias Schunter	Intel Labs, Germany

Publicity Chair

Manolis Stamatogiannakis	Vrije Universiteit Amsterdam, The Netherlands

Local Organizing Committee

Nikolaos Petroulakis	FORTH, Greece
Panos Chatziadam	FORTH, Greece
Theodosia Bitzou	FORTH, Greece

Program Committee

Giulio Aliberti	Università degli Studi Roma 3, Italy
Magnus Almgren	Chalmers University of Technology, Sweden
Elias Athanasopoulos	FORTH, Greece
Liqun Chen	Hewlett-Packard Laboratories, UK
Manuel Costa	Microsoft Research, UK
Francesco Di Cerbo	SAP Research Sophia-Antipolis, France

Xuhua Ding	Singapore Management University, Singapore
Sascha Fahl	Leibniz University Hannover, Germany
Michael Franz	University of California, Irvine, USA
Peter Gutmann	University of Auckland, New Zealand
Sotiris Ioannidis	FORTH, Greece
Limin Jia	Carnegie Mellon University, USA
Rüdiger Kapitza	TU Braunschweig, Germany
Ghassan Karame	NEC Laboratories Europe, Germany
Stefan Katzenbeisser	TU Darmstadt, Germany
Michael Locasto	University of Calgary, Canada
Federico Maggi	Politecnico di Milano, Italy
Mohammad Mannan	Concordia University, Canada
Jonathan McCune	Google, USA
Aziz Mohaisen	Verisign Labs, USA
Sachar Paulus	Hochschule Mannheim, Germany
Marcus Peinado	Microsoft Research, USA
Milan Petkovic	Philips Research Laboratories, The Netherlands
Christina Pöpper	Ruhr University Bochum, Germany
Vassilis Prevelakis	TU Braunschweig, Germany
Steffen Schulz	Intel Labs, Germany
Sean Smith	Dartmouth College, USA
Manolis Stamatogiannakis	Vrije Universiteit Amsterdam, The Netherlands

Contents

Hardware-Enhanced Trusted Execution

PUF-Based Software Protection for Low-End Embedded Devices

Florian Kohnhäuser(✉), André Schaller, and Stefan Katzenbeisser

Security Engineering Group, TU Darmstadt, Darmstadt, Germany
{Kohnhauser,Schaller,Katzenbeisser}@seceng.informatik.tu-darmstadt.de
http://www.seceng.de/

Abstract. In recent years, low-end embedded devices have been used increasingly in various scenarios, ranging from consumer electronics to industrial equipment. However, this evolution made embedded devices profitable targets for software piracy and software manipulation. Aggravating this situation, low-end embedded devices typically lack secure hardware to effectively protect against such attacks. In this work, we present a novel software protection scheme, which is particularly suited for already deployed low-end embedded devices without secure hardware. Our approach combines techniques based on self-checksumming code with Physically Unclonable Functions (PUFs) to establish a hardware-assisted software protection. In this way, we can tie the execution of a software instance to a specific device and protect its program code against manipulations. We show that our software protection scheme offers a high level of security against static adversaries and demonstrate that dynamic adversaries require considerable resources to perform a successful attack. To explore the feasibility of our solution, we implemented the protection scheme on an ARM-based low-end commodity microcontroller. A further performance evaluation shows that the implemented solution exhibits a fair overhead of ten percent.

1 Introduction

In recent years, the Internet of Things (IoT) [2] became one of the biggest buzzwords in the technology industry. With the IoT, billions of smart, interconnected embedded systems are proliferating virtually every aspect of our life. Nowadays, those devices can already be found in many everyday-life objects, such as consumer electronics, mobile devices, cars, smart-meters, or home appliances. On top of that, low-end embedded devices are widely used in industrial automation environments. However, the fact that embedded systems are increasingly deployed and typically lack effective security mechanisms aroused the interest of hackers, who started to realize that embedded devices are profitable targets. In practice, there are many attack scenarios on embedded devices.

One of the most tempting scenarios is the illegitimate reproduction of embedded systems, where an adversary reproduces existing devices by copying their firmware to counterfeit, cheaper hardware. Selling those cloned devices, adversaries cause financial loss for the manufacturer of the original system. In 2005,

© Springer International Publishing Switzerland 2015
M. Conti et al. (Eds.): TRUST 2015, LNCS 9229, pp. 3–21, 2015.
DOI: 10.1007/978-3-319-22846-4_1

KPMG estimated the sales lost to counterfeiters for fake electronic goods at 100 billion dollars [17]. Another attack scenario is the removal of license checking code, also referred to as software cracking. As an example, the attacker's mobile device may contain an application which requires a license. Instead of purchasing a license, the attacker bypasses the license check by manipulating the software. A further scenario is the play-back of Digital Rights Management (DRM) pro-tected media on hardware media players, such as TV streaming devices. An attacker might insert code in the decryption function of the DRM player to intercept and extract the decrypted media. A famous example is the bypass of the DVD DRM encryption system CSS [26].

In order to protect against such attacks, the execution of the software must both be tied to a particular device and be secured against manipulations. To realize an effective hardware-software binding, hardware support is required. With hardware support, the security of a protected program rests on a secret, e.g., a cryptographic key or a piece of code implemented in a physical module. Prominent examples are the Trusted Platform Module (TPM), USB dongles, and cryptographic coprocessors. Nevertheless, integrated circuits dedicated to security are complex in their design, provoke deployment issues, occupy addi-tional space on the underlying board, and lead to higher production costs. For this reason, especially legacy or low-end embedded devices lack hardware secu-rity mechanisms. However, as these devices are widely deployed and increasingly become the target of attacks [25], there is the need for a security solution that requires no specifically designed hardware.

1.1   Contributions

In this work, we explore a novel software protection approach, which is particularly suited for low-end embedded devices. Our approach combines and extends a self-checksumming code technique [15] with SRAM PUFs in commodity hardware [24] to protect a program against modifications and tie its execution to a dedicated device. Due to the usage of an intrinsic PUF as a secure key storage, our approach does not require any hardware modifications and thus can be easily retrofitted to already deployed devices. Furthermore, relying on a PUF significantly decreases the attack surface, as the secret is stored involving the PUF's physical properties. This makes physical attacks much more complicated compared to solutions based on non-volatile memory [1]. In order to explore the applicability of our solution, we implemented the proposed scheme on a low-cost ARM Cortex microcontroller. Various security parameters allow for a balancing between security and perfor-mance. Finally, a security and performance evaluation reveals that we achieve a substantial level of security with a performance penalty of ten percent.

1.2   Structure

In Sect. 2 we introduce PUFs and summarize existing work on tamper-resistant software. Section 3 presents our software protection solution. In Sect. 4 we evaluate the security of our approach. Section 5 depicts our implementation and evaluates its performance. Eventually, Sect. 6 concludes this work.

2 Related Work

Physically Unclonable Functions. Physically Unclonable Functions (PUFs) are physical objects that exhibit unique physical microstructures induced by manufacturing process variations. When a PUF is queried with a stimulus (challenge), it generates an unpredictable but repeatable response, which depends on the challenge and the PUF's physical structure. Typically, a PUF is assumed to exhibit characteristics of robustness, unclonability, unpredictability and tamper-evidence [22] (see Sect. 5.1). There exist various PUF implementations, ranging from optical and analogue PUFs to electronic PUFs [22]. The most significant PUFs for electronic circuits are delay- and memory-based PUFs. The former, e.g., arbiter PUFs or ring oscillator PUFs, utilize delays in their electronic circuits to generate the response. Memory-based PUFs exploit metastable states of digital memory primitives, such as SRAM or flip-flops, whose cells show a tendency to either initialize with the value zero or one. As not all memory bits show a stable initialization behavior, those bits introduce noise, which needs to be taken care of. For this purpose, Fuzzy Extractors are applied that remove the noise effect, which enables a robust reconstruction of an identifier [11].

Software Integrity Protection. Software integrity protection techniques deter attackers from modifying a particular software. They prevent adversaries from performing unauthorized actions, such as skipping a license check or playing a DRM-protected media file without the correct key.

Self-checksumming code is a common approach to protect a program against tampering [3,7,15]. The idea behind this concept is to equip a program with the functionality to verify its own integrity at runtime by calculating checksums for parts of its code. After a checksum is computed, it is compared to a pre-computed reference checksum, indicating if the checked code has been tampered with. In this case a tamper-response (e.g., program termination) is initiated.

Oblivious hashing techniques pursue another approach. Instead of verifying parts of the program's machine-code, oblivious hashing mechanisms compute a hash value over the program's execution trace. In order to verify the program integrity, this hash value is then compared to a reference value. Typically, the hash value is computed over assignments and execution branches. Thus, instructions that monitor changes to variables and control flow are interweaved with the original code [8,16].

Result checking is a simple mechanism where, instead of verifying the program's code integrity, the result of certain computational operations is verified [5]. Checking the outcome of a computation can be considerably faster than performing the computation itself. For instance, a general sorting computation has order of $\mathcal{O}(n \cdot log(n))$ time complexity, whereas validating a sorted sequence takes $\mathcal{O}(n)$ time.

PUF-Based Software Protection. Gora, Maiti and Schaumont [12] proposed a system that implements a PUF instance on an FPGA to protect software and bind it to one hardware instance. At device start, they derive an 128-bit AES key from the PUF, utilize this key to decrypt the actual software code that was stored encrypted beforehand, and finally execute the decrypted software.

In a similar work of Schaller et al. [24], the authors presented an anti-counterfeiting solution which exploits inherent PUF characteristics from on-chip static random-access memory (SRAM) found in commodity devices. The authors propose to extract a unique device-dependent key from the SRAM PUF found in commodity devices. Using this key, the second-stage bootloader as well as the kernel of the device is decrypted during device start-up.

Nithyanand and Solis [23] show that traditional PUFs cannot solve the software protection problem in offline settings because they are vulnerable to *observe once, run everywhere* (OORE) attacks. To solve this problem, the authors propose the use of *intrinsic personal PUFs* (IP-PUFs). IP-PUFs are PUFs that are intrinsically and continuously involved in the computation of the program to be protected. In their proposed system, an IP-PUF computes the ordering of nodes in the control flow graph and enforces a random permutation of those nodes.

In summary, there are existing approaches that allow software to be integrity protected and tied to one device using PUFs. However, the security level existing solutions provide is comparatively low, since an adversary can dump the decrypted software at runtime. Once the adversary is in possession of the decrypted software, he can modify it or run it on other devices. By contrast, this work pursues a different approach, where self-checksumming code is combined with PUF responses to additionally provide security against attacks at runtime. Furthermore, the developed solution does not require any hardware modifications, which allows the deployment on commodity or legacy devices.

3   PUF-Based Software Protection Solution

Our software protection solution consists of four basic mechanisms: two *check* and two *response* functions. Check functions measure the authenticity of the device and the integrity of the program. Response functions read these measurements, decide whether they indicate a healthy or a manipulated state, and initiate a program misbehavior if a manipulation has been detected. In order to protect a software with our protection scheme, both functions are repeatedly integrated into the software's program code.

In more detail, the first check function measures the integrity of the software by hashing its native program code (see Sect. 3.1). The second check function computes a unique bitstream on the basis of a device-dependent SRAM PUF response to measure the authenticity of the device (see Sect. 3.2). If those two measurements indicate a manipulated state, the first response function redirects branches to random locations in the program text segment and the second response function corrupts the program's execution stack (see Sect. 3.3). Hence, if the program or the execution environment has been manipulated, both response functions cause a malfunction of the program.

3.1 Code Integrity Check

Principles. The integrity of the executable is measured by multiple self-check-summing code segments at runtime. Each segment consists of a hash function which computes a hash value over a predefined section in the program's text segment. The hash value represents the integrity status of the checked section. It is later used by response functions to decide whether the program has been tampered with. Depending on the spatial separation of the hash function and the response function, a hash value is either stored in a register or on the stack.

For stealth and security reasons, each hash function is inlined in the code, preferably with some spatial separation to other hash functions, and gets executed as the control flow passes the code location where the hash function is inserted. It is desirable that each inserted hash function is executed at least once at runtime, but not so frequently that the protected program suffers from a huge runtime overhead. In practice, profiling tools can be utilized to identify suitable code locations. We propose to let multiple hash functions measure a contiguous and relatively small part of the program. Thus, each integrity measurement consumes only little time. In addition, the effort for an attacker to remove the software protection increases.

In order to increase the effort even more, each code segment is measured multiple times by different hash functions. The so-called *overlap factor* indicates how often a code section is checked by different hash functions. Its value must be well-chosen to achieve a balance between security and performance according to the application scenario. To avoid that hash functions suspiciously measure large parts of the program, we recommend to split the program code in sections of equal size. These code regions are then uniformly assigned to hash functions till the overlap factor for each code region is saturated.

Hash Function Design. The design of our hash function is based on the work by Horne et al. [15]. With $d = [d_1, ..., d_n]$ being data in a code section which is protected by a hash function h, c being an odd multiplier constant, and $h_i(d)$ being the hash value in iteration i, our hash function can formally be defined as:

$$h_i(d) = \begin{cases} 0, & i = 1 \\ h_{i-1}(d) + c \cdot d_i. & 1 < i \leq n \end{cases} \tag{1}$$

We deviated from Horne's approach by not multiplying $h_{i-1}(d)$ with c in each iteration. This allows us to construct arbitrary complex mutually checking code regions (see Sect. 3.4). One reason we build on the code integrity check by Horne et al. is the hash function's size and speed. A large and slow hash function would fairly expand program size as well as runtime overhead, since the hash function is inlined frequently into the original program. However, the most important reason is stealth. An attacker who can locate all hash functions is able to break the code integrity check, for instance, by overwriting hash functions with code that always writes the respective expected hash value in memory. The proposed hash function neither contains any suspicious operations nor provides any characteristic pattern. In addition, its implementation in native program code can easily be diversified. Thus, each hash function can be customized, leaving the attacker no weak point for pattern matching attacks (see Sect. 4.1).

In order to customize hash functions, the odd constant c can be randomized, the addition can be replaced by a subtraction or an XOR operation, or a further constant can be added or subtracted after the multiplication with c. In addition, the hash function's implementation in native program code can be diversified, among others, by permuting the instruction order, permuting the assignment of variables to CPU registers, or diversifying particular instructions. A further possibility is to split the hash function code into multiple segments which are inserted with spatial separation in the original program code. With these techniques, it is straightforward to generate multiple million different hash function implementations.

Another attack vector is the code read operation performed by the hash function. It allows an attacker to find the location of hash functions by searching the code for addresses within the text segment, or observing if and where certain registers obtain values within the text segment at runtime. To mitigate this threat, we propose to implement Horne's memory access obfuscation approach [15] which uses an additional offset when addressing data in the program text segment (e.g., with the instruction LDR Rd, [Rn, Rm] on ARM-based platforms). In this way, text section addresses neither appear in the code nor in a register at runtime.

3.2   Device Authenticity Check

Principles. Recent work by Schaller et al. [24] have shown that SRAM modules present in several microcontrollers can be used as a PUF instance. In the device authenticity check mechanism, we use the microcontroller's SRAM PUF start-up values to compute a device-dependent bitstream. Since the SRAM PUF is unique and highly integrated in the microcontroller, the bitstream is unique for each embedded device. For these reasons, our response functions utilize the bitstream to authenticate the device at runtime.

The code for the bitstream generation is inserted into the device's bootloader. Hence, the bitstream is generated each time the device is starting up. In particular, a pseudorandom number generator (PRNG) is applied to allow for a variable bitstream length. In this way, a tradeoff between performance and security can be achieved. A larger bitstream takes more time to compute at device start-up but provides more unique values that can later be verified by response functions. Alternatively, it would be possible to gradually create the bitstream during program execution. However, as this further increases the execution overhead, we decided to precompute the entire bitstream in advance.

PRNG Bitstream Generation. Generating the PRNG bitstream comprises an enrollment and a reconstruction phase. The enrollment phase is performed at a trusted site, e.g., by the software integrator, and involves taking a reference

PUF measurement and equipping the device's bootloader with code and helper data to reconstruct a unique and reliable bitstream. During reconstruction, which is performed after deployment at the side of the user, the equipped bootloader is executed. Thus, the actual bitstream is generated using the PUF start-up values and additional error correction methods. To correct the raw PUF start-up values from noise, they are processed by error correction mechanisms. For this purpose, we integrate a Fuzzy Extractor (FE) based on the design by Bösch et al. [6] in the bootloader. The techniques used in the following to restore a predefined secret from SRAM cells are based on the work by Schaller et al. [24].

The *enrollment phase* is performed during the deployment of our software protection scheme once for each device. Initially, a unique random secret S is chosen. Using the FE with a reference PUF measurement and the secret S as input, so-called Helper Data is generated and stored on the device. The Helper Data is required in the reconstruction phase to retrieve S from a single noisy PUF measurement. Afterwards, the length for the PRNG bitstream is set, balancing security, speed, and storage consumption for the particular device and use case. At last, it is set at which location the bitstream is stored in memory during the reconstruction phase.

The *reconstruction phase* is executed each time the device is started. Initially, the bootscript measures and stores the noisy SRAM PUF values R'. Next, the FE reconstructs a secret S' using the current PUF measurement R' and the stored Helper Data as input. If the PUF measurement R' corresponds to the respective Helper Data, the reconstructed secret S' will match the original secret S. S' is then used to initialize the PRNG which finally generates a PRNG bitstream of the set length in memory.

3.3 Response Functions

Principles. Before a response function is inserted into the code, it is randomly selected whether the response function verifies a hash value, a value of the PRNG bitstream, or both values at once. If a response function verifies a hash value, it uses the hash value of the nearest preceding hash function. This ensures that hash values are verified shortly after they are measured, thwarting code manipulations promptly after they have been detected. If a response function verifies a value of the PRNG bitstream, it uses a random preferably nonrecurring bitstream value. The basic idea is to use a unique address in each PRNG bitstream access. Thus, a single address cannot be used as an attack vector for pattern matching attacks or as a watchpoint in dynamic analyses. However, if there are less PRNG bitstream values than deployed response functions available, some addresses must be used multiple times.

The overall goal of our two response functions is to provoke a malfunction of the protected program if the measured code integrity or device authenticity values are invalid. We would like to point out that a malfunction of the program may lead to a damage of the machine that is controlled by the program. However, the alternative to perform a deterministic action (e.g., a controlled program shutdown) would provide an easy attack vector for the adversary. In this scenario, the adversary could simply observe where the program shutdown is initiated, to locate the response functions in the code.

Indirect Branch Response. The indirect branch response is applicable on any branch in the program. When applied, an original branch is converted to an indirect branch whose target address is dependent on the verified values, i.e., either on a hash value, on a value of the PRNG bitstream, or on both values. The exact target address of the indirect branch is determined by a computation which meets the following requirements.

The output of the computation must equal the target address of the replaced original branch if the verified values correspond to their expected values. If at least one of the verified values is corrupted, the outcome of the computation must be a random address that lies within the program text segment. The latter requirement ensures that the computed target address is always a valid instruction that can be executed. If the computation of the target address would not generate a valid address in the text segment, program manipulations would immediately cause memory access violations. This would be very suspicious and allows the attacker to easily locate the response function with backtraces.

In practice, the behavior of the indirect branch tamper response is highly dependent on the program size and the structure of the program code (e.g., the number of functions in the program). We observed, on average, about two function calls until a memory access violation occurred after the indirect branch response was executed.

As an additional requirement, the computation of the target address must be simple. In order to improve stealth, its implementation should be short and should not contain unusual instructions. To improve stealth even more, each deployment of the indirect branch response function should be customized, for instance, with the techniques presented in Sect. 3.1.

Stack Manipulation Response. In contrast to the indirect branch response, the stack manipulation response can be deployed at arbitrary locations in the program code. When deployed, we propose to use one stack manipulation response per hash function to ensure that each code measurement is eventually verified by a response function.

The idea behind the stack manipulation response is to corrupt the execution stack if the verified values are invalid. Hence, in case of an unauthorized modification, local variables, function arguments, register copies, return addresses, and other data that lies on the stack, are altered. As a result, the program continues execution with incorrect values.

A simple way to accomplish a modification of all values on the stack is to shift the stack pointer. Shifting the stack pointer has two benefits. First, it mixes up stack frames, which complicates a backtracing the program. Second, it modifies the return address and thus provokes a program crash when the currently executed function returns. If an eventual program crash as a tamper-response is not desirable, we propose to alter values on the stack directly.

3.4   Mutually Checking Code Regions

Since the presented protection mechanisms secure the entire program code and at the same time are also part of the program code, they secure each other against modifications as well. Although this enhances the security of a protected software, it comes at the cost of emerging circular dependencies in the deployment process. These mutual dependencies occur because at some point code protection measures, consisting of a hash function and a response function which verifies the hash function's value, circularly check each other.

In the work by Horne et al. [15], code regions are assigned to hash functions in a left-to-right pass which generates no mutual dependencies. However, with this approach, the overlap factor is comparatively low at the beginning and the end of the program code. In fact, their overlap factor goes down to a factor of one in the first and last few bytes of the program code. By contrast, we propose a uniform assignment of hash functions to code regions and a subsequent solving of the upcoming circular dependencies. Thus, we can ensure a consistent overlap factor throughout the entire program code.

When solving cyclic checks, the first step is to transform mutually checking code regions into an equation system. For this purpose, we initially deploy all protection mechanisms into the software and build a temporary protected binary. The protected binary contains the final code, except for the response functions' reference values and additional placeholder values. We propose to insert one freely selectable 32-bit placeholder value per code integrity measure to facilitate solving the equation system. Next, we utilize the fact that hash values can be written as the sum of multiple data values. With $d = [d_1, ..., d_r, ..., d_p, ..., d_n]$ being a list of n 32-bit words in a code section, where d_r is a reference value, d_p is a placeholder value, and c being the hash function's multiplier constant, a hash function h which measures this code section on a 32-bit microprocessor can be written as:

$$h(d) \equiv \underbrace{c \cdot d_r + c \cdot d_p}_{l} + \underbrace{\sum_{\substack{i=1 \\ i \neq r \\ i \neq p}}^{n} c \cdot d_i}_{r} \quad (mod\ 2^{32})\ . \tag{2}$$

In this way, hash values are divided in a variable part l, containing the reference value d_r and the additional placeholder value d_p which are to be solved, and a fixed part r, containing the rest of the code segment. Since the code data d_i and the multiplier constant c are fixed after deployment, r can easily be computed. Next, reference values must be expressed in relation to hash values and PRNG bitstream values. The exact dependence between PRNG, hash, and reference value is given by the response function in which the reference value is used. Finally, these relations are combined to one linear Diophantine equation system which is then solved according to the approach of Lazebnik [20].

4   Security Evaluation

Information security mechanisms like cryptographic primitives or secure protocols are commonly designed to be secure in the black-box model. However, we assume a much more challenging scenario where the attacker is in possession of the endpoint devices and thus has access to the implementation and power over the execution environment. This security model is referred to as white-box model [14]. Taking the white-box model as a basis, we specify two attacker models, the *static attacker* and the *dynamic attacker*. We generally expect both attackers to be familiar with our software protection model, albeit we assume that they do not know the particular deployed protection code, the location of the protection code, and aspects of our protection scheme which are randomized at deployment. The following sections specify the attacker models and evaluate the security of our software protection scheme against the respective model.

4.1   Static Attacker Model

Specification. A static attacker has the ability to perform static analysis on a device in his possession, i.e., he can read and modify all the data stored on the device. For instance, the attacker can read and modify the content of the external memory, like the flash memory or the RAM, or the internal memory, including the software with its hard-coded secrets and cryptographic keys. Additionally, we presume that the static attacker can run the program and observe its input-output behavior.

The static attacker model is a reasonable assumption for an experienced attacker who lacks the ability to debug the protected program. This may be the case due to the employment of anti-debugging techniques implemented in software (e.g., the exhaustion of breakpoint registers, or the use of API functions to check if a debugger is present) or in hardware (e.g., the physical removal of debugging ports).

Evaluation. Using a disassembler, a static attacker can analyze native program code and reverse engineer the protected program. In the worst case, the attacker would comprehend the complete code and thereby know how he can circumvent our protection mechanisms. In practice, though, this task is highly laborious, as even a small program consists of a few thousand lines of machine code.

One possibility to accelerate the analysis process is to look for outstanding instructions or specific patterns in the code. In a pattern matching attack, the attacker reveals the location of the protection code by extracting a pattern from found protection mechanisms and then searching the entire program code for that pattern. Therefore, we specifically avoided the use of suspicious operations by performing short and common computations only. The implementation of our hash function requires approximately 30 bytes (48 bytes with code access obfuscation) and the response function between 12 and 18 bytes. Additionally, we demonstrated in Sect. 3 that both mechanisms can easily be diversified repeatedly.

In another technique called collusion or differential attack, an adversary compares multiple versions of a protected program to spot the location of the inserted protection mechanisms in their differences. In order to protect against this attack, we can distribute our protection scheme to many devices with the same deployment preferences. In this way, a collusion attack would only reveal the location of the Helper Data which does not leak any information. A further approach would be to diversify the entire program in the deployment process [18].

A very common technique applied during a static analysis is the examination of the program's execution flow. With the deployment of the indirect branch response function, branches are replaced with indirect branches whose target addresses are dependent on hash values and values of the PRNG bitstream. As both values are not known to a static analysis tool, our approach can significantly reduce the amount of useful information that an attacker can extract from a control flow analysis.

The unpredictability of the PRNG bitstream in offline attacks has an additional advantage. Since both response functions occasionally utilize a value of the PRNG bitstream for their operation, their exact behavior cannot be predicted with static analysis techniques. Furthermore, both response functions can be used to perform essential operations in the program, i.e., branches or stack allocations. As a result, it is hardly possible for a static attacker to remove the hardware-software binding.

4.2   Dynamic Attacker Model

Specification. A dynamic attacker inherits all abilities from the static attacker. Furthermore, the dynamic attacker has the ability to read and modify all the data on a device at runtime. With these abilities, the attacker can interrupt a program at any time, single-step through the program code, and inspect or modify memory values at runtime. Moreover, the attacker has the capability to modify a program's execution environment. He might force the program to use bogus dynamic libraries, altered operating system functionalities, or run the program in a virtual machine.

We are aware that an attacker with the stated abilities and enough resources in time and money is capable of breaking any software security mechanism. Therefore, our goal is to increase the effort for a successful attack to a level where an attack becomes uneconomical.

Evaluation. One of the most powerful debugging features when analyzing a protected program are watchpoints. Watchpoints are used to halt the execution whenever the program accesses predefined memory locations. A dynamic attacker can use this technique to locate a large fraction of all response functions by recurrently setting watchpoints on values of the PRNG bitstream while executing the program with various input. In addition, by setting watchpoints on addresses within the program text segment, the attacker can locate hash functions. A subsequent tracing of the hash functions' hash values can reveal the location of all remaining response functions. Having located all response functions, the attacker can remove the verification of hash and PRNG bitstream values and thus disable our software protection. Although the described approach is eventually successful, it requires a significant amount of effort from an attacker. Furthermore, the effort can be arbitrarily augmented by increasing the number of hash functions, setting a higher overlap factor, or obfuscating access on hash values and values of the PRNG bitstream.

Another common dynamic analysis technique is tracing. Tracing a program involves logging information during the program's execution, such as the execution path, memory values, or register values. A dynamic attacker may trace back program crashes or abnormal program behavior to localize response functions. During the design of our response functions, we ensured that there is a large spatial and temporal separation between the execution of the response function and its impact on the program, i.e., a program crash or a program misbehavior. Thus, the attacker has to examine a large portion of the trace back to finally localize a single response function.

Profiling is an additional dynamic analysis technique which involves measuring particular runtime performance values. In general, our protection mechanisms do not consume exceptionally much CPU time or memory. But yet, profiling a protected program may reveal the location of deployed hash functions when the execution of a hash function takes exceptionally long time compared to the execution time of the original program. Anyhow, profiling requires about the same effort as the above described approach with watchpoints, as the protected program must be examined multiple times with different input. On top of that, the profiling approach is less reliable than the watchpoint approach, because code that is often run through need not be part of a hash function.

Emulation is a further dynamic analysis technique. An emulator is software which simulates the behavior of a particular hardware platform. With emulation, an adversary can bypass the hardware-software binding by emulating particular PUF start-up values. In addition, an adversary can redirect data access to the unmodified version and code access to the modified version of a protected program, to bypass our code integrity protection. Nevertheless, emulation attacks are unpractical, because the software has to run in an emulator and cannot run directly on the hardware of an embedded system. In addition, the performance is slower, an emulator is hard to implement, and the protected programs PRNG bitstream must be extracted.

With temporary modifications or on-the-fly writes in memory, the attacker modifies a code region before its execution and recovers it to its original form afterwards. If an adversary inserts his modification just before it is executed and restores the original code immediately after the modified code has been executed, we cannot defend against this attack. However, this requires the attacker to permanently attach a debugger to the program, to write a debugger script which performs the attack without manual intervention, and to accept a loss in performance because of multiple code manipulations at runtime.

5 Proof of Concept

In order to explore the applicability of our software protection scheme, we implemented and evaluated it on the Stellaris EK-LM4F120XL microcontroller. The Stellaris board is a low-end embedded system featuring an 80 MHz ARM Cortex-M4F microprocessor. During deployment, the protection mechanisms are inserted into the source code of the program to be protected. Subsequently, the LLVM compiler framework [19] with Clang front-end [10] is used to compile the equipped source code to the final protected binary. For this purpose, we wrote a Python script which controls LLVM, Clang, and additional external tools and libraries to automatically build the protected program. In the following sections we give details on the intrinsic PUF instance of the Stellaris board, the implementation of the protection scheme, and the performance of our implementation.

5.1 PUF Characteristics

Before using a SRAM PUF instance in security critical applications, it is crucial to characterize the SRAM start-up values for constructing an efficient Fuzzy Extractor (FE) and extracting a secret with full entropy. In order to obtain sufficient measurements, we used a hardware setup comprising 15 Stellaris boards. The Stellaris boards were connected to a custom microcontroller, which in turn was connected to our terminal PC. This setup allowed us to repeatedly query each of the boards automatically. In particular, the microcontroller was programmed to toggle an individual device, executing the modified bootloader (see below for details) and sending the SRAM start-up values over UART back to the microcontroller. Subsequently, the measurements were forwarded to the terminal PC, where they were saved and post-processed. Using this setup we generated 1000 measurements per device.

In the following we present numbers for metrics, which are generally used to evaluate the quality of a PUF instance. The *Hamming Weight* (HW) of measurements from the same device indicates a potential bias towards zero or one. This metric provides a first impression on the entropy present in the start-up values. The *Within-Class Hamming distance* (WCHD) indicates the robustness of measurements from a single device. In particular, it shows how many bits were flipped during repeated start-ups and therefore represents the noise level. The *Between-Class Hamming distance* (BCHD) reveals the independence of start-up

Table 1. Metrics from 15 Stellaris boards with 1000 measurements per device.

Metric	Value [%]
Fractional HW (min; max)	43.29; 53.69
Fractional WCHD (max)	5.25
Fractional (avg)	49.33
min-entropy (min)	5.86

values from different devices and thus shows whether the PUF can be used to uniquely identify a given device. Lastly, the *min-entropy* was calculated to quantify the randomness of the start-up values. To do so, we adapted the well-known approach to calculate min-entropy [21], assuming independence between all bits from the start-up pattern [4,9] and each individual bit to be a binary source. In Table 1 numbers for these metrics are shown, attesting that the Stellaris board has almost ideal PUF characteristics.

5.2   Implemented Protection Mechanisms

Hash Function. In Sect. 3 we stated that it is vital for the security of our protection scheme to deploy syntactically different hash functions. In order to have precise control over the hash function's native program code, we inline hash functions as ARM assembler code in the program source code. To avoid the usage of unusual instructions in our ARM assembler version of the hash function, we implemented the hash function in C and compiled it to get an assembly language prototype. A so generated ARM assembly prototype is show in the following code snippet. It hashes a code region from address 0x26c to 0x2ac with the multiplier constant c = 3:

```
1: movs  r1, #0                    // hash = 0
2: movw  r2, 0x26c                 // start = 0x26c
3: movw  r3, 0x2ac                 // end = 0x2ac
4: loop:
5: ldr   r4, [r2], 4               // tmp = data[i], start++
6: add   r4, r4, r4, LSL#1         // tmp = 3*tmp
7: add   r1, r4                    // hash = hash + 3*tmp
8: cmp   r2, r3                    // if (start < end)
9: blt   loop                      // then goto loop
```

PRNG Bitstream Generation. During deployment, we substitute the pre-existing Stellaris bootloader with a modified version that contains our PRNG bitstream generation code. Besides the standard initialization code, the modified bootloader contains code for the extraction of the PUF start-up values, a FE based on the design by Bösch et al. [6], Helper Data to reconstruct a predefined secret, and a PRNG based on the Keccak (SHA-3) implementation of Herrewege et al. [13]. At first, the bootloader extracts 240 bytes of PUF start-up values. For this purpose, we added ASM code to the power-on reset vector, which configures a GPIO to be used as a UART port. In a next step the code iterates over the memory region of the SRAM, putting each byte out over UART. Afterwards, the original code is resumed, relocating the firmware to SRAM and executing it. Next, the FE reconstructs a predefined 128 bit secret using the PUF start-up values and the Helper Data. Here, we reuse Keccak in the privacy amplification phase of the FE. The reconstructed secret is used to initialize the PRNG. We use Keccak as a PRNG, primarily because of its compact size and speed on ARM devices. For the length of the bitstream, we suggest to use 2^{17} bits, which provides

4096 unique values and consumes 16 KiB of memory at runtime. Nevertheless, the bitstream length can be set to an arbitrary value, for instance, to consume less storage.

Indirect Branch Response Function. During deployment, existing branches in the original source code are overwritten with the code of the indirect branch response function. The target address of the indirect branch is computed by the sum of the verified values and a specific offset, modulo a unique value, plus a unique value. The following code snippet in C syntax illustrates an indirect branch to a function, which takes no argument and returns void (e.g., void foo(void)):

```
void (*foo)(void);
foo = ((*hash_value + *puf_prng_value + *offset) % *modulo) + *shift;
foo();
```

If the hash value and the PRNG value match their expected values, *off-set*, *modulo*, and *shift* adjust the indirect branch to match the original target address. In order to provide no constant value as an attack vector for pattern matching attacks, *modulo* and *shift* are randomized between certain bounds in each deployment of the indirect branch response function.

Stack Manipulation Response Function. We insert each stack manipulation response function randomly between the location of the corresponding hash function and the subsequently executed hash function. Our implemented stack manipulation response function sums all values to be verified and checks whether the result is equal to the expected value. If it is not, the stack pointer is either incremented or decremented by a random value between 4 and 24 bytes.

5.3 Performance Evaluation

Due to the lack of open source applications for the Stellaris platform, we developed our own evaluation program. The evaluation program encrypts and decrypts a 16 bytes string using AES 128 bit, sends the plaintext and the cipher-text to the UART port, and measures the amount of CPU cycles consumed from the start to the end of the main function.

For the deployment of our software protection scheme, we used the following security settings. We inserted one code integrity check mechanism in each function of the evaluation program. As 9 of the 11 deployed functions are executed at runtime, we generate a coverage of 82 %. This is a realistic scenario, as a real application will certainly contain functions that are not always executed at runtime (e.g., whose execution depends on specific user input). In addition, we used a PRNG bitstream length of 2^{17} bits, which corresponds to a size of 16 KiB. For the deployment of the response functions, we inserted the stack manipulation response in each circular dependent code region and the indirect branch response in the remaining code.

Runtime Performance. In our runtime evaluation, we deployed the evaluation program with the above mentioned security settings and a variable overlap factor. Figure 1 illustrates the relative average runtime overhead for various overlap factor preferences. The runtime of the original unprotected program is represented with an overlap factor of zero and an overhead factor of one. As the overlap defines how many times a code region is checked by different hash functions, an increasing overlap factor increments the amount of code lines that each hash function has to check. With an overlap factor of nine, each hash function almost checks the complete text segment, which generates an overhead of approximately half of the original runtime. It is evident that such an overhead is not acceptable in most applications. On the other hand, even when each code region is checked by three different hash functions, the runtime overhead is below 5 %. As this slow-down will only be noticed by sensitive users, we can easily recommend an overlap factor of three for a conservative usage.

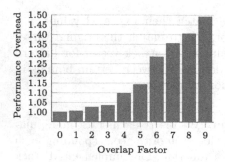
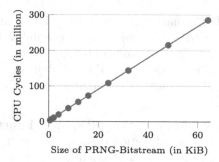

Fig. 1. Runtime performance comparison with different overlap factor settings.

Fig. 2. Start-up runtime performance with varying bitstream size.

Another performance overhead originates from the generation of the PRNG bitstream at device start-up. Figure 2 depicts the amount of CPU cycles that is required to compute a bitstream of a specific length. For comparison, the original program consumes roughly 1.8 million CPU cycles.

The figure illustrates that there is almost a proportional relationship between the size of the PRNG bitstream and the amount of CPU cycles. Thus, compared with the calculation of the pseudorandom values, the extraction of the PUF start-up values and the execution of the Fuzzy Extractor barely uses any CPU time. The figure also shows that the generation of the PRNG bitstream consumes much more CPU resources than the execution of the actual program. However, it must be considered that the PRNG bitstream is only generated at device start-up. Assuming the embedded devices is clocked at 50 MHz, a bitstream size of 16 KiB delays the start of the device by 1.5 s which is likely to be acceptable for most applications.

Storage Consumption. The program size overhead of a protected program is dependent on the number of inserted hash functions, the choice of the response function, and the number of inserted response functions. For evaluation, we deployed our protection mechanisms using the previously mentioned security settings. In this way, we obtained a protected program which was on average 63 % larger than the equivalent unprotected program. Another storage overhead arises at runtime due to the operating of both check mechanisms. However, the hash functions' memory consumption is negligible, as each value resides just a short time in memory and only occupies 4 bytes of storage. In contrast, the values of the PRNG bitstream are kept in memory permanently and they consume 16 KiB of memory for our proposed bitstream length. Nevertheless, by setting another bitstream length, the runtime memory overhead can be adjusted as required.

6 Conclusion

In this work, we explored a novel hardware-assisted software protection approach, which combines existing software-based techniques with PUFs. Using a microcontroller's SRAM as a PUF instance, we overcome the drawbacks of traditional hardware tamper-proofing solutions. Our software protection scheme ties the execution of a software instance to a specific device, protects its program code against manipulations, and can easily be retrofitted to already deployed devices. To demonstrate our approach, we implemented it on a low-cost ARM-based microcontroller. By adjusting certain security parameters, we are able to balance security with performance. We showed that our software protection scheme offers a high level of security against a static adversary and demonstrated that a dynamic adversary requires a considerable amount of resources to perform a successful attack. A further performance evaluation showed that an extensive level of security is achievable with an acceptable performance degradation of ten percent.

References

1. Armknecht, F., Maes, R., Sadeghi, A.-R., Sunar, B., Tuyls, P.: Memory leakage-resilient encryption based on physically unclonable functions. In: Sadeghi, A.-R., Naccache, D. (eds.) Towards Hardware-Intrinsic Security. Information Security and Cryptography, pp. 135–164. Springer, Heidelberg (2010)
2. Atzori, L., Iera, A., Morabito, G.: The internet of things: a survey. Comput. Netw. 54(15), 2787–2805 (2010)
3. Aucsmith, D.: Tamper resistant software: an implementation. In: Anderson, R. (ed.) Information Hiding, vol. 1174, pp. 317–333. Springer, Heidelberg (1996)
4. van den Berg, R., Skoric, B., van der Leest, V.: Bias-based modeling and entropy analysis of PUFs. In: ACM Proceedings of the 3rd International Workshop on Trustworthy Embedded Devices TrustED (2013)
5. Blum, M., Kannan, S.: Designing programs that check their work. J. ACM JACM 42(1), 269–291 (1995)
6. Bösch, C., Guajardo, J., Sadeghi, A.-R., Shokrollahi, J., Tuyls, P.: Efficient helper data key extractor on FPGAs. In: Oswald, E., Rohatgi, P. (eds.) CHES 2008. LNCS, vol. 5154, pp. 181–197. Springer, Heidelberg (2008)

7. Chang, H., Atallah, M.J.: Protecting software code by guards. In: Sander, T. (ed.) DRM 2001. LNCS, vol. 2320, pp. 160–175. Springer, Heidelberg (2002)
8. Chen, Y., Venkatesan, R., Cary, M., Pang, R., Sinha, S., Jakubowski, M.H.: Oblivious hashing a stealthy software integrity verification primitive. In: Petit-colas, F.A.P. (ed.) Information Hiding. LNCS, vol. 2578, pp. 400–414. Springer, Heidelberg (2003)
9. Claes, M., van der Leest, V., Braeken, A.: Comparison of SRAM and FF PUF in 65nm technology. In: Laud, P. (ed.) NordSec 2011. LNCS, vol. 7161, pp. 47–64. Springer, Heidelberg (2012)
10. Clang: A C language family frontend for LLVM. http://www.clang.llvm.org/
11. Dodis, Y., Reyzin, L., Smith, A.: Fuzzy extractors: how to generate strong keys from biometrics and other noisy data. In: Cachin, C., Camenisch, J.L. (eds.) EUROCRYPT 2004. LNCS, vol. 3027, pp. 523–540. Springer, Heidelberg (2004)
12. Gora, M.A., Maiti, A., Schaumont, P.: A flexible design flow for software IP binding in commodity FPGA. In: IEEE Symposium on Industrial Embedded Systems IEEE SIES (2009)
13. van Herrewege, A., Verbauwhede, I.: Software only, extremely compact, keccak-based secure PRNG on ARM Cortex-M. In: ACM Proceedings of the 51st Annual Design Automation Conference (2014)
14. Herzberg, A., Shulman, H., Saxena, A., Crispo, B.: Towards a theory of white-box security. In: Gritzalis, D., Lopez, J. (eds.) SEC 2009. IFIP AICT, vol. 297, pp. 342–352. Springer, Heidelberg (2009)
15. Horne, B., Matheson, L., Sheehan, C., Tarjan, R.E.: Dynamic self-checking tech-niques for improved tamper resistance. In: Sander, T. (ed.) DRM 2001. LNCS, vol. 2320, pp. 141–159. Springer, Heidelberg (2002)
16. Jacob, M., Jakubowski, M.H., Venkatesan, R.: Towards integral binary execution: implementing oblivious hashing using overlapped instruction encodings. In: ACM Workshop on Multimedia & Security MM&Sec (2007)
17. KPMG: Managing the Risks of Counterfeiting in the Information Technol-ogy Industry. http://www.agmaglobal.org/press_events/press_docs/Counterfeit_WhitePaper_Final.pdf. Accessed 23 June 2015
18. Larsen, P., Homescu, A., Brunthaler, S., Franz, M.: SoK: automated software diver-sity. In: IEEE Symposium on Security and Privacy S&P (2014)
19. Lattner, C., Adve, V.: LLVM: a compilation framework for lifelong program analy-sis & transformation. In: IEEE Symposium on Code Generation and Optimization (2014)
20. Lazebnik, F.: On systems of linear diophantine equations. In: Mathematics Maga-zine (1996)
21. van der Leest, V., van der Sluis, E., Schrijen, G.-J., Tuyls, P., Handschuh, H.: Efficient implementation of true random number generator based on SRAM PUFs. In: Naccache, D. (ed.) Cryphtography and Security: From Theory to Applications. LNCS, vol. 6805, pp. 300–318. Springer, Heidelberg (2012)
22. Maes, R., Verbauwhede, I.: Physically unclonable functions: a study on the state of the art and future research directions. In: Sadeghi, A.-R., Naccache, D. (eds.) Towards Hardware-Intrinsic Security, pp. 3–37. Springer, Heidelberg (2010)
23. Nithyanand, R., Solis, J.: A theoretical analysis: physical unclonable functions and the software protection problem. In: IEEE Symposium on Security and Privacy S&P (2012)

24. Schaller, A., Arul, T., van der Leest, V., Katzenbeisser, S.: Lightweight anti-counterfeiting solution for low-end commodity hardware using inherent PUFs. In: Holz, T., Ioannidis, S. (eds.) Trust 2014. LNCS, vol. 8564, pp. 83–100. Springer, Heidelberg (2014)
25. Schneier on Security: Security Risks of Embedded Systems. https://www.schneier.com/blog/archives/2014/01/security_risks_9.html. Accessed 23 June 2015
26. Wikipedia: DeCSS. http://www.en.wikipedia.org/wiki/DeCSS. Accessed 23 June 2015

Why Attackers Win: On the Learnability of XOR Arbiter PUFs

Fatemeh Ganji$^{(\boxtimes)}$, Shahin Tajik, and Jean-Pierre Seifert

Security in Telecommunications, Technische Universität Berlin
and Telekom Innovation Laboratories, Berlin, Germany
{fganji,stajik,jpseifert}@sec.t-labs.tu-berlin.de

Abstract. Aiming to find an ultimate solution to the problem of secure storage and hardware authentication, Physically Unclonable Functions (PUFs) appear to be promising primitives. While arbiter PUFs utilized in cryptographic protocols are becoming one of the most popular PUF instances, their vulnerabilities to Machine Learning (ML) attacks have been observed earlier. These attacks, as cost-effective approaches, can clone the challenge-response behavior of an arbiter PUF by collecting a subset of challenge-response pairs (CRPs). As a countermeasure against this type of attacks, PUF manufacturers shifted their focus to non-linear architectures, such as XOR arbiter PUFs with a large number of arbiter PUF chains. However, the natural question arises whether an XOR arbiter PUF with an arbitrarily large number of parallel arbiter chains can be considered secure. On the other hand, even if a mature ML approach with a significantly high accuracy is adopted, the eventual delivery of a model for an XOR arbiter PUF should be ensured. To address these issues, this paper presents a respective PAC learning framework. Regarding our framework, we are able to establish a theoretical limit on the number of arbiter chains, where an XOR arbiter PUF can be learned in polynomial time, with given levels of *accuracy* and *confidence*. In addition, we state how an XOR arbiter PUF with noisy responses can be provably PAC learned. Finally, on the basis of learning theory concepts, we conclude that no secure XOR arbiter PUF relying on current IC technologies can be manufactured.

1 Introduction

An increasing demand for secure storage of encryption mechanisms as well as hardware fingerprinting stimulates research on possible solutions. Techniques depending on storing a secret key in non-volatile memory (NVM) have been shown to be subject to physical attacks [12]. Other methods relying on the implementation of cryptographic primitives are less practical due to the constraints of the IC technology [5]. To deal with the above-mentioned issues, Physically Unclonable Functions (PUFs) have been introduced [8,20]. From a general point of view, the security-related functionality of PUFs, more specifically their challenge-response behavior, is offered by the manufacturing variations of an IC. One of the most celebrated types of PUF instances are arbiter PUFs, which

© Springer International Publishing Switzerland 2015
M. Conti et al. (Eds.): TRUST 2015, LNCS 9229, pp. 22–39, 2015.
DOI: 10.1007/978-3-319-22846-4_2

are widely utilized in several different cryptographic protocols [5,13,17]. The challenge-response behavior of an arbiter PUF is characterized by slightly different propagation delays of identical paths, caused by chip imperfections. These slight differences are further exploited to generate unique responses.

While authentication and fingerprinting methods enjoying this privilege have been emerging, it has been demonstrated that arbiter PUFs are vulnerable to different types of attacks. Different ML techniques contribute to the success of non-invasive ML attacks against arbiter PUFs [13]. Aiming at mathematically *cloning* an arbiter PUF, the attacker collects a set of challenge-response pairs (CRPs), and *attempts* to provide a model that can *approximately* predict the response of the PUF to an arbitrarily chosen challenge. Most of the ML attacks benefit from the linear additive model of an arbiter PUF. This forces a migration to modified structures of arbiter PUFs, in which non-linear effects are added to the PUF in order to impair the effectiveness of ML attacks. To this end, XORing the responses of multiple arbiter PUFs has been demonstrated as a promising solution [28].

However, it has been shown that more advanced ML techniques can still break the security of an XOR arbiter PUF (briefly called XOR PUF in this paper) with a limited number of arbiter chains (here called chains) [23]. Going beyond this limited number is suggested as a countermeasure by PUF manufacturers, although they have encountered serious problems, namely the increasing number of noisy responses as well as optimization of the silicon area required on the respective chip [21]. Even in this case, physical side-channel attacks, such as photonic emission analysis, can physically characterize XOR PUFs regardless of the number of XORs [29]. In another attempt a combination of ML attacks with non-invasive side channel attacks (e.g., power and timing) is suggested to model XOR PUFs, with the number of chains exceeding the previously established limit [24].

The latter attack is cost-effective due to its non-invasive nature, and therefore, it might be preferred to the semi-invasive one in practice. However, in contrast to pure ML techniques (i.e., without any side channel information), using side channel information in combination with ML techniques requires physical access to the device and reconfiguration of the circuits on the chip, which are not always feasible in a real scenario [24]. Therefore, it is still tempting to develop new pure ML techniques to break the security of XOR PUFs, with an arbitrary number of chains. Nevertheless, it is still unclear how many chains should be XORed to ensure the security of arbiter PUFs against ML attacks. Moreover, when applying current ML attacks, the maximum number of CRPs required for modeling an XOR PUF, with given levels of *accuracy* and final model delivery *confidence*, is not known today.

Only recently, it has been shown how a single chain arbiter PUF under the Deterministic Finite Automata (DFA) representation can be learned for given levels of accuracy and confidence [7]. It is further proved that the run time of their proposed algorithm is polynomial in the size of the DFA. We claim that for the XOR PUFs, a more compact representation can be adopted to improve the time complexity of this attack. Furthermore, to deal with noisy responses of an XOR PUF more efficiently, in contrast to their method, an approach not relying on majority voting can be applied.

We present a new framework to prove that XOR PUFs can be learned in polynomial time, for given levels of accuracy and confidence. The main contributions of our framework are summarized as follows:

Finding a theoretical limit for ML techniques to learn XOR PUFs in polynomial time. Under a well-known representation of an XOR PUF, we provide a theoretical limit as a function of the number of arbiter PUF stages and the number of chains, where an XOR PUF can be provably learned in polynomial time.

Learning of an XOR PUF for given levels of accuracy and confidence. With regard to the proposed limit, we present an algorithm, which learns the challenge-response behavior of an XOR PUF, for given levels of accuracy and confidence. The run time of this algorithm is polynomial in the number of the arbiter PUF stages, the number of chains, as well as the levels of accuracy and confidence. Moreover, our approach requires no side channel information.

Modeling the XOR PUF even if the responses are noisy. A celebrated model of noise fitting the purpose of our ML framework is applied to prove that even in the presence of noise, the run time of our algorithm is still polynomial in the number of the arbiter PUF stages, the number of chains, levels of accuracy and confidence, and the noise rate. Finally, through a comprehensive discussion, we will explain why secure XOR PUFs cannot be manufactured on chips based on current technologies.

2   Notation and Preliminaries

This section focuses on the background information and notations required to understand the general concept of arbiter PUFs, XOR PUFs, fundamentals of LTFs, the perceptron algorithm, the PAC model, and finally PAC learning with the Perceptron algorithm.

2.1   Arbiter and XOR PUFs

PUFs are most often related to the intrinsic silicon properties of a chip. They are physical input to output mappings, which generate a *response* for a given *challenge*. Let $\mathcal{C} = \{0,1\}^n$ and $\mathcal{Y} = \{0,1\}$ be the set of challenges and the set of responses, respectively. A PUF can be described by the function $f_{\mathrm{PUF}} : \mathcal{C} \rightarrow \mathcal{Y}$ where $f_{\mathrm{PUF}}(c) = y$.

PUFs are *evaluable*, which means that for a given PUF, f_{PUF} can be evaluated in polynomial time. Given a set of PUF instantiations, each PUF is *unique* and different from other PUFs with regards to its response set $\mathcal{Y}$. A response $y = f_{\mathrm{PUF}}(c)$ is *reproducible* in a sense that different evaluations of the same challenge yield "close" responses with respect to the considered distance metric.

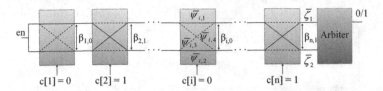

Fig. 1. Schematic of an arbiter PUF with n multiplexer stages and an arbiter at the end of the chain. Each multiplexer stage consists of four different delays. Based on the applied challenge, when the enable signal (denoted by "en") is fed, either the direct paths or the crossed paths are utilized for the signal propagation. Upon arrival of the first signal, the arbiter generates a binary response.

As the name implies, PUFs are *unclonable*, i.e., it is nearly impossible to construct another physical mapping (device) g_{PUF}, where $g_{\mathrm{PUF}} \neq f_{\mathrm{PUF}}$, but g_{PUF} and f_{PUF} have a similar challenge response behavior. Moreover, PUFs are *unpredictable*, which means that despite knowing a set $U = \{(c_i, y_i) \mid y_i = f_{\mathrm{PUF}}(c_i)\}$, it is practically impossible to predict $y_r = f_{\mathrm{PUF}}(c_r)$, where c_r is a random challenge with $(c_r, \cdot) \notin U$. Finally, PUFs are *one-way*, i.e., for a given $y = f_{\mathrm{PUF}}(c)$, the probability that a probabilistic polynomial time algorithm or a physical procedure $\mathcal{A}$ can output c is negligible, where c is drawn from a uniform distribution on $\{0,1\}^n$ [25].

Utilizing the timing differences of symmetrically designed electrical paths on a chip is the core idea of arbiter PUFs. The chain of an arbiter PUF consists of n connected switches, or so called *stages*, and an arbiter at the end, see Fig. 1. A challenge is an n-bit string $c = c[1] \cdots c[n]$, where the ith bit is fed into the ith stage. There are four different paths in each stage. If $c[i] = 1$, the signal propagates through the crossed paths, otherwise the direct paths are utilized, see Fig. 1. Enabling the inputs of the first stage leads to the propagation of two electrical signals on two symmetrically designed paths terminated by the arbiter. Due to the imperfections on the chip the two signals arrive at the end of the chain at different times. With regard to the arrival time of the signals, the arbiter generates a binary response.

We define a random variable Ψ_i related to the delay within the ith stage, which follows a Gaussian distribution with the mean μ_i and the deviation σ_i [7,22]. The realizations of the random variable Ψ_i are certain $\overline{\psi}_{i,1}$, $\overline{\psi}_{i,2}$, $\overline{\psi}_{i,3}$, and $\overline{\psi}_{i,4}$. $\overline{\psi}_{i,1}$ and $\overline{\psi}_{i,2}$ are the delays of the upper and lower direct paths, whereas $\overline{\psi}_{i,3}$ and $\overline{\psi}_{i,4}$ are the delays of the upper and lower crossed paths, respectively, see Fig. 1. The delay differences between the upper and lower outputs of the ith stage are denoted by $\overline{\beta}_{i,0} = \overline{\psi}_{i,1} - \overline{\psi}_{i,2}$ and $\overline{\beta}_{i,1} = \overline{\psi}_{i,4} - \overline{\psi}_{i,3}$, for direct paths and crossed paths, respectively.

Let $\mathcal{Z}$ be a random variable which corresponds to the total delay between the enable point and the outputs of the nth stage of the arbiter PUF. With regard to the linear additive model of an arbiter PUF, we have $\mathcal{Z} = \sum_{l=1}^{n} \Psi_l$ [7,13]. $\overline{\zeta}_1$ and $\overline{\zeta}_2$ are the realizations of $\mathcal{Z}$ at the upper and lower output, respectively, see Fig. 1. Let $\kappa > 0$ denote the precision of the arbiter. By comparing $\overline{\zeta}_1$ and $\overline{\zeta}_2$,

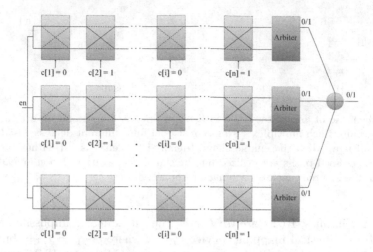

Fig. 2. Schematic of an XOR PUF. It consists of k chains of n-bit arbiter PUFs. The responses of all arbiters are XORed together to generate the final binary response.

the arbiter makes a decision whether the output is either "1" or "0". More formally, we assume that the output of the PUF is "1" if $\overline{\Delta} = \overline{\zeta}_1 - \overline{\zeta}_2 > \kappa$, whereas it is "0" if $\overline{\Delta} < -\kappa$. If $|\overline{\Delta}| \leq \kappa$, the arbiter is assumed to be in a metastable condition.

Following the procedure introduced in [7], in each stage, e.g., i^{th} stage, $\overline{\psi}_{i,j}$ can be mapped into an integer value $\psi_{i,j}$ ($1 \leq j \leq 4$). It is known that $\overline{\psi}_{i,j} \in [\mu_i - 3\sigma_i, \mu_i + 3\sigma_i]$ with probability 99.7%. Now we define the mapping f_{int} : $\mathbb{R} \mapsto \mathbb{Z}$ so that for all $\overline{\psi}_{i,j} \in [\mu_i - 3\sigma_i, \mu_i + 3\sigma_i]$, we have $\psi_{i,j} = f_{int}(\overline{\psi}_{i,j}) = \left\lceil (\overline{\psi}_{i,j} - \mu_i + 3\sigma_i)/\kappa \right\rceil$. Without loss of generality, we assume that $\mu_1 = \cdots = \mu_n$ and $\sigma_1 = \cdots = \sigma_n$. Hence, by performing the mapping f_{int} the maximum and the minimum of the real valued delays $\overline{\psi}_{i,j}$ ($1 \leq i \leq n$ and $1 \leq j \leq 4$) are mapped into $m = \left\lceil \frac{6\sigma}{\kappa} \right\rceil$ and 0, respectively (for more details see [7]). Furthermore, similarly, $\overline{\Delta}$ can be mapped with a high probability to an integer value Δ lying within a finite interval. In this case, the response of the arbiter is "1" if $\Delta > 0$, whereas it is "0" if $\Delta < 0$. The arbiter is in the metastable condition, if $\Delta = 0$.

To improve the security of arbiter PUFs against machine learning attacks, a modified construction called XOR PUF was suggested by [28]. An XOR PUF consists of k different chains, all with the same number of stages n. The responses of all arbiter PUFs are XORed together to generate the final response, see Fig. 2. The response of the XOR PUF can be defined as $f_{XOR}(c) = \bigoplus_{j=1}^{k} f_{j^{\text{th}} \text{ arbiter PUF}}(c)$.

2.2   Linear Threshold Functions

We begin with the definition of a Perceptron (i.e., single-layer Perceptron), where P_n denotes an n-input and single output Perceptron. P_n is represented by the function $\Omega \rightarrow H$, where the vector $\omega = (\boldsymbol{A}[1], \boldsymbol{A}[2], \cdots, \boldsymbol{A}[n], \theta)$ denotes a state, and the set $\Omega \subset \mathbb{R}^{n+1}$ is the set of states. The function $h_\omega \in H$ with $h_\omega : \mathbb{R}^n \mapsto \{0, 1\}$ is defined as follows:

$$h_\omega = \begin{cases} 1, & \text{if } \sum_{i=1}^n \boldsymbol{A}[i]\boldsymbol{\Phi}[i] - \theta \geq 0 \\ 0, & \text{otherwise.} \end{cases} \tag{1}$$

The sets of positive and negative examples of h_ω are half-spaces S^1 and S^0, where $S^1 = \{\boldsymbol{\Phi} \in \mathbb{R}^n| \sum_{i=1}^n \boldsymbol{A}[i]\boldsymbol{\Phi}[i] \geq \theta\}$ and $S^0 = \{\boldsymbol{\Phi} \in \mathbb{R}^n| \sum_{i=1}^n \boldsymbol{A}[i]\boldsymbol{\Phi}[i] < \theta\}$. Alternatively, by applying the mapping $f_{\text{map}} : \{0,1\} \mapsto \{1, -1\}$, so that $f_{\text{map}}(0) = 1$ and $f_{\text{map}}(1) = -1$, we have:

$$h_\omega = sgn(\boldsymbol{\Phi} \cdot \boldsymbol{A} - \theta), \tag{2}$$

where the inner product of the vector $\boldsymbol{A}$ and $\boldsymbol{\Phi}$ is denoted by $\boldsymbol{\Phi} \cdot \boldsymbol{A}$. Equation (2) denotes a linear threshold function (LTF), whose decision regions are S^1 and S^0 bounded by the hyperplane $\mathcal{P} : \boldsymbol{\Phi} \cdot \boldsymbol{A} = \theta$ (for further details see [2]).

2.3 Perceptron Algorithm

The Perceptron algorithm is an *online* algorithm invented to learn LTFs efficiently. By online we mean that providing the learner (i.e., learning algorithm) with each example, e.g., $\boldsymbol{\Phi}_i$, it attempts to predict the response to that example. Afterwards, the actual response (i.e., the label, for instance $\mathfrak{p}(\boldsymbol{\Phi}_i)$) is presented to the learner, and then it can improve its hypothesis by means of this information. The learning process continues until all the examples are provided to the learner [14].

Let the input of the Perceptron algorithm be a sequence of r labeled examples $((\boldsymbol{\Phi}_1, \mathfrak{p}(\boldsymbol{\Phi}_1), \cdots, (\boldsymbol{\Phi}_r, \mathfrak{p}(\boldsymbol{\Phi}_r))$. The output of the algorithm is the vector $\boldsymbol{A}$ classifying the examples. Executing the Perceptron algorithm, it initially begins with $\omega_0 = (\boldsymbol{A}_0[1], \boldsymbol{A}_0[2], \cdots, \boldsymbol{A}_0[n], \theta) = (0, \cdots, 0)$. When receiving each example (e.g., $\boldsymbol{\Phi}_j$), the algorithm examines whether $\boldsymbol{A}_j[i] \cdot \boldsymbol{\Phi}_j[i] \geq \theta_j$ and compares its prediction with the received label. If the label and the prediction of the algorithm differ, ω_j is updated as follows:

$$\omega_{j+1}[k] = \begin{cases} \boldsymbol{A}_j[k] - \mathfrak{p}(\boldsymbol{\Phi}_j) \cdot \boldsymbol{\Phi}_j[k] & 1 \leq k \leq n \\ \theta_j - \mathfrak{p}(\boldsymbol{\Phi}_j) & k = n + 1. \end{cases}$$

Note that if the prediction and the label of an example agree, no update is performed [26].

Quantifying the performance of an on-line algorithm, the prediction error (i.e., number of mistakes) of the algorithm is taken into account. In this way, the upper bound of the mistakes is defined as a measure of the performance. The Perceptron convergence theorem gives an upper bound of the error that can occur while executing the Perceptron algorithm [6]:

Convergence Theorem of the Perceptron Algorithm: *Considerr labeled examples which are fed into the Perceptron algorithm, and* $\|\mathbf{\Phi}_i\| \leq R$ *(*$\|\cdot\|$ *denotes the Euclidean length). Let* $\mathbf{u}$ *be the solution vector with* $\|\mathbf{u}\| = 1$ *whose error is denoted by* ε *(*$\varepsilon > 0$*). The deviation of each example is defined as* $d_i = \max\{0, \varepsilon - \mathfrak{p}(\mathbf{\Phi}_i)(\mathbf{u} \cdot \mathbf{\Phi}_i)\}$*, and* $D = \sqrt{\sum_{i=1}^{r} d_i^2}$*. The upper bound of the mistakes of the Perceptron algorithm is*

$$N_{mis} = \left(\frac{R+D}{\varepsilon}\right)^2.$$

For the proof, the reader is referred to [6]. Let the parameter σ be the minimum distance of any example from $\mathcal{P}$, i.e.,

$$\sigma = \min_{\mathbf{\Phi} \in \Phi} \frac{\|\mathbf{\Phi} \cdot \mathcal{A}\|}{\|\mathcal{A}\|}, \tag{3}$$

where Φ is the set of all $\mathbf{\Phi}$'s. The order of $1/\sigma$ determines whether the data is linearly separable. It has been demonstrated that when $1/\sigma$ is exponential in n, the data is not linearly separable, and consequently, the Perceptron algorithm cannot classify the data [4, 26]. On the other hand, if $1/\sigma$ is polynomial in n, the Perceptron algorithm can be applied.

2.4 PAC Model

As the name implies, the concept of PAC (Probably Approximately Correct) model aims at learning an unknown target (i.e., a concept class $\mathfrak{C}_n$) under the following circumstances: (a) after the learning phase, the output of the algorithm is a hypothesis approximating $\mathfrak{C}_n$, and (b) with a high probability the learner can deliver a good hypothesis.

To formalize the above mentioned definition, let $\mathfrak{C}_n$ be defined over the instance space $X_n = \{0,1\}^n$. Furthermore, $X = \cup_{n \geq 1} X_n$ and $\mathfrak{C} = \cup_{n \geq 1} \mathfrak{C}_n$. We have also $\mathfrak{H}_n$ as the *hypothesis space*, and $\mathfrak{H}$ defined in a similar fashion. The learner is provided with a finite number of examples drawn randomly with respect to the probability distribution D. For the target concept $c \in \mathfrak{C}$, the error of the hypothesis is $error(h) := \Sigma_{x \in h \triangle c} D(x)$, where $\triangle$ is the symmetric difference. Now we can define PAC learnability as followings.

Let $p(\cdot, \cdot, \cdot)$ be a polynomial, ε and δ be arbitrary values such that $0 < \varepsilon, \delta < 1$, and a distribution D on the instance space X_n (arbitrary distribution). When a PAC learning algorithm $\mathcal{L}$ is fed by $p(n, 1/\varepsilon, 1/\delta)$ independent examples drawn randomly with respect to D, then with probability at least $1 - \delta$ the output of $\mathcal{L}$ is a hypothesis $h \in \mathfrak{H}_n$ such that $error(h) \leq \varepsilon$. The sample complexity of $\mathcal{L}$ is the smallest polynomial p. With regard to the relation between $\mathfrak{C}$ and $\mathfrak{H}$, we define that $\mathfrak{C}$ is *properly* PAC learnable, when $\mathfrak{C} = \mathfrak{H}$. Otherwise, if $\mathfrak{H}$ can be evaluated on given instances in polynomial time, and $\mathfrak{C}$ is PAC learnable by $\mathfrak{H}$, $\mathfrak{C}$ is called *PAC learnable*.

2.5 PAC Learning of LTFs with Perceptron Algorithm

Several studies have focused on the PAC learning of an unknown LTF from labeled examples by applying the Perceptron algorithm (for an exhaustive survey see [26]). Here we briefly describe how the Perceptron algorithm, as an online algorithm, can be converted to a PAC learning algorithm, following the conversion procedure defined in [26].

The learner has access to an Oracle EX, providing labelled examples. By calling EX successively, a sequence of labeled examples is obtained and fed into the online algorithm. Hypotheses generated by the algorithm are further stored. At the second stage, the algorithm again calls EX to receive a new sequence of labeled examples. This new sequence is used to calculate the error rate of the hypotheses stored beforehand. The output of the procedure is a hypothesis with the lowest error rate. Let ε and δ be the accuracy and the confidence levels of the obtained PAC learning algorithm. Suppose that N_{mis} is the upper bound of the mistakes made by the original online algorithm for the concept class $\mathfrak{C}$. The following theorem is proved by Littlestone [15].

Theorem 1. *Suppose that the online algorithm L_{on} improves its hypothesis, only when its prediction and the received label of the example do not agree. The total number of calls that the obtained PAC algorithm $\mathcal{L}$ makes to EX is $O\left(1/\varepsilon(\log 1/\delta + N_{mis})\right)$.*

From the convergence theorem of the Perceptron algorithm and Theorem 1, it is straightforward to prove the following corollary [26]:

Corollary 1. *Let the concept class $\mathfrak{C}_n$ over the instance space $X_n = \{0,1\}^n$ be the class of linear threshold functions such that the weights $A_i \in \mathbb{Z}$, and $\sum_{i=1}^{n} |\mathcal{A}[i]| \leq \mathfrak{A}$, where $\mathfrak{A} \in \mathbb{Z}$ is the maximum sum over the weights. Then the Perceptron algorithm can be converted to a PAC learning algorithm running in time $p(n, \mathfrak{A}, 1/\varepsilon, 1/\delta)$.*

3 PAC Learning of XOR PUFs

In this section we first present how and why an XOR PUF can be PAC learned by the Perceptron algorithm. Furthermore, we provide the theoretical limit for the learnability of XOR PUFs in polynomial time. Finally, the theoretical results will be verified against experimental results from existing literature.

3.1 LTF-Based Representation of XOR PUFs

Here we briefly describe the LTF-based representation of an XOR PUF, which is widely adopted [9,19,23]. Consider the delay vector $\mathcal{A}^T$ defined as follows:

$$\mathcal{A}^T = (\alpha_1, \alpha_2, \ldots, \alpha_{n+1}) \text{ with } \begin{cases} \alpha_1 = \frac{\beta_{i,0} - \beta_{i,1}}{2} \\ \alpha_i = \frac{\beta_{i-1,0} + \beta_{i-1,1} + \beta_{i,0} - \beta_{i,1}}{2}, 2 \leq i \leq n \\ \alpha_{n+1} = \frac{\beta_{n,0} + \beta_{n,1}}{2} \end{cases} \quad (4)$$

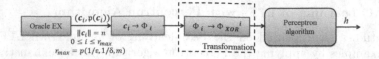

Fig. 3. Block diagram of the PAC learning framework. By calling the Oracle EX at most r_{max} times, a sequence of examples is collected. Φ_i is fed into the third block corresponding to our problem transformation. The output of the third block is fed into the Perceptron algorithm.

where the integer valued $\beta_{i,j}$ ($1 \le i \le n$ and $0 \le j \le 1$, as shown in Fig. 1) are the delay differences at the output of the ith stage. Wrt. the discretization process described in Sect. 2.1, it is straightforward to show that $\beta_{i,j}$ lies within the interval $[-m, m]$, hence, α_i ($1 \le i \le n+1$) lies within the interval $[-2m, 2m]$.

Consider a challenge string represented by a vector $\mathbf{c} = (c[1], \cdots, c[n])$. $\mathbf{\Phi} = (\mathbf{\Phi}[1], \cdots, \mathbf{\Phi}[n], 1)$ is the encoded challenge vector, where $\mathbf{\Phi}[i] = \prod_{j=i}^{n}(1 - 2c[j])$. We defined Δ as the delay difference at the outputs of the last stage. According to the linear additive model of the arbiter PUF, we have $\Delta = \mathbf{\mathcal{A}}^T \cdot \mathbf{\Phi}$, cf. [13,23]. Now let $f_{\text{map}} : \mathcal{Y} \mapsto \{1, -1\}$, so that $f_{\text{map}}(0) = 1$ and $f_{\text{map}}(1) = -1$. The output of the arbiter can be defined as

$$f_{PUF} = sgn(\Delta) = sgn(\mathbf{\mathcal{A}}^T \cdot \mathbf{\Phi}). \tag{5}$$

From Eq. (5), it is obvious that an arbiter PUF can be represented by an $(n+1)$-dimensional LTF. In a similar fashion, an XOR PUF can also be represented by an LTF, when the final response ($\mathcal{Y}_{XOR}$) is mapped to $\{1, -1\}$, cf. [23]:

$$f_{XOR} = \prod_{j=1}^{k} sgn(\mathbf{\mathcal{A}}^T \cdot \mathbf{\Phi}) = sgn\left(\bigotimes_{j=1}^{k} \mathbf{\mathcal{A}}^T \cdot \bigotimes_{j=1}^{k} \mathbf{\Phi}_j \right) = sgn(\mathbf{\mathcal{A}}_{XOR}^T \cdot \mathbf{\Phi}_{XOR}) \tag{6}$$

where $\mathbf{\mathcal{A}}_{XOR} = \otimes_{j=1}^{k} \mathbf{\mathcal{A}}_j^T$ is the tensor product of the vectors $\mathbf{\mathcal{A}}_j^T$, and similarly $\mathbf{\Phi}_{XOR} = \otimes_{j=1}^{k} \mathbf{\Phi}_j$.

3.2   PAC Learning of XOR PUFs with Perceptron

We claim that by adopting a simple transformation the Perceptron algorithm can be applied, particularly in our case. Comparing Eqs. (5) and (6), it can be seen that the $(n + 1)^k$-dimensional vectors $\mathbf{\mathcal{A}}_{XOR}$ and $\mathbf{\Phi}_{XOR}$ are substituted for $(n + 1)$-dimensional vectors $\mathbf{\mathcal{A}}^T$ and $\mathbf{\Phi}$. In other words, XOR-ing k $(n + 1)$-dimensional LTFs results in an $O((n + 1)^k)$-dimensional LTF. Therefore, if we transform the problem of learning the XOR of k $(n + 1)$-dimensional LTFs into an $O((n + 1)^k)$ dimensional space, this problem can be solved by applying the Perceptron algorithm. In order to support our claim, we begin with the following theorem stating that examples are linearly separable in $\mathbb{R}^{n+1}$.

Theorem 2. *For an XOR PUF, with fixed k, represented by an LTF in an $O\left((n+1)^k\right)$ dimensional space, $1/\sigma$ is polynomial in n.*

Proof. As described in Sect. 2, $\mathcal{A}_{XOR}$ contains integer elements lying within the limited interval $[-2m,2m]$. Furthermore, elements of Φ_{XOR} are in $\{-1,1\}$. Now we have

$$\sigma = \min_{\Phi_{XOR} \in \Phi_{XOR}} \frac{\|\Phi_{XOR} \cdot \mathcal{A}_{XOR}\|}{\|\mathcal{A}_{XOR}\|} = \min_{\Phi_{XOR} \in \Phi_{XOR}} \frac{\sqrt{\sum_{i=1}^{(n+1)^k} \alpha_i^2}}{\sqrt{(n+1)^k}}, \quad (7)$$

where Φ_{XOR} is the set of all Φ_{XOR}'s. Due to a non-trivial challenge-response behavior of the given PUF, at least one of the elements of $\mathcal{A}_{XOR}$ must be equal to ± 1. Therefore, $\min \left(\sum_{i=1}^{(n+1)^k} \alpha_i^2\right)^{1/2} = 1$, and $1/\sigma = (n+1)^{k/2}$. ∎

Figure 3 illustrates how the perceptron algorithm is applied in our PAC learning framework. The learner has access to an Oracle EX, which is related to the XOR PUF as follows: $EX := f_{XOR}$. At the first stage, the Oracle EX is called successively to collect CRPs. The maximum number of calls is denoted by r_{max}. For each CRP (e.g., $(\mathbf{c}_i, \mathfrak{p}(\mathbf{c}_i))$) a vector Φ_i is generated. Afterwards, Φ_i is transformed to Φ_{XOR}^i, which is in an $O\left((n+1)^k\right)$ dimensional space. The Perceptron algorithm predicts the response to Φ_{XOR}^i, and if its prediction and $\mathfrak{p}(\mathbf{c}_i)$ disagrees, its hypothesis will be updated.

Now we will elaborate on the upper mistake bound in our framework. Following the convergence theorem of the Perceptron algorithm and Theorem 2, when $\|\Phi_{XOR}\| \leq (n+1)^{k/2}$, we have $N_{mis} = (n+1)^k/\varepsilon^2$. As an immediate corollary, we have:

Corollary 2. *Let k be constant and consider the class of XOR PUFs over the instance space $X_n = \{0,1\}^{(n+1)^k}$ which is that class of linear threshold functions such that $\alpha_i \in \mathbb{Z}$, and $\sum_{i=1}^{(n+1)^k} |\alpha_i| \leq 2m(n+1)^k$. Then the Perceptron-based algorithm running in time $p((n+1)^k, 4m^2, 1/\varepsilon, 1/\delta)$ can PAC learn an XOR PUF by calling EX at most $O\left(\log(1/\delta)/\varepsilon + 4m^2(n+1)^k/\varepsilon^3\right)$ times.*

There are some key implications from this corollary. First, with regard to the PAC model, the hypothesis delivered by the algorithm must be evaluable in polynomial time. The point here is that the term $(n+1)^k$, related to the Vapnik-Chervonenkis dimension of the representation [3], may grow significantly if k is not a constant. In this case, our algorithm cannot find a hypothesis in polynomial time, since the number of examples is super-polynomial in n. However, in Sect. 5 we will see that in practice, k cannot exceed the bound $\lceil \ln n \rceil$, and therefore, XOR PUFs realized in practice are PAC learnable, as k must be reasonable small and can be seen as constant when compared with n.

Second, it is tempting that an increase in m can help to ensure the security of an XOR arbiter PUF. The upper bound for the number of CRPs calculated according to the Corollary 2, for $\delta = 0.0001$, $k = 5$ for $n = 64$ and $n = 128$, is depicted in Fig. 4. This figure can provide a better understanding of the impact of

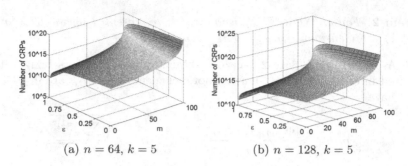

(a) $n = 64, k = 5$ (b) $n = 128, k = 5$

Fig. 4. Upper bound of the number of CRPs. The x-axis indicates m, whereas the y-axis shows ϵ. The z-axis corresponds to the upper bound of the number of CRPs.

m on the learnability of an XOR arbiter PUF. A marginal increase in m cannot dramatically increase the number of CRPs required for modeling an XOR arbiter PUF. Although an arbitrarily large m can be suggested to ensure the security of an XOR arbiter PUF, as stated in [7], m is restricted by technological limits (i.e., the yield and many other factors), and thus cannot be arbitrarily large. In Sect. 5 the impact of an increase in m on the learnability will be further discussed.

3.3   Validation of the Theoretical Results

We compare our theoretical findings with several experimental results reported in [16,23]. As reported in [16], until now no *effective* pure ML attack has been launched on XOR PUFs with $k \geq 5$ ($n = 64$). Pure ML attacks proposed in the literature are conducted on XOR PUFs with the maximum n being equal to 128 [23,24]. Taking into account the long run time of pure ML algorithms, even on the powerful machines employed by [23], XOR PUFs with $n = 256$ and $n = 512$ have been targeted only by combined modeling attacks [24]. Therefore, unfortunately, in the literature no practical limit for pure ML techniques has been reported for XOR PUFs with $n \geq 128$.

As an attempt to compare our theoretical results to what has been observed in practice, we focus on the results reported in [23]. Note that although the algorithm applied in [23] (Logistic Regression) differs from our algorithm, we can compare the number of CRPs required by them to learn an XOR PUF with a given accuracy. The argument supporting this claim is that the hypothesis class of LR can be "discretized" so that it becomes finite [27]. Furthermore, due to the fact that the delay values can be mapped to a finite interval of integer values, the loss function of LR is also bounded. Therefore, LR can be converted to a PAC learning algorithm, and the maximum number of EX calls made by the obtained algorithm is polynomial in n, k, $1/\epsilon$ and $1/\delta$. Moreover, note that the theoretical limit of learning an XOR PUF in polynomial time is established by the Vapnik-Chervonenkis dimension of the LTF representation of an XOR PUF, as used in [23] as well. These enable us to compare their experimental results with our findings.

The authors of [23] have attempted to model 64-bit and 128-bit XOR PUFs with up to 6 and 5 chains, respectively. Their results demonstrate that the proposed model can predict responses to a set of arbitrary chosen challenges with 99 % accuracy. However, the number of CRPs required for modeling a 64-bit XOR PUF with $k = 5$ and $k = 6$ is increased drastically, comparing to those with $k \leq 4$. In this regard, the number of CRPs collected to predict the response is increased from 12000 to 80000 and 200000 for $k = 5$ and $k = 6$, respectively ($\epsilon = 0.01$). As a result, the time spent to build a model is increased from a few minutes to several hours, which shows an exponential growth. For a 128-bit XOR PUF with $k = 5$, 500000 CRPs are required to model the XOR PUF, with 99 % accuracy, while for a PUF with $k = 4$, this number is only 24000. Consequently, the learning time is again increased exponentially.

In the above-mentioned cases, an exponential growth in the number of CRPs and the learning time can be clearly observed, when k exceeds 4. This matches the theoretical limit proposed in Sect. 3.2.

4 PAC Learning of Noisy XOR PUFs

In the previous section, we have explained how the Perceptron algorithm can be applied to PAC learn an XOR PUF. The natural and important question would be whether the proposed framework is applicable in the case of noisy responses. The term *noisy response* here refers to the response of the XOR PUF to a challenge under either the metastable condition or the impact of environment noise. Although it has been accepted that metastablity of an XOR PUF must be solved by the PUF manufacturer, we consider this particular case for completeness. From the point of view of PAC learning, this condition results in incorrect labels generated by the Oracle EX. We aim to state that an XOR PUF can be PAC learned by applying the Perceptron algorithm, even if noisy responses are included in the collected set of CRPs.

Several versions of the Perceptron algorithm, which can tolerate noise, i.e., incorrect labels of examples, have been developed (for a comprehensive survey see [11]). Here we follow the work by [1] to demonstrate that the original Perceptron algorithm can be further applied in the case of noisy responses. In this case, the number of CRPs required to be collected is polynomial in the number of noisy responses.

At the first stage, we define a simple but effective model of noisy Oracle EX_η [1]. In our model, the examples are drawn with respect to the relevant distribution D, and the label of each example is chosen in an independent random fashion. More specifically, after drawing an example, an unfair coin (head with probability $1 - \eta$) is flipped. If the outcome is head, the correct label is provided, otherwise the label is incorrect. It is clear that $\eta < 1/2$, since $\eta = 1/2$ means that no relevant information is provided by EX_η, and the case of $\eta > 1/2$ is irrelevant. We assume that an upper bound on η, denoted by η_b, is known. Even if this assumption may not be the case in practice, following the procedure defined in [1], η_b can be estimated. It is shown that the sample size is increased very slightly in the case of unknown η_b (for further information and the proof see [1]).

The Convergence Theorem of the Perceptron algorithm states that in the case of noisy responses the condition $\mathfrak{p}(\boldsymbol{\Phi}_i)(\mathbf{u}.\boldsymbol{\Phi}_i) \geq 0$ cannot always be met. This condition relates the accuracy of the prediction performed by the Perceptron algorithm to the labels provided that afterwards update the respective hypothesis. In the case of noisy examples, we suggest that this condition should be modified so that it reflects the accuracy of the Perceptron algorithm in the presence of noise. Suppose that an example, such as $(\boldsymbol{\Phi}_i, \mathfrak{p}(\boldsymbol{\Phi}_i))$, is provided by EX_η. The probability that this example disagrees with any hypothesis $\mathbf{u}$ can be calculated as following:

$$\Pr[\mathfrak{p}(\boldsymbol{\Phi}_i)(\mathbf{u} \cdot \boldsymbol{\Phi}_i) < 0] \leq (1 - \eta)\varepsilon + \eta(1 - \varepsilon) < \eta_b + \varepsilon(1 - 2\eta_b) \qquad (8)$$

From Eq. (8) it can be inferred that the expected rate of disagreement is at least η for the ideal hypothesis $\mathbf{u}$. Therefore, the separation factor of at least $\varepsilon(1 - 2\eta)$ should be between an ideal hypothesis and an approximation of that cf. [1]. As stated in the following theorem, the maximum number of mistakes that can be made by the Perceptron algorithm is polynomial in this separation.

Theorem 3. *Consider r labeled examples which are fed into the Perceptron algorithm, and let $\|\boldsymbol{\Phi}_i\| \leq R$. In the case of noisy labels, let $\mathbf{u}_n$ be the solution vector with $\|\mathbf{u}_n\| = 1$, and $\mathfrak{p}(\boldsymbol{\Phi}_i)(\mathbf{u}_n.\boldsymbol{\Phi}_i) \geq \varepsilon(1 - 2\eta_b) > 0$. Then*

$$N_{mis} = \left(\frac{R}{\varepsilon(1 - 2\eta_b)} \right)^2.$$

The key idea is that a separation factor of at least $\varepsilon(1 - 2\eta_b)$ must exist between $\mathbf{u}$ and $\mathbf{u}_n$. It is straightforward to prove this theorem, and for more details the reader is referred to [1].

Theorem 4. *When PAC learning the noisy XOR PUF, the maximum number of mistakes that the Perceptron algorithm can make is $N_{mis} = (n + 1)^k / (\varepsilon^2(1 - 2\eta_b)^2)$. Furthermore, the maximum number of CRPs required for PAC learning a noisy XOR PUF is $O\big(\log(1/\delta)/(\varepsilon(1 - 2\eta_b)) + 4m^2(n + 1)^k / (\varepsilon^3(1 - 2\eta_b)^3)\big)$.*

Proof. Following Corollary 2 and Theorem 3, this can be easily shown.   ∎

The most important message is that this maximum number of CRPs is polynomial in n, ε, δ as well as the upper bound of η. According to experimental results when the noise rate is 2 %, the number of CRPs required to learn a 128-bit XOR PUF ($k = 4$) is approximately increased by the factor 2, in comparison to the noiseless scenario with approximately the same ϵ [23]. For the same XOR PUF, increasing the noise rate to 5 % and 10 %, the number of CRPs is increased 2 times and 8 times, comparing with the case of $\eta_b = 0.02$. It has been concluded that the number of CRPs collected to model the XOR PUF is polynomial in the noise rate [23], which agrees with our theoretical result.

5 Discussion

5.1 Theoretical Considerations

By providing the proof of vulnerability of XOR PUFs to PAC learning we have demonstrated how fragile the security of this kind PUF is. The concept of PAC learning of XOR PUFs was almost catched by Hammouri et al. [10]. Although the authors benefit from one of the most adequate representations of the XOR PUFs, which is LTF-based [9], they could not prove the PAC learnability of the XOR PUFs. As the Vapnik-Chervonenkis dimension of an LTF representing an arbiter PUF is equal to $n + 1$, this family of PUF primitives is subject to PAC learning attacks [7]. It is straightforward to further prove that the Vapnik-Chervonenkis dimension of the LTF representing an XOR PUF is $(n+1)^k$. Therefore, for constant k an XOR PUF with k chains (each with n stages) is also PAC learnable. In this paper, instead of sticking to this obvious fact, we introduced an algorithm that can PAC learn an XOR PUF, even in the case of noisy responses. However, the key argument supporting our claim is that the Vapnik-Chervonenkis dimension of the proposed LTF-based representation should be finite. Wrt. this argument, we have shown that by applying the Perceptron algorithm its run time is polynomial in n, $1/\varepsilon$, $1/\delta$, and k.

Another important aspect of our framework is the representation of an XOR PUF. As mentioned earlier, it is clear that according to what has been observed in [7], an XOR PUF can also be represented by a DFA with $O(n^k m^{2k})$ states. Therefore, their proposed algorithm makes $O\left((1 + 2/\varepsilon \ln(1/\delta))n^k M^{2k} + 2/\varepsilon n^{2k} M^{4k}\right)$ calls to EX. Comparing this number of calls with the number of calls that our algorithm makes to EX (see Corollary 2), it is clear that the numbers of calls made by both algorithms are polynomial in n, m, $1/\varepsilon$, and $1/\delta$. However, our algorithm outperforms in terms of the number of calls, and consequently its time complexity.

Of crucial importance for our framework is how the algorithm deals with noisy responses. In this paper we have proposed a model of noise, which is well-studied in the PAC learning related literature, and agrees with what can be seen in practice. Towards launching a machine learning attack, the adversary applies a set of challenges and collects the responses, where the latter might be noisy. From the lessons learnt from practice, the number of noisy response of an XOR PUF is virtually equal to the sum of the number of noisy response of each individual arbiter PUF [21]. In the literature majority voting is suggested as a solution to deal with noisy responses [18, 23]. This can impair the performance of the proposed learning algorithm, when the attacker can observe each CRP only once and cannot do majority voting. It is even suggested that in order to reduce the effectiveness of ML attacks, the noise rate that can be observed by an attacker can be artificially increased, while the verifier still observes only a small noise rate [31]. In this latter scenario the majority voting cannot be helpful. On contrary, we have proved that XOR PUFs can be PAC learned without the need for majority voting.

We have stated that the maximum number of mistakes that the Perceptron algorithm can make, and consequently, the maximum number of CRPs required for PAC learning is polynomial in n, k, $1/\varepsilon$, $1/\delta$ as well as $1/(1-2\eta)$ in the case of noisy responses. Since we have mainly aimed to prove this, the maximum number of CRPs calculated in Sect. 3 ensures that the algorithm delivers an approximation of the desired hyperplane, with the probability at least $1-\delta$. The proposed upper bound of the number of CRPs can be improved to even reduce the number of required CRPs (see for instance [3]).

5.2 Practical Considerations

When proving that the Perceptron algorithm can be applied to PAC learn an XOR PUF, we take the advantage of the lessons learnt from practice, namely (a) the delay values can be mapped to a finite interval of integer values, and (b) the number of chains contained in an XOR PUF (k) cannot exceed a certain value. The importance of the first fact can be recognized in the recent proof of the PAC learnability of an XOR PUF (see Corollary 2). The second fact confirms that the Vapnik-Chervonenkis dimension of the LTF representing an XOR PUF is finite. Whereas the first fact has been already reflected in [7], the second one has been only partially discussed in the literature.

The results of experiments clearly demonstrate that XORing more than a certain number of chains is not feasible [21]. In their experiments, different XOR PUFs designed on 10 Xilinx Virtex 5 (LX110) FPGAs at the nominal condition (temperature = 35° C and VDD = 1V) are employed. For $k = 4$, it is reported that the noise rate is $\eta = 23.2\%$, and a change in the condition (e.g., reducing VDD) may result in an increase in the noise rate up to 43.2%. Their most impressive achievement demonstrates that the noise rate of an XOR PUF is approximately equal to the sum of the noise rate of each individual arbiter PUF. For an arbiter PUF designed on 65 nm technology, a typical value of the noise rate is about 4% [21]. Therefore, it can be approximated that the maximum of k can be ideally equal to 12, where the noise ratio would be approximately 50%. Under this condition, even majority voting cannot be helpful so that the PUF cannot be verified. Another important factor limiting k is the silicon area used for constructing an XOR PUF. Based on a rough estimation reported in [16], the silicon area required for constructing an XOR PUF with k chains is k times larger than a single arbiter PUF.

Despite the implementation and technological limits on k, we have proved theoretical limits on when an XOR PUF can be learned in polynomial time. In practical studies it is not stated how the learnability is theoretically limited, even though the empirical upper bound reported in [16] and the experimental results in [23] are in line with our theoretical limit. Moreover, the experimental results presented in [30] are also evidences that support our findings. It has been shown that when $n = 64$ and $k \geq 4$, the number of CRPs required for the ML attack, and consequently the time complexity, is increased drastically. The same observation is repeated for $n = 128$ and $k \geq 5$. These emphasize the importance of our approach, in which not only the limit of the learnability in polynomial time is identified but also no side channel information is required to PAC learn the XOR PUFs under this limit. To evaluate the security of an XOR PUF with respect to this theoretical limit, the following scenarios can be distinguished:

- n is small (e.g., $n \leq 32$): in this case, the security can be easily broken by adopting a brute-force strategy.
- n is large (i.e., no brute-force strategy is applicable) and $k \gg (\ln n)$: under this condition, the XOR PUF cannot be learned in polynomial time. However, no practical implementation of such an XOR PUF is feasible due to the technological limits, more specifically the noisy responses.
- n is large and $k \ll (\ln n)$: the XOR PUF can be PAC learned.

In the latter scenario, it can be thought that an increase in m may lead to a more secure XOR PUF. Neither is this a valid theoretical approach nor it is possible in practice. From a theoretical point of view, although more CRPs are required for PAC learning an XOR PUF with large m, the number of CRPs is still polynomial in m, n and levels of accuracy and confidence. On the other hand, from a practical perspective, a chip designed with the large σ neither might work properly nor it can be utilized as a general purpose device [7]. Moreover, it can be suggested to produce arbiters with high precision in order to enlarge m. In this case, the cost of the chip is increased dramatically.

In previous studies, e.g., [23,24], powerful and costly machines have been employed to prove the concept of learnability of XOR PUFs. It might not be convenient to run a ML algorithm on such machines, particularly for XOR PUFs with large k and n. Since our concrete proofs state how the security of XOR PUFs can be broken in polynomial time, it seems redundant to conduct a simulation or an experiment concerning this issue. Last but not least, we emphasize that protocols relying on the security of XOR PUFs cannot be considered as an ultimate solution to the issue of insecure arbiter PUFs. As it has been also stated in [5], none of the XOR PUF-based protocols in its current form can be thought of as being perfectly secure.

6   Conclusion

We have developed a PAC learning framework, which clearly states how an XOR PUF can be learned, for given levels of accuracy and confidence. Furthermore, a theoretical limit for ML attacks as a function of the number of the chains and the number of arbiter PUF stages has been established. Moreover, we have proved that the maximum number of CRPs required for our framework is polynomial in the number of arbiter PUF stages, the pre-defined level of accuracy and confidence. It is further shown that our approach deals with the noisy responses in an efficient fashion so that in this case, the maximum number of CRPs collected by the attacker is polynomial in the noise rate. Our rigorous mathematical approach matches the results of experiments, which can be found in the literature. The observation made to reveal the technological limits on the number of chains contributes to the proof of vulnerability of XOR PUFs to PAC learning attacks.

Last but not least, on the basis of learning theory concepts, this study explicitly states that the current form of XOR PUFs cannot be considered as an ultimate solution to the problem of insecure arbiter PUFs. Furthermore, we believe that this work can provide an insight not only into the academic research but also for the design and manufacturing of delay-based PUFs.

References

1. Angluin, D., Laird, P.: Learning from noisy examples. Mach. Learn. **2**(4), 343–370 (1988)
2. Anthony, M.: Computational Learning Theory. Cambridge University Press, Cambridge (1997)
3. Blumer, A., Ehrenfeucht, A., Haussler, D., Warmuth, M.K.: Learnability and the Vapnik-Chervonenkis dimension. J. ACM **36**(4), 929–965 (1989)
4. Bylander, T.: Learning linear threshold functions in the presence of classification noise. In: Proceedings of the Seventh Annual Conference on Computational Learning Theory, pp. 340–347 (1994)
5. Delvaux, J., Gu, D., Schellekens, D., Verbauwhede, I.: Secure lightweight entity authentication with strong PUFs: mission impossible? In: Batina, L., Robshaw, M. (eds.) CHES 2014. LNCS, vol. 8731, pp. 451–475. Springer, Heidelberg (2014)
6. Freund, Y., Schapire, R.E.: Large margin classification using the perceptron algorithm. Mach. Learn. **37**(3), 277–296 (1999)
7. Ganji, F., Tajik, S., Seifert, J.P.: PAC Learning of Arbiter PUFs, Security Proofs for Embedded Systems-PROOFS (2014). https://eprint.iacr.org/2015/378. pdf. Accessed 18 May 2015
8. Gassend, B., Clarke, D., Van Dijk, M., Devadas, S.: Silicon physical random functions. In: Proceedings of the 9th ACM Conference on Computer and Communications Security, pp. 148–160 (2002)
9. Gassend, B., Lim, D., Clarke, D., Van Dijk, M., Devadas, S.: Identification and authentication of integrated circuits. Concurrency Comput. Pract. Experience **16**(11), 1077–1098 (2004)
10. Hammouri, G., Öztürk, E., Sunar, B.: A tamper-proof and lightweight authentication scheme. Pervasive Mobile Comput. **4**(6), 807–818 (2008)
11. Khardon, R., Wachman, G.: Noise tolerant variants of the perceptron algorithm. Journal Mach. Learn. Res. **8**, 227–248 (2007)
12. Kömmerling, O., Kuhn, M.: Design principles for tamper-resistant security processors. In: USENIX Workshop on Smartcard Technology (1999)
13. Lee, J.W., Lim, D., Gassend, B., Suh, G.E., Van Dijk, M., Devadas, S.: A technique to build a secret key in integrated circuits for identification and authentication applications. In: Symposium on VLSI Circuits, 2004. Digest of Technical Papers, pp. 176–179 (2004)
14. Littlestone, N.: Learning quickly when irrelevant attributes abound: a new linear-threshold algorithm. Mach. Learn. **2**(4), 285–318 (1988)
15. Littlestone, N.: From on-line to batch learning. In: Proceedings of the Second Annual Workshop on Computational Learning Theory, pp. 269–284 (1989)
16. Maes, R.: Physically Unclonable Functions: Constructions, Properties and Applications. Springer, Heidelberg (2013)

17. Maes, R., Verbauwhede, I.: Physically unclonable functions a study on the state of the art and future research directions. In: Sadeghi, A.-R., Naccache, D. (eds.) Towards Hardware-Intrinsic Security. Information Security and Cryptography, pp. 3–37. Springer, Heidelberg (2010)
18. Majzoobi, M., Koushanfar, F., Devadas, S.: FPGA PUF using programmable delay lines. In: 2010 IEEE International Workshop on Information Forensics and Security (WIFS), pp. 1–6 (2010)
19. Majzoobi, M., Koushanfar, F., Potkonjak, M.: Lightweight secure PUFs. In: Proceedings of the 2008 IEEE/ACM International Conference on Computer-Aided Design, pp. 670–673 (2008)
20. Pappu, R., Recht, B., Taylor, J., Gershenfeld, N.: Physical one-way functions. Science 297(5589), 2026–2030 (2002)
21. Rostami, M., Majzoobi, M., Koushanfar, F., Wallach, D., Devadas, S.: Robust and reverse-engineering resilient puf authentication and key-exchange by substring matching. IEEE Trans. Emerg. Top. Comput. 2(1), 37–49 (2014)
22. Ruhrmair, U., Solter, J., Sehnke, F., Xu, X., Mahmoud, A., Stoyanova, V., Dror, G., Schmidhuber, J., Burleson, W., Devadas, S.: PUF modeling attacks on simulated and silicon data. IEEE Trans. Inf. Forensics Secur. 8(11), 1876–1891 (2013)
23. Rührmair, U., Sehnke, F., Sölter, J., Dror, G., Devadas, S., Schmidhuber, J.: Modeling attacks on physical unclonable functions. In: Proceedings of the 17th ACM Conference on Computer and Communications Security, pp. 237–249 (2010)
24. Rührmair, U., Xu, X., Sölter, J., Mahmoud, A., Majzoobi, M., Koushanfar, F., Burleson, W.: Efficient power and timing side channels for physical unclonable functions. In: Batina, L., Robshaw, M. (eds.) CHES 2014. LNCS, vol. 8731, pp. 476–492. Springer, Heidelberg (2014)
25. Sadeghi, A.R., Naccache, D. (eds.): Towards Hardware-Intrinsic Security: Foundations and Practice, 1st edn. Springer, Heidelberg (2010)
26. Servedio, R.A.: Efficient Algorithms in Computational Learning Theory. Harvard University, Cambridge (2001)
27. Shalev-Shwartz, S., Ben-David, S.: Understanding Machine Learning: From Theory to Algorithms. Cambridge University Press, Cambridge (2014)
28. Suh, G.E., Devadas, S.: Physical unclonable functions for device authentication and secret key generation. In: Proceedings of the 44th Annual Design Automation Conference, pp. 9–14 (2007)
29. Tajik, S., Dietz, E., Frohmann, S., Seifert, J.-P., Nedospasov, D., Helfmeier, C., Boit, C., Dittrich, H.: Physical characterization of arbiter PUFs. In: Batina, L., Robshaw, M. (eds.) CHES 2014. LNCS, vol. 8731, pp. 493–509. Springer, Heidelberg (2014)
30. Tobisch, J., Becker, G.T.: On the Scaling of Machine Learning Attacks on PUFs with Application to Noise Bifurcation (2015). https://www.emsec.rub.de/research/publications/ScalingPUFCameraReady/. Accessed 18 May 2015
31. Yu, M.D.M., Verbauwhede, I., Devadas, S., MRaihi, D.: A noise bifurcation architecture for linear additive physical functions. In: 2014 IEEE International Symposium on Hardware-Oriented Security and Trust (HOST), pp. 124–129 (2014)

A Unified Security Analysis of Two-Phase Key Exchange Protocols in TPM 2.0

Shijun Zhao[1]([✉]) and Qianying Zhang[2]

[1] TCA Lab, Institute of Software Chinese Academy of Sciences,
Beijing 100190, China
{zqyzsj,zsjzqy}@gmail.com
[2] College of Information Engineering, Capital Normal University,
Beijing 100048, China

Abstract. The Trusted Platform Module (TPM) version 2.0 provides an authenticated key exchange functionality by a single key exchange primitive, which can be called to implement three key exchange protocols (denoted as two-phase key exchange protocols in TPM 2.0): the Full Unified Model, the MQV, and the SM2 key exchange protocols. However, some vulnerabilities have been found in all of these protocols. Fortunately, it seems that protections provided by the TPM can deal with vulnerabilities of these protocols. This paper investigates whether the TPM key exchange primitive provides a secure key exchange functionality under protections of the TPM. We first perform an informal analysis of the TPM key exchange primitive which helps us to model in a precise way. Then we formally analyze the TPM key exchange primitive in a security model for AKE, based on which all the protocols adopted by TPM 2.0 can be analyzed in a unified way. Our analysis indicates under what conditions the TPM 2.0 can provide a provable secure key exchange functionality. In the end, we give suggestions on how to leverage the TPM key exchange primitive properly, and suggestions on how to improve the security of current TPM key exchange primitive to enable its wide use in practice.

Keywords: Authenticated key exchange · Security model · Security analysis · Min-entropy · TPM 2.0

1 Introduction

Authenticated key exchange (AKE) is a very important public key primitive in modern cryptography, which allows two parties to establish a shared secret session key via the public insecure communication while providing mutual authentication. To achieve security against active attackers, who control the public communication channels, AKE protocols commonly use digital signatures or message authentication codes (MAC) to explicitly authenticate the messages exchanged. Some typical examples include: STS [5], SIGMA [8], TLS [11], and JFK [3]. However, the authentication mechanism to resist active attacks incurs

© Springer International Publishing Switzerland 2015
M. Conti et al. (Eds.): TRUST 2015, LNCS 9229, pp. 40–57, 2015.
DOI: 10.1007/978-3-319-22846-4_3

a significant increase in both the computation and communication complexity compared to the basic Diffie-Hellman key exchange protocol.

In 1986, Matsumoto et al. first put forth the design of implicitly AKE protocols [20] which only required basic Diffie-Hellman exchanges while providing identities authentication by combining the ephemeral keys and long-term keys in the derivation of the session key. The implicitly AKE protocols achieve efficiency in both communication and computation, so they are widely studied and many protocols are proposed [13,14,16–19,21,23,27,29–31]. Among these protocols, the HMQV protocol [16] marks the milestone of the development of the implicitly AKE protocols because it provides the first formal analysis of implicitly AKE protocols within a modern AKE security model (the CK model). By now, it becomes a basic requirement for AKE protocols to achieve the security defined by modern AKE security models, such as the CK [7] model or eCK [17] model. The core security property defined by modern AKE security models guarantees that the corruption of one session would not compromise the security of other sessions. In modern AKE security models, a session of implicitly AKE protocols is identified by a quadruple $(\hat{A}, \hat{B}, X, Y)$ where $\hat{A}$ is the identity of the holder of the session, $\hat{B}$ the peer, X the outgoing ephemeral public key, and Y the incoming ephemeral public key.

In this work, we focus on the two-phase key exchange primitive defined in the new released TPM 2.0 specification [25], which supports three implicitly AKE protocols: the Full Unified Model and Full MQV protocols described in SP800-56A [4], and the SM2 key exchange protocol [29]. The three protocols are described as two-phase key exchange protocols in TPM 2.0 as they require two phases. In the first phase, the TPM generates an ephemeral DH key to be sent to the other party. In the second phase, the TPM generates the unhashed shared secret by combining ephemeral keys and long-term keys, and then the host of the TPM uses the unhashed shared secret to derive the session key.

We first introduce some preliminaries used in the three protocols. Let G' be a finite Abelian group of order N, $G \subseteq G'$ be a subgroup of prime order q. Denote by g a generator of G, by 1_G the identity element, by $G \backslash 1_G = G - \{1_G\}$ the set of elements of G except 1_G and by $h = N/q$ the cofactor. We use multiplicative notation for the group operation in G'. Let $u \in_R Z_q$ denote randomly selecting an integer u between 1 and $q - 1$. Note that G actually is an elliptic curve in this work as all the three protocols are based on elliptic curve cryptography. Let $P.x$ denote the x-coordinate of point P. The party having A as its public key will be denoted by $\hat{A}$. The Full Unified Model, Full MQV and SM2 key exchange protocols are described in Fig. 1. $H_1()$ and $H_2()$ are cryptographic hash functions. The Full Unified Model protocol analyzed in this paper includes the ephemeral public keys exchanged as suggested by [15]. The Full MQV protocol is a variant of the original MQV protocol [21] (which doesn't include parties' identifiers in the session key derivation, i.e., $K = H_2(Z_A) = H_2(Z_B)$).

$$\hat{A} : (a, A = g^a) \qquad\qquad\qquad\qquad\qquad\qquad \hat{B} : (b, B = g^b)$$

$$X = g^x \xrightarrow{\hspace{2cm} X \hspace{2cm}} Y = g^y$$

$$\xleftarrow{\hspace{2cm} Y \hspace{2cm}}$$

$$Z_A = (YB^e)^{h(x+da)}, Z_B = (XA^d)^{h(y+eb)}$$

Full Unified Model: $K = H_1(Z_1, Z_2, \hat{A}, \hat{B}, X, Y)$, where $Z_1 = g^{ab}$, $Z_2 = g^{xy}$

Full MQV: $K = H_2(Z_A, \hat{A}, \hat{B}) = H_2(Z_B, \hat{A}, \hat{B})$, where

$$d = avf(X) \stackrel{\text{def}}{=} 2^l + (X.x \bmod 2^l),$$

$$e = avf(Y) \stackrel{\text{def}}{=} 2^l + (Y.x \bmod 2^l), l = \lceil q/2 \rceil$$

SM2 Key Exchange: $Z_A = (BY^e)^{h(a+dx)}, Z_B = (AX^d)^{h(b+ey)}$

$$K = H_2(Z_A, \hat{A}, \hat{B}) = H_2(Z_B, \hat{A}, \hat{B}), \text{ where}$$

$$d = avf'(X) \stackrel{\text{def}}{=} 2^l + (X.x \bmod 2^l),$$

$$e = avf'(Y) \stackrel{\text{def}}{=} 2^l + (Y.x \bmod 2^l), l = \lfloor q/2 \rfloor$$

Fig. 1. The full unified model, full MQV, and SM2 key exchange protocols

1.1   Weaknesses of AKE Protocols in TPM 2.0

Unfortunately, all the three AKE protocols adopted by TPM 2.0 are not secure[1]. We summarize their weaknesses in the following.

We find that the Full Unified Model key exchange protocol is completely insecure if an attacker is able to learn the intermediate information $Z_1 = g^{ab}$ of some session established by $\hat{A}$ with $\hat{B}$: the attacker transmits an ephemeral key $X' = g^{x'}$ generated by himself to party $\hat{B}$ and receives an ephemeral public key Y' from $\hat{B}$, then he can compute the session key $K = H(Z_1, Y'^{x'}, \hat{A}, \hat{B}, X', Y')$, i.e., the attacker is able to impersonate $\hat{A}$ to $\hat{B}$ indefinitely.

Kaliski presented an unknown-key share (UKS) attack [15] on the original MQV protocol in which the attacker $\mathcal{M}$ interfaces with the session establishment between two honest parties $\hat{A}$ and $\hat{B}$ such that $\hat{A}$ is convinced that he is sharing a key with $\hat{B}$, but $\hat{B}$ believes that he is sharing the same session key with $\mathcal{M}$. $\mathcal{M}$ can mount Kaliski's UKS attack by (a) registering with the CA a specific key $C = g^c$, and (b) sending a specific ephemeral public key X' to $\hat{B}$. c and X' are cleverly computed by $\mathcal{M}$ such that session keys of sessions $(\hat{A}, \hat{B}, X, Y)$ and $(\hat{B}, \mathcal{M}, Y, X')$ are identical. Although the Full MQV protocol tries to overcome the UKS weakness by including identities in the session key derivation, we find that it still cannot achieve the security defined by modern AKE models if $\mathcal{M}$ is able to learn the unhashed shared Z value: $\mathcal{M}$ performs the same steps above, learns Z_B by corrupting the session $(\hat{B}, \mathcal{M}, Y, X')$, then $\mathcal{M}$ can compute the session key of session $(\hat{A}, \hat{B}, X, Y)$, i.e., corruption of the session $(\hat{B}, \mathcal{M}, Y, X')$

---

[1] The TPM 2.0 specification notes that the Full MQV and SM2 key exchange protocols "may be susceptible to unknown key-share (UKS) attacks" [25].

helps $\mathcal{M}$ to compromise another session $(\hat{A}, \hat{B}, X, Y)$. In the following of this paper, we use MQV to denote the Full MQV.

Xu et al. introduced two attacks [29] on the SM2 key exchange protocol in which an honest party $\hat{A}$ is coerced to share a session key with the attacker $\mathcal{M}$, but $\hat{A}$ thinks that he is sharing the key with another party $\hat{B}$. Both attacks requires $\mathcal{M}$ to reveal the unhashed shared Z_B in $\hat{B}$. Besides, the first attack requires $\mathcal{M}$ to register with the CA a specific key $C = Ag^e$ where $e \in_R Z_q$, and the second attack requires $\mathcal{M}$ to perform some computations using his private key after obtaining Z_B.

From above attacks we can see that the three AKE protocols cannot achieve the security property defined by modern AKE security models if the attacker is able to get the unhashed Z values. Unfortunately, this is exactly how the TPM 2.0 two-phase key exchange primitive implements these three AKE protocols: Z_1 of the Full Unified Model, unhashed Z value of the MQV and SM2 key exchange protocols are returned to the host, whose memory is vulnerable to attacks. So it seems that the TPM 2.0 key exchange primitive is not secure.

1.2 Motivations and Contributions

Fortunately, protections provided by the TPM improve the security of the TPM key exchange primitive. We use tpm.KE to denote the TPM key exchange primitive in this paper. First, all long-term keys are generated by TPM chip randomly, so the attacker cannot use the TPM chip to generate a specific key such as the cleverly computed key $C = g^c$ in Kaliski's UKS attack or $C = Ag^e$ in Xu's first attack. Second, the TPM only provides fixed functionalities through TPM commands [26] in a black-box manner: when a TPM command is invoked, the TPM chip executes the pre-defined computation procedure, and returns the computation result. The second feature constrains the attacker from using the key to perform computations at will. It seems that above two features can prevent Kaliski's UKS attack and Xu's attacks, and Zhao et al. [32] show that protections provided by the TPM indeed help the SM2 key exchange protocol to resist Xu's two attacks by an informal analysis. However, Zhao et al. don't model the two features above in their formal analysis, but perform their formal analysis by adopting an easier approach: they modify tpm.KE not to return the unhashed Z value but the session key, thus Z is not available to the attacker. This leads to our first motivation:

1. *How to precisely model protections provided by the TPM, and check whether the protections can help current* tpm.KE *to be proven secure?*

Although protections provided by the TPM help the MQV and SM2 key exchange protocols to resist current attacks, the $avf()$ and $avf'()$ used in the MQV and SM2 key exchange protocols respectively make that no analysis can prove these two protocols to be secure. Consider such a group G that the representation of its elements satisfies that the $\lceil q/2 \rceil$ least significant bits (LSBs) of the representation of points' x-coordinate are fixed. In this case, the attacker can mount the so-called group representation attacks on MQV and SM2 key exchange protocols, in which the attacker can impersonate $\hat{A}$ to $\hat{B}$ without knowing the private key of $\hat{A}$. A group representation attack on MQV is described in [16], and a similar attack on the SM2 key exchange protocol can be found in [32]. To make this type of attacks more convincing, [32] proposes an approach to construct such an elliptic curve in theory. HMQV, a variant of MQV proved secure in the CK model, prevents this type of attack by replacing $avf()$ with a cryptographic hash function. [32] also suggests replacing the $avf'()$ of the SM2 key exchange protocol with a cryptographic hash function. However, group representation attacks are not practical as in practice it's difficult to find an elliptic curve whose $\lceil q/2 \rceil$ LSBs of the representation of points' x-coordinate are fixed. On the contrary, the generation of the $avf()$ and $avf'()$ seems to range in a uniform way over all possible values. This leads to our second motivation:

2. *Can we give a quantitative measure of the amount of randomness (entropy) contained in the practical output distribution of $avf()$ and $avf'()$, and check whether $avf()$ and $avf'()$ provide enough entropy to prevent group representation attacks?*

The tpm.KE is designed to support three implicitly AKE protocols through a unified interface. However, current modern AKE security models only consider how to formally analyze one single protocol. To the best of our knowledge, all AKE protocols proven secure in the literature are analyzed separately. For example, [32] only analyzes the SM2 key exchange protocol in TPM 2.0, and doesn't model the other two protocols. However, this analysis approach is insufficient for tpm.KE. Suppose an honest party $\hat{A}$ tries to establish a secure channel with $\hat{B}$ through MQV, and the TPM of $\hat{B}$ has a long-term key of the type SM2, which is controlled by the attacker. Is the session key of $\hat{A}$ still secure if the attacker leverages the key of the type SM2 to complete the session? In this case, it's desirable for tpm.KE to protect the session key of $\hat{A}$. We denote this security property by *correspondence property*. However, current security models don't capture this security property. This leads to our third motivation:

3. *Can we build a unified security AKE model, based on which we can give a formal analysis of tpm.KE, which supports three AKE protocols?*

Contributions. We summarize the contributions of this paper as follows:

1. We leverage the min-entropy, a notion from information theory, to give a quantitative measure of the amount of randomness in the output distribution of $avf()$ and $avf'()$. We measure several series of elliptic curves used in practice, covering all elliptic curves adopted by TPM 2.0 [24]. We also compare the measurement with a cryptographic hash function, SHA-2. The comparison results show that $avf()$ and $avf'()$ provide almost the same level of randomness as cryptographic hash functions.
2. We model the protections provided by the TPM by modeling the interfaces of tpm.KE as oracles, and present a unified AKE security model for tpm.KE, which captures not only the security property defined by modern AKE models but also the correspondence property.

3. We give a formal analysis of tpm.KE in our new model, and prove that tpm.KE is secure under the condition that the unhashed shared secrets are not available to the attacker. This condition can be achieved by slightly modifying the Full Unified Model functionality of TPM 2.0 or proper implementation of the host's software which derives the session key.
4. The tpm.KE defined by current TPM 2.0 specification opens a window of opportunity to actually mount impersonate attacks, so we give suggestions on how to avoid such attacks. We also give some suggestions on how to modify TPM 2.0 specification to achieve a more secure tpm.KE.

1.3 Organization

In the rest of this paper, Sect. 2 gives some preliminaries. Section 3 introduces the two-phase key exchange primitive defined by TPM 2.0 specification, gives a quantitative measure of several series of elliptic curves used in practice, and presents an informal analysis of tpm.KE. Section 4 presents our unified security model for tpm.KE. Section 5 gives a formal description of tpm.KE. Section 6 proves the unforgeabilities of the functionalities of MQV and SM2 key exchange provided by tpm.KE, which can simplify our analysis. Section 7 formally analyzes tpm.KE in our new model. Section 8 discusses some further security properties, and gives our suggestions on how to implement secure AKE protocols based on current tpm.KE and how to modify current TPM 2.0 specification to achieve a more secure key exchange primitive. Section 9 concludes this paper and gives our future work.

2 Preliminaries

This section first introduces the notion of min-entropy and two commonly used methods to calculate the min-entropy, then introduces CDH (Computational Diffie-Hellman) and GDH (Gap Diffie-Hellman) assumptions used in this paper.

2.1 Min-entropy

Min-entropy is a notion from information theory, which provides a very strict information-theoretical lower bound (i.e., worst-case) measure of randomness for a random variable. High min-entropy indicates that the distribution of the random variable is close to the uniform distribution. Low min-entropy indicates that there must be a small set of outcomes that has an unusually high probability, and the small set can help the attacker to perform the group representation attack. Take the two extreme cases for example: if the min-entropy of a random variable is equal with the length of the outcome, the distribution is a uniform distribution, and if the min-entropy of a random variable is zero, the outcomes of the random variable are a fixed value. From the two extreme cases we can see that the higher the min-entropy is, the harder for the attacker to mount group representation attacks. There are usually two methods to measure the min-entropy of a random variable:

1. NIST SP 800-90. This method is described in NIST specification 800-90 for binary sources. The definition for min-entropy of one binary bit is: $H = -log_2(p_{max})$, where $p_{max} = max\{p_0, p_1\}$, and p_0, p_1 are probabilities of the binary bit outputs zero and one respectively. The min-entropy of an n-bit binary string is defined by:

$$H_{total} = \sum_{i=1}^{n} H_i \tag{1}$$

2. Context-Tree Weighting compression. Context-Tree Weighting (CTW) [28] is an optimal compression algorithm for stationary sources and is commonly used for estimate the min-entropy.

2.2   CDH and GDH Assumptions

Definition 1 (CDH Assumption). *Let G be a cyclic group of order p with generator g. The CDH assumption in G states that, given two randomly chosen points $X = g^x$ and $Y = g^y$, it is computationally infeasible to compute $Z = g^{xy}$.*

Definition 2 (GDH Assumption). *Let G be a cyclic group generated by an element g whose order is p. We say that a decision algorithm $\mathcal{O}$ is a Decisional Diffie-Hellman (DDH) Oracle for a group G and generator g if on input a triple (X, Y, Z), for $X, Y \in G$, oracle $\mathcal{O}$ outputs 1 if and only if $Z = CDH(X, Y)$. We say that G satisfies the GDH assumption if no feasible algorithm exists to solve the CDH problem, even when the algorithm is provided with a DDH-oracle for G.*

3   The TPM Key Exchange Primitive

This section first presents how tpm.KE is implemented in TPM 2.0 and introduces relevant TPM commands. Then we give an informal analysis of tpm.KE. In our informal analysis, we present our solutions to prevent impersonation attacks on the Full Unified Model protocol, and a quantitative measure of the randomness of the output distribution of $avf()$ and $avf'()$ on a wide range of elliptic curves which have been widely used in practice.

3.1   Introduction of tpm.KE

tpm.KE consists of two phases. In the first phase, the TPM generates an ephemeral key which is transferred to the other party. In the second phase, the TPM generates the unhashed secret values according to the specification of the selected protocol, then the host derives the session key from the unhashed secret values. Before running the two phases, the **Key Generation** procedure should be invoked first to generate the long-term key. As we aim to analyze the whole AKE protocols adopted by TPM 2.0, tpm.KE introduced below not only includes the key exchange functionality provided by the TPM, but also the session key derivation procedure performed on the host.

Key Generation. The relevant commands are TPM2_Create() and TPM2_CreatePrimary(). They take as input public parameters including an attribute identifying the key exchange scheme for the long-term key. The scheme should be one of the following three: TPM_ALG_ECDH, TPM_ALG_ECMQV, and TPM_ALG_SM2. In this procedure, the TPM performs the following steps: if the command is TPM2_Create(), it picks a random $a \in_R Z_q$ and computes $A = g^a$, and if the command is TPM2_CreatePrimary(), it derives a from a primary seed using a key derivation function and computes $A = g^a$; finally it returns A, and a key handle identifying a.[2]

First Phase. The relevant command is TPM2_EC_Ephemeral(). This command is used to generate an ephemeral key. The TPM performs the following steps:

1. Generate $x = \mathsf{KDFa}(Random, Count)$, where KDFa() is a key derivation function described in [9], $Random$ is a secure random value stored inside the TPM, and $Count$ is a counter.
2. Set $ctr = Count$, $A[ctr] = 1$, $Count = Count + 1$, where $A[]$ is an array of bits used to indicate whether the ephemeral key has been used.
3. Set $x = x \bmod q$, and generate $X = g^x$.
4. Return X and ctr.

Note that the TPM doesn't need to store the ephemeral private key x as it can be recovered using KDFa() and ctr.

Second Phase. The relevant command is TPM2_ZGen_2Phase(), which is the main command of tpm.KE. This command takes the following items as input:

$scheme$ a scheme selector indicating to the TPM which of the supported schemes is to be used

$keyA$ the key handle identifying the long-term private key a generated in the Key Generation procedure

ctr the counter used to identify the ephemeral key generated in the first phase

B the public key of $\hat{B}$, with which $\hat{A}$ wants to establish a session

Y the ephemeral public key received from $\hat{B}$

1. The TPM first does the following checks:
   (a) Whether $scheme$ equals the scheme designated for key A in the key generation procedure.
   (b) Whether B and Y are on the curve associated with A.
   (c) Whether $A[ctr] = 1$.
2. If the above checks succeed, the TPM recovers $x = \mathsf{KDFa}(Random, ctr)$, and performs the following steps:
   (a) Compute unhashed values according to the value of $scheme$:
        Case TPM_ALG_ECDH:
          set $Z_1 = B^a$, $Z_2 = Y^x$;
        Case TPM_ALG_ECMQV:
          set $Z_1 = (YB^e)^{h(x+da)}$, Z_2=NULL, where $d = avf(X)$ and $e = avf(Y)$;

---

[2] Actually TPM2_Create() returns a key blob encrypted by a storage key, and the TPM2_Load() command loads the key blob and returns the key handle. For simplicity, we let TPM2_Create() directly return the key handle.

Case TPM_ALG_SM2:

set $Z_1 = (BY^e)^{h(a+dx)}$, Z_2=NULL, where $d = avf'(X)$ and $e = avf'(Y)$;

(b) Set $A[ctr] = 0$.

(c) Return Z_1 and Z_2.

3. Finally, the host computes the session key after obtaining Z_1 and Z_2. Note that when TPM2_ZGen_2Phase() completes successfully, the TPM clears $A[ctr]$, which ensures that the ephemeral private key x can only be used once.

3.2   Informal Analysis

We have shown that two weaknesses in the design of tpm.KE prevent it from achieving security property defined by modern AKE security models. One weakness is that tpm.KE returns Z_1 of the Full Unified Model protocol to the host whose memory is vulnerable to attacks, which makes Z_1 be available to the attacker. If the attacker obtains Z_1, the Full Unified Model protocol would be completely insecure as we have shown in Sect. 1.2. The other one is the weakness caused by the $avf()$ and $avf'()$, which results in group representation attacks on the MQV and SM2 key exchange protocols. Although this type of attacks is not feasible, it makes the two protocols cannot be proven secure.

We give two solutions to overcome the first weakness:

1. Perform the entire session key computation of Full Unified Model in the secure environment of the TPM, i.e., modify the TPM2_ZGen_2Phase() command not to return Z_1 and Z_2 but the session key, i.e., $K = H_1(Z_1, Z_2, \hat{A}, \hat{B}, X, Y)$.
2. Protect Z_1 and Z_2 from malicious code running on the host as much as possible such as keeping them only available in kernel mode, and delete Z_1 and Z_2 as soon as the session key is derived.

The first solution requires modifying the current TPM 2.0 specification, and the second one requires that the software code of session key derivation running on the host must be implemented properly and should be included in the Trusted Computing Base (TCB). The two solutions have the same purpose: protecting Z_1 from the attacker, which helps us exclude Z_1 of Full Unified Model from the session state which the attacker can obtain in our formal analysis in Sect. 7.

As it seems that the second weakness only happens in theory, we perform a quantitative measure of the min-entropy contained in the output distribution of $avf()$ and $avf'()$ to check whether this weakness can happen in practice. We measure several series of widely deployed elliptic curves: the NIST series [12], the BN series [2], the SECG series [22], and an SM2 elliptic curve [1]. Our measure totals 17 elliptic curves and covers all elliptic curves adopted by TPM 2.0 [24]. We generate 16384 points for each elliptic curve, apply $avf'()$ to points of SM2 P256 curve, and apply $avf()$ to points of the rest curves[3]. We also apply the cryptographic hash function SHA-2 to the generated points of all curves. Then we

---

[3] $avf'()$ is defined only for SM2 key exchange, and $avf()$ is for MQV.

measure the min-entropy of the output distributions of $avf()$ $(avf'())$ and SHA-2. The min-entropy results calculated using method of NIST SP 800-90 (formula 1) and CTW compression are summarized in Table 1. Table 1 also compares the min-entropy of the two output distributions. To our surprise, the min-entropy of the output distribution of $avf()$ and $avf'()$ is very close to the min-entropy of the output distribution of SHA-2: the former is only about 1 bit less than the latter. What's more, the measure results indicate that the output distribution of $avf()$ and $avf'()$ is close to the uniform distribution. Take the measurement of BN P256 for example, the min-entropy calculated by the NIST's method is 126.93, very close to the output length of $avf()$ which is $129 = \lceil 256/2 \rceil + 1$, and the CTW ratio is 98.08 % which is close to 1. Our practical measure indicates that the outputs of $avf()$ $(avf'())$ on different elliptic curve points are almost independent, and it is impractical for an attacker to mount group representation attacks on protocols based on practical elliptic curves. So in our formal analysis we model $avf()$ and $avf'()$ as random oracles.

Table 1. Min-entropy results

Elliptic Curves		NIST 800-89		CTW Ratio	
		$avf()$	SHA-2	$avf()$	SHA-2
NIST Series	P192	95.19	95.94	97.13 %	97.92 %
	P224	111.01	111.99	97.68 %	98.33 %
	P256	126.86	127.89	98.08 %	98.65 %
	P384	190.19	191.30	98.95 %	99.31 %
	P521	258.73	259.80	100.01 %	100.11 %
BN Series	P192	95.09	96.15	97.13 %	97.91 %
	P224	111.03	111.95	97.67 %	98.34 %
	P256	126.93	127.95	98.08 %	98.67 %
	P384	190.23	191.19	98.95 %	99.32 %
	P512	253.62	254.80	99.35 %	99.60 %
	P638	314.97	316.13	100.04 %	100.23 %
SECG Series	P192	95.17	95.99	97.13 %	97.92 %
	P224	110.98	111.98	97.68 %	98.34 %
	P256	126.63	127.90	98.07 %	98.65 %
	P384	190.39	191.28	98.95 %	99.31 %
	P521	258.64	259.62	100.08 %	100.11 %
SM2	P256	125.81	126.89	100.14 %	100.17 %

4   A Unified Security Model

This section presents our unified security model for tpm.KE, and describes the attacker model which models the capabilities of the attacker by some queries.

In our security model, each party has a long-term key generated by the TPM and a certificate (issued by a Certificate Authority (CA)) that binds the public key to the identity of that party. The long-term key can be one of the following three types: TPM_ALG_ECDH, TPM_ALG_ECMQV, and TPM_ALG_SM2. A party can be activated to invoke the interfaces of tpm.KE to run an instance of the protocol supported by the long-term key, and an instance of a protocol is called a session. In each session, a party can be activated as the role of initiator to send the first ephemeral public key or responder to send the second ephemeral public key by invoking the interface of the first phase of tpm.KE, and a party can complete the session by invoking the interface of the second phase of tpm.KE and computing the session key.

In previous AKE security models, a session is identified by a quadruple $(\hat{A}, \hat{B}, X, Y)$ where $\hat{A}$ is the identity of the owner of the session, $\hat{B}$ the peer party, X the outgoing ephemeral public key from $\hat{A}$, and Y the incoming ephemeral public key from $\hat{B}$. This kind of session identifier cannot identify a session established by tpm.KE as tpm.KE supports more than one scheme (protocol). So we use a quintuple $(sc, \hat{A}, \hat{B}, X, Y)$ to identify a session where sc denotes the scheme of the session. The session $(sc, \hat{B}, \hat{A}, Y, X)$ (if it exists) is said to be **matching** to session $(sc, \hat{A}, \hat{B}, X, Y)$, and the session $(sc', \hat{B}, \hat{A}, Y, X)$ where $sc' \neq sc$ (if it exists) is said to be **message-matching** to session $(sc, \hat{A}, \hat{B}, X, Y)$.

The introduction of sc to the session identifier brings an issue we must address: how about the security of the session $(sc, \hat{A}, \hat{B}, X, Y)$ if it has a corrupted message-matching session? Previous AKE security models don't capture this attack as they don't support formal analysis of multiple kinds of protocol in a unified way. However, this attack can happen on tpm.KE as it supports three AKE schemes and the TPM specification doesn't force the TPM to check the key type of its peer party. We say tpm.KE satisfies *correspondence property* if it can resist above attack, i.e., the session $(sc, \hat{A}, \hat{B}, X, Y)$ is secure if its message-matching session is compromised.

4.1   Attacker Model

The experiment involves multiple honest parties and an attacker $\mathcal{M}$ connected via an unauthenticated network. The attacker is modeled as a probabilistic Turing machine and has full control of the communications between parties. $\mathcal{M}$ can intercept and modify messages sent over the network. $\mathcal{M}$ also schedules all session activations and session-message delivery. In addition, in order to model potential disclosure of secret information, the attacker is allowed to access secret information via the following queries:

- **SessionStateReveal(s)**: $\mathcal{M}$ queries directly at session s while still incomplete and learns the session state for s. In our analysis, the session state includes the values returned by interfaces of tpm.KE and intermediate information stored and computed in the host.
- **SessionKeyReveal(s)**: $\mathcal{M}$ obtains the session key for the session s.

- **Corruption**($\hat{P}$): In other AKE security models, this query allows $\mathcal{M}$ to learn the plaintext of the long-term private key of party $\hat{P}$. In our model, $\mathcal{M}$ doesn't learn anything about the plaintext of the private key but obtains the black-box access of the long-term key via TPM interfaces.
- **Test(s)**: This query may be asked only once throughout the game. Pick $b \xleftarrow{R} 0, 1$. If $b = 1$, provide $\mathcal{M}$ the session key; otherwise provide $\mathcal{M}$ with a value r randomly chosen from the probability distribution of session keys. This query can only be issued to a session that is "clean". A completed session is "clean" if this session as well as its matching session (if it exists) is not subject to above three queries. A session is called *exposed* if $\mathcal{M}$ performs any one of above three queries to this session.

Note that our model differs from previous AKE security models in that the **Corruption** query to some party doesn't provide the attacker with the plaintext of the long-term private key of the party, but the black-box access of the long-term key which is randomly generated and protected by the TPM. This difference models the two protection features (see description in Sect. 1.2) provided by the TPM for tpm.KE.

The security is defined based on a game played by $\mathcal{M}$, in which $\mathcal{M}$ is allowed to activate sessions and perform SessionStateReveal, SessionKeyReveal, and Corruption queries. At some time, $\mathcal{M}$ performs the Test query to a clean session of its choice and gets the value returned by Test. After that, $\mathcal{M}$ continues the experiment, but is not allowed to expose the test session and its matching session (if it exists). Eventually $\mathcal{M}$ outputs a bit b' as its guess, then halts. $\mathcal{M}$ wins the game if $b' = b$. The attacker with above capabilities is called a **KE-attacker**. The formal security is defined as follows.

Definition 3. tpm.KE *is called secure if the following properties hold for any KE-attacker $\mathcal{M}$ defined above:*

1. *When two uncorrupted parties complete matching sessions, they output the same session key, and*
2. *The probability that $\mathcal{M}$ guesses the bit b (i.e., outputs $b' = b$) from the Test query correctly is no more than $1/2$ plus a negligible fraction.*

The first condition is a "consistency" requirement for sessions completed by two uncorrupted parties. The second condition is the core property for the security of tpm.KE: it guarantees that exposure of one session doesn't help the attacker to compromise the security of another session. Note that our security definition of tpm.KE allows the attacker to expose the message-matching session, that is to say, the test session is still secure even if the message-matching session is exposed by the attacker. Thus our model captures the correspondence property.

5 Formal Description of TPM.KE

This section formally describes tpm.KE from the view of how two-phase key exchange protocols can be implemented leveraging the TPM.

We use $\mathsf{ephem}_A()$ to model the interface of the first phase of tpm.KE where A is the long-term key of $\hat{A}$: once invoked, $\mathsf{ephem}_A()$ generates an ephemeral private/public key pair $(r, R = g^r)$, and returns an index ctr identifying the private key r in the TPM. We model as oracles the black-box manner of the key exchange functionalities provided by the second phase of tpm.KE. The Full Unified Model, MQV, and SM2 key exchange functionalities provided by the second phase of tpm.KE are modeled as oracle $\mathcal{O}_A^{EC}$, oracle $\mathcal{O}_A^{MQV}$, and oracle $\mathcal{O}_A^{SM2}$ respectively. $\mathcal{O}_A^{EC}$ takes as input the input of TPM2_ZGen_2Phase(), and returns the session key generated according to the specification of Full Unified Model. Note that we model our solutions to the first weakness of tpm.KE by letting $\mathcal{O}_A^{EC}$ directly return the session key but not Z_1 and Z_2. $\mathcal{O}_A^{MQV}$ and $\mathcal{O}_A^{SM2}$ take as input the input of TPM2_ZGen_2Phase(), and return the unhashed value according to specifications of the MQV and SM2 key exchange protocols respectively. We now formally describe tpm.KE by giving the following three session activations.

1. Initiate($sc, \hat{A}, \hat{B}$): $\hat{A}$ invokes $\mathsf{ephem}_A()$ of its TPM to obtain an ephemeral public key X and an index ctr_x identifying the ephemeral private key x stored in the TPM, creates a local session which it identifies as (the incomplete) session $(sc, \hat{A}, \hat{B}, X)$ where sc is the key exchange scheme supported by the long-term key A, and outputs X as its outgoing ephemeral public key.
2. Respond($sc, \hat{B}, \hat{A}, X$) (sc is the scheme supported by B): After receiving X, $\hat{B}$ performs the following steps:
   (a) Invoke $\mathsf{ephem}_B()$ of its TPM to obtain an ephemeral public key Y and an index ctr_y identifying the ephemeral private key y stored in the TPM.
   (b) With input $(sc, keyB, ctr_y, A, X)$ where $keyB$ is the key handle of B, invoke corresponding oracle according to the value of sc:
       Case TPM_ALG_ECDH: Invoke $\mathcal{O}_B^{EC}$, set the session key K to be the return result of $\mathcal{O}_B^{EC}$.
       Case TPM_ALG_ECMQV: Invoke $\mathcal{O}_B^{MQV}$, obtain Z_B from the return result, and compute the session key $K = H_2(Z_B, \hat{A}, \hat{B})$.
       Case TPM_ALG_SM2: Invoke $\mathcal{O}_B^{SM2}$, obtain Z_B from the return result, and compute the session key $K = H_2(Z_B, \hat{A}, \hat{B})$.
   (c) Complete the session with identifier $(sc, \hat{B}, \hat{A}, Y, X)$.
3. Complete($sc, \hat{A}, \hat{B}, X, Y$): $\hat{A}$ checks that it has an open session with identifier $(sc, \hat{A}, \hat{B}, X)$, then performs the following steps:
   (a) With input $(sc, keyA, ctr_x, B, Y)$ where $keyA$ is the key handle of A, invoke corresponding oracle according to the value of sc:
       Case TPM_ALG_ECDH: Invoke $\mathcal{O}_A^{EC}$, set the session key K to be the return result of $\mathcal{O}_A^{EC}$.
       Case TPM_ALG_ECMQV: Invoke $\mathcal{O}_A^{MQV}$, obtain Z_A from the return result, and compute the session key $K = H_2(Z_A, \hat{A}, \hat{B})$.
       Case TPM_ALG_SM2: Invoke $\mathcal{O}_A^{SM2}$, obtain Z_A from the return result, and compute the session key $K = H_2(Z_A, \hat{A}, \hat{B})$.
   (b) Complete the session with identifier $(sc, \hat{A}, \hat{B}, X, Y)$.

6   Unforgeability of MQV and SM2 Key Exchange Functionalities

In this section, we first give formal definitions of MQV and SM2 Key Exchange functionalities provided by tpm.KE, and formally prove their unforgeabilities with a constraint on the attacker. The unforgeabilities can simplify our formal analysis of tpm.KE.

Definition 4 (MQV Functionality of tpm.KE). *The functionality, denoted by $\mathcal{O}_B^{MQV}$, is provided by a party possessing a private/public key pair $(b, B = g^b)$. A challenger, possessing a private/public key pair $(a, A = g^a)$, provides $\mathcal{O}_B^{MQV}$ with a challenge $X = g^x$ (x is chosen and kept secret by the challenger). With the pair (A, X), $\mathcal{O}_B^{MQV}$ first computes an ephemeral private/public key pair $(y, Y = g^y)$, and returns $Z = (XA^d)^{y+eb}$ where $d = avf(X)$ and $e = avf(Y)$. The challenger can verify the return result (Y, Z) with respect to challenge X by checking whether $Z = (YB^e)^{x+da}$.*

Definition 5 (SM2 Key Exchange Functionality of tpm.KE). *The functionality, denoted by $\mathcal{O}_B^{SM2}$, is provided by a party possessing a private/public key pair $(b, B = g^b)$. A challenger, possessing a private/public key pair $(a, A = g^a)$, provides $\mathcal{O}_B^{SM2}$ with a challenge $X = g^x$ (x is chosen and kept secret by the challenger). With the pair (A, X), $\mathcal{O}_B^{SM2}$ first computes an ephemeral private/public key pair $(y, Y = g^y)$, and returns $Z = (AX^d)^{b+ey}$ where $d = avf'(X)$ and $e = avf'(Y)$. The challenger can verify the return result (Y, Z) with respect to challenge X by checking whether $Z = (BY^e)^{a+dx}$.*

Theorem 1. *Under the CDH assumption, with $avf()$ modeled as a random oracle, given a challenge X, it is computationally infeasible for an attacker to forge a return result of $\mathcal{O}_B^{MQV}$ on behalf of a challenger whose public key is A under the constraint that (a, x) is unknown to the attacker.*

Theorem 2. *Under the CDH assumption, with $avf'()$ modeled as a random oracle, given a challenge X, it is computationally infeasible for an attacker to forge a return result of $\mathcal{O}_B^{SM2}$ on behalf of a challenger whose public key is A under the constraint that (a, x) is unknown to the attacker.*

Due to the space limitation, we omit the proof of Theorems 1 and 2, and the complete proof of the two theorems are given in the full version [33].

7   Security Analysis of tpm.KE

In this section, we analyze the security of tpm.KE in the security model defined in Sect. 4. We first define the session state allowed to be revealed by the attacker.

Session State. In order to simulate the protections provided by the TPM, we specify that a session state stores the results returned by the TPM and the information stored in the host. For the Full Unified Model scheme, the session state is the session key; for the MQV and SM2 key exchange schemes, the session state is the unhashed value returned by the TPM.

Theorem 3. *Under the CDH and GDH assumptions, with hash functions $H_1()$ and $H_2()$, $avf()$, and $avf'()$ modeled as random oracles, tpm.KE is secure in our unified model.*

Due to the space limitation, we give the complete proof of above theorem in the full version [33].

8   Discussion and Suggestions

In this section, we first discuss some further security properties for AKE protocols, then give suggestions on how to use tpm.KE securely and suggestions on how to improve the security of tpm.KE.

8.1   Further Security Properties

Besides the basic security property defined by modern security models, it's desirable for AKE protocols to achieve the following security properties: (1) the key-compromise impersonation (KCI) resistance property; that is, the knowledge of a party's long-term private key doesn't enable the attacker to impersonate *other, uncorrupted, parties* to the party; and (2) the Perfect Forward Secrecy (PFS) property; that is, the expired session keys established before the compromise of the long-term key cannot be recovered.

Note that our security model doesn't capture the KCI resistance property and PFS property as our model doesn't allow the attacker to obtain the plaintext of the long-term private key but only allows the attacker to control the handle of the long-term key. The reason that we put such constraint on the attacker, which is used to model protections provided by the TPM hardware chip, is that we aim to check whether the tpm.KE defined by current TPM specification can provide a secure key exchange functionality (Note that in scenarios where long-term keys can be obtained by the attacker, for example keys are not protected by hardware tokens, all the three protocols adopted by TPM 2.0 are not secure).

Although tpm.KE cannot achieve the rigorous KCI resistance and PFS properties, it can satisfy weak forms of the two properties: (1) constrained KCI; that is, the control of a party's long-term key handle doesn't enable the attacker to impersonate *other, uncontrolled, parties* to the party; and (2) the constrained PFS property; that is, the expired session keys established before the attacker controls the handle of the long-term key cannot be recovered. To prove weak forms of the two properties, all is needed is to note that the proof of tpm.KE in Sect. 7 still holds if we allow the attacker to corrupt $\hat{A}$ and $\hat{B}$ which are the related parities of the test session, i.e., all the simulators don't abort when $\hat{A}$ and $\hat{B}$ are corrupted. The proof remains valid since the abort operations are never used in the proof.

8.2   Suggestions

TPM 2.0 is an important industrial specification which might be deployed widely in practice, so a formal analysis of its key exchange primitive is critical. In this work we formally show that tpm.KE can achieve the basic security property defined by modern AKE models. However, this goal is achieved under some constraints on the attacker, and if the host of a TPM doesn't code its software properly, tpm.KE would be vulnerable to attacks. In order to ensure proper use of tpm.KE, we give the following suggestions:

1. As only in the environment that all long-term keys are protected by the TPM can tpm.KE achieve rigorous security property, we suggest that the Certificate Authority only issues certificates for keys that are generated by TPM chips. This can be done via the Privacy CA protocol [10] or the direct anonymous attestation (DAA) protocol [6] if higher anonymity is required.
2. Note that the Full Unified Model scheme would be definitely insecure if the unhashed value Z_1 is compromised by the attacker. We suggest that the software running on the host which derives the session key from the return results of the TPM should be well protected, and the software should delete the return results of the TPM (especially Z_1 of the Full Unified Model scheme) immediately after the session key is derived.

In real world environments, it's common that some parties are equipped with the TPM and others are not, and some CAs only issue certificates for keys protected by the TPM (for example, via Privacy CA or DAA protocol) and some CAs issue certificates for keys no matter whether they are protected by the TPM. For the keys that are not protected by the TPM, it's feasible for the attacker to obtain their plaintexts, and these keys open a window of opportunity to mount Kaliski's UKS attack and Xu's attacks on tpm.KE: the attacker can register specific long-term keys or long-term keys whose plaintexts are available to him to compromise sessions of other honest parties. So current tpm.KE is not suitable for use in real world environments. For the sake of enabling tpm.KE to achieve rigorous security in real world environments, where plaintexts of some parties' long-term private keys are vulnerable to attacks, we give the following suggestions:

1. Perform the session key derivation in the TPM rather than on the host, i.e., perform $H_1()$ and $H_2()$ in the TPM. This modification to tpm.KE only adds a hash to the TPM which is negligible compared to the elliptic curve scalar multiplication. We have shown that protecting the unhashed value Z_1 is a basic requirement for the security of the Full Unified Model protocol. Protecting the unhashed value Z is also necessary for the security of MQV and SM2 key exchange in real world environments: it has been shown in [16] and [32] that the disclosure of Z of a session can lead to the vulnerability of other sessions. That's why Krawczyk mandates the hashing of Z in the HMQV (a proven secure variant of MQV), and Zhao et al. suggest putting the session key derivation of SM2 key exchange into the TPM.
2. Replace $avf()$ and $avf'()$ with cryptographic hash functions. Although we have shown that $avf()$ and $avf'()$ can be modeled as random oracles as they provide strong enough randomness, it's still preferred to replace them with cryptographic hash functions.

9   Conclusions and Future Work

In this paper, we present a formal analysis of the key exchange primitive of TPM 2.0 in a unified way. One feature of our analysis is that we eliminate specific assumptions on the representation of group elements by measuring the entropy contained in the output of the $avf()$ and $avf'()$. The entropy measurement results enable us to model $avf()$ and $avf'()$ as random oracles convincingly. Another feature of our analysis is that we consider protections provided by the TPM. Our analysis shows that the TPM 2.0 indeed can provide a proven secure key exchange functionality if the following requirements are satisfied: all honest parties use the TPM (or other hardware security tokens) to protect their long-term keys, and the CA only issues certificates for keys from legitimate TPMs. However, these requirements are somewhat impractical, which limit the use of tpm.KE in real world environments. So we give suggestions on how to improve the security level of tpm.KE to enable its use in real world environments. A formal security analysis of the improved tpm.KE based on our unified security model can be done in the future work.

References

1. GM/T 0003.5-2012: Public Key Cryptographic Algorithm SM2 Based on Elliptic Curves Part 5: Parameter definition
2. ISO/IEC 15946–5:2009 Information technology - Security techniques - Cryptographic techniques based on elliptic curves - Part 5: Elliptic curve generation
3. Aiello, W., Bellovin, S.M., Blaze, M., Canetti, R., Ioannidis, J., Keromytis, A.D., Reingold, O.: Just fast keying: key agreement in a hostile internet. ACM Trans. Inf. Syst. Secur. (TISSEC) 7(2), 242–273 (2004)
4. Barker, E.B., Johnson, D., Smid, M.E.: NIST SP 800–56A. recommendation for pair-wise key establishment schemes using discrete logarithm cryptography (2007) (revised)
5. Blake-Wilson, S., Menezes, A.: Unknown key-share attacks on the station-to-station (STS) protocol. In: Imai, H., Zheng, Y. (eds.) PKC 1999. LNCS, vol. 1560, pp. 154–170. Springer, Heidelberg (1999)
6. Brickell, E., Camenisch, J., Chen, L.: Direct anonymous attestation. In: Proceedings of the 11th ACM Conference on Computer and Communications Security, pp. 132–145. ACM (2004)
7. Canetti, R., Krawczyk, H.: Analysis of key-exchange protocols and their use for building secure channels. In: Pfitzmann, B. (ed.) EUROCRYPT 2001. LNCS, vol. 2045, pp. 453–474. Springer, Heidelberg (2001)
8. Canetti, R., Krawczyk, H.: Security Analysis of IKE's Signature-Based Key-Exchange Protocol. In: Yung, M. (ed.) CRYPTO 2002. LNCS, vol. 2442, pp. 143–161. Springer, Heidelberg (2002)
9. Chen, L.: Recommendation for key derivation using pseudorandom functions. NIST Spec. Publ. **800**, 108 (2008)
10. Chen, L., Warinschi, B.: Security of the tcg privacy-ca solution. In: 2010 IEEE/IFIP 8th International Conference on Embedded and Ubiquitous Computing (EUC), pp. 609–616. IEEE (2010)
11. Dierks, T.: The transport layer security (tls) protocol version 1.2. (2008)

12. FIPS, PUB: 186–2. Digital Signature Standard (DSS). National Institute of Standards and Technology (NIST) (2000)
13. Gennaro, R., Krawczyk, H., Rabin, T.: Okamoto-Tanaka revisited: fully authenticated Diffie-Hellman with minimal overhead. In: Zhou, J., Yung, M. (eds.) ACNS 2010. LNCS, vol. 6123, pp. 309–328. Springer, Heidelberg (2010)
14. Jeong, I.R., Katz, J., Lee, D.-H.: One-round protocols for two-party authenticated key exchange. In: Jakobsson, M., Yung, M., Zhou, J. (eds.) ACNS 2004. LNCS, vol. 3089, pp. 220–232. Springer, Heidelberg (2004)
15. Kaliski Jr., B.S.: An unknown key-share attack on the MQV key agreement protocol. ACM Trans. Inf. Syst. Secur. (TISSEC) $4(3)$, 275–288 (2001)
16. Krawczyk, H.: HMQV: a high-performance secure Diffie-Hellman protocol. In: Shoup, V. (ed.) CRYPTO 2005. LNCS, vol. 3621, pp. 546–566. Springer, Heidelberg (2005)
17. LaMacchia, B.A., Lauter, K., Mityagin, A.: Stronger security of authenticated key exchange. In: Susilo, W., Liu, J.K., Mu, Y. (eds.) ProvSec 2007. LNCS, vol. 4784, pp. 1–16. Springer, Heidelberg (2007)
18. Lauter, K., Mityagin, A.: Security analysis of KEA authenticated key exchange protocol. In: Yung, M., Dodis, Y., Kiayias, A., Malkin, T. (eds.) PKC 2006. LNCS, vol. 3958, pp. 378–394. Springer, Heidelberg (2006)
19. Law, L., Menezes, A., Qu, M., Solinas, J., Vanstone, S.: An efficient protocol for authenticated key agreement. Des. Codes Crypt. $28(2)$, 119–134 (2003)
20. Matsumoto, T., Takashima, Y.: On seeking smart public-key-distribution systems. IEICE Trans. (1976–1990) $69(2)$, 99–106 (1986)
21. Menezes, A., Qu, M., Vanstone, S.: Some new key agreement protocols providing mutual implicit authentication. In: Second Workshop on Selected Areas in Cryptography (SAC 1995) (1995)
22. SEC, Secg. 2: Recommended elliptic curve domain parameters (2000). http://www.secg.org
23. Skipjack and NIST. KEA algorithm specifications (1998)
24. TCG: TCG Algorithm Registry Family 2.0, Level 00 Revision 15 January 2014
25. TCG: Trusted platform module library part 1: Architecture, family 2.0, level 00 revision 07 January 2014
26. TCG: Trusted Platform Module Library Part 3: Commands Family 2.0, Level 00 Revision 07 January 2014
27. Ustaoglu, B.: Obtaining a secure and efficient key agreement protocol from (H)MQV and NAXOS. Des. Codes Crypt. $46(3)$, 329–342 (2008)
28. Willems, F.M., Shtarkov, Y.M., Tjalkens, T.J.: The context-tree weighting method: basic properties. IEEE Trans. Inf. Theo. $41(3)$, 653–664 (1995)
29. Xu, J., Feng, D.: Comments on the SM2 key exchange protocol. In: Lin, D., Tsudik, G., Wang, X. (eds.) CANS 2011. LNCS, vol. 7092, pp. 160–171. Springer, Heidelberg (2011)
30. Yao, A.C., Zhao, Y.: A new family of implicitly authenticated diffie-hellman protocols. Technical report
31. Yao, A.C.-C., Zhao, Y.: OAKE: a new family of implicitly authenticated diffie-hellman protocols. In: Proceedings of the 2013 ACM SIGSAC Conference on Computer & Communications Security, pp. 1113–1128. ACM (2013)
32. Zhao, S., Xi, L., Zhang, Q., Qin, Y., Feng, D.: Security analysis of SM2 key exchange protocol in TPM2. 0. security and communication. Networks $8(3)$, 383–395 (2015)
33. Zhao, S., Zhang, Q.: A Unified Security Analysis of Two-phase Key Exchange Protocols in TPM 2.0. http://eprint.iacr.org/2015/611

On Making Emerging Trusted Execution Environments Accessible to Developers

Thomas Nyman[1]([⊠]), Brian McGillion[1], and N. Asokan[2,3]

[1] Intel Collaborative Research Institute for Secure Computing (ICRI-SC)
at Aalto University, Espoo, Finland
{thomas.nyman,brian.mcgillion}@aalto.fi
[2] Aalto University, Espoo, Finland
[3] University of Helsinki, Helsinki, Finland
asokan@acm.org

Abstract. New types of Trusted Execution Environment (TEE) architectures like TrustLite and Intel Software Guard Extensions (SGX) are emerging. They bring new features that can lead to innovative security and privacy solutions. But each new TEE environment comes with its own set of interfaces and programming paradigms, thus raising the barrier for entry for developers who want to make use of these TEEs. In this paper, we motivate the need for realizing standard TEE interfaces on such emerging TEE architectures and show that this exercise is not straightforward. We report on our on-going work in mapping GlobalPlatform standard interfaces to TrustLite and SGX.

1 Introduction

For more than a decade the vast majority of smartphones and tablets have been equipped with hardware security functionality, usually referred to as *Trusted Execution Environments* (TEEs) [3]. A TEE is an isolated and integrity-protected processing environment where sensitive computations, such as cryptographic operations, can be safely carried out. Until recently, application developers have not had the means to make use of TEEs to enhance the security and privacy of their applications. New standardization efforts, such as GlobalPlatform (GP) [5], and open source implementation initiatives, such as OP-TEE [8] and Trusted Little Kernel [11] have the potential for ushering in widespread use of TEEs by application developers.

Although the deployed base of mobile devices with TEEs is very large, numbering in hundreds of millions, they predominantly follow the same architectural pattern: a computing device containing a physical or logical TEE where small amounts of sensitive computation can be carried out in conjunction with a larger software components operating outside the TEE. The chief example of such a TEE architecture is ARM TrustZone [1] which is widely deployed in smartphones.

Recently new types of TEE architectures have been proposed. They range from TEEs like TrustLite [7] and SMART [4] designed for tiny resource constrained

© Springer International Publishing Switzerland 2015
M. Conti et al. (Eds.): TRUST 2015, LNCS 9229, pp. 58–67, 2015.
DOI: 10.1007/978-3-319-22846-4_4

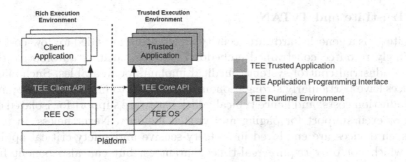

Fig. 1. Abstract view of computing device equipped with a TEE [5]

devices to Intel Software Guard Extensions (SGX) [10] intended primarily for servers and desktops. They provide novel functionality but come with their own *Application Program Interfaces* (APIs) and development environments. This constitutes a high barrier for entry for developers making it more difficult for them to benefit from such TEE functionality. A natural solution approach to this problem would be to support a set of standard TEE interfaces, such as those specified by GP, on these emerging TEE architectures thereby allowing developers familiar with the standard interfaces to readily make use of the new TEEs. However, subtle differences in architectural assumptions pose some challenges in mapping GP interfaces to these TEEs. In this work-in-progress paper, we examine these challenges.

Our contribution is two-fold. First, we briefly juxtapose the features of the emerging TEE architectures with the assumptions behind TEE standards (Sect. 2). We then show the subtleties and challenges in realizing the GlobalPlatform model on two such example TEE architectures: TrustLite and SGX (Sect. 3). We briefly describe our experience so far in resolving these challenges.

2 Background

The isolation and integrity-protection of the processing environment in a TEE can be achieved in different ways. Contemporary TEE architectures commonly utilize either a dedicated security co-processor or CPU extensions that allow one physical processor to operate efficiently in two distinct isolated modes in a so called *split-world* configuration. In either case, the device may be viewed as having two separate environments, each with its own set of features, as shown in Fig. 1. The *Rich Execution Environment* (REE) refers to the operating environment that houses the conventional OS and applications. In contrast, the TEE typically only has a limited set of features that are only intended to address security critical functionality offloaded onto the TEE by *Client Applications* (CAs) in the REE. The isolation of the TEE itself and discrete pieces of software inside the TEE, referred to as *Trusted Applications* (TAs) is realized by means of hardware support. Services and APIs available to TAs, such as access to trusted storage, are provided by a TEE OS, part of the TEE *Trusted Computing Base* (TCB).

2.1   TrustLite and TyTAN

TrustLite [7] is a generic hardware security architecture intended for low-cost and exceedingly resource constrained embedded systems, such as automotive electronics, industrial control systems, medical implants or wearables. Such classes of devices have particularly strong economic incentives to minimize development and production costs, and hence typically lack hardware support for isolated execution or even support for paging and virtual memory. Nevertheless, in many cases such devices are employed in security-sensive and safety-critical applications, which not only require real-time guarantees, but can also benefit from certain security features, such as strong isolation and the possibility of attesting local state to a (remote) verifier.

Lacking a conventional *Memory Management Unit* (MMU), memory access in these constrained environments is typically mediated by a *Memory Protection Unit* (MPU), which can be programmed in supervisor mode by the device OS with memory access rules for the next task scheduled to run. In TrustLite the basis for strong isolation between tasks is an *Execution Aware Memory Protection Unit* (EA-MPU), which not only enforces access control on all memory accesses, but does so considering the current program counter value when validating a particular access to memory. Hence, a platform equipped with an EA-MPU can enforce fine-grained access control based on the individual code regions executed independently of the OS. TrustLite also introduces a secure exception engine which maintains the memory isolation of secure tasks protected by the EA-MPU even in the case of hardware and software interrupts.

Later work by Brasser et. al. leverages the TrustLite architecture to realize TyTAN [2], a security architecture for embedded systems that provides strong isolation of dynamically configurable tasks assisted by hardware features introduced in TrustLite, as well real-time scheduling guarantees. TyTAN utilizes the secure exception engine of TrustLite to provide a secure *Inter Process Communication* (IPC) mechanism, where both sender and receiver can be authenticated using the digest of respective tasks measured upon loading. TyTAN does not provide any built-in access control for IPC. Instead, e.g., the task on the receiving end of an IPC call can make access control decisions based on the verified identity of the sender. TyTAN differs from the traditional TEE model in Fig. 1 in that normal and secure tasks co-exist in a single environment[1], and rely on scheduling provided by an untrusted (real time) operating system. The OS is assumed to schedule tasks fairly without starvation. Normal tasks are isolated from other tasks but are fully controlled and accessible by the OS. In contrast, secure tasks are isolated by the EA-MPU from the rest of the system, including the OS. Whereas CAs in Fig. 1 are thought to include the advanced domain logic of an application, and TAs only very limited security sensitive functionality, all tasks in TyTAN are relatively simple. The primary concern in TyTAN is the correct operation of secure tasks, even in the face of an adversary who has full control of the untrusted OS and normal tasks running on the platform.

---

[1] Instead, the class of devices TrustLite represents may potentially be used as part of a programmable secure co-processor.

2.2   Intel SGX

Intel Software Guard Extensions [10] is another hardware-based approach to realize an isolated environment for preserving the confidentiality and integrity of sensitive code and data. SGX consists of a set of new CPU instructions and memory access changes to the Intel CPU architecture, which allows parts of the application code and data residing in main memory to be encrypted using a key accessible only in the CPU core. The protected portions of the application's virtual address space together with the corresponding SGX control data structures are referred to as an *enclave*. Enclave creation and initialization is handled via two dedicated instructions, *Enclave CREATE* (`ECREATE`) and *Enclave INIT* (`EINIT`). When an enclave is operated on, a dedicated hardware unit on the CPU package decrypts incoming, and encrypts outgoing traffic between the main memory and CPU package, so that sensitive code and data never leave the CPU package unencrypted. Transfer of execution into and out of an enclave is strictly controlled.

Entry to an enclave occurs via a dedicated *Enclave ENTER* (`EENTER`) CPU instruction, which causes any cached page table translations overlapping with the protected address region of an enclave to be invalidated and transfers control to code inside the enclave. While the CPU is executing in *enclave mode*, it has access to the protected pages belonging to the currently executing enclave, as well as any unprotected pages in the current processes's virtual address space. Accesses to protected pages belonging to other enclaves are prevented. Outside of enclave mode, access attempts by the CPU to enclave pages are treated as references to nonexistent memory, as are physical memory accesses by other agents, such as DMA access by capable disk drive controllers, graphics cards etc. Furthermore, `SYSENTER` and `SYSCALL` instructions are prohibited while in enclave mode, requiring the enclave to be exited before making system calls.

Exit from an enclave may occur either as a result of an *Enclave EXIT* (`EEXIT`) instruction, or asynchronously, such as when exceptions or interrupts occur during enclave execution. In the latter case, an *Asynchronous Enclave eXit* (`AEX`) event causes the processor state to be securely saved inside protected enclave memory and the CPU registers to be scrubbed in order to avoid leakage of sensitive data. Finally, the CPU leaves enclave mode. The enclave may subsequently be re-entered with an *Enclave RESUME* (`ERESUME`) instruction, which restores the execution state of the enclave. In both cases, any cached page translations referring to the enclave's protected address region are cleared.

In contrast to conventional split-world-based isolated execution approaches, such as ARM TrustZone [1], the SGX hardware architecture results in much simpler transitions to and from the secure CPU mode. There is no need to manually transfer data back and forth between a secure and normal world, as the isolated enclaves execute within the address space of the host process. In addition there is no need for a separate operating environment to provide further isolation between enclaves, as each enclave is already isolated from other processes in the system, including it's own host process and other enclaves.

2.3   Standardization

To date there have been many proprietary APIs developed for TEEs. Almost every vendor of TEE technology has supplied their own implementations, with varying levels of complexity and functionality. Many of these solutions are aimed at the same market segments. They thus impact the consumers, namely *Original Equipment Manufacturers* (OEMs) and operators in this case, in similar ways. This fragmentation has been partly to blame for the slow uptake in the use of TEE technology. OEMs find that they need to provide more engineering effort to support essentially the same functionality on different hardware platforms. With ever increasing demands for more services and growing awareness of end users' need for privacy protection, OS vendors such as Google are mandating that more of the security critical components of the OS are protected by hardware security mechanisms.

This fragmentation and the need for OEMs to pass *Compliance Test Suites* (CTSs), designed to test that the platform protects the security critical components as mandated by the OS vendor, have led to the need to address this through some form of standardization. There have also been a number of efforts to address this by providing a standard operating system to run within the TEE, such as Nvidia's *Trusted Little Kernel* [11] (TLK) and Linaro's *OP-TEE* [8]. Though a common operating system is a good start to help adoption as it removes a lot of engineering effort, it does not go far enough to address the needs of application developers on platforms such as Android or iOS. To benefit these application developers there must be a consistent API by which TEE functionality can be accessed.

To this end *GlobalPlatform* (GP) [5], a non-profit association focused on promoting the industry wide adoption of security standards, has been formulating and driving standards for TEE APIs. Within the scope of the TEEs that we describe in this paper, i.e. extensible TEEs that allow for the deployment of trusted third-party code, GP has defined two main standards. The *TEE Client API*, running in the host operating system, and the *TEE Core API*, running inside the TEE. This provides standardization of both the TAs (so they can be deployed in any GP compliant TEE irrespective of the HW vendor) and the CAs that run on the host operating system. GP's architecture is built around the model defined in Fig. 1 where a CA running in the REE creates one or more sessions to TAs in the TEE. This session establishes an effective *Remote Procedure Call* (RPC) mechanism through which it is possible for the CA to invoke commands in the TA. Via a well defined API a TA is able to provide its services while also protecting itself from misuse. The first column in Table 1 summarizes the GP TEE Core API internal TA interface.

To date GP is the forerunner in TEE standardization – numerous GP implementations are starting to emerge. Both TLK and OP-TEE provide some form of GP compliance, though the exact extent of the compliance is unknown as the GP compliance test suite is not readily available.

2.4   Open-TEE

In our previous work [9], while recognizing the efforts that have been undertaken to address the issue of TEE compliance, we highlight other issues that hinder

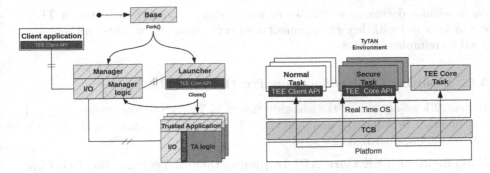

Fig. 2. Open-TEE architecture [9]   **Fig. 3.** GP architecture on TyTAN

widespread adoption of TEEs. Chief among them are the lack of access to debug-enabled versions of existing TEEs and the difficulty of developing applications for the TEE. This insight led to the development of Open-TEE, a virtual TEE that complies with the GP standard and provides a fast and efficient proto-typing platform for TAs / CAs. Fig. 2 shows the Open-TEE architecture as a series of processes running on a development machine, thus allowing developers to leverage the tools, e.g. editors and debuggers, that they are familiar with. The *Manager* process provides the TEE runtime with services usually expected from the TEE OS. Unlike a proper TEE OS, which would be self-contained and run on bare hardware, the implementation of Manager utilizes APIs provided by the host OS, in this case POSIX and a small number of APIs specific to Linux. The sole purpose of the *Launcher* process is to pre-load the shared library implement-ing the TEE Core API and serve as a base process used to clone the actual TA processes, which are subsequently reparented onto Manager. Each TA process is divided into two separate threads; the *I/O* thread and *TA logic* thread. The I/O thread facilitates communication with Manager, whereas the TA logic thread executes the TA logic. Open-TEE is publicly available[2] under the permissive Apache-V2 license.

3 Mapping GlobalPlatform Interfaces to New TEE Architectures

Although not conventional TEE environments with their own OSs, TrustLite and SGX provide the same security assurances i.e. integrity and confidential-ity of both code and data. They do not enforce the split world view that has become the de facto standard for extensible TEEs. However, there are still a number of use cases where applying the GP concepts and having access to a GP compliant implementation can be beneficial. First and foremost is the question of portability – GP compliant applications should be readily deployable in any compliant TEE. Second is the notion of a services framework – there are many

---

[2] http://open-tee.github.io/

cases when a developer would like to use existing services provided by a TEE, e.g. a keystore with key management and cryptographic routines, without the need to reimplement these.

3.1   Realizing GP Interfaces on TrustLite / TyTAN

In Sect. 2.1 we noted how the isolation model in TyTAN differs from the typical GP model. Consequently, mapping the GP APIs to platforms such as TyTAN presents some challenges:

Placement of TEE Core API Implementation. Typically, the TEE Core API and support for CA-to-TA communication would be provided as services by the TEE OS. In TrustLite and TyTAN the OS itself is excluded from the platform TCB; thus the TEE Core API implementation needs to be provided in some other manner. An obvious alternative would be to provide it purely in a library linked to each trusted task designated as a GP-style TA. This has a number of drawbacks. First, due the lack of paging memory management and caching, this leads to suboptimal memory utilization as identical functionality would be replicated in each TA. Second, the implementation of certain APIs, such as trusted storage access would be greatly simplified by platform support for centralized secure storage. Therefore TEE Core API functionality could either be provided directly by the TyTAN TCB, or in a less invasive approach, by a separate secure task, referred to as *TEE Core task*, separately protected by the EA-MPU. The TEE Core API library linked to TAs can then invoke IPC calls to the TEE Core task, which resolves such calls appropriately. The overall architecture is shown in the Fig. 3. In this case, the challenge stems from the fact that the strong isolation provided by TrustLite is not based on a completely separate environment, but on per-task isolation. Therefore, there is no separate trusted OS part of the TCB as is the case in established TEEs.

Session Access Control. The TEE Client API is used for communication between normal and secure tasks. The TEE Core API also provides an Internal Client API, which allows one TA to act as a client to another TA. With regards to TyTAN tasks, this can be utilized for communication from one secure task to another. One challenge with this mapping is the need to enforce access restrictions on the TEE Core task so that only secure tasks are allowed to invoke TEE Core API functionality. In addition, the TEE Client API provides session-based access to TAs. As noted in Sect. 2.1, TyTAN does not provide any IPC access control by itself, but leaves this up to individual secure tasks based on the hash digest of the sender as reported by the IPC primitives part of the TyTAN TCB. One approach would be to implement sessions, TEE Core task multiplexing and access control in each secure task individually. However, providing this functionality as part of a proxy in the TyTAN TCB has the same advantages as the centralized TEE Core placement which is an important consideration in the highly resource constrained environments that TyTAN targets. The challenge here stems from a large disparity in levels of IPC abstraction between TyTAN, and the GP specifications.

Table 1. Mapping TEE Core API internal TA entry points to SGX instructions

GP TEE Core API internal TA entry points	SGX instructions and events
TA_CreateEntryPoint	ECREATE, EINIT, EENTER, EEXIT
TA_DestroyEntryPoint	EENTER, EEXIT
TA_OpenSessionEntryPoint	EENTER, AEX, ERESUME, EEXIT
TA_CloseSessionEntry	EENTER, AEX, ERESUME, EEXIT
TA_InvokeCommandEntryPoint	EENTER, AEX, ERESUME, EEXIT

Other Issues. Apart from the Internal Client API, the TEE Core API provides the TAs with internal programming interfaces for trusted storage, cryptographic operations, time API, and an arithmetic API intended as building blocks for developers to implement further asymmetric cryptographic algorithms. For performance reasons, platforms based on TrustLite may require additional cryptographic hardware accelerators to meet operational requirements, hence full coverage of the TEE Core API is not only impractical, but also unnecessary for many intended use cases. Due to its nature, it is likely that instantiations of TrustLite for different use cases will have varying degrees of hardware support for aforementioned features, and it is unlikely that a one-size-fits-all solution would be applicable for devices of this scale.

3.2   Realizing GP with SGX Through Open-TEE

Open-TEE was conceived as a GP compliant tool for fast prototyping. However, throughout its design, choices were made that would allow it to work as a fully functional TEE environment when combined with the right hardware security mechanisms, like SGX enclaves. An enclave is a ring-3 construct. As such code in an enclave cannot make systems calls or other external interactions. Due to these restrictions, an enclave must synchronize with the non-enclave part of the application to perform external tasks on its behalf.

If we take a common usage scenario of a CA wishing to interact with a TA that performs some operation involving access to secure storage, we can see how Open-TEE's architecture (Fig. 2) can be mapped to SGX [6]. The choice to split the TA process into two distinct threads, one handling I/O, and the other logic functionality facilitates this mapping. The I/O thread is responsible for all communication with Manager and CA. It is also responsible for all system interactions that may be required. The TA logic thread is where the TA code, which can make use of the TEE Core API, is executed. Manager provides secure storage functionality as a service to TA processes.

The CA initiates an open session call towards the TA. Manager noticing that the TA is not running requests Launcher to create a TA process. At this point the TA is a standard process and loads in accordance with the OS requirements. Once the TA is created we must initialize the TA logic code which conforms to the GP standard [5] by invoking TA_CreateEntryPoint(). As all of the GP conformant functionality is implemented within the enclave it is at this point that the enclave must be created. The TA hands over the enclave code along with any additional configuration data to the enclave creation service running in supervisor mode. Once the enclave has been created and initialized control is handed back to the TA application which enters the enclave to finalize the TA initialization and establish the session to the CA.

Now that the session is established between the CA and the TA, the CA can invoke TA commands using TEEC_InvokeCommand(). Imagine that the CA wishes to provision some data to the secure storage. It invokes the corresponding TA command when the TA logic thread wants to access the secure storage. This requires a read or write operation to the storage media, which is a system call and is thus prohibited by SGX. In this case the Open-TEE implementation of the TEE Core secure storage API initiates an interrupt towards the I/O thread causing an AEX event which stores the enclave state and control is passed back to the I/O thread. The I/O thread then invokes the Manager to read/write encrypted data from/to persistent storage. When this action has been completed the TA can resume execution in the TA logic thread. When the invoked task is complete the enclave can be exited thereby returning control to the I/O thread which can then respond to the CA on the status of the invoked command. Other system services needed in the TEE Core API such as time functionality can be handled in a similar fashion. Table 1 summarizes the mapping of TEE Core API internal TA entry points to SGX instructions and events.

4 Conclusion

The GP TEE interfaces were designed to support split-world-based TEEs. We have shown that, even though potentially beneficial for easing the adoption of new, emerging TEE environments, mapping existing GP interfaces to them has a number of challenges. In ongoing work we are implementing the GP TEE Client API, and a subset of the TEE Core API on TyTAN. We are also exploring practical subsets of the TEE Core API applicable to different use cases. In future work we plan to investigate possible extensions to the TEE Core API relevant for small scale devices as well as realize Open-TEE on SGX.

References

1. ARM Security Technology - Building a Secure System using TrustZone Technology (2009). http://infocenter.arm.com/help/topic/com.arm.doc.prd29-genc-009492c/PRD29-GENC-009492C_trustzone_security_whitepaper.pdf
2. Brasser, F., et al.: TyTAN: tiny trust anchor for tiny devices. In: 52nd Design Automation Conference (DAC) June 2015
3. Ekberg, J., Kostiainen, K., Asokan, N.: The untapped potential of trusted execution environments on mobile devices. IEEE Secur. Priv. 12(4), 29–37 (2014). http://dx.doi.org/10.1109/MSP.2014.38
4. Eldefrawy, K., Tsudik, G., Francillon, A., Perito, D.: SMART: secure and minimal architecture for (establishing dynamic) root of trust. In: 19th Annual Network and Distributed System Security Symposium, NDSS 2012, San Diego, California, USA, February 5–8 (2012). The Internet Society (2012). http://www.internetsociety.org/smart-secure-and-minimal-architecture-establishing-dynamic-root-trust

5. GlobalPlatform: Device specifications for trusted execution environment. http://www.globalplatform.org/specificationsdevice.asp
6. Intel: Software Guard Extensions Programming Reference (2013). https://software.intel.com/en-us/isa-extensions/intel-sgx
7. Koeberl, P., Schulz, S., Sadeghi, A.R., Varadharajan, V.: TrustLite: a security architecture for tiny embedded devices. In: Proceedings of the Ninth European Conference on Computer Systems, pp. 10:1–10:14. EuroSys 2014. ACM, New York, NY, USA (2014). http://doi.acm.org/10.1145/2592798.2592824
8. Linaro: OP-TEE. https://wiki.linaro.org/WorkingGroups/Security/OP-TEE
9. McGillion, B., Dettenborn, T., Nyman, T., Asokan, N.: Open-TEE - an open virtual trusted execution environment. Technical report. Aalto University (2015). http://arxiv.org/abs/1506.07367
10. McKeen, F., et al.: Innovative instructions and software model for isolated execution. In: Proceedings of the 2nd International Workshop on Hardware and Architectural Support for Security and Privacy, pp. 10:1–10:1. HASP 2013. ACM, New York, NY, USA (2013). http://doi.acm.org/10.1145/2487726.2488368
11. NVIDIA: Trusted Little Kernel (TLK). http://nv-tegra.nvidia.com/gitweb/?p=3rdparty/ote_partner/tlk.git;a=summary

Trust and Users

Computing Trust Levels Based on User's Personality and Observed System Trustworthiness

Michalis Kanakakis[1], Shenja van der Graaf[2], Costas Kalogiros[1(✉)], and Wim Vanobberghen[2]

[1] AUEB, 76, Patission Str., 1034 Athens, Greece
{kanakakis, ckalog}@aueb.gr
[2] iMinds-SMIT, Brussels, Belgium
{a.van.der.graaf, wim.vanobberghen}@vub.ac.be

Abstract. In this article, we describe an approach for computing the current trust level of individual users towards an online system and present initial validation results from a small-scale experiment. This trust computational model relies upon survey research for identifying the set of key trust attributes and grouping users into four segments of expected behaviors. Each user's initial trust level is computed based on a set of assumptions tailored to the specific segment she belongs to, while the trust level evolution takes additionally into account the system outcomes she has experienced so far. More specifically, the trust update follows a machine learning approach, where during the training phase that consists of a small number of system outcomes, users are asked to report their actual trust levels. Finally, we demonstrate the trustors' segmentation validity and trust estimation accuracy by performing a small-scale experiment in the context of a fictitious online security service.

Keywords: Trust computational model · Trust · Trustworthiness · Trustor attributes · Survey

1 Introduction

The increasing complexity to attain trust in trustworthy Information and Communications Technology (ICT) systems and the conditions that affect it, has warranted continuous scrutiny from researchers in various domains. While trust is important in the real world too, it is said to be especially complex to achieve and sustain in Internet-based marketplaces due to the lack of the providers' physical presence and in certain settings the rare frequency of transactions between two entities [1, 2]. In this view, the need for models of trust and credibility in technology-mediated interactions can be detected, particularly, those that are not-domain specific and technology-independent [3]. These models can offer guidance for researchers across disciplines examining a range of technologies and contexts, thereby highlighting multiple subcomponents, such as associated with antecedents (i.e. preconditions of trust), processes of trust building (e.g., interdependence), the context of shaping trust-building (e.g., social relations, regulation), decision-making processes in trust (e.g., rational choice, routine, habitual),

© Springer International Publishing Switzerland 2015
M. Conti et al. (Eds.): TRUST 2015, LNCS 9229, pp. 71–87, 2015.
DOI: 10.1007/978-3-319-22846-4_5

implications and uses of trust (e.g., interpersonal entrepreneurial relations, moralistic trust), and lack of trust, distrust, mistrust and repair (e.g., risks, over-trust, trust violations) [4]. In addition, much of this research seems to mainly address how to optimize user trust.

In this study, we have taken the, arguably, complimentary perspective to examine how different trust-related user experiences are guided by different sets of trustor's attributes underpinned by aspects of well-placed trust and trustworthy behaviors. The reason for developing an approach conditioning the trust levels to individual entities, is that trust formation is a dynamic, or, contextual, yet subjective process, drawing attention to the presence of drivers, such as of a social, economic and legal nature [4, 5, 7]. More specifically, trust is approached as a property of an entity (known as the trustor) reflecting the strength of her belief that engaging in an online system (called the trustee) for some purpose will produce an acceptable outcome [8]. Here, a trustee's trustworthiness is defined as an objective measure (probability) of the provider's ability to produce an acceptable outcome, assuming consensus on the criterion for determining whether an outcome is acceptable or not. We argue that whenever such a criterion is not obvious it could be defined by a regulatory authority, or in the extreme case set by the dominant provider.

Estimating the current user's trust level can be useful for a provider of ICT systems/services both at design-time and run-time. In the former case, knowing the trustors' current trust level and the effects of both desirable and undesirable outcomes on them would allow her to predict the actual demand and set the optimal combination (s) of trustworthiness level and price. Obviously, failing to predict the true demand would result either in missed opportunities for higher revenues, or higher costs. In the latter case, a provider should meet users' expectations in order to avoid customer churn and do so in a cost-effective way at run-time. Thus, whenever the provider believes that a user's trust is lower than a certain threshold the former could make the necessary changes to system in order to regain its trust.

Our main contribution, therefore, is to propose a conceptual trust computational model that allows a provider to estimate the trust level of candidate trustors. Our approach differentiates among trustors based on their attributes and highlights their influence on trust. Our aim is to cover all the phases of the computation process: before engaging with the system and after observing evidences about its performance. For example, it is expected that a successful system outcome will not decrease the user's trust in the system, and similarly, an unsuccessful outcome should not cause an increase. Thus, the trust computational model is based on system behavior instead of user behavior (such as eye gaze). Against the standard methodology of the well-known Bayesian models, which follows common initialization and evolution of trust among individuals, we introduce a modification to capture the attributes making trust subjective. The wide range of attributes affecting reactions of trust vis-à-vis ICT systems, motivated us to execute a user survey and identify the key drivers to be considered as trust indicators. Based on this analysis, the trustors were grouped into segments of expected behaviors and their properties are formulated via the variables of the modified Bayesian model. In order to demonstrate the validity of our approach we performed a small-scale experiment in the context of a fictitious online security service.

The remaining sections are structured as follows; Sect. 2 introduces the basic computational model that forms the basis for the proposed models. Section 3 presents the trustors' segments, using survey research, that were found to be statistically significant and Sect. 4 describes the initialisation and update process of the personalised trust computational model. Then, Sect. 5 presents the experiment setup and the validation results, while Sect. 6 motivates our work by providing an overview of trust computational models that explicitly consider trustor attributes. Finally, we conclude the paper and provide our future steps in Sect. 7.

2 The Basic Trust Computational Model

We consider a system characterized by a wide range of trustworthiness factors, notated as J, e.g. reliability, availability, etc. In this work, we focus on factors resulting in outcomes of binary form, i.e. they may be characterized either as a success or a failure. The performance of the system for factor $j \in J$, is determined by its actual trustworthiness notated as $w_{j,s}$; the probability of a successful transaction.

For each of them, any individual trustor estimates the trustworthiness in terms of a random variable θ which follows the Beta distribution and is determined by two parameters "α, β" for specifying the current beliefs. The choice of this particular distribution is inline with the related work (e.g., see [10] for more details). Given that these parameters can capture all factors that result in trust being subjective (for instance different trustor attributes) we use the notation $\alpha_{i,s}^{j}(t)$ and $\beta_{i,s}^{j}(t)$, where the indicators i, j, s, t stand for the trustor, the metric, the system and the time respectively. From now onwards, we simplify this notation by keeping only the indicators i, j and using s, t when necessary. Thus, for each trustworthiness factor there is an objective probability quantifying its trustworthiness level and a subjective trust level estimating the former. Such a fine-grained approach should give the provider the flexibility to identify, at run-time, the reason(s) for low trust and react accordingly.

Mathematically: $\theta | \alpha_i^j, \beta_i^j \sim Beta(\alpha_i^j, \beta_i^j)$, with probability density function (PDF):

$$f(\theta; \alpha_i^j, \beta_i^j) = \frac{\theta^{\alpha_i^j - 1}(1 - \theta)^{\beta_i^j - 1}}{\int_0^1 y^{\alpha_i^j - 1}(1 - y)^{\beta_i^j - 1} dy}, \alpha_i^j, \beta_i^j > 0 \tag{1}$$

Over this context, trust should be considered as the subjective probability that the system will provide a successful outcome in the next single transaction, and equals the expected value of the $Beta(\alpha_i^j, \beta_i^j)$:

$$\tau_i^j = E[\theta | \alpha_i^j, \beta_i^j] = \frac{\alpha_i^j}{\alpha_i^j + \beta_i^j} \tag{2}$$

Utilizing a PDF allows us to calculate not only trust, but also the confidence, i.e. the probability that the actual trustworthiness lies within an acceptable error range around trust. In general, higher value of α parameter indicates higher trust level (for equal values of β), while confidence depend on their respective sum (for equal trust values).

The values of these parameters can evolve over time, reflecting the trustor's ability to interact with the system further and use those outcomes for getting a more accurate idea of its trustworthiness. The Beta distribution is also appropriate for the update phase, mainly because the process results to the same prior-posterior distributions (before and after an outcome is observed). Indeed, if x stands for the binary outcome of a single transaction, then x follows the Bernoulli distribution with parameter θ, i.e.

$$x|\theta \sim Bern(\theta) \rightarrow f(x|\theta) = \theta^x(1-\theta)^{1-x}, x = 0, 1 \tag{3}$$

Thus, for prior $Beta(a_i^j, \beta_i^j)$ the posterior distribution for parameter θ is as follows:

$$\theta|x, \alpha_i^j, \beta_i^j \sim Beta(x + \alpha_i^j, 1 - x + \beta_i^j) \tag{4}$$

Note that if the outcome is successful ($x = 1$), the α_i^j parameter will be increased by one, while β_i^j parameter will be increased by one in the opposite case, ($x = 0$).

3 Trustors Segmentation

For the examination of the conceptual dynamics underpinning trust-related user experiences and sets of trustor attributes, input from different stakeholders was sought. The focus was to yield insights into their trust perceptions and appetite towards digital technologies, in particularly the Internet. A two-step approach was followed. The first step consisted of survey and interview research where the stakeholders targeted were derived from members of the public (or, (end)users), the business community, and governmental institutions. Based on a thorough literature review focusing on designing ICTs supporting (mediated) transactions, the exploratory empirical investigation focused on drawing out several key aspects of trust, particularly, antecedents, processes of trust building, the context of shaping trust-building, decision-making processes in trust, implications and uses of trust, and lack of trust, distrust, mistrust and repair [4].

In doing so, we sought to draw out the combined underpinnings of relevant (socio-legal-economic) trust drivers, and which guided the main categories for which data were collected. Questions were asked about the disposition to and perceptions of trust, cost of trust, content and information quality, legal constraints, organisational trust, and demographics (user, organizations). These constructs were operationalized with using five-point rating scales open questions, checklist questions, and ranking questions.

As it was the aim to have a reliable question format and a good wording and order, the questions were pre-tested with a group of 142 respondents determining the effectiveness, the strengths and weaknesses of the questions. A principle factor analysis (PCA), therefore, was conducted to detect relationships within the data set generated by the survey in order to yield insight into the underlying structure of trust elements. PCA works by revealing existing linear components in the data set and the way specific variables contribute to that component. First, 49 items were checked for their suitability by screening for high correlations ($R < .9$) and significance values over .05 ($N = 142$).

This led to the removal of one item. The Kaiser-Meyer-Olkin value was .850 and Bartlett's Test of Sphericity was highly significant (p < .001), both indicating a good sampling adequacy. The PCA revealed 11 components with eigenvalues exceeding 1. The first component explained 14.7 % of the total variance and all components combined, explained 61.1 % of the total variance. A closer inspection of the scree plot and running the Monte Carlo parallel analysis indicated that the first few eigenvalues for the randomly generated data matrix scored below the observed eigenvalues from the reduced matrix of data. As a result, it was decided to retain five components based on their explained variance and the outcome of the reliability analysis (>.3). Together they accounted for 50.01 % of the total variance. A Varimax rotation was used to help in interpreting the components: Disposition to trust (e.g. stance towards trusting another person or organization), trust management (e.g., tradeoff between personal information disclosure vs accessing an application), trust constraints (e.g., availability of legal guarantees, price), information and content quality (e.g., trust cues, transfer). The results from pre-testing were then used to adjust problematic questions in the questionnaire before releasing the questionnaires to the target groups. In February and March 2013, N = 203 responses served as input.

While the first step served mainly to learn about combined constructs in trust-related experiences and attributes [8], the second step was to conduct a 'segment-specific' analysis so as to learn about different types of subjective trust-related user experiences in this context. Examining the results of the (end user) survey (N = 90) linkages between different sets of trustor attributes could be associated with trust-related concepts of (1) Trust stance: the tendency of people to trust other people across a wide range of situations and persons; (2) Trust beliefs in general professionals; (3) Institution-based trust; (4) General trust sense levels in online applications and services; (5) ICT-domain specific sense of trust levels; (6) Trust-related seeking behavior; (7) Trust-related competences; and, (8) Perceived importance of trustworthiness design elements. And, which underpin the segmentation of trust-related user experiences on trustor attributes.

For the analytical exercise, a K-means clustering was performed for segmentation purposes and an Anova analysis was conducted to test for each item whether statistical significance differences could be retrieved between the uncovered trust-related user experience segments. Some iterative clustering and testing led us to a four segments solution to best explain differences in trust-related user experiences. These segments can be represented by the following terms, with the corresponding abbreviation to be used for the remaining of this article: "High trust" (HT), "Ambivalent (A) trust", "Highly active trust seeking" (HATS) and "Medium active trust seeking" (MATS). They differ on a number of aspects (see below), however, based on our analyses, three major concepts are sufficient to explain their core differences. The three underpinning concepts are 'trust stance' (e.g., 'I usually trust a person until there is a reason not to'), 'motivation to engage in trust-related seeking behavior' (e.g., 'I look for guarantees regarding confidentiality of the information that I provide') and 'trust-related competences' (e.g., 'I'm able to understand my rights and duties as described by the terms of the application provider'). They could be measured on 3, 7 and 4 item-scale with a reliability coefficient of .69, .89 and .87 respectively. From this a few items could be further reduced to the summarized Table shown below:

Table 1. Segmentation results for the three underpinning concepts.

	Total (n = 90)	HT (n = 24)	HATS (n = 28)	MATS (n = 18)	A (n = 20)	Anova	
	Mean	Mean	Mean	Mean	Mean	F	Sig.
Trust stance	3,22	3,85	3,15	2,86	3,50	7,260	,000
Trust related seeking behaviour	3,52	3,14	4,27	3,34	3,01	24,383	,000
Trust related competences	2,44	2,71	2,42	2,94	1,44	13,361	,000

The user experience for the "HT" segment can be characterized by a high level trust stance. This means an overall high trust level for the various online applications, such as social networks and online banking, accompanied by only few trust seeking behaviors, such as checking trust seals, even though the competences are present to cognitively assess the trustworthiness of online applications and services.

For the "HATS" segment, the user experience can be highlighted in terms of a high level of trust seeking behavior beyond the mere scanning of trustworthiness cues. It also suggests that individuals are informed about procedures in case of harms and misuse. It points to the capacity of certain competence level that facilitate the assessment of trustworthiness and to possess, at least, a minimal understanding of the rules and procedures to look for in case of complaints and misuse. Varied trust stance and trust levels could be observed including medium to low trust stance/trust levels.

For the "MATS" segment, the user experience is similar to the "Highly active" one, yet, here, trust seeking behavior is not so apparent. Thus, while drivers for trust seeking behavior, such as a low trust stance, are present as well as competences to assess trustworthiness, people's motivation may be absent to look for trustworthiness cues.

The "A" trust segment seems to highlight a clear perceived inability to assess the trustworthiness of online applications and services and which may be explained by the personal competence level. Hence, only few active trust seeking behaviors can be observed, yet do not equal low trust levels per se. Trust seems to be derived from either the general trust stance or basic heuristics, such as 'public organizations are more trustworthy than commercial companies'. It seems that the "Ambivalent" nature of this user experience can be explained by a failure to cognitively assess the trustworthiness and a certain need to trust in order to avoid, or to lower the omnipresence of cautious and other negative feelings, and which is a so-called 'forced trust' (that is, trust without trustworthiness evidence and with a possible presence of cautious feelings). These findings point to understanding trustworthiness indicators based on the experience of others (referrals), as the main source of 'trustworthiness information' that is accessible for this cluster, and underlying the outcome of the trustworthiness assessment.

4 Model Parameterization, Based on Segments' Properties

In this section, we will present our methodology for transferring the fundamental properties of each segment into the Bayesian trust computational model, both in the initialization and evolution phases. Doing so will allow us to take into account user's personality when estimating it's trust level.

4.1 Trust Initialization

The initial trust level of a user who has never interacted with the system in question before could be based on information present on the system's welcome screen, its past experiences in using other systems, the opinion of others users etc. Here we assume that the user has a glimpse of the actual system trustworthiness by looking at information present on the system's welcome screen (e.g., a page containing certifications, attractive layout, etc.). We call this information 'look and feel' elements. The users willing to invest sufficient amount of time in gaining information about system trustworthiness (or, equivalently those being extremely capable of finding evidences of trustworthiness) before using it would always have a good estimation of the actual trustworthiness. Furthermore, this will be the case regardless of how advanced strategies a provider had followed in order to deceive users (adopting for example techniques from social engineering).

Let d_l, m_l, c_l stand for mean values of trust stance, motivation and competence respectively, where $l = 1, 2, 3, 4$ indicates the segment "HT", "HATS" "MATS" and "A" respectively. Additionally, let $e_l = \frac{m_l + c_l}{2}$ be the factor quantifying the aggregate impact of the two latter concepts.

In general, we consider that the closeness of initial trust to actual trustworthiness, depends on the combined impact of both the motivation to engage in seeking behavior and competences concepts, while trust stance determines whether it is under or overestimated. In order to compute the error magnitude and its sign we utilize the segmentation results (see Table 1). More specifically we follow a normalization approach using the second segment (HATS) as a benchmark, since it was found to achieve the highest "e" factor among all and thus users therein estimate trustworthiness accurately. Trustors in all other segments make an estimation error proportionally correlated to the normalized value of "e", i.e.: $\tilde{e}_l = \frac{e_2 - e_l}{e_2}$. Furthermore, under or overestimation is determined by the correlation of the trust stance values, e.g., if $(d_l - d_2) > 0$ the estimation error is added to the actual trustworthiness level.

In a mathematic formulation, the initial trust of user i in segment l is given by:

$$\tau_{i \in l, s}^j(0) = \frac{\alpha_{i \in l, s}^j(0)}{\alpha_{i \in l, s}^j(0) + \beta_{i \in l, s}^j(0)} = \begin{cases} \min\left(\max\left(0, w_{j,s} + \tilde{e}_l\right), 1\right), & \text{if } d_l > d_2 \\ \min\left(\max\left(0, w_{j,s} - \tilde{e}_l\right), 1\right), & \text{if } d_l \leq d_2 \end{cases}, l = 1, 2, 3, 4,$$

(5)

where we have restricted its value in the [0, 1] interval because it estimates the success probability.

Notice that 'trust level' alone, is not enough to calculate the exact values of a and β parameters, as an infinite number of their combinations may result to the same outcome. In Sect. 2, we mentioned that for equal trust values, their sum reflects the trustor's confidence. We reasonably assume that the level of confidence proportionally depends on the value of e_l coefficient and the number of look and feel elements with respect to factor j, notated as k_s^j. The equivalent mathematical expression is:

$$\alpha_{i \in l,s}^j(0) + \beta_{i \in l,s}^j(0) = e_l * k_s^j \tag{6}$$

Using (5) and (6) one can compute a pair of Beta parameters for each segment that depend on Table 1 and thus will reflect the personality of the users in that segment. Then, the initial trust level for each segment's users can be computed using Eq. (2).

4.2   Trust Evolution with Observations Following a Machine Learning Approach

Contrary to the standard process where each outcome is equally weighted, here we consider that trustors apply greater importance to a success or failure: thus, biasing their trust to over or under estimate the corresponding trustworthiness respectively. The reason for doing so is that trust levels are subjective; two users having observed the exact same sequence of system outcomes can have significantly different estimation about the trustworthiness of the system in question. The subjectivity of trust will be demonstrated in the next section (see Figs. 2 and 3), where the averages of the trust levels being reported in a small-scale experiment varied significantly. Aligned with Eq. (4), for each factor j a trustor in segment l updates her personal parameters as follows:

$$\alpha_l^j(t+1) = \alpha_l^j(t) + A_l^j \text{ and } \beta_l^j(t+1) = \beta_l^j(t) + B_l^j \tag{7}$$

where A_l^j and B_l^j stand for the increment coefficients of segment l, after each success and failure observed with respect to trustworthiness factor j.

The parameters' values determining the trust evolution may be adjusted so that the theoretical model results to any given value "m", after a specific number of outcomes. This is easily feasible by setting:

$$\frac{\alpha_l^j(0) + s(t)A_l^j}{\alpha_l^j(0) + s(t)A_l^j + \beta_l^j(0) + f(t)B_l^j} = m(t), \tag{8}$$

where $s(t)$ and $f(t)$ stand for the number of successes and failures observed until time t respectively. Note that if we apply this rule for the initial trust and two additional different time moments ($t_1 \neq t_2$), then we get a unique pair of increment coefficients, assuming that they remain constant for all observations.

The value of factor m, may be derived by any assumption concerning the impact of personal attributes on trust and trustworthiness correlation or may stand for actual measurements based on trustor's real responses. In this paper, we follow the latter approach: the trusts levels, as reported by participants, will be averaged per segment and fed into the theoretical model to reset the parameters so that they closely reflect the former. The initial trust may be either explicitly provided or may be derived by the relevant formula in the previous section. For completeness, we note that in this approach (three points equation), the estimated trust is unique and does not depend on the number of look and feel elements.

5 Validation Results

5.1 Experiment Setup

The experiment took place in October 2014 inviting participants to test and evaluate an online security service. A fictitious provider was offering a service, called Distributed Attack Detection and Visualization (DADV), for detecting virtual attacks on devices connected to the Internet, such as personal computers. The approach followed for attracting attackers was to deploy special decoy hosts in the subscribers' network that imitate vulnerable machines. All participants were assumed to be part of the same organization requesting protection and thus a single set of honeypots was deployed.

Real-time information about those incidents was sent to the provider for further processing so that the attack is prevented from expanding to other machines in the network. The experiment was performed for two versions of the online service; the Vanilla DADV where administrators are responsible for detecting and mitigating attacks and the Automated one where all tasks are performed by sophisticated tools [9].

The first step was for the participants to fill in the online segmentation-related (intake) questionnaire (See Sect. 5.2 below). In order to validate the trust initialization approach, participants were asked to report their initial trust towards the system before having any other evidence for its performance. To do so, each participant engaged with the DADV system, separately for each version during two different days, starting with the Vanilla DADV and then with the Automated one. After logging in to the online website (and before any attack was performed), they were given the opportunity to access the "about page" and familiarize themselves with the activated version. This webpage provided general information of the system functionality and a high-level description of its expected trustworthiness. Furthermore, users who had noticed and clicked on a distinguishable hyperlink were redirected to a more detailed webpage, which explicitly mentioned each system's actual trustworthiness in terms of the metric under interest. In this way we could validate the effects of "seeking motivation" on the initial trust level of each segment.

Afterwards, they observed the service performance for a sequence of 10 attacks that were identical for both DADV cases. During each attack, they could navigate to the "health statistics page", which was providing a holistic view of the system status. More specifically the subjects could judge whether an attack was taking place by observing the current CPU/memory/network load and observe the number of attempts initiated by a compromised sensor to the rest network hosts. At the end of each attack a message was appearing indicating whether the provider succeeded in preventing any network host from being attacked, or not. These pop-up messages also contained a link to a questionnaire where users were asked to indicate their current trust level that the provider would prevent future attacks from compromised honeypots to their computers. In other words, the metric of interest was the number of successfully mitigated attacks of each DADV system over the total number of attacks. This step provided the actual trust values, which after taking the average per segment, were utilized for training the trust computational model (see Sect. 5.3).

The attacks resulted to the following sequences of outcomes, as depicted in Fig. 1. The Automated DADV version outperformed the Vanilla one in preventing a connection from being initialized since adminstrators had higher reaction times than their counterparts. Remember that all users observed exactly the same sequence of outcomes. This is essential to guarantee that the trust level was consistently monitored and, hence, any differentiations were guided by different sets of trustor's attributes only.

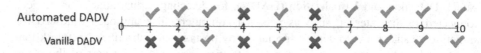

Fig. 1. The sequence of outcomes evidenced for each DADV version.

5.2 Validating Trustors' Segmentation

In order to assess whether the four segmentation solution described in Sect. 3 could be deployed, additional empirical research was carried out. For this purpose the intake survey was dispersed using several Living Lab panels in September 2014. While 108 started the survey, 89 people from 11 European countries fully completed the survey and these were used for further analysis. Some 55 % were aged between 25 and 34, followed by 32 % that were aged between 35 and 44, and a few younger and older. Also, some 65 % reported to have a university degree. The same steps were followed as in Sect. 3. Thus, a K-means clustering to segment different trust-related user experiences and an Anova analysis was performed to test the statistical significance for each item, thereby highlighting statistical differences between uncovered trust-related user experience segments. The results are shown in Table 2 below, where the absolute differences from Table 1 appear inside the parentheses.

Despite the minor variations between the two exploratory analyses presented below, the dominant drivers that seem to characterize users in each segment appear to be relatively constant. Thus, the findings seem to correspond to the previous ones indicating that the three underpinning users' attributes appear as statistically significant difference. More specifically, we observe that the combined aggregate factor of "competences" and "seeking motivation" is again higher for the HATS segment. This finding justifies our approach to correlate higher values of this factor with a more accurate estimation (Eq. 5). Furthermore, it is confirmed that a high level of "trust stance" results to trustworthiness overestimation (misplaced trust) and vice versa (presence of overcautious users).

Table 2. Intake survey segmentation results (n = 89 participants)

	Total (n = 89)	HT (n = 25)	HATS (n = 20)	MATS (n = 32)	A (n = 12)	Anova	
	Mean	Mean	Mean	Mean	Mean	F	Sig.
Trust stance	2,65 (−057)	3,42 (−0.43)	2,45 (−0.7)	2,33 (−0.53)	2,25 (−1.25)	27,053 (19.8)	,000 (0)
Trust related seeking behaviour	2,38 (−1.14)	2,14 (−1)	3,02 (−1.25)	2,16 (−1.18)	2,44 (−0.57)	28,361 (3.98)	,000 (0)
Trust related competences	3,65 (1.21)	3,88 (1.17)	4,29 (1.87)	3,63 (0.69)	2,17 (0.73)	53,592 (40.2)	,000 (0)

5.3 Validating the Trust Computational Model

In order to validate the trust computational model described in Sect. 4 we employ two additional variations and compare the evolution of the computed trust levels with the actual ones, as reported by the participants. Before proceeding, we mention that while N = 89 were asked to fill in an online segmentation-related questionnaire, a subset N = 27 decided to also take part in the experiment. Table 3 below shows the output of the segmentation process and the mean values of the three trust-related concepts that were used for setting the initial values of the Beta parameters $\alpha_l^j(0), \beta_l^j(0)$ for each segment l, as described in Sect. 4.1.

Table 3. Intake survey segmentation results for experiment participants (n = 27)

	Total (n = 27)	HT (n = 5)	HATS (n = 4)	MATS (n = 10)	A (n = 8)	Anova	
	Mean	Mean	Mean	Mean	Mean	F	Sig.
Trust stance	2,65	3,40	2,63	2,30	2,63	4,519	,012
Trust related seeking behaviour	2,16	2,06	2,82	1,89	2,25	6,879	,002
Trust related competences	3,53	3,80	4,13	3.58	3.58	3,067	,048

In Figs. 2 and 3 we juxtapose the actual trust values with those derived by the three variations of the trust computational model (T1, T2 and T3), for the Vanilla DADV experiment. Similar results are obtained for the Automated DADV, but omitted for brevity.

The approaches used for the initialization and update phase for each of the three variations T_o (where $o = 1, 2, 3$ denotes the number of actual trust values used as input to the model) are described below:

The T1 model computes the initialization parameters $\alpha_l^j(0), \beta_l^j(0)$ for each segment using the average of the actual trust values, as reported by their members before using the system. Note that in this case, the number of "look and feel" elements affects the initial values of the Beta parameters and consequently the graph oscillations. After observing the actual trust values and especially the significant trust degradation following each negative outcome we have set their number to one ($k = 1$). Furthermore, T1 relies on the standard unitary update coefficient for all segments ($a = 1$, $\beta = 1$) and thus follows the basic Bayesian model for the update (see Sect. 2).

The T2 model uses Eqs. (5) and (6) for deriving the initial trust value and thus follows the approach described in Sect. 4.1. For the update process, the respective coefficients A_l^j and B_l^j are computed based on two measurements only using Eq. (8). More specifically, we used the actual trust values after the 2nd and 8th outcome. These four pairs of values, one for each segment, are denoted as (2, 8).

The T3 model requires three input values from the actual responses and can be seen as a hybrid of T1 and T2. More precisely, T3 follows the same initialization process as with T1, while the update process is similar to T2.

We observe that the models are aligned with the expected user reactions for most segments; namely trust should not decrease after a success and should not increase after a failure. The only exception is T2 for the "MATS" segment, which appears to constantly increase with the number of trials. This can be attributed to the error in estimating that particular initial value; in such cases the system of Eqs. (7)–(8) may result in negative values for one or both update coefficients. Notice that T2 succeeds in computing a very accurate initial trust value for the High Trust and Highly Active Trust Seeking segments, while the relative error for the Ambivalent and Medium Active Trust Seeking segments is 10 % and 20 %, respectively. Before proceeding further, recall that T1 and T3 are initialized explicitly from the initial values, thus the effect described above is avoided over these two methods.

Additionally, observe that T2 and T3 manage to closely estimate the average trust of the HATS and Ambivalent segments, while for the rest segments the deviations tend to vanish as the number of observed system outcomes increases. Concerning the T1 graph, it is easy to see that this naïve approach fails to capture the segment differentiations in the trust evolution and thus its estimation is outperformed by both T2 and T3. Intuitively the common update coefficients of T1, result in all segments converging to the same value (which equals the actual trustworthiness) despite the personalized initial trust values. Thus, any potential different reactions among the segments are not captured on the trust evolution computation and the impact of the different initial values fades out as the number of observations increases.

We now compare the accuracy of the three versions of the computational model for different input pairs. More specifically, we fix the first part of the input data (always after the second trial) and vary the second one. We consider the evaluation metric "AAD" standing for the average absolute difference of estimated and actual values. In order for the comparison to be fair the "AAD" is computed over the non-provided points in each case, meaning that it is the average of 10, 9 and 8 points for T1, T2 and T3 respectively. In Table 4, we report the measurements for the Vanilla version only, for both T3 and T2 (when meaningful). For T1, this metric has a single value, as the update coefficients are static and thus the input pair is not considered.

First note that the average absolute difference decreases, as we delay the second input value for all segments over both T2 and T3. This is because the second trust value

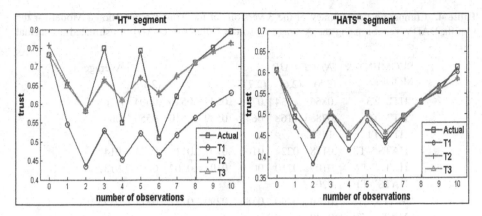

Fig. 2. Actual and estimated trust values for the "HT" (left) and "HATS" (right) segments.

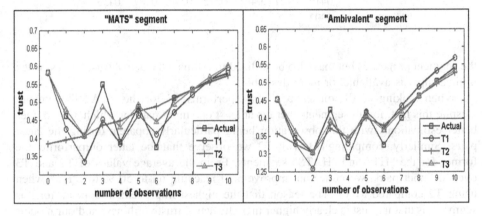

Fig. 3. Actual and estimated trust values for the "MATS" (left) and "A" (right) segments.

provides collective knowledge about the user's reaction at the intermediate trials, even though the actual trust at these moments is not explicitly given in the model. Although "AAD" is not always decreasing (meaning that we don't always achieve a more accurate trust estimation with more experimental trials), it seems to converge at acceptable levels for input pairs where users have observed adequate evidence from the system performance and consequently their trust appears with small variations (last four trials). We expect that in a larger-scale experiment with increased number of trials, "AAD" will reach even lower values, as more trust measurements will be available.

Concerning the comparison between T2 and T3, we can observe that the former is more accurate for "HT" and "HATS", despite the fact that it requires fewer user responses. This seems to be due to the close estimation of initial trust in these two segments, and which is also justified by the "A" segment where this property does not hold and consequently T3 outperforms T2. Thus, T2 and T3 have similar performance, meaning that our methodology for the trust initialization not only achieves to capture

Table 4. Comparing the accuracy of the 3 versions of the Trust Computational Model for the Vanilla DADV version using the Average Absolute Difference (AAD) of estimated and actual values.

SEGMENT & MODEL	INPUT PAIR						Average
	(2,5)	(2,6)	(2,7)	(2,8)	(2,9)	(2,10)	
"HT"- T3	.0866	.1334	.0706	.0549	.0549	.0604	.0768
"HT"- T2	.0788	.1168	.0643	.0509	.0510	.0559	.0696
"HT"- T1	.1399						
"HATS"–T3	.0118	.0224	.0106	.0107	.011	.0221	.0148
"HATS"-T2	.0109	.0210	.0099	.0101	.0102	.0202	.0137
"HATS"-T1	.0206						
"MATS"–T3	.0286	.0790	.0386	.0299	.0287	.0311	.0393
"MATS"–T1	.0340						
"A" –T3	.0246	.0500	.0285	.0222	.0222	.0236	.0285
"A"-T2	.0419	.0721	.0448	.0372	.0370	.0387	.0453
"A"-T1	.0302						

the segment properties but may also be utilized to estimate the actual trust values, when limited input is available, or more desirable.

When looking at T1, on average, it outperforms T3 for the "MATS" segment. Despite this fact, for all segments there is at least one input pair for which T3 provides better estimations, with this observation being particularly apparent during the latest pairs. Similarly, comparing T1 with T2 we observe that the latter outperforms the former for the "HT" and "HATS" segments. From the average values of T2 and T3 over all input pairs, we notice an improvement reaching up to 50 % for "HT" when using T2 compared to T1. The reason that the highest improvement appears for this segment, is that its trust is clearly higher than the actual trustworthiness and our models capture this deviation. This fact is less intense for the other segments, thus the improvement is less impressive, but still remarkable: Notice that even though trust of "HATS", is the most accurate estimation of trustworthiness among all segments, our approaches provide interesting results in this case also. This is because the evolution of estimated trust levels closely matches the actual ones, another important property apart from the accuracy in the long-run.

Thus, we may conclude that our approach to cluster users into segments and update their trust level according to the segment they belong to seem to provide valuable results towards a more accurate trust estimation.

6   Related Work

Significant research effort can be evidenced to understand the factors that affect a trustor's trust and build trust computational models that can be configured to make autonomous decisions that mimic a personalized mental process. The rationale behind this is that trust formation has been found to be a rather subjective and dynamic process. Such computational models are usually initialized using reputation systems that aggregate experiences of other trustors. Later, as users interact with the system/service and get direct observations, their trust levels are updated. Below, we provide an overview of trust computational models that explicitly consider trustor attributes and how these differ from our model. For a comprehensive overview of such models the interested reader is redirected to, for example, [10].

In [11] the following personal trust factors are considered when initializing a trust level: (a) the effects of stereotypes such as appearance, the context and existence of certificates proving expertise (b) trustor characteristics like general propensity to trust, user expertise and user need, as well as, (c), similarity between persons (and empathy when the trustee is a system). Even though the authors did not quantify the effect of these personal factors, their importance has been validated via experiments. Furthermore, the resulting trust level is a single value (not a probability density function, or PDF) and thus the confidence cannot be determined.

In [12] a computational model is provided that allows to reason about the produced trust level by analyzing and formalizing the dynamics of trust in the light of experiences. Furthermore, they hypothesize that trustors can be grouped into sets based on their attributes, which, however, were not produced following a statistical approach nor were associated with trustor attributes (such as trustor expertise).

In [13] a trust computational model is proposed that takes into account the following personal attributes for trust update only: (a) trust flexibility that expresses how much each system outcome counts, (b) trust decay that defines how fast the trust level goes back to a neutral state in absence of new experiences, and (c) autonomy that indicates whether the trust level to one trustee is affected by the trust level to other trustees. Even though the importance of these attributes has not been validated (using surveys etc.) in the sequel paper [14] the authors suggested and compared four techniques that could be used for estimating the values of these parameters from subjects' responses.

A different approach for estimating a user's trust level is based on user (as opposed to system) behavior. In [15] they performed an experiment to identify that different eye gaze and heart rate patterns could indicate different trust levels.

Our trust computational model builds upon a set of trust concepts that were found to be statistically significant; (a) general propensity to trust, (b) user expertise, and (c) motivation to search for stereotypes that prove provider trustworthiness. Thus, although these concepts focus on trustor characteristics only, there is significant overlap with the findings in [11, 12]. In addition, we utilize those trustor attributes to suggest how the trust level of each segment should be initialized, as well as, updated after successful or unsuccessful system outcomes. Thus, we argue that we follow a more holistic approach compared to papers [11, 12, 13, 14].

7 Conclusions and Future Work

In this paper, we have drawn out the conceptual background for our proposed a trust computational model that allows a provider to estimate the trust level of candidate trustors, using a holistic approach. We also demonstrated the validity of our results via a small-scale experiment in the online security service context. More specifically, we have identified four segments with statistically significant differences which affect both the initial level but also the evolution of trust towards a system. These differences are captured by means of a modified Bayesian inference model, where the system outcomes have a weighted impact on the trust of each segment. We observed that our approach, i.e., to feed in the model with actual data so as to identify the individual weights, results to remarkably improved trust estimation compared to the standard process where the personal attributes are not considered in the trust update.

In the future we plan to revisit the initialization steps for the Medium Active Trust Seeking and Ambivalent segments and perform another experiment, possibly in another domain, where participants would engage with the system for more transactions. In this way, it allows to accurately estimate all users' trust level with a small subset of actual trust values provided by the trustors themselves. Furthermore, we will validate that the number of transactions necessary for the trust level to converge is limited ($\sim$ 10–15) and, thus, the trust computational model can afterwards be used for helping the provider to meet customers' expectations at run-time.

References

1. Habib, S.M., et al.: Trust as a facilitator in cloud computing: a survey. J. Cloud Comput. 1(1), 1–18 (2012)
2. Riegelsberger, J., Sasse, M.A., McCarthy, J.D.: The mechanics of trust: a framework for research and design. Int. J. Hum Comput Stud. 62(3), 381–422 (2005)
3. McKnight, D., Chervany, N.L.: Trust and distrust definitions: one bite at a time. In: Falcone, R., Singh, M., Tan, Y.-H. (eds.) AA-WS 2000. LNCS (LNAI), vol. 2246, pp. 27–54. Springer, Heidelberg (2001)
4. Lyon, F., Möllering, G., Saunders, M.N.K. (eds.): Handbook of Research Methods on Trust. Edward Elgar, Cheltenham (2012)
5. Li, F., Kowski, D.P., van Moorsel, A., Smith, C.: Holistic framework for trust in online transactions. Int. J. Manag. Rev. 14, 85–103 (2012)
6. Sztompka, P.: Trust: A Sociological Theory. Cambridge University Press, Cambridge (1999)
7. Gambetta, D.: Can we trust trust? In: Gambetta, D. (ed.) Trust: Making and Breaking Cooperative Relations, pp. 213–238. Basil Blackwell, Oxford (1990)
8. Surridge, M., et al.: OPTET D2.1 – Socio-economic requirements for trust and trustworthiness. Technical report, OPTET consortium (2013)
9. Gol Mohammadi, N., Bandyszak, T., Moffie, M., Chen, X., Weyer, T., Kalogiros, C., Nasser, B., Surridge, M.: Maintaining trustworthiness of socio-technical systems at run-time. In: Eckert, C., Katsikas, S.K., Pernul, G. (eds.) TrustBus 2014. LNCS, vol. 8647, pp. 1–12. Springer, Heidelberg (2014)
10. Pinyol, I., Sabater-Mir, J.: Computational trust and reputation models for open multi-agent systems: a review. Artif. Intell. Rev. 40(1), 1–25 (2013)
11. Masthoff, J.: Computationally modelling trust: an exploration. In: Proceedings of the SociUM Workshop Associated with the User Modeling Conference, Corfu, Greece (2007)
12. Jonker, C.M., Treur, J.: Formal analysis of models for the dynamics of trust based on experiences. In: Garijo, F.J., Boman, M. (eds.) MAAMAW 1999. LNCS, vol. 1647, pp. 221–231. Springer, Heidelberg (1999)

13. Hoogendoorn, M., Jaffry, S., Treur, J.: Modeling Dynamics of Relative Trust of Competitive Information Agents. In: Klusch, M., Pěchouček, M., Polleres, A. (eds.) CIA 2008. LNCS (LNAI), vol. 5180, pp. 55–70. Springer, Heidelberg (2008)
14. Hoogendoorn, M., Jaffry, S.W., Treur, J.: An adaptive agent model estimating human trust in information sources. In: Proceedings of the 2009 IEEE/WIC/ACM International Joint Conference on Web Intelligence and Intelligent Agent Technology (2009)
15. Leichtenstern, K., Bee, N., André, E., Berkmüller, U., Wagner, J.: Physiological measurement of trust-related behavior in trust-neutral and trust-critical situations. In: Wakeman, I., Gudes, E., Jensen, C.D., Crampton, J. (eds.) Trust Management V. IFIP AICT, vol. 358, pp. 165–172. Springer, Heidelberg (2011)

Enhancing the Trustworthiness of Service On-Demand Systems via Smart Vote Filtering

Christos V. Samaras$^{(\boxtimes)}$, Ageliki Tsioliaridou, Christos Liaskos,
Dimitris Spiliotopoulos, and Sotiris Ioannidis

Foundation of Research and Technology - Hellas (FORTH), Heraklion, Greece
{csamaras,atsiolia,cliaskos,dspiliot,sotiris}@ics.forth.gr

Abstract. Service on-demand (SoD) systems allow their users to regulate the sharing of common resources via a voting process. A common application example is the collaborative scheduling of multimedia
transmissions in e-radio or video streaming services. Therefore, high user
commitment and participation is critical to the success of a SoD system.
Securing a SoD system against common attacks, such as vote flooding,
can impose client anonymity retraction, online registering and access
control mechanisms. Nonetheless, such processes can degrade the users'
quality of experience, discouraging user participation. The present study
proposes a defense mechanism against vote flooding attacks that can
operate under complete vote anonymity and without any user access
restrictions. The novel scheme is implemented as a vote filtering scheme,
executed prior to each service scheduling decision. The proposed scheme
has linear complexity and is shown via simulations to considerably mitigate or completely negate the effects of several attacks types.

Keywords: Service on-demand · Client anonymity · Security · Query
filtering

1 Introduction

Service on-demand (SoD) systems constitute a particularly attractive means of
resource sharing and large-scale information dissemination. Users of SoD systems
can influence how often a server supplies a service via a voting system. For
instance, users of video-on-demand or e-radio systems can regulate the broadcast
frequency of multimedia files [25,27]. Therefore, high and unobstructed user
participation is critical to the operation and economic viability of SoD systems,
accentuating the need for user-friendliness. To this end, SoD systems may need
to operate on anonymous user votes and without any access control method
that may degrade the users' quality of experience [26]. On the other hand, such
requirements facilitate the misuse by malevolent users who may, e.g., flood the
system with vast amounts of votes for personally preferred services, degrading
the trustworthiness of the process.

SoD systems typically follow a centralized architecture, comprising a server
and a set of clients in a virtual star topology. The server supports a set of

M. Conti et al. (Eds.): TRUST 2015, LNCS 9229, pp. 88–103, 2015.
DOI: 10.1007/978-3-319-22846-4_6

actions that are provided in a cyclic fashion. After the end of an action, the server proceeds to select the next action for execution. The selection is derived from the votes of the users, which arrive continuously at the server and are promptly enqueued. The selection process can consider the arrival times of the votes at the server, as well as the total number of votes pertaining to each supported action. Typical selection processes are the First Come-First Served, Most Requests First and the RxW scheduler which takes into account both considerations [13]. Given that the arrival time of a vote at the server cannot be tampered with, a malevolent user may seek to influence the total number of votes pertaining to one or more actions. Thus, the selection process can be forced to produce results that no longer correspond to the preferences of the normal (benevolent) users of the system.

Existing voting systems employ access control and user identification mechanisms in order to: (i) discourage or disable vote-flooding attacks and (ii) detect the perpetrator in case of a successful attack [9,20]. A commonly followed access control approach is to employ CAPTCHAs, automated challenge-response Turing tests, to disable vote flooding by bots [32,39]. However, the process is time-consuming and degrades the quality of experience of the normal users. Furthermore, the users may be requested to register to the system with an online account, compromising their anonymity. Some approaches employ an intermediate anonymization server, which removes personal information from the vote of a user prior to forwarding it to the SoD system [11]. Nonetheless, this approach simply delegates the identification and access control process to another system and still degrades the quality of experience. Furthermore, the approach requires additional equipment, increasing the capital and operational expenses of the system.

The present paper proposes a mechanism for defending against vote flooding attacks in SoD systems, which requires no access control and does not compromise the anonymity of the users, even under attack. It can be classified as a first-line, low-complexity defense mechanism that is implemented as a vote filtering mechanism. The methodology of the presented scheme comprises an attack detection and an actuation process. For the detection purposes, the votes of the users are mapped to a stream of alarm indications, each designating the presence or absence of malevolent behavior. A specially-designed, low-complexity variation of the Misra-Gries algorithm [31] deduces the most frequent indication, thus raising an alarm or deducing normal operation. In the case of an alarm, the actuation process is activated and proceeds to filter the users' votes prior to every new scheduling decision. The success of an attack is measured in terms of the increase it induces to the user query service ratio and service times. In retaliation, the proposed scheme succeeds in keeping these metrics close to their normal operation counterparts under several attack cases. Thus, it can promote the trustworthiness of a SoD system, without compromises in the users' quality of experience.

The remainder of this paper is organized as follows. The related work on trustworthy voting systems is given in Sect. 2. The prerequisites for the presentation and presentation of the novel scheme follow in Sect. 3. The scheme is detailed in Sect. 4 and evaluated via simulations in Sect. 5. Finally, the conclusion is given in Sect. 6.

2 Related Work

Research on secure service-on-demand systems has not proposed a voting mechanism that can operate on anonymous users with no access restrictions, to the best of the authors knowledge. However, there exists a considerable amount of work on electronic voting systems and polling protocols in general, which has concentrated on a diverse set of desired properties and functionality such as accuracy, privacy, verifiability, eligibility, coercion resistance, availability and fault-tolerance. A number of protocols, models, prototypes, and real-world systems have been proposed and implemented to support e-voting and polling functions.

Electronic voting schemes are mainly divided into three categories, based on the technique used to anonymize votes: (i) Homomorphic encryption allows computations to be carried out on ciphertext, thus generating an encrypted result which, when decrypted, matches the result of operations performed on the plaintext. Protocols based on homomorphic encryption generally have a complex mathematical structure thus inducing high computational costs. (ii) In blind signature approaches the content of message/vote is disguised (blinded) before it is signed, thus the signer (authenticator) is not given any knowledge about the message. The voter unblinds the signed vote and submits it to the tallier through an anonymized channel. Blind signature protocols usually exhibit the advantages of simplicity, low computational costs and being ballot independent. (iii) A mix network (mixnet) is a multistage system that uses cryptography and permutations to provide anonymity. The design of a mixnet is based on providing anonymity for a batch of inputs, by changing their appearance and removing the order of arrival information. In mix network schemes, voters authenticate and submit encrypted votes; votes are anonymized using a mix; and anonymized votes are then decrypted. Mix network protocols involve less voter's interactions, but require complex proofs of correctness.

E-voting and polling have been an active area of research posing several new challenges [2,16,19,23,34,38]. Comparison of existing voting schemes reveals common security property tradeoffs [35]. REVS [22] is an electronic voting system based on blind signatures and designed for distributed and faulty environments, which exploits server replication to allow a certain degree of failures. Sensus [11] is a secure and private system for polling that requires at least two servers, namely a validator and a tallier, for conducting an election or a survey (i.e., a generic term of polling is considered). In [3] authors propose a prototype implementation of SEAS, which is a portable and flexible system that preserves the limited number of servers of the above-mentioned Sensus, but it avoids a vulnerability that allows one of the entities involved in the election process to cast its own votes in place of those that abstain from the vote. Civitas [9] is based on mix networks and enforces verifiability (an integrity property) and coercion resistance (a confidentiality property), whereas it does not rely on trusted supervision of polling places, making it a remote voting system.

In the literature there also exist studies on polling protocols [5,14,17,20,21, 37], which cover areas such as: distributed polling, privacy, secret sharing, scalability, social networks, peer-to-peer networks, and reputation systems. However, anonymity systems are of significant practical relevance because they are the best means of providing privacy for users. Further works relating to e-voting and to methods for achieving anonymity and providing privacy for users, can be seen in [4,6–8,10,15,24,28–30,41].

Given that existing systems do not cover the needs of SoD systems for complete client anonymity and unrestricted access, the authors proposed an initial solution based on early filtering of client queries [26]. The study defined probable attack types and proposed a defense mechanism based on the Dendritic algorithm, a nature-inspired process for intrusion detection based on danger and safety signals. However, being a nature-inspired heuristic, the mechanics of the Dendritic algorithm are still not well understood [18]. Particularly, it is not clear how to parametrize and map the danger and safety signals to real attributes of a given system. Thus, while the proposed Sensor Swarm Filter process was shown to efficiently defend against several attack types, it could not account for common attacks, such as random query flooding.

The present study proposes a superior query filtering process that: (i) is based on the well-studied Misra-Gries classification algorithm [31], and (ii) utilizes parameters that have an intuitive and clear meaning within the context of the voting system.

3   Prerequisites

We assume a service-on-demand system, comprising a server and a set of connected clients. The server hosts a number of service "items" (actions), each with its own service time. The clients post queries in order to vote for the next action to be taken by the server. In order to derive the next service action, the server employs the RxW scheduler without preemption support, but enhanced to handle actions with different processing times [1,36]. The RxW scheduler selects the action with the highest number of hits, multiplied by the queuing time of its oldest query.

The preferences of each client regarding the service actions are unknown to the server, and are expressed as personal probability mass functions (p.m.f.):

$$p_{c,i}, \, c = 1\ldots C, \, i = 1\ldots N, : \sum_{i=1}^{N} p_{c,i} = 1 \tag{1}$$

which denotes the percentage of queries of client $c = 1\ldots C$ that refer to action i.

In order to establish a dependable ground-through on the popularity of each action, an external, trusted entity provides the server with an approximate, per-action p.m.f. as:

$$\mathbb{P}_i, \, i = 1\ldots N : \sum_{i=1}^{N} \mathbb{P}_i = 1 \tag{2}$$

For example, in the case of a video on-demand service, the popularity of each movie "item" can be derived by its ranking in online services (e.g., the Internet Movie Database), hits in social networks (e.g., Tweets) or direct polling of trustworthy, authenticated users (critics).

Each service action may be requested multiple times over the operation of the system by any user, without restrictions. On the client-side, each benevolent user poses a query for a single service action and awaits for a maximum time interval D (deadline). The server is oblivious to deadline expiration events, since such an ability would be open to extensive misuse, even by non-expert users. If D elapses and the server has not started to process the requested action, the client abandons the query. Regardless of the outcome (served or not) a client poses a new query after a random $ThinkTime$ [25]. The service ratio of the system is defined as the total number of served queries over all clients divided by the total number of posed queries.

Finally, the attacker model of [26] is assumed. According to it, a malevolent user performs query flooding in order to tip the RxW scheduler to their favor. An attack by a malevolent user is defined as:

$$\{target, \bar{T}, t_s, t_e\} \tag{3}$$

where t_s is the time moment when the user begins posting consecutive queries with mean interarrival $\bar{T}$ until time t_e. The $target$ of these queries, i.e., the action that is being requested, defines the attack types introduced in [26]:

- **Needed action.** "Selfish" behavior which constitutes at flooding the scheduler with requests for the personally needed service action.
- **Random action.** Flooding the server with random queries.
- **Less popular action.** The scheduler is flooded with multiple requests for the less wanted service action.
- **Lengthiest action.** The scheduler is forced to yield the most time-consuming service, delaying all other actions.
- **Smallest popularity-to-size ratio** action, which combines the preceding attacks.

The last three attack types assume that a malevolent user has obtained an approximation of the the the $\mathbb{P}_i$ p.m.f..

The proposed scheme seeks to improve the trustworthiness of the system by (ideally) keeping the service/expiration ratio and the mean service time unaltered, despite the presence of an increasing number of malevolent users.

4   Misra-Gries-Based Query Filtering

A service-on-demand system defines a cycle of operation given in Fig. 1. A server selects and executes an action from a given pool, based on the preceding votes of the users. While the action is executed, the server enqueues all incoming votes in a single queue, logging their arrival times as well. Once the execution

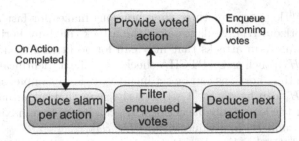

Fig. 1. State chart of the service on-demand system, combined with the proposed defense mechanism.

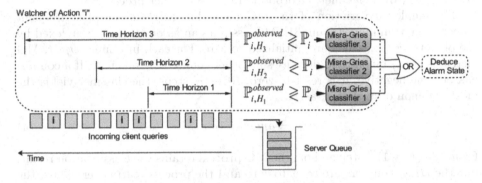

Fig. 2. Operation of an action "watcher", responsible for raising an alarm when the observed rate of incoming queries for the action, $\mathbb{P}^{observed}$, consistently surpasses the expectation $\mathbb{P}$.

of the current action is complete, the server proceeds to select the next action for execution, given the user votes and the employed scheduler (e.g., RxW). The proposed defense mechanism takes action before the execution of the scheduler, by filtering the votes accumulated at the queue of the server. In this aspect, the proposed mechanism has the added advantage of not disrupting the normal operation of the used scheduler.

The defense mechanism comprises two components: the *threat detection module* and the *actuation module* (i.e., query filtering).

The operation of the *threat detection module* is illustrated in Fig. 2. It comprises a set of N *watcher* processes running as daemons on the server. Each watcher is responsible for detecting suspicious queries pertaining to a single action offered by the server, with $1 - 1$ correspondence. The watcher of action i processes all incoming client queries before they enter the server's queue, and logs the running ratio of i–query occurrences, $\mathbb{P}^{observed}_{i,H}$, over three different time horizons, H_1, H_2, H_3. For example, if the span of time horizon H_1 is $S = 100$ incoming client votes and action i was requested $n = 10$ times within this window, then $\mathbb{P}^{observed}_{i,H} = n/s = 0.1$.

The $\mathbb{P}_{i,H}^{observed}$ logging over three time horizons makes for fast attack detection (smaller horizon, H_1), vigilance after the attack (medium horizon, H_2) and indications of long-term attacks that may call for additional security measures (large horizon, H_3), such as CAPTCHA checks and client identification requests. The span of the time horizons can be set intuitively. For example, assuming that $min\{\mathbb{P}_i\} = p$, H_1 can be set at $\lceil 1/p \rceil$, i.e., the span that accentuates the presence of votes for the least probable actions. H_3 can be set to a maximum allowed attack duration, and H_2 in a value within $[H_1, H_3]$.

Once the $\mathbb{P}_{i,H}^{observed}$ values have been derived for each horizon, the attack detection module proceeds to compare them to the $\mathbb{P}_i$ expectations and deduce whether they constitute threat indications. This task is accomplished by the Misra-Gries (MG) classifier, incorporated to the watcher process.

The employed variation of the MG algorithm extracts the most frequent object from a running stream [31]. MG assumes an associative array indexed by the objects, ctr_{obj}, which are initialized to zero. For each incoming $object$, MG increases ctr_{obj} by one and decreases all other counters by one unit. If a counter has become negative, it is reset to zero. After K steps, the classifier yields the most common object, obj^*, as:

$$obj^* = argmax\{ctr_{obj}\} \tag{4}$$

From the $(K + 1)^{th}$ step and on, the MG process retains the classification result, but the ctr_{obj} counters are reset to zero and the process starts over. Thus, the classification result is updated at the $(2 \cdot K)^{th}$ step. The storage overhead of MG is $O(m)$, where m is the total number of possible objects, while its complexity is constant, $O(1)$.

In the case of the proposed defense mechanism, the MG objects are the Boolean outcomes of the comparisons:

$$\mathbb{P}_{i,H}^{observed} > \mathbb{P}_i \tag{5}$$

i.e., $m = 2$. In other words, MG deduces whether the votes pertaining to an action i are persistently higher than the expectations, implying that an attack may be in progress. In this case, MG is said to raise an "alarm". Three MG instances are used within each action watcher, each deducing the alarm state over the three time horizons. The action watcher then yields an alarm state for the monitored action if any of the three MG processes is positive.

The set of watchers, one per available server action, thus yield a Boolean alarm level per action, $\mathbb{A}_i$, at any requested time moment.

The *actuation module* (query filtering process of Fig. 1, formulated as Algorithm 1) takes place before relinquishing operation to the RxW scheduler.

At first, Algorithm 1 counts the number of occurrences of each query for action i within the server queue (lines $3 - 5$). The Algorithm then proceeds to calculate the expected (proper) occurrences for each action with a raised alarm flag, $\mathbb{A}_i$ (lines $8 - 12$). However, it is possible that certain actions have presently zero occurrences within the queue (e.g., when the corresponding $\mathbb{P}_i$ is low).

Algorithm 1. Query filtering process.

INPUTS:

1. Presently Enqueued Queries $\mathbb{Q}_k$, $k = 1 \ldots Q$;
2. Expectations $\mathbb{P}_i$, $i = 1 \ldots N$;
3. Binary Alarm State per Action $\mathbb{A}_i$, $i = 1 \ldots N$.

1:   $times_i \leftarrow 0$, $\forall i = 1 \ldots N$;
2:   $proper\_times_i \leftarrow 0$, $\forall i = 1 \ldots N$;
3:   **for** $k = 1 \ldots Q$
4:     $times_{\mathbb{Q}_k} = times_{\mathbb{Q}_k} + 1$;
5:   **end for**
6:   $s \leftarrow 1 - \sum_{i:\{1 \ldots N | times_i = 0\}} \mathbb{P}_i$;
7:   $proper\_times_i \leftarrow times_i$, $i = 1 \ldots N$;
8:   **for** $i = 1 \ldots N$
9:     **if** $times_i > 0$ **and** $\mathbb{A}_i$
10:      $proper\_times_i \leftarrow \left\lfloor \frac{\mathbb{P}_i \cdot Q}{s} \right\rfloor$;
11:    **end if**
12:   **end for**
13:   **for** $i = 1 \ldots N$
14:     **if** $times_i > proper\_times_i$
15:      Remove the most recent $proper\_times_i - times_i$ queries for action i from the server queue.
16:    **end if**
17:   **end for**

The cumulative probability of these actions is logged (line 6) and is distributed to other actions with $times_i \neq 0$ within the queue (line 10). This approach ensures a less aggressive but more fair query filtering, since it takes into account that zero action occurrences within the queue are normal from time to time.

The actual query filtering then takes place at lines $13 - 17$. The occurrences of each query type are reduced to their expected values by discarding the newest queries first. Notice that the RxW scheduler schedules then next action for execution by checking the product of occurrences multiplied by the maximum query waiting time for each action. Therefore, given the importance of waiting times, discarding newest queries first ensures that older, potentially legitimate queries are not harmed by the filtering process.

The maximum storage overhead and complexity of Algorithm 1 is $O(N)$, which also represents the complexity of the complete defense mechanism, given that static requirements of the MG and $\mathbb{P}_{i,H}^{observed}$ logging sub-processes.

5   Simulations

In this Section, the performance of the proposed Misra-Gries Filtering (MGF) is compared via simulations to the Sensor Swarm Filtering (SSF) of [26]. The simulator, implemented on the Anylogic platform [40], represents a broadcast on-demand system, where "actions" correspond to "Web page items" with dynamic content. The runs evaluate the ability to maintain acceptable service ratios and mean service times while the system is under attack.

The system configuration assumes a star topology comprising a broadcast on-demand server, connected to $C = 100$ clients via $20Mbps$ links. The upstream direction (client-to-server, for posting queries) is considered trivial.

The server schedules its transmissions by employing the $R \times W$ on-demand scheduler. Each transmission pertains to an item selected from a static pool of $N = 100$ items with random sizes $l_i \in [1, 10]\,KBytes$ (uniformly distributed), representing simple Web pages.

The query deadline is set to $100\,msec$ due to the low item size/channel rate ratio. Should the deadline be exceeded, the query is dropped and global query service ratio is updated. Else, the query is answered successfully, and the average, global service time is updated. The clients' $ThinkTime$ is picked uniformly within $[0, 10]\,sec$.

The client query posing process operates as follows. Each client c has preset preferences in the form of a p.m.f. over the items, $p_{c,i}$, $i = 1 \ldots N$, which is unknown to the server. $\mathbb{P}_i$ is derived from a distributed consensus process. We assume that the clients participate in a separate social network. The server also participates as a single peer. In this network, each peer has a random number of friends (other peers), which are represented as a connected graph. Each peer c assigns a random weight $g_{c,k} \in (0, 1)$ (uniformly distributed) to each member of his local network $k = 1 \ldots K$, which comprises himself and his friends. A distributed consensus is a rumor propagation process and $g_{c,k}$ expresses the effect of a friendly peer on the formation of the personal opinion. A peer may also use different sets of $g_{c,k}$ weights for each data item i (i.e., $g_{c,k,i}$). The sole restriction that must hold is $\sum_{i=1}^{K} g_{c,k,i} = 1$.

The consensus process then operates as follows. Each peer initializes its estimate, $\mathbb{P}_{c,i}^{(self)}$, as his personal preferences, $p_{c,i}$, $i = 1 \ldots N$. This estimate is then sent to his immediate friends. Each peer collects the incoming estimates of all his friends and updates his estimate as:

$$\mathbb{P}_{c,i}^{(self)} \leftarrow \mathbb{P}_{c,i}^{(self)} \cdot g_{c,self,i} + \sum_{k=1\ldots K,\, k \neq self} \mathbb{P}_{c,i}^{(k)} \cdot g_{c,k,i}, \forall i \tag{6}$$

As proven in [12], the process converges iteratively, leading to $\mathbb{P}_{c,i}^{(self)} \approx \mathbb{P}_i$, $\forall c, \forall i$. Normalization is finally applied to ensure that $\sum \mathbb{P}_i = 1$. The $\mathbb{P}_{c,i}^{(self)}$ update period was set to $1\,sec$ and convergence was typically achieved in $10\,sec$. The $p_{c,i}$ preferences were set to yield a Zipfian p.m.f., $\mathbb{P}_i \propto i^{-0.9}$, which has been observed to describe client requests for Web pages [33]. Thus, both the server and the malevolent users acquire $\mathbb{P}_i$ anonymously, without knowledge of the individual $p_{c,i}$. At that point, a varying number of malevolent users, ranging from $1 - 10\% \cdot C$, attack with a period of $\bar{T} = 1\,msec$ each. The percentage of malevolent users is assumed not to surpass 10% of the total users. Notice that an on-demand system serves common needs. Thus, if the malevolent users were the majority, or even a considerable minority, the system would inevitably abide

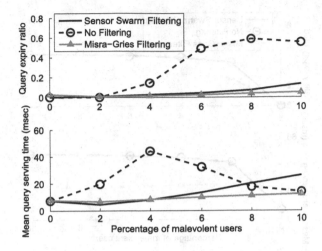

Fig. 3. Effects of the "Needed action" attack on the performance of the system.

by their preferences. Furthermore, assuming a great percentage of highly skilled users is not expected in general.

The proposed MGF uses a single *watcher* per item, monitoring the incoming client queries over three horizons, $h_1 = 10$, $h_2 = 30$ and $h_1 = 50$ (measured in number of queries). Each internal Misra-Gries process yields a classification result every $K = 20$ threshold events. Thus, the watcher process may deduce the alarm state every 200, 600 and 1000 queries. Given that $min\{\mathbb{P}_i\} = 0.02$, the horizons h_{1-3} take the values of 4, 12 and 20, which roughly correspond to ≈ 1, ≈ 10 and 20 appearances of the less popular item per threshold event. Finally, all SSF parameters are taken directly from [26].

The query service/expiration ratio and mean service time are logged and the simulation ends when a 95% confidence has been attained. The results presented below correspond to mean values derived over 10 Monte Carlo runs, randomly varying the item sizes and the client preferences.

Figure 3 studies the robustness of the proposed MGF under a progressively aggravating "Needed action" attack. MGF is shown to surpass SSF, while essentially nullifying the attack. The query expiry ratio is kept at near-zero, while the mean service time is constant, regardless of the increasing number of attackers. On the other hand, SSF mitigates the attack for up to $\approx 5\%$ malevolent user percentage. From that point and on, the query expiry ratio and the service time increases steadily, with a rate double than the proposed MGF. The behavior of the system in absence of any filtering is provided to show the impact of the attack. Without any defense mechanism, approximately 60% of the queries are dropped. The service time decreases only when a considerable amount of queries has been dropped. Therefore, MGF can be used to provide non-disrupted system performance, even under attack.

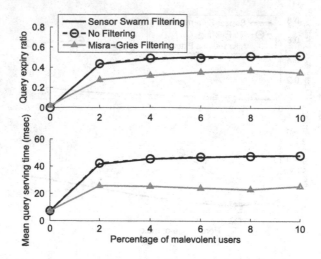

Fig. 4. The "Random action" query flooding is the most effective attack type. The proposed SSF is the only one offering a considerable degree of resilience.

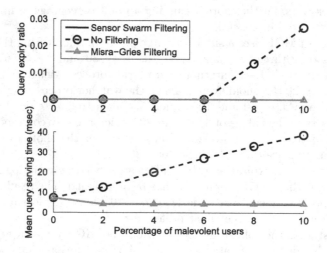

Fig. 5. The behavior of the system under a "Less popular action" attack.

Malevolent users may also attempt to flood the server with random queries. This case is examined in Fig. 4. According to [26], this type of attack is the most effective in the examined voting systems. This can be explained if we consider that a random attack of just a few users is tantamount to a high number of attackers launching a "Needed action" attack. As a result, SSF is not able to offer any defense against a "Random item" attack, even when the number of malevolent users is very low. On the other hand, the proposed MGF performs better, bounding the expiry ratio at ≈ 35 % in the worst case, while keeping the

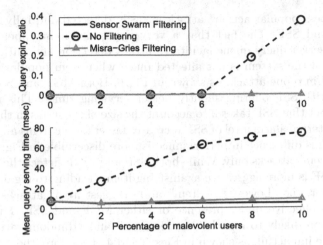

Fig. 6. Operation under false queries for the item with the lowest $\mathbb{P}_i/l_i$ ratio (popularity-to-size).

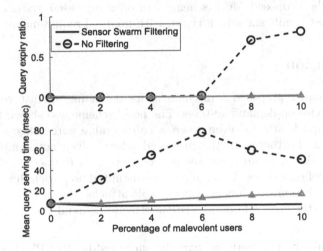

Fig. 7. Flooding the server with queries for the biggest item can yield slightly increased service times.

average service time constant at $\approx 25\,msec$. While the attack is not mitigated, the system exhibits an increased degree of robustness against this attack type. Figure 4 also accentuates the fact that the nature-inspired, Dendritic attack detector of SSF is still not well understood [18]. The present simulations can certainly not preclude that a different mapping of the nature-inspired process to real-world attributes may perform better. However, such a mapping is not straightforward and a well-defined process does not exist up to date.

Figures 5, 6 and 7 study the less probable attacks of "Less popular action", "Lowest $\mathbb{P}_i/l_i$ action" and "Lengthiest action" (i.e., biggest item). As shown in

Fig. 5, the "Less popular action" attack is easily detected and fully negated by both MGF and SSF. The fact that a very unpopular item appears multiple times in the server query queue facilitates attack detection and mitigation. The performance of the system is not affected much when item popularity and size are combined into one attack, as shown in Fig. 6. Both MGF and SSF mitigate the attack, with SSF offering slightly better servicing times. This behavior is owed to the fact that SSF takes into account the size of the items in the detection phase. The internal alarm level of SSF increases faster for big items and slower for small ones. This difference in performance is more discernible in Fig. 7, focusing on "Biggest item" attacks only. While both SSF and MGF detect the attack, the filtering of SSF is more aggressive against big items, leading to a gain in service times. However, the "Lowest $\mathbb{P}_i/l_i$ item" and "Biggest item" attacks cannot be considered as effective under presence of either MGF and SSF. Furthermore, a hacker is more likely to launch "Needed item" and "Random" attacks, since these are more impactful, as shown in Figs. 3 and 4. Therefore, the $+2\,msec$ and $+10\,msec$ service time advantage of SSF over the proposed MGF in "Lowest $\mathbb{P}_i/l_i$ item" and "Biggest item" is not deemed significant. Coupled with $O(N)$ complexity, the proposed MGF scheme can offer increased system robustness under the most significant attack types, with minimal requirements.

6 Conclusion

The present paper proposed a mechanism for defending against vote flooding attacks in service on-demand systems. The novel scheme was shown to suppress the effects of such attacks, even when a considerable percentage of the users are malevolent. Furthermore, the proposed scheme does not compromise the anonymity of the users and imposes no access control that could degrade the users' quality of experience. Combining non-disrupted user-friendliness and non-obstructed operation even under considerable attacks, the propose scheme can constitute an attractive add-on for trustworthy on-demand systems.

Acknowledgment. This work was partially supported by EU FP7 project OPTET (Grant no.317631).

References

1. Aksoy, D., Franklin, M.: R×W: a scheduling approach for large-scale on-demand data broadcast. IEEE/ACM Trans. Network. **7**(6), 846–860 (1999)
2. Backes, M., Hritcu, C., Maffei, M.: Automated verification of remote electronic voting protocols in the applied pi-calculus. In: Proceedings of the 21st IEEE Computer Security Foundations Symposium (CSF 2008), pp. 195–209, Pittsburgh, 23–25 June 2008 (2008). http://doi.ieeecomputersociety.org/10.1109/CSF.2008.26
3. Baiardi, F., Falleni, A., Granchi, R., Martinelli, F., Petrocchi, M., Vaccarelli, A.: Seas, a secure e-voting protocol: design and implementation. Comput. Secur. **24**(8), 642–652 (2005). http://dx.doi.org/10.1016/j.cose.2005.07.008

4. Benkaouz, Y., Erradi, M.: A distributed protocol for privacy preserving aggregation with non-permanent participants. Computing. J. **3**, 1–20 (2014). doi:10.1007/s00607-013-0373-6
5. Benkaouz, Y., Guerraoui, R., Erradi, M., Huc, F.: A distributed polling with probabilistic privacy. In: IEEE 32nd Symposium on Reliable Distributed Systems (SRDS 2013), pp. 41–50, Braga, 1–3 October 2013 (2013). http://dx.doi.org/10.1109/SRDS.2013.13
6. Camenisch, J.L., Lysyanskaya, A.: An efficient system for non-transferable anonymous credentials with optional anonymity revocation. In: Pfitzmann, B. (ed.) EUROCRYPT 2001. LNCS, vol. 2045, pp. 93–118. Springer, Heidelberg (2001)
7. Chaum, D.: Security without identification: transaction systems to make big brother obsolete. Commun. ACM **28**(10), 1030–1044 (1985). http://doi.acm.org/10.1145/4372.4373
8. Chen, Y., Jan, J., Chen, C.: The design of a secure anonymous internet voting system. Comput. Secur. **23**(4), 330–337 (2004). http://dx.doi.org/10.1016/j.cose.2004.01.015
9. Clarkson, M.R., Chong, S., Myers, A.C.: Civitas: Toward a secure voting system. In: 2008 IEEE Symposium on Security and Privacy (S&P 2008), pp. 354–368, Oakland, 18–21 May 2008. http://dx.doi.org/10.1109/SP.2008.32
10. Cortier, V., Smyth, B.: Attacking and fixing helios: an analysis of ballot secrecy. J. Comput. Secur. **21**(1), 89–148 (2013)
11. Cranor, L.F., Cytron, R.: Sensus: a security-conscious electronic polling system for the internet. In: 30th Annual Hawaii International Conference on System Sciences (HICSS-30), pp. 561–570, Maui, 7–10 January 1997. http://doi.ieeecomputersociety.org/10.1109/HICSS.1997.661700
12. Degroot, M.H.: Reaching a consensus. J. Am. Stat. Assoc. **69**(345), 118–121 (1974)
13. Dykeman, H.D., Ammar, M.H., Wong, J.W.: Scheduling algorithms for videotex systems under broadcast delivery. In: Proceedings of the International Conference on Communications (ICC 1986), pp. 1847–1851, Toronto, June 1986
14. Englert, B., Gheissari, R.: Multivalued and deterministic peer-to-peer polling in social networks with reputation conscious participants. In: 12th IEEE International Conference on Ubiquitous Computing and Communications (IUCC-2013), pp. 895–902, Melbourne, July 16–18 2013. http://dx.doi.org/10.1109/TrustCom.2013.109
15. Fan, C., Sun, W.: An efficient multi-receipt mechanism for uncoercible anonymous electronic voting. Math. Comput. Model. **48**(9–10), 1611–1627 (2008). http://dx.doi.org/10.1016/j.mcm.2008.05.039
16. Frith, D.: E-voting security: hope or hype? Netw. Secur. **2007**(11), 14–16 (2007)
17. Gambs, S., Guerraoui, R., Harkous, H., Huc, F., Kermarrec, A.: Scalable and secure polling in dynamic distributed networks. In: IEEE 31st Symposium on Reliable Distributed Systems (SRDS 2012), pp. 181–190, Irvine, 8–11 October 2012. http://dx.doi.org/10.1109/SRDS.2012.63
18. Greensmith, J., Aickelin, U., Tedesco, G.: Information fusion for anomaly detection with the dendritic cell algorithm. Inf. Fusion **11**(1), 21–34 (2010)
19. Gritzali, D.: Principles and requirements for a secure e-voting system. Comput. Secur. **21**(6), 539–556 (2002). http://dx.doi.org/10.1016/S0167-4048(02)01014-3
20. Guerraoui, R., Huguenin, K., Kermarrec, A., Monod, M., Vigfusson, Y.: Decentralized polling with respectable participants. J. Parallel Distrib. Comput. **72**(1), 13–26 (2012). http://dx.doi.org/10.1016/j.jpdc.2011.09.003
21. Hoang, B., Imine, A.: Efficient polling protocol for decentralized social networks. CoRR abs/1412.7653 (2014). http://arxiv.org/abs/1412.7653

22. Joaquim, R., Zúquete, A., Ferreira, P.: Revs-a robust electronic voting system. IADIS Int. J. WWW/Internet **1**(2), 47–63 (2003)
23. Jonker, H., Mauw, S., Pang, J.: Privacy and verifiability in voting systems: Methods, developments and trends. Comput. Sci. Rev. **10**, 1–30 (2013). http://dx.doi.org/10.1016/j.cosrev.2013.08.002
24. Li, C., Hwang, M., Liu, C.: An electronic voting protocol with deniable authentication for mobile ad hoc networks. Comput. Commun. **31**(10), 2534–2540 (2008). http://dx.doi.org/10.1016/j.comcom.2008.03.018
25. Liaskos, C., Petridou, S., Papadimitriou, G.: Towards realizable, low-cost broadcast systems for dynamic environments. IEEE/ACM Trans. Netw. **19**(2), 383–392 (2011)
26. Liaskos, C., Papadimitriou, G., Douligeris, C.: Sensor swarm query filtering: heightened attack resilience for broadcast on-demand services. In: IEEE Symposium on Computers and Communications (ISCC 2013), pp. 000312–000317. IEEE (2013)
27. Liaskos, C., Tsioliaridou, A., Papadimitriou, G., Nicopolitidis, P.: Minimal wireless broadcast schedules for multi-objective pursuits. IEEE Transactions on Vehicular Technology p. preprint (2014)
28. Malkhi, D., Margo, O., Pavlov, E.: E-voting without cryptography. In: Financial Cryptography, 6th International Conference (FC 2002), pp. 1–15, Southampton, 11–14 March 2002. http://dx.doi.org/10.1007/3-540-36504-4_1
29. Meng, B.: A critical review of receipt-freeness and coercion-resistance. Inf. Technol. J. **8**(7), 934–964 (2009)
30. Meng, B., Li, Z., Qin, J.: A receipt-free coercion-resistant remote internet voting protocol without physical assumptions through deniable encryption and trapdoor commitment scheme. J. Softw. **5**(9), 942–949 (2010)
31. Misra, J., Gries, D.: Finding repeated elements. Sci. Comput. Program. **2**(2), 143–152 (1982)
32. Pardede, E., Taniar, D., Awan, I., Al-Sudani, W., Gill, A., Li, C., Wang, J., Liu, F.: Protection through multimedia CAPTCHAs. In: Proceedings of the 8th International Conference on Advances in Mobile Computing and Multimedia (MoMM 2010), p. 63. ACM Press (2010)
33. Pietronero, L., Tosatti, E., Tosatti, V., Vespignani, A.: Explaining the uneven distribution of numbers in nature: the laws of Benford and Zipf. Physica A **293**(1–2), 297–304 (2001)
34. Qadah, G.Z., Taha, R.: Electronic voting systems: Requirements, design, and implementation. Computer Standards Interfaces **29**(3), 376–386 (2007). http://dx.doi.org/10.1016/j.csi.2006.06.001
35. Sampigethaya, K., Poovendran, R.: A framework and taxonomy for comparison of electronic voting schemes. Comput. Secur. **25**(2), 137–153 (2006). http://dx.doi.org/10.1016/j.cose.2005.11.003
36. Sharaf, M.A., Chrysanthis, P.: On-Demand Broadcast: new Challenges and Scheduling Algorithms. In: Proceedings of the 1st Hellenic Conference on the Management of Data (2002)
37. Sieka, B., Kshemkalyani, A.D., Singhal, M.: On the security of polling protocols in peer-to-peer systems. In: 4th International Conference on Peer-to-Peer Computing (P2P 2004), pp. 36–44, Zurich, 15–17 August 2004. http://doi.ieeecomputersociety.org/10.1109/PTP.2004.1334929
38. Smart, M., Ritter, E.: True trustworthy elections: remote electronic voting using trusted computing. In: Calero, J.M.A., Yang, L.T., Mármol, F.G., García Villalba, L.J., Li, A.X., Wang, Y. (eds.) ATC 2011. LNCS, vol. 6906, pp. 187–202. Springer, Heidelberg (2011)

39. Tsioliaridou, A., Zhang, C., Liaskos, C.: Fast and fair handling of multimedia captcha flows. International Journal of Interactive Mobile Technologies (2015). (To appear)
40. XJ Technologies: The AnyLogic Simulator (2013). http://www.xjtek.com/anylogic/
41. Zwierko, A., Kotulski, Z.: A light-weight e-voting system with distributed trust. Electr. Notes Theor. Comput. Sci. **168**, 109–126 (2007). http://dx.doi.org/10.1016/j.entcs.2006.12.004

Design and Field Evaluation of PassSec: Raising and Sustaining Web Surfer Risk Awareness

Melanie Volkamer[1,3], Karen Renaud[2], Gamze Canova[1],
Benjamin Reinheimer[1], and Kristoffer Braun[1 (✉)]

[1] Technische Universität Darmstadt, Darmstadt, Germany
{melanie.volkamer,gamze.canova,benjamin.reinheimer,
kristoffer.braun}@secuso.org
[2] University of Glasgow, Glasgow, UK
karen.renaud@glasgow.ac.uk
[3] Karlstad University, Karlstad, Sweden

Abstract. This paper presents PassSec, a Firefox Add-on that raises user awareness about safe and unsafe password entry while they surf the web. PassSec comprises a two-stage approach: highlighting as the web page loads, then bringing up a just-in-time helpful dialogue when the user demonstrates an intention to enter a password on an unsafe web page. PassSec was developed using a human-centred design approach. We performed a field study with 31 participants that showed that PassSec significantly reduces the number of logins on websites where password entry is unsafe.

1 Introduction

Web surfers can be at risk: (1) if the website itself is masquerading as the genuine entity; (2) the web page does not secure communications with the server by using HTTPS. In this paper, we focus on the latter as 10 % of the top 100 sites in the study country currently fail to do this (including the 8th, 9th and 11th most popular sites, including three major email providers). Insecure transmission has two consequences: communications being sniffed or the page itself being manipulated by third parties. Web browsers could refuse to load insecure pages but this relies on their being able to judge situations with 100 % reliability, an unrealistic expectation. Failing this, users need to be wary, to protect themselves when pages are insecure.

Popular web browsers currently do a poor job of supporting users in this respect. *Firstly*, the main security indicator (HTTP or HTTPS with a padlock) is usually placed in the address bar where it is easily missed [2,12,15,23,34]. *Secondly*, web browsers usually reassure rather than signal problems, with indicators appearing only when communications *are* secured (padlock and/or highlighted in green). This is counter-intuitive since people's attention is generally deliberately drawn to risk; they are not only told to relax in similar contexts.

To support users more effectively we developed a Firefox Add-On called PassSec (see Fig. 1) to raise awareness in two stages: (1) highlight the password

M. Conti et al. (Eds.): TRUST 2015, LNCS 9229, pp. 104–122, 2015.
DOI: 10.1007/978-3-319-22846-4_7

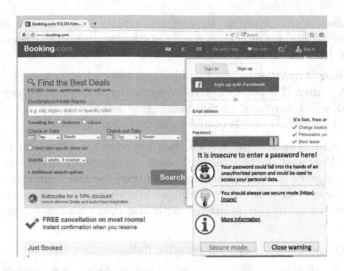

Fig. 1. Screenshot of PassSec: highlighted password field and helpful dialogue as HTTPS is not in place and the password field is focused.

field either in red with an icon to *draw attention*, or in green with a lock icon to *reassure*, as the web page loads; (2) bring up a helpful dialogue when the user is about to enter a password insecurely. The add-on was developed iteratively using a human-centred approach. We performed a field study with 31 participants and found that PassSec significantly reduced the number of logins on unsafe web pages.

2 Development Process

We derived a list of guidelines from the literature to inform effective implementation of PassSec's security indicators [6,11,13,21,29,31,32]. PassSec's *raison dêtre* is to raise awareness [17,27], to make security visible, thereby helping people to understand risk. Guidelines apply either to the indicator mechanism as a whole, or are specific to the delivered message. The *overall* guidelines for warning indicators are that they should meet the following requirements:

Be Noticeable. According to the C-HIP model [29] and the human-in-the-loop security framework [11], it is important to grab the user's attention and then maintain it [2,5,12,15,34].

Draw Attention and Reassure. The currently deployed HTTPS indicator and address bar padlock icon only reassure. One cannot expect users to interpret the lack of reassurance as something to be concerned about. Both must be provided.

Do Not Overstate. This risks habituation if people get used to dismissing advice because it appears gratuitously. For example [19] report on warning systems in hospitals and explain that when warnings appear too often or falsely they lead to confusion and irritation. Breznitz [7] explain that repeated alarms dull reactions so it is vital for indicators to signal genuine problems. This admonition is confirmed by [26].

Respect User Autonomy. The final decision rests with the user, not with the software. Wichman [28] points out that autonomy is a universal psychological human need, which is related to well-being. Humans always strive to meet their needs, so not respecting this is bound to be less than helpful.

Minimise Annoyance. Any advice that intrudes too often can be counter-productive. Politis *et al.* [20] tested speech warnings for drivers in terms of urgency, annoyance and effectiveness and argue for the importance of min-imising annoyance in delivering warnings. Wogalter [30] also caution against causing annoyance since it interferes with the user's ability to interpret the communication.

The *message-specific* guidelines for security indicators are that they should:

Be Explicit. Wolf *et al.* [33] recommend using simple and explicit language in communications. Wogalter *et al.* [31,32] say interventions should identify the problem, explain the consequences and offer directives for how to avoid the problem. It is important for people to understand why wariness is recommended, maximising personal relevance [22].

Offer Alternatives. Users do not like to abandon their intended action [16] so offering them an alternative (where possible) is preferable to advising abandon-ment.

Be Understandable. Many active warnings fail in this respect [12] so we need to maximise understandability deliberately by using a human-centred design approach.

Be Succinct and Minimise Effort. Too much text is likely to be daunting and become ineffective [3]. Humans are "cognitive misers" [14] meaning that they prefer to use intuition than to engage in effortful thinking. Moreover, we can not rely on people clicking on explanatory links such as "More Information" [2] so we should ensure that the most important information is displayed upfront.

These guidelines are not orthogonal. For example, understandability can help to raise awareness and offering alternatives minimises annoyance. On the other hand, a respect for autonomy can be taken too far: it could be used to jus-tify removing interventions altogether, but that would not align with the 'raise awareness' guideline. In effect, for each design decision we had to rank the guide-lines and use the most relevant one to guide our decision. This list helped us to make optimal design decisions, acknowledging the trade-offs that were sometimes unavoidable.

2.1   Design Decisions

When to Intervene? We identified relevant contexts for raising awareness. For each, we evaluated whether the password would be at risk while entering

Table 1. Risk in different contexts and how it is addressed.

Context	At Risk		Current	With
	Entry	Send	Browsers	PassSec
HTTP e.g. http://edition.cnn.com	Yes	Yes	– –	Draw Attention
HTTPS with unencrypted main page e.g. http://www.booking.com	Yes	No	– –	Draw Attention
HTTPS e.g. https://www.amazon. com	No	No	Reassures: lock icon	Reassures
HTTPS with mixed passive content [1] e.g. https://www.answers.com	No	No	Draw Attention: icon	Reassures
HTTPS with mixed active content [1] e.g. https://www.answers.com	No	No	Blocks active content, shield icon	Reassures
HTTPS with certificate issues	Maybe	Maybe	Active warning	Reassures

or sending (Table 1). We deliberately do not warn about certificate issues since these are only relevant when the website itself is fake, as is the case of websites masquerading as the genuine entities. Web browsers routinely warn about certificate issues and there is no point replicating this.

Redirect to HTTPS. It is technically possible to forward users to the secure web page automatically[1], if available, but automatic redirecting might be unnecessary if users do not plan to enter their password (*not overstate*). The other option is to advise them to switch. We decided on the second approach to let users decide, because it allows users to retain control: not treating them like children (*autonomy*). It also allows users to learn about securing communications and sustain awareness of insecure websites. Finally, it allows users to make the decision to use the unsecured web page, which they might do because they know that it is safe, despite appearances to the contrary (e.g. an internal company website or due to a trash account being used for this web page) (*autonomy*). We contemplated whether PassSec should provide an explanation or an easy-to-use button to authorise redirection. While the first option might be preferable with respect to raising awareness, we were concerned that it constituted too much effort for the user (*minimising effort*). We thus provide a button.

Keep History. The next decision is related to whether to ask users whether to switch to the HTTPS website every time an insecure web page is visited, or only once per specific page. Both have advantages (better awareness when asked each time) and disadvantages (likely to annoy). We incorporated a historical function to store details of those web pages where the user decided to switch to

---

[1] One could e.g. use the HTTPS-Everywhere Firefox Add-On https://www.eff.org/https-everywhere (last access: June 23, 2015).

the secure option. Any time a user visits a web page that appears in the history, PassSec automatically redirects them to the secure web page (*minimising effort & annoyance*).

Intervention Strategy. PassSec deploys a two-stage approach to maximise effectiveness. The *first* stage is a specific passive security indicator that appears as soon as the web page is loaded to immediately draw attention to a problem. To achieve this, password fields are highlighted either to raise awareness or to provide reassurance (*raise awareness & reassure*). The *second* a helpful dialogue appears next to the password field as soon as users start entering their password (just-in-time). Noticeability and effectiveness were evaluated in the field study.

2.2   Security Indicator Design

In [10], we showed that the combination of a red background and a yellow icon attracts attention effectively in an unsafe context (cf. Fig. 2). To reassure, we gave the input field a green border and a padlock icon (cf. Fig. 2). This proposal was developed through several iterations incorporating feedback from potential users. We started off with a green check mark but that confused people as they were accustomed to seeing it when they entered their data correctly. We settled on a padlock icon since it was perceived to be security-related. A green border was used instead of utilising a green background that was perceived to be too intrusive. The obvious concern with colour coding is that colour-blind users will be disadvantaged. It is true that the red background will not attract colour-blind users' attention as reliably, but the icon, being yellow, will serve to attract their attention. By using two independent indicators we make it less likely that colour-blind users will miss the signal.

Fig. 2. Highlighting of password fields to draw attention (left) if HTTPS is not in place; and to reassure (right) if HTTPS is in place.

2.3   Security Dialogue Design

The structure of the dialogues is based on Wogalter *et al.* [31,32] who recommend that such dialogues should consist of four core components: (1) Signal word to attract attention, (2) Identification of problem, (3) Explanation of consequences, and (4) Directives to avoid problem. While this structure is in line with the guidelines, we adapted it slightly. First, we do not utilise one signal word to attract attention (1). Here, we share the opinion of Bauer *et al.* [4] that a signal word is not necessary but that a corresponding icon should suffice to draw attention. As an icon is already used in the highlighted field, we decided not to add another in the dialogue. Second, we provide additional information about the problem and the consequences for those who want to learn more (*understandability* and *raise awareness*). We ensure, however, that the most important information is available without any extra effort being expended. We decided to formulate the identified problem (2) as headline.

Icons. Based on feedback on first mockups of our dialogues, we realised we had to incorporate meaningful icons. Wolf *et al.* [33] advise the use of icons to reduce the amount of text (*minimise effort*). Thus, instead of using headlines for the different elements of our dialogues we use corresponding icons. The icons were chosen from other areas to maximise ease of association with the type of information being provided (*understandable*). We used a light bulb to denote recommendations and the well-known "i" icon with blue background for information. After some iterations with potential users, we settled on a spy icon to depict the potential consequences.

Options. Users receiving dialogues have two options. One is to dismiss the dialogue and the other is to detour to the safe route, which is only possible if HTTPS is available. We facilitated the latter (secure) course of action by providing a button with green font based on findings about the efficacy of colour in this respect [10]. We allowed them to add exceptions when HTTPS was not available.

Background Colour. We considered two background colours: neutral (grey) or yellow. The first is less *annoying* while the second is more likely to be *noticed*. We decided to go with the grey background since the dialogue already comes with the password field highlighted in red. The design of a PassSec dialogue is shown in Fig. 3.

Fig. 3. Design proposal for dialogues (Color figure online)

2.4   Dialogue Content

We conducted a feasibility study in order to test the viability of different terms for different aspects as well as different phrases for different parts of the intervention to maximise understandability and effectiveness. We studied in surveys:

Term for 'Eve': The following terms were studied to find a common usage term for what we understand by 'Eve': Unauthorised people, criminals, hackers, attackers, and con men. The most promising common-usage term for 'Eve' turned out to be *'unauthorised person'*.

Headline. The following headlines were evaluated: 'You are not protected here', 'Your password is endangered here', 'The connection is not encrypted' as potential titles of the dialogue. 'Your password is endangered here' was promising, but it turned out that some people thought that 'endangered' was the wrong term. Therefore, we rephrased this proposal to *'It is insecure to enter a password'*.

Consequences. A number of alternative phrases were mooted to find a common usage phrase that is concrete, understandable and effective in depicting Eve's actual action: access, capture, reveal, publish, forward, distribute personal data *as well as* use, have access to, abuse the account/data at your account. To describe her malicious actions in the consequence 'access your personal data' was the preferred option. Furthermore, during the discussion we realised the importance of mentioning the password again to explain how access is granted. The final consequence reads: *'Your password could fall into the hands of unauthorised persons and could be used to access your personal data'*.

Recommendation. The recommendation depends on whether HTTPS is available, or not. The dialogue text recommends switching to HTTPS whenever possible. This is the only recommended option (see Fig. 3) and the consequence is that the web page will, in future, always be opened using HTTPS. Note, we decided to use the term *'Secure mode'* instead of using the term HTTPS to avoid technical terms and maximise *understandability*. The actual text is: *"You should always use secure mode (https). Click on the 'secure mode' button and you will be redirected to secure mode automatically in the future."*

If HTTPS *is not* available, the risk can be reduced by not re-using the password entered on this web page. Consequently, the text reads: *"This website does not offer a secure option (https). If you decide to log in anyway, you should at least use a different password for other websites."* We are aware of the fact that this lacks substance, but being more explicit and prescriptive would result in a long paragraph and might lead to users not reading it at all (*minimise effort* and *annoyance*).

Options. The options provided in the dialogue depend on whether HTTPS is available, or not. The recommended option for our context is to open the web page via HTTPS whenever available, that is, the secure option. If HTTPS is not available, there are two options. The first is for the user to add an exception. This ensures that the decision is recorded and PassSec does not annoy the user by asking him or her to re-affirm every time they access the page. The other option is for the user to dismiss the dialogue by clicking on 'Close'. The risk of the first option is that an HTTPS option might be available in the future and the exception would prevent PassSec from checking for the availability of HTTPS. On the other hand, if the exception is not added this will lead to a dialogue appearing every time, which is bound to lead to annoyance.

Amount of Visible Text. To balance *succinctness* and *understandability*, we show the headline, the entire consequence, and the first part of the recommendation (when HTTPS is available) as well as the entire recommendation (when HTTPS is not available); with a link to more information. We ensure that the most important information is always visible and does not require any additional action by the user as clicking on a link such as "More Information".

2.5 Firefox Add-On

The described concepts were implemented as a Firefox Add-On called *PassSec*. The dialogues are depicted in Figs. 4 and 5. PassSec acts after the browser has judged the web page (what the browser blocks, stays blocked). In summary, PassSec satisfies the guidelines identified in Sect. 2 as depicted in Table 2.

Fig. 4. A PassSec screenshot for when HTTPS is not available. The expanded version is shown.

Fig. 5. A PassSec screenshot for when HTTPS is not available. The expanded version is shown.

3 Field Evaluation

Testing security-related behaviour in a laboratory setting leads to unrealistic and overly positive results. We thus carried out a field test to evaluate PassSec's noticeability, understandability and the succinctness of the dialogue text. Acceptability was also considered in terms of the System Usability Scale[2] (SUS) and feedback questions as this would be a necessary pre-condition for PassSec's potential success in the future. One cannot test security-related behaviour reliably in a laboratory setting since you get unrealistic and overly positive results.

---

[2] http://www.usability.gov/how-to-and-tools/methods/system-usability-scale.html (last access: June 23, 2015).

Table 2. Mapping guidelines to PassSec Add-On design.

GUIDELINE	HOW ACHIEVED
noticeability	locate next to password field
draw attention & reassure	highlight field and add icon
not overstate	redirect not enforced
respects user autonomy	user decides whether to redirect or not
minimise annoyance	appear only when password field focused
explicit	dialogue design
offer alternatives	'Secure mode'
understandability	feasibility testing
be succinct	'[more]' links
minimise effort	remember whitelist decisions

3.1   Study Design

Participants were told that the study was part of our research into Internet-related warnings but we did not specify the types of risky situations we were interested in. The field study comprised three phases. Participants used a deactivated Add-On to record baseline performance. After three to four weeks, participants installed a logging PassSec. A link to a web page detailing the functionality of PassSec, including information about the logging, was provided. Two weeks later participants uninstalled PassSec and filled out an online survey. The online survey elicited demographics, posed SUS usability-related questions [8] and questions relating to PassSec acceptability and the choices they made during their usage of PassSec.

3.2   Study Prototype

The Pre-Study Add-On logged the following information together with time-stamps whenever users focused on a password field: (1) Hash of the domain (sub and top level domain) of the visited website, (2) Whether this was done via HTTPS, (3) Whether users submitted their password via HTTP and (4) Whether HTTPS was available (if not used by default). The PassSec Add-On additionally logged whether and which of the buttons in the dialogue were pressed, whether participants clicked on the 'more information' link, whether they submitted their passwords via HTTP or HTTPS. The hashed domains were destroyed once they were tallied to support analysis to preserve the privacy of our participants.

3.3   Recruitment, Reimbursement, and Ethics

Flyers were distributed across town, emailed to mailing lists, posted on web pages and to social networks. Those we reached were asked to advertise the study to get more participants, using a snowball approach. We did not pay participants but they could win one of two iPad minis if they participated in all three phases. Guidelines on ethical issues regarding research involving humans are provided by an ethics commission at the host University. The relevant requirements for this research relating to respondent consent and data privacy were satisfied. Logged data, as well as survey data, was not linked to individuals and only used for the purposes of this research. Visited domain details were hashed. Participants could withdraw at any time and request that their stored logs be deleted.

4   Results

In total, 51 participants installed the Pre-Add-On and 37 installed the PassSec Add-On. The final online survey was completed by 31 participants (sixteen female and fifteen male), whose data informed our analysis. The average age was 31, ranging from 19 to 73 with a standard deviation of 10.64. Out of the 31 participants, 14 people had something to do with IT (e.g. postgraduate or undergraduate degree). The free-text responses were independently coded by two of the authors using an inductive coding approach. Both reviewed the answers and identified categories from participants' responses. These were discussed and iteratively developed.

4.1   Noticeability

There are two ways of testing noticeability. If one tests something in the lab you can use eye-tracking equipment to see if people look at the part of the screen where the dialogue appears, or you can ask people if they saw it. With a field evaluation you cannot do this, so you have to use an indirect measure to detect noticeability. In our case we tested whether people carried out fewer insecure actions with the PassSec dialogues appearing. If we see a reduction in insecure actions, one can assume that the dialogue must have been noticed, and affected behaviour. We studied the impact of PassSec on participants' behaviour. For the purposes of this discussion we will use the following terms: for access via HTTP we will use the term *insecure* and for access via HTTPS we will use the term *secure*. Table 3 presents participants (P), attempting (A) to login to websites on different domains (D) in phase-1 (Pre-Add-On) and phase-2 (PassSec). Figure 6 provides an overview of participants' behaviour with PassSec (based on the logs and survey responses).

Insecure Logins (HTTPS Available:): In total there were 476 insecure login attempts executed by 19 participants on 19 different domains. With PassSec there were 30 insecure login attempts by nine participants on 15 different domains. Seven of these attempts happened after the participant had previously switched to 'secure mode' to log in. This might have happened if participants used PassSec on different devices. Seven of the nine participants subsequently switched to secure mode. One participant only logged in once insecurely (he/she · did not return to the website thereafter). Another logged in five times on the

Table 3. Number of insecure login attempts with and without PassSec.

	HTTP Login Attempts	By Participants	At Domains
HTTPS Available	476	19	19
HTTPS Available (PassSec)	30	9	15
HTTPS Unavailable	105	7	9
HTTPS Unavailable (PassSec)	87	19	24

same insecure website. For the evaluation, we considered for each participant (who – at least once – logged in insecurely) the difference between insecure login attempts *without* and *with* PassSec. We first used the Kolmogorov-Smirnov test to determine whether these differences were normally distributed. This hypotheses had to be rejected ($p = 0.011$, $p < 0.001$). Therefore we applied a one-tailed Wilcoxon signed-rank test to determine statistical significance. These differences differ from zero in a highly significant manner ($p < 0.001$). Thus PassSec was successful.

Switch to HTTPS: 17 participants switched to secure mode a total of 43 times. Ten did so whenever the option was offered. In the online survey participants were asked why they did not switch to the 'Secure Mode' (if applicable). Five of the seven participants who failed to switch stated that they always switched to the 'secure mode' before they logged in and two stated that they switched to secure version of the website themselves.

Insecure Logins (HTTPS Unavailable): There were 105 insecure login attempts on nine different domains without PassSec. Seven participants did this at least once. There were 87 login attempts on 24 domains with PassSec. Fifteen participants did this at least once.

Exceptions Added: Ten exceptions were added by five participants. Participants were asked to share their reasons for adding exceptions. One participant cited the irrelevance of the dialogue for the specific website. Another said that he/she was annoyed by the dialogue. Three said they had no alternative because they wanted to log into their account so abandonment was not an option. Some entries in the logfiles showed that dialogues were ignored whereas the expected log entry detailing the dialogue was missing. We tried to reproduce this exception and noticed that we had failed to anticipate the fact that some people allow the browser to store their passwords. In this case the browser populates the credentials automatically and the dialogue would not appear since it is triggered only when the password is focused.

Background Colour: The survey contained a screenshot of the dialogue, as shown in Fig. 4 and one with the same content but with a yellow background. We asked participants to rate their appeal and ability to grab attention and asked which one they would recommend. In terms of appeal and recommendation,

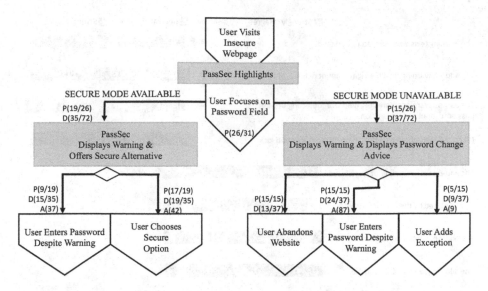

Fig. 6. Impact of PassSec on participants behaviour when faced with either of the messages (P=Participants, D=Domains, A=Attempts/ Number of Actions).

both performed equally. With respect to grabbing attention, the yellow one was much preferred. We tested the difference in grabbing attention with a two-tailed Wilcoxon signed-rank test and it reached significance with p = 0.028.

4.2 Understandability and Succinctness

Participants were asked whether the message texts were easy to understand. On a scale from 1 (not at all) to 5 (very understandable), the median of the answers was 4. For the boxplot see Fig. 7. Participants were also asked whether they were aware of the PassSec recommendation to consider changing their other passwords One was indeed aware of the message text but 23 were not and two were unsure. We also asked whether they changed their password based on the recommendation. Seven answered 'no' and 19 argued that there was no recommendation.

Confusion regarding the '*Close*' button was identified from the free text answers on feedback. Some participants seemed unsure of the consequences of clicking on this button. It was sometimes interpreted as "leave this web page". Participants were asked whether the dialogues had the right amount of text. On a scale from 1 (totally agree) to 5 (totally disagree), the median of the answers is 2. For the boxplot see Fig. 7. The survey also contained a screenshot of a shorter message text version (only headline and buttons and a link to get more information) and a long version (as shown in Fig. 4). Participants were asked whether the long version should be displayed immediately, or not. The longer version was preferred by the majority of participants (21 out of 31).

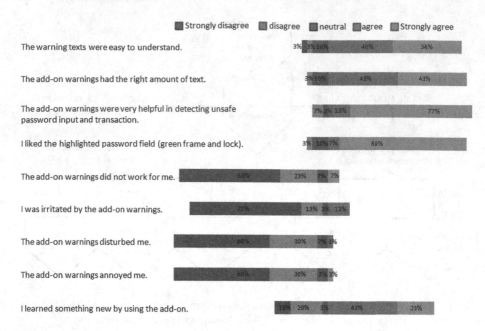

Fig. 7. Result for the survey questions related to amount and understandability of the provided text, as well as satisfaction related questions.

4.3   Acceptability

Satisfaction. PassSec received an SUS score of 81.91. A score over 80 implies a good-to-excellent result. Besides the SUS score, we asked the participants several questions about its usability. Responses and ratings are depicted in Fig. 7. For most of the questions the rating was *very good* (median). This includes helpfulness in detecting unsafe contexts, appreciating reassurance, not disturbing, not irritating, and not annoying.

Intention to Use PassSec in Future. 18 participants wanted to continue to use PassSec after the study; and ten were undecided. Three did not plan to use it in future (all male). Examples of positive comments were: '*easy to notice*', '*increased attention that passwords are also requested on* HTTP *websites*', '*feeling more secure*', '*does not disturb me but helpful*', and '*easy to switch to* HTTPS'. Examples of negative comments: '*too few technical details*' '*Firefox was only used to participate in the study*', '*design should be improved first*', '*other Add-Ons installed such as https-everywhere*', '*slows down browser*', and '*not enough protection*'. We categorised them as negative and positive and not according the three groups (wants to use it, not decided, does not want to use it again) because in all three groups we found both negative and positive arguments.

Nice to have Features. In order to collect input regarding possible future functionality and modifications, we requested suggestions for improvement from the participants. They responded: '*cover more critical form fields; e.g. bank account* *details*', '*allow users to enable* HTTPS *everywhere*', '*provide more information about algorithms/criteria*' '*improve performance*', '*not easy enough to see whether* HTTPS *is available or not*', '*option to close does not function as expected*' (as the dialogue is displayed every time the password field is focused) and '*improve recommendation for insecure situation*'. Furthermore, we provided a list of possible *form fields* which could also trigger PassSec dialogues in future versions. Bank account number and credit card were selected 28 times, TANs 25 times, email addresses 16 times, postal addresses 15 times, and name 13 times.

5 Discussion

Noticeability: PassSec significantly reduced the number of insecure login attempts. Most participants who logged in insecurely either dismissed the dialogue or added an exception. The dialogues must have been noticed. It also became clear that the highlighting of the password field was insufficient indication since participants with stored passwords logged in despite the password field being highlighted in red. Thus, in PassSec 2.0 we need to ensure messages are also displayed in this context, to improve noticeability. There are actually two options: (1) detect the auto-fill of the password field and then show the dialogue (not two-stage but still passive) or (2) detect the auto-fill of the password field and show the dialogue when user clicks the login button. In this case the login would not be executed when clicked. It would be enabled again once the dialogue was displayed (two-stage but active since it interferes with the user's activity and demands attention). Both require evaluation in a future study. The survey answers indicate that noticeability could be further improved by using a yellow background colour for the text which seems to improve noticeability without increasing annoyance or decreasing appeal.

Understandability: The overall understandability rating was good but we identified a number of areas for improvement. The semantics and consequences of the 'close' and the 'add exception' buttons were unclear. There was no explanation in the dialogue, an unfortunate omission. 'Close' may have confused participants because it reappeared every time the user focused the password field. This may also explain why one participant became annoyed by the dialogue. We propose renaming the 'close' button to 'Ok, got it' in PassSec 2.0, and adding a sentence: 'If you do not want to see this dialogue again, add an exception'. Moreover, we will ensure that the dialogue only appears once per page. Another issue was the recommendation to 'change' passwords on other websites. The phrase '*If you decide to log into this website anyway, you should use a different password your other websites*' was unclear. We propose to rephrase this to '*If you decide to log into this website anyway and you use the same password for other website accounts, you should change them immediately.*'

Succinctness: Users accepted the amount of text and most voted against showing less text. PassSec 2.0 will provide an option to switch to the short version. Participants complained that it was difficult to distinguish between websites that could be opened securely from websites which could not, at first glance. Initially the only difference was the green font versus the black font on the other button. To make the difference more obvious, PassSec 2.0 will use a green background for the secure mode button and a red one for the exception button.

Acceptability: PassSec performed very well with respect to usability. The free text answers revealed a number of positive comments revealing ease of use, minimal disturbance and low annoyance. Many will continue to use PassSec, others wanted their comments about usability addressed before they would consider adoption. The main areas for improvement were performance and the amount of information displayed. The performance issues were caused by the logging as well as by the way that PassSec was implemented: It initially loaded the HTTP page, then checked whether the user had previously elected to be redirected, and, if so, loaded the HTTPS page. If not, it checked for the domain on the exception list. The performance was particularly poor with slow Internet connections. This has been improved in PassSec 2.0 by optimising the checks and directly loading the HTTPS page if the website is in the secure mode list. We plan to extend the provided information and to provide a link to the website in the 'More information' part of the dialogue.

All participants recommended extending the mechanism to cover other kinds of data entry. PassSec 2.0 identifies banking data related fields as well as name, address, and email address fields. While most of these issues can, and will, be addressed, there is a trust issue that appears when trying to recruit users. People tend to mistrust Add-Ons in general, since they do not know whether additional information is collected. This issue can be addressed if PassSec's functionality is integrated into browsers.

Limitations: Participants used PassSec for different lengths of time due to recruitment difficulties and a fixed end date. Due to the fact that we conducted a field evaluation, we do not know whether we logged data only from the actual participant or whether he/she shared the device with others (which six stated they did, three on a daily basis). Participants were told that we were going to log their actions, and this might have influenced their behaviour, perhaps biasing them towards behaving more securely than usual.

6   Related Work

Researchers have come up with a variety of innovative mechanisms to make users aware of the dangers to their data while using the Internet. Based on the literature there seem to be three ways of approaching this problem: (1) Educating web surfers, (2) passive (non-blocking) security indicators, and (3) using active (blocking) warnings that interrupt the user's current workflow. A prominent *educational* approach is Anti-Phishing Phil by Sheng *et al.* [24]. Their game was designed to help users to differentiate between secure and fake URLs in a playful way. They were able to show that their approach was superior to existing teaching material. As other Phishing detection mechanisms cannot provide 100 %

protection, it is important not to discount the benefits of education; it is an essential first step in making users more aware of threats. To warn about insecure communications, technology can reliably check whether HTTPS is in place or not and then either reassure or warn, augmenting the educational approach. Some notable approaches in the field of *passive* approaches are LinkExtend[3] and research such as published by Shepherd *et al.* [25]. LinkExtend is a Firefox Add-On considering many different security indicators including whether HTTPS is in place or not. However, it displays the relevant information at the top of the web browser while other research has shown that indicators in the address bar are unlikely to be noticed [2,12,15,34]. Their approach is unlikely to be effective.

Active warnings have been studied e.g. by Brustoloni and Villamarín-Salomón [9]. They evaluated their approach in a user study with 26 participants and this led to participants being more risk averse. The active approach is likely to annoy people in our case as they would get a warning even though they only want to surf on the corresponding page. Maurer *et al.* [18] use a mix of passive and active warnings. A warning dialogue is displayed whenever critical data type fields are focused and the corresponding website is not yet white listed. They call their approach "semi-blocking" as it does not actively interrupt the user's current workflow but requires deliberate action before submission is possible. Their main purpose is to make users aware that they are about to enter sensitive data and that they should make sure it is transmitted securely and the website is not a Phishing website. Users can elect to add the web page to a whitelist in order to reduce warnings, or just dismiss the warning. The system aimed to reduce warnings and only display them when really required in order to reduce both annoyance and minimise habituation effects. Their solution was comprehensibly tested, both in the lab and in the field. In the lab, they tested whether people could detect Phishing web sites with the help of their warning system. In the seven day field study they focused on how their approach was perceived by real users. As opposed to our work, their field study did not quantitatively evaluate whether the tool reduced insecure behaviours in the wild but rather on whether the number of warnings decreased over time.

In summary, education is definitely worthwhile in our context but augmenting it with warnings is likely to improve matters even further. Existing approaches proposing passive and passive indicators have their limitations. The approach that most closely mirrors ours is the semi-blocking approach written about by Maurer *et al.* [18]. Their main focus was on masquerading websites. They have yet to test its effectiveness in reducing insecure behaviours in the field.

7   Conclusion and Future Work

We developed a Firefox Add-On, called PassSec, to effectively support users in detecting insecure communications. By ensuring that we satisfied a number of guidelines identified from the literature, and by applying a human-centered

---

[3] https://addons.mozilla.org/de/firefox/addon/linkextend-safety-kidsafe-site/ (last access: June 23, 2015).

design approach (both for the content and design of its dialogue) we were able to achieve our aim. PassSec significantly reduced the number of insecure logins. We have identified ways to improve PassSec 2.0. We delivered dialogues using a Firefox Add-On, but it would be preferable for this functionality to be embedded within current browsers. The results for the first phase of the field study indicated that passwords are at risk in many situations and it became clear that such an Add-On could lead to more secure behaviour. While PassSec is not the first Add-On to attempt to support users in this respect, it is, to the best of our knowledge the first that has been evaluated in a field study which is as close to ecological validity as is possible in a controlled field study. For future work, we plan to distribute PassSec 2.0. Since PassSec significantly reduced insecure logins we hope that PassSec 2.0 will improve the situation even further.

References

1. Mixed Content Blocking Enabled in Firefox: 23! (2013). https://blog.mozilla.org/tanvi/ (last Access: June 2, 2015)
2. Akhawe, D., Felt, A.P.: Alice in warningland: A large-scale field study of browser security warning effectiveness. In: Usenix Security. pp. 257–272, Washington DC, 14–16 August 2013
3. Ayres, T.J., Gross, M.M., Wood, C.T., Horst, D.P., Beyer, R.R., Robinson, J.N.: What is a warning and when will it work? In: Proceedings of the Human Factors and Ergonomics Society Annual Meeting, vol. 33, pp. 426–430. SAGE Publications (1989)
4. Bauer, L., Bravo-Lillo, C., Cranor, L., Fragkaki, E.: Warning design guidelines. Technical report, Carnegie Mellon University (2013). CMU-CyLab-13-002
5. Bravo-Lillo, C., Cranor, L.F., Downs, J., Komanduri, S., Sleeper, M.: Improving computer security dialogs. In: Campos, P., Graham, N., Jorge, J., Nunes, N., Palanque, P., Winckler, M. (eds.) INTERACT 2011, Part IV. LNCS, vol. 6949, pp. 18–35. Springer, Heidelberg (2011)
6. Bravo-Lillo, C., Komanduri, S., Cranor, L.F., Reeder, R.W., Sleeper, M., Downs, J., Schechter, S.: Your attention please: designing security-decision UIs to make genuine risks harder to ignore. In: Proceedings of the Ninth Symposium on Usable Privacy and Security (SOUPS 2013), pp. 6:1–6:12. ACM (2013)
7. Breznitz, S.: Cry Wolf: The Psychology of False Alarms. Psychology Press, New York (2013)
8. Brooke, J.: SUS: a Retrospective. J. Usability Stud. 8(2), 29–40 (2013)
9. Brustoloni, J.C., Villamarín-Salomón, R.: Improving security decisions with polymorphic and audited dialogs. In: Proceedings of the 3rd symposium on Usable privacy and security, pp. 76–85. ACM (2007)
10. Canova, G., Volkamer, M., Bergmann, C., Borza, R.: NoPhish: an anti-phishing education app. In: Mauw, S., Jensen, C.D. (eds.) STM 2014. LNCS, vol. 8743, pp. 188–192. Springer, Heidelberg (2014)
11. Cranor, L.F.: A framework for reasoning about the human in the loop. In: Proceedings of the 1st Conference on Usability, Psychology, and Security (UPSEC 2008), pp. 1:1–1:15. USENIX Association (2008)
12. Dhamija, R., Tygar, J.D., Hearst, M.: Why phishing works. In: Proceedings of the SIGCHI Conference on Human Factors in Computing Systems, pp. 581–590. ACM (2006)

13. Egelman, S., Cranor, L.F., Hong, J.: You've been warned: an empirical study of the effectiveness of web browser phishing warnings. In: Proceedings of the SIGCHI Conference on Human Factors in Computing Systems, pp. 1065–1074. ACM (2008)
14. Kahneman, D.: Thinking Fast and Slow. Farrar Strauss, Giroux, New York (2011)
15. Lin, E., Greenberg, S., Trotter, E., Ma, D., Aycock, J.: Does domain highlighting help people identify phishing sites? In: Proceedings of the SIGCHI Conference on Human Factors in Computing Systems (CHI 2011), pp. 2075–2084. ACM (2011)
16. Locke, E.A.: Relationship of success and expectation to affect on goal-seeking tasks. J. Pers. Soc. Psychol. 7(2), 125–134 (1967)
17. Maurer, M.E.: Bringing effective security warnings to mobile browsing. In: 2nd International Workshop on Security and Privacy in Spontaneous Interaction and Mobile Phone Use (in Conjunction with Pervasive 2010), Helsinki (2010)
18. Maurer, M.E., De Luca, A., Kempe, S.: Using data type based security alert dialogs to raise online security awareness. In: Proceedings of the Seventh Symposium on Usable Privacy and Security, p. 2. ACM (2011)
19. Meredith, C., Edworthy, J.: Are there too many alarms in the intensive care unit? An overview of the problems. J. Adv. Nurs. 21(1), 15–20 (1995)
20. Politis, I., Brewster, S., Pollick, F.: Speech tactons improve speech warnings for drivers. In: Proceedings of the 6th International Conference on Automotive User Interfaces and Interactive Vehicular Applications (AutomotiveUI 2014), pp. 4:1–4:8. ACM, New York (2014). http://doi.acm.org/10.1145/2667317.2667318
21. Potgieter, M., Marais, C., Gerber, M.: Fostering content relevant information security awareness through browser extensions. In: Dodge Jr., R.C., Futcher, L. (eds.) WISE 6/7/8. IFIP AICT, vol. 406, pp. 58–67. Springer, Heidelberg (2013)
22. Ruiter, R.A., Abraham, C., Kok, G.: Scary warnings and rational precautions: a review of the psychology of fear appeals. Psychol. Health 16(6), 613–630 (2001)
23. Schechter, S.E., Dhamija, R., Ozment, A., Fischer, I.: The emperor's new security indicators. In: IEEE Symposium on Security and Privacy (SP 2007), pp. 51–65. IEEE (2007)
24. Sheng, S., Magnien, B., Kumaraguru, P., Acquisti, A., Cranor, L.F., Hong, J., Nunge, E.: Anti-phishing Phil: the design and evaluation of a game that teaches people not to fall for phish. In: Proceedings of the 3rd Symposium on Usable Privacy and Security, pp. 88–99. ACM (2007)
25. Shepherd, L.A., Archibald, J., Ferguson, R.I.: Reducing risky security behaviours: utilising affective feedback to educate users. In: International Conference on Cyber Forensics, Glasgow, 23–24 June 2014
26. Sunshine, J., Egelman, S., Almuhimedi, H., Atri, N., Cranor, L.F.: Crying wolf: an empirical study of ssl warning effectiveness. In: USENIX Security Symposium, pp. 399–416 (2009)
27. West, R.: The psychology of security. Commun. ACM 51(4), 34–40 (2008)
28. Wichmann, S.S.: Self-determination theory: the importance of autonomy to well-being across cultures. J. Humanistic Couns. 50(1), 16–26 (2011)
29. Wogalter, M.S.: Communication-human information processing (C-HIP) model. In: Wogalter, M.S. (ed.) Handbook of Warnings. Lawrence Erlbaum Associates, Mahwah (2006)
30. Wogalter, M.S., Conzola, V.C.: Using technology to facilitate the design and delivery of warnings. Int. J. Syst. Sci. 33(6), 461–466 (2002)
31. Wogalter, M.S., Desaulniers, D.R., Brelsford, J.W.: Consumer products: how are the hazards perceived? In: Proceedings of the Human Factors and Ergonomics Society Annual Meeting, vol. 31, pp. 615–619. SAGE Publications (1987)

32. Wogalter, M.S., Godfrey, S.S., Fontenelle, G.A., Desaulniers, D.R., Rothstein, P.R., Laughery, K.R.: Effectiveness of warnings. Hum. Factors J. Human Factors Ergon. Soc. **29**(5), 599–612 (1987)
33. Wolf, M.S., Davis, T.C., Bass, P.F., Curtis, L.M., Lindquist, L.A., Webb, J.A., Bocchini, M.V., Bailey, S.C., Parker, R.M.: Improving prescription drug warnings to promote patient comprehension. Arch. Intern. Medicine **170**(1), 50–56 (2010)
34. Wu, M., Miller, R.C., Garfinkel, S.L.: Do security toolbars actually prevent phishing attacks? In: Proceedings of the SIGCHI Conference on Human Factors in Computing Systems. pp. 601–610. ACM, Montreal, 22–27 April 2006

Trusted Systems and Services

Trustworthy Memory Isolation
of Linux on Embedded Devices

Hamed Nemati[1], Mads Dam[1], Roberto Guanciale[1]([✉]), Viktor Do[2],
and Arash Vahidi[2]

[1] KTH Royal Institute of Technology, Stockholm, Sweden
{hnnemati,mfd,robertog}@kth.se
[2] SICS Swedish ICT, Lund, Sweden
{viktordo,arash}@sics.se

Abstract. The isolation of security critical components from an untrusted OS allows to both protect applications and to harden the OS itself, for instance by run-time monitoring. Virtualization of the memory subsystem is a key component to provide such isolation. We present the design, implementation and verification of a virtualization platform for the ARMv7-A processor family. Our design is based on direct paging, an MMU virtualization mechanism previously introduced by Xen for the x86 architecture, and used later with minor variants by the Secure Virtual Architecture, SVA. We show that the direct paging mechanism can be implemented using a compact design, suitable for formal verification down to a low level of abstraction, without penalizing system performance. The verification is performed using the HOL4 theorem prover and uses a detailed model of the ARMv7-A ISA, including the MMU. We prove memory isolation of the hosted components along with information flow security for an abstract top level model of the virtualization mechanism. The abstract model is refined down to a HOL4 transition system closely resembling a C implementation. The virtualization mechanism is demonstrated on real hardware via a hypervisor capable of hosting Linux as an untrusted guest.

1 Introduction

A basic security requirement for systems that allow software to execute at different levels of security is memory isolation: The ability to store secret information within a designated part of memory and prevent the contents of this memory to be affected by, or leaked to, parts of the system that are not authorized to access it. Without the usage of special hardware, trustworthy memory isolation relies on the correct implementation of the OS kernel. However, given the size and complexity of modern OSs, the vision of comprehensive and formal commodity OS verification is as distant as ever.

An alternative to verifying the entire OS is to delegate critical functionality to special low-level execution platforms such as hypervisors, separation kernels, or microkernels. Such an approach has some significant advantages. First, the size

© Springer International Publishing Switzerland 2015
M. Conti et al. (Eds.): TRUST 2015, LNCS 9229, pp. 125–142, 2015.
DOI: 10.1007/978-3-319-22846-4_8

and complexity of the execution platform can be made much smaller, potentially opening up for rigorous verification. The literature has many recent examples of this, in seL4 [16], Microsoft's Hyper-V project [17], Green Hills' CC certified INTEGRITY-178B separation kernel [22], and the PROSPER separation kernel [10]. Second, the platform can be opened up to public scrutiny and certification, independent of application stacks. Virtualization-like mechanisms can also be used to support various forms of application hardening against untrusted OSs. Examples of this include KCoFi [7] based on the Secure Virtual Architecture [9], Overshadow [5], Inktag [14], and Virtual Ghost [8]. All these cases rely crucially on memory isolation to provide the required security guarantees, typically by virtualizing the memory management unit (MMU) hardware. MMU virtualization, however, can be exceedingly tricky to get right, motivating the use of formal methods for its verification.

In this paper we present an MMU virtualization API for the ARMv7 family of processors (which is one of the widely adopted architectures for embedded devices) that has been formally verified down to a low level of abstraction. The API uses direct paging, a virtualization mechanism introduced by Xen [4] and used later with some variations by the Secure Virtual Architecture [9]. In direct paging, page tables are kept in guest memory and allowed to be read and directly manipulated by the untrusted guest OS (when they are not in active use by the MMU). Xen demonstrated that this approach has better performance than other software virtualization approaches (e.g. shadow page tables) on the x86 architecture [4]. Moreover, since direct paging does not require shadow data structures, this approach has small memory overhead. The engineering challenge we posed ourselves was to design a minimal API that is (i) sufficiently expressive to host a paravirtualized Linux, (ii) introduces an acceptable overhead and (iii) whose implementation is sufficiently small to be subject to pervasive verification for commodity CPU architecture such as ARMv7.

The security objective is to allow a malicious guest system to operate freely, invoking the hypervisor at will, without being able to access memory or processor resources that the guest has not received static permission for. The verification is performed using a formal model of the ARMv7 architecture [11], implemented in the HOL4 interactive theorem prover.

The verification is built on top a model, the top level specification (TLS), which describes the ideal behavior of hypervisor's handlers implementing the virtualization mechanism, alternating with user mode execution under control of a possibly malicious guest. Parts of the security state is stored in a model state, by construction outside the reach of the guest. However, page tables are stored in memory. This is a key complication forced by the direct paging approach, and the solution to this problem is a key contribution of the paper. The upshot is that it is no longer self-evident that the desired memory isolation properties, non-exfiltration and non-infiltration in the terminology of [13], hold for the TLS, and an important part of the verification is therefore to formally validate this fact.

To keep the TLS as simple and abstract as possible, the TLS addresses page tables directly using their physical addresses. A real implementation cannot do this, but must appeal to virtual addresses instead, in addition to managing its internal data structures. To this end we introduce an implementation model, essentially a state transition model operating on the real ARMv7-A state through transitions that directly reflect handler execution at the binary level. We exhibit a refinement from the TLS to the implementation model, prove its correctness, and show, as a corollary, that the memory isolation properties proved at top level transfer to the implementation level.

The verification highlighted three classes of bugs in the initial design of the virtualization mechanism:

(i) Arithmetic overflows, bit field and offset mismatches, and signed operators where the unsigned ones were needed.
(ii) Missing checks of self referencing page tables.
(iii) Approval of guest requests that cause unpredictable behaviors of the ARMv7 MMU.

Moreover, the verification of the implementation model identified additional bugs exploitable by requesting the validation of physical blocks residing outside the guest memory. This last class of bugs was identified because the implementation model takes into account the virtual memory mapping used by the handlers.

We report on a port of Linux kernel 2.6.34 and demonstrate the prototype implementation of a hypervisor for which the core component is the verified MMU virtualization API. Experiments demonstrate that the hypervisor can run with reasonable performance on real hardware (Beagleboard-xM based on the Cortex-A8 CPU).

2   Related Work

The ability to isolate security critical components from an untrusted OS allows non critical parts of a system to be implemented while the critical software remains adequately protected. This isolation can be used both to protect applications from an untrusted OS as well as to protect the OS itself from internal threats. For example, KCoFI [7] uses Secure Virtual Architecture [9] to isolate the OS from a run-time checker. The checker instruments the OS and monitors its activities to guarantee the control-flow integrity of the OS itself. Related examples are application hardening frameworks such as Overshadow [5], Inktag [14], and virtual ghost [8]. In all these cases some form of virtualization of the MMU hardware is a critical component to provide the required isolation guarantees.

Shadow page tables (SPT) is a common approach to MMU virtualization. The virtualization layer maintains a shadow copy of page tables created and maintained by the guest OS. The MMU uses only the shadow pages, which are updated after the virtualization layer validates the OS changes. The Hyper-V hypervisor, which uses shadow pages on x86, has been formally verified using the semi automated VCC tool [17]. Related work [3,21] uses shadow page tables to provide full virtualization, including virtual memory, for "baby VAMP", a simplified MIPS, using VCC. This work, along with later work on TLB virtualization for an abstract mode of x64 [2], has been verified using Wolfgang Paul's

VCC-based simulation framework. Also, the OKL4-microvisor uses shadow paging to virtualize the memory subsystem [12]. However, this hypervisor has not been verified.

Some modern CPUs provide native hardware support for virtualization. The ARM Virtualization Extensions augment the CPU with a complete new execution mode and provide a two stage address translation. Using this mechanism, the MMU virtualization does not need to be implemented in software. Even though such hardware support can significantly reduce the complexity of the virtualization layer [24], it does not make software based solutions obsolete. For example, the recent Cortex-A5 (used in feature-phones) and the legacy ARM11 cores (used in the 2014 "New Nintendo 3DS") do not make use of such extensions. Today, the IoT and wearable computing are dominated by microcontrollers (e.g. Cortex-M). As the recent Intel Quark demonstrates, the necessity of executing legacy stacks (e.g. Linux) is pushing towards equipping these microcontrollers with a MMU. Quark and the upcoming ARMv8-R both support an MMU and lack two stage page-tables. Furthermore, solutions based on FPGAs and softcores (e.g. LEON) can benefit from software based virtualization since the gates that are not used for virtualization extensions can be used to implement the application specific logic (e.g. digital signal processing, software-defined radio, cryptography).

Our Contributions. We present the first trustworthy virtualization mechanism based on "direct paging", an approach inspired by the paravirtualization mechanism of Xen [4]. The design of the platform is sufficiently slim to enable its formal verification without penalizing the system performance. The verification is done down to a detailed model of the architecture, including a detailed model of the ARMv7 MMU. This enable our threat model to consist of an arbitrary guest that can execute any ARMv7 instruction in user mode. We prove complete mediation of the MMU configurations, memory isolation of the hosted components, and information flow correctness. We demonstrate the platform via a prototype hypervisor that is capable of hosting a Linux system while provably isolating it from other services.

3   The Memory Virtualization API

The memory virtualization API supports two types of clients: (i) an untrusted commodity OS guest (Linux) running non-critical software (e.g. GUI, browser, server, games), and (ii) a set of trusted services such as controllers that drive physical actuators, run-time monitors, sensor drivers, or cryptographic services.

To support this use case the memory virtualization subsystem needs to provide two main functionalities:

- Isolation of memory resources used by the trusted components.
- Virtualization of the memory subsystem to enable the untrusted OS to dynamically manage its own memory hierarchy, and to enforce access restrictions.

switch	Select the active L1
L1create	Create page table of type L1
L2create	Create page table of type L2
L1free	Change the type of an L1 block to *data*
L2free	Change the type of an L2 block to *data*
L1unmap	Clear an entry of an L1 page table
L2unmap	Clear an entry of an L2 page table
L1map	Set an entry of an L1 page table
L2map	Set an entry of an L2 page table

Fig. 1. The virtualization API

The physical memory region allocated to each type of client is statically defined. Inside its own region the guest OS is free to manage its own memory, and the virtualization API is designed to provide the same guarantees to the guest OS as when it is running in native mode.

3.1 Memory Management

The ARMv7 MMU uses a two level translation scheme. The first level (L1) is a 4096 entry table that divides up to $4GB$ of memory into $1MB$ sections. These sections can either point to an equally large region of physical memory or to a level 2 (L2) page table with 256 entries that maps the $1MB$ section into $4KB$ physical pages.

We use direct paging [4] to virtualize the memory subsystem. Direct paging allows the guest to allocate the page tables inside its own memory and to directly manipulate them while the tables are not in active use by the MMU. Once the page tables are activated, the hypervisor must guarantee that further updates are possible only via the virtualization API to modify, allocate and free the page tables.

Physical memory is fragmented into blocks of 4 KB. Since L1 and L2 page tables have size 16 KB and 1 KB respectively, an L1 page table is stored in four contiguous physical blocks and a physical block can contain four L2 page tables. We assign a type to each physical block, that can be:

- *data*: the block can be written by the guest.
- *L1*: contains part of an L1 and is not writable in user mode.
- *L2*: contains four L2 and is not writable in user mode.

The virtualization API shown in Fig. 1 is very similar to the MMU interface of the Secure Virtual Architecture [9] and consists of 9 hypercalls that selects, creates, frees, maps, or unmaps memory blocks or page tables.

3.2 Enforcing the Page Type Constraints

Each API call needs to validate the page type, guaranteeing that page tables are write-protected. This is illustrated in Fig. 2. The table in the center represents the physical memory and stores the virtualization data structures for each physical

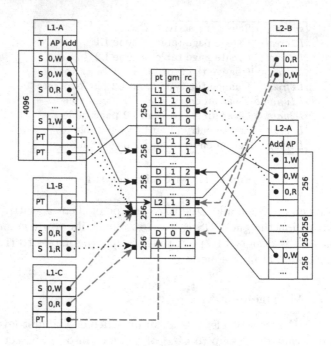

Fig. 2. Direct-paging mechanism

block; the page type (pt), a flag informing if the block is allocated to the guest partition (gm), and a reference counter (rc).

The four top most blocks contain an L1 page table, whose 4096 entries are depicted by the table *L1-A*. The top entry of the page table is a section descriptor $(T = S)$ that grants write permission to the guest $(AP = (0, w))$. This entry points (Add) to the second physical section, which consists of 256 physical blocks. Three other section descriptors of the L1 are depicted in the table: the first one grants write accesses to the guest, the second one gives read-only permission to the guest $(0, r)$, the third descriptor prevents any guest access and enables write permission for the privileged mode $(1, w)$. The last two entries of the L1 are PT-descriptors. These two entries point to two different L2 page tables that are stored in the same physical block.

The API calls manipulating an L1 enforce the following policy; Any section descriptor that allows the guest to access the memory must point to a section for which every physical block resides in the guest memory space. Moreover, if a descriptor enables guest to write then each block must be typed *data*. Finally, all PT-descriptors must point to physical blocks of type *L2*.

The Figure depicts two additional L1 page tables; *L1-B* and *L1-C*. The type of a physical block containing *L1-B* can be transformed to *L1* by invoking *L1create*. On the other hand, a block containing *L1-C* is rejected by *L1create* since the block contains three entries that violate the policy. In fact,

(i) the first descriptor grants guest write permission over a section which has at least one non data block, in this case *L2*,

(ii) the second section descriptor allows the guest to access a section of the physical memory in which there exists a block that is outside the guest memory, and

(iii) the third entry is a PT-descriptor, but points to a physical block that is not typed *L2*.

The table *L2-A* depicts the content of a physical block typed *L2* and that contains four L2 page tables, each consisting of 256 entries. Each hypercall that manipulates an L2 enforces the following policy: if any entry of the four L2 page tables grants access permission to the guest then the pointed block must be in the guest memory. If the entry also enables guest write access then the pointed block must be typed *data*. For example a block containing *L2-B* is rejected by *L2create*, since the block contains at least two entries that violate the policy.

A naive run-time check of the page-type policy is not efficient, since it requires to re-validate the L1 page table whenever the *switch* hypercall is invoked. To efficiently enforce that only blocks typed *data* can be written by the guest the hypervisor maintains a reference counter, which tracks for each block the sum of (i) the number of descriptors providing writable access in user mode to the block, and (ii) the number of PT-descriptors that point to the block.

In Fig. 2 we use solid arrows to represent the references that are counted and dashed arrows to represent the other references. The intuition is that a hypercall can change the type of a physical block (e.g. allocate or free a page table) only if the corresponding reference counter is zero.

3.3   Hypervisor Guest Page Table Access

The hypervisor APIs must be able to read and write guest page tables in order to check the soundness of the requests and to apply the corresponding changes. The naive solution requires handlers to change the current page table, enabling a master page table whenever the guest memory must be accessed and then re-enabling the original page table before the guest is restored. This solution is expensive as it requires to flush TLB and caches. A solution tailored for Unixes can rely on the injective mapping built by the guest, which can be used to access the guest kernel memory. However, in our setting the hosted guest is not trusted, thus this solution can not guarantee that the injective mapping is obeyed by the guest. Instead, our design reserves a subset of the virtual address space for hypervisor use. The hypervisor master page table is built so that this address space is always mapped according to an injective translation (1-to-1) allowing to easily compute the virtual address for each physical address in the guest memory, similar to the direct memory maps supported by FreeBSD and Linux.

3.4   Memory Model and Cache Effects

The presence of data caches and memory aliasing raise further issues. In ARMv7 CPUs such as the Cortex-A8 the MMU consults the data caches on TLB misses.

When a virtual mapping is changed, the hypervisor must in general invalidate the corresponding TLB entries to guarantee that the MMU uses the updated page descriptors. However, the ARM architecture reference manual [1] predicates only weak cache coherence properties, even for single-core processors. For example, in Cortex-A8 sequential consistency is not guaranteed if the same physical address is accessed with mappings having different cacheability attributes. Thus, without knowledge of the specific processor platform, care must be taken. To ensure that the model remains valid we are forced to apply a conservative cache eviction strategy. For this reason, the hypervisor must flush the cache before accessing data stored by the guest.

More aggressive approaches (e.g. evicting only the necessary physical addresses, or avoiding flushing altogether) may be adopted for some processor implementations, but require a more fine-grained modeling including caches for their justification.

4 Verification Approach

The TLS models user mode execution of an arbitrary guest system on top of an ARMv7 CPU with MMU support, alternating with abstract handler events. These events model invocations of the hypervisor handlers as atomic transformations H_a operating on an abstract machine state. Abstract states are concrete ARMv7 states extended by auxiliary (model) data such as page types or reference counters that reflect the internal hypervisor state. Handler events represent the execution of ARMv7 instructions at privileged level, in response to exceptions or interrupts. Modeling handler effects as atomic state transformations is possible, since the hypervisor is non-preemptive, i.e. nested exceptions/interrupts are ruled out by the implementation.

4.1 TLS Consistency Properties

Since guest systems can directly manipulate inactive page tables, the TLS needs to explicitly store page tables in memory. We must show first that this does not introduce unwanted interference between guest and hypervisor state:

1. The hypervisor must act as a security monitor for the MMU settings. If *complete mediation* of the MMU settings is violated, then an attacker can bypass the access policies and compromise the security of the entire system.
2. Executions of an arbitrary guest can not affect the "trusted world", i.e. the parts of the state the guest is not supposed to be able to write, such as non-guest memory, inaccessible processor registers and status flags, and the abstract state. We view this as an integrity property, similar to the non-exfiltration property of [13].
3. Dually, absence of information flow from the "trusted world" to the guest, confidentiality, similar to non-infiltration, must be guaranteed.

These properties, as in [13], are qualitatively different: The integrity property is first-order, and concerns the inability of the guest to directly write some other state variables. Since it is under guest control when and how to invoke the virtualization API, there are plenty of indirect communication channels connecting guests to the hypervisor. For instance, a guest decision to allocate or deallocate an L1 block affects large parts of the hypervisor state, without ever directly writing to any internal hypervisor state variable. Enforcing this is in a sense the very purpose of the hypervisor. On the other hand, the hypervisor should be unable to affect guest state even indirectly: The only desired effects of hypervisor actions should be to allocate/deallocate, map, remap, and unmap virtual memory resources, leaving any observation a guest may make unaffected. This is essentially a second-order information flow property, needed to break guest-to-guest (or guest-to-service) information channels in much the same way as intransitive noninterference is used in [19] to break guest-to-guest channels passing through the scheduler in seL4.

4.2 Refinement

Accordingly, the first verification task is to establish the model consistency properties 1, 2 and 3 above. Extending this to an actual implementation, however, requires more work, because of the TLS abstract state, and since the TLS handlers access memory using the physical addresses. The virtualization code need to execute under the same address translation as the guest, in order to minimize the number of context switches. To show implementation soundness we exhibit a refinement property relating TLS states to implementation states. We demonstrate that the refinement relation is preserved by all atomic hypervisor operations; reads and updates of the page tables, reads and updates of the hypervisor data structures. Moreover, we prove that the refinement relation directly transfers both the consistency properties and the information flow properties of the TLS to the implementation level, completing the overall memory isolation proof.

4.3 Processor Model

The verification uses the HOL4 model of ARMv7-A developed at Cambridge [11]. This model has been extensively tested and is phrased in a manner that retains a high resemblance to the pseudocode used by ARM in the architecture reference manual [1]. The Cambridge model has been extended by ourselves to include MMU functionality. The resulting model gives a highly detailed account of the ISA level instruction semantics at the different privilege levels, including relevant MMU coprocessor effects. It must be noted that the Cambridge ARM model assumes linearizable memory, and so can be used out of the box only for processor and hypervisor implementations that satisfy this property, for instance through adequate cache flushing as discussed in Sect. 3.

We outline the HOL4 ARMv7 model in sufficient detail to make the formal results presented later understandable. An ARMv7 machine state is a record $\sigma = \langle regs, psrs, coregs, mem \rangle \in \Sigma$, where $regs$, $psrs$, mem and $coregs$, respectively, represent the registers, program status registers, memory, and coprocessors. The function $mode(\sigma)$ returns the current privilege execution mode in the state σ, which can be either $PL0$ (non-privileged or user mode, used by the guest) or $PL1$ (privileged mode, used by the hypervisor). The memory is the function $mem \in 2^{32} \rightarrow 2^8$. The coprocessor registers $coregs$ control the MMU.

System behavior is modeled by the state transition relation $\rightarrow_{l\in\{PL0,PL1\}} \subseteq \Sigma \times \Sigma$, where a transition is performed by the execution of an ARM instruction. Non-privileged transitions $(\sigma \rightarrow_{PL0} \sigma')$ start from and end in states that are

in non-privileged execution mode (i.e. $mode(\sigma) = mode(\sigma') = PL0$). All the other transitions $(\sigma \rightarrow_{PL1} \sigma')$ involve at least one state in privileged level. The raising of an exception is modeled by a transition that enables the level $PL1$. An exception can be raised because: (i) a software interrupt (SWI) is executed, (ii) the current instruction is undefined, or (iii) a memory access is attempted that is disallowed by the MMU. Whenever an exception occurs, the CPU disables the interrupts and jumps to a predefined address in the vector table to transfer the control to the corresponding exception handler.

MMU behavior is modeled by the function $mmu(\sigma, PL, va, req)$, which takes a state σ, a privilege level, a virtual address va and an access request $req \in \{rd, wt, ex\}$ (representing read, write and execute accesses) and yields $pa \in 2^{32} \cup \{\bot\}$, where pa is the translated physical address or an access denied. The state transition relation queries the MMU whenever a virtual address is accessed, and raises an exception if the requested access mode is not allowed.

5 Formalizing the Proof Goals

A TLS state is a tuple $\langle \sigma, h \rangle$, consisting of an ARMv7 state σ and an abstract hypervisor state h of the form $\langle pgtype, pgrefs \rangle$ where $pgtype$ indicates memory block types and $pgrefs$ maintains reference counters. Specifically, $pgtype \in 2^{20} \rightarrow \{D, L1, L2\}$ tracks the type of each 4kb physical block; a block can either be (D) memory writable from the guest or data page, (L1) contain a L1 page table or (L2) contain a L2 page table. The map $pgrefs \in 2^{20} \rightarrow 2^{30}$ tracks the references to each physical block, as described in Sect. 3.

The TLS interleaves standard non-privileged transitions with abstract handler invocations. Formally, the TLS transition relation $\langle \sigma, h \rangle \rightarrow_{i\in\{0,1\}} \langle \sigma', h' \rangle$ is defined as follows:

- If $\sigma \rightarrow_{PL0} \sigma'$ then $\langle \sigma, h \rangle \rightarrow_0 \langle \sigma', h \rangle$; instructions executed in non-privileged mode that do not raise exceptions behave equivalently to the standard ARMv7 semantics and do not affect the abstract hypervisor state.
- If $\sigma \rightarrow_{PL1} \sigma'$ and $mode(\sigma) = PL0$ then $\langle \sigma, h \rangle \rightarrow_1 H_a(\langle \sigma', h \rangle)$; whenever an exception is raised, the hypervisor is executed, modeled by the abstract handler H_a.

In our setup the trusted services and the untrusted guest are both executed in non-priviledged mode. To distinguish between these two partitions, we use

ARM domains. In the ARM architecture domains are the primarily access control mechanism used by the MMU. This mechanism is orthogonal to the CPU execution modes. The architecture provides sixteen domains, each of them can be activated independently. We reserve the domains 2-15 for the secure services. In the following we use the predicate $S(\sigma)$ to identify if the active partition is the one hosting the secure services: the predicate holds if at least one of the reserved domain is enabled.

5.1   TLS Consistency

We introduce a system invariant $I(\langle \sigma, h \rangle)$ used to constrain the set of consistent initial states of the TLS. The invariant is needed, for instance, to ensure that guests have write access to page tables only when they are inactive. We use Q_I to represent the set of all possible TLS states that satisfy the invariant. We thus need to show:

Theorem 1. *Let* $\langle \sigma, h \rangle \in Q_I$ *and* $i \in \{0, 1\}$. *If* $\langle \sigma, h \rangle \rightarrow_i \langle \sigma', h' \rangle$ *then* $I(\langle \sigma', h' \rangle)$.

We say that two states are *MMU-equivalent* if for any virtual address va the MMU yields the same translation and the same access permissions. Formally, $\sigma \equiv_{mmu} \sigma'$ if and only if

$$mmu(\sigma, PL, va, req) = mmu(\sigma', PL, va, req)$$

for any va, PL, req. Complete mediation (MMU-integrity) is demonstrated by showing that neither the guest nor the secure services are able to directly change the content of the page tables and affect the address translation mechanism.

Theorem 2. *Let* $\langle \sigma, h \rangle \in Q_I$. *If* $\langle \sigma, h \rangle \rightarrow_0 \langle \sigma', h' \rangle$ *then* $\sigma \equiv_{mmu} \sigma'$.

We use the approach of [13] to analyze the hypervisor data separation properties. The observations of the guest in a state $\langle \sigma, h \rangle$ is represented by the structure $O_g(\langle \sigma, h \rangle) = \langle uregs, cpsr, mem_g, coregs \rangle$ of user registers $uregs$, control register $cpsr$, guest memory mem_g and coprocessor registers $coregs$. The register $cpsr$ and the coprocessor registers are visible to the guest since they directly affect guest behavior, and do not contain any information the guest should not be allowed to see. Evidently, however, all writes to the coprocessor registers must be mediated by the hypervisor.

The remaining part of the state (i.e. the content of the memory locations that are not part of the guest memory, special registers) and, again, the coprocessor registers constitute the secure observations $O_s(\langle \sigma, h \rangle)$ of the state, which guest transitions are not supposed to affect.

The following theorem demonstrates that the context switch between the untrusted guest and the trusted services is not possible without the mediation of the hypervisor. The proof is straightforward, since S only depends on coprocessor registers that are not modifiable in nonprivileged mode.

Theorem 3. *Let* $\langle \sigma, h \rangle \in Q_I$. *If* $\langle \sigma, h \rangle \rightarrow_0 \langle \sigma', h' \rangle$ *then* $S(\sigma) = S(\sigma')$.

The *non-exfiltration* property guarantees that a transition executed by the guest does not modify the secure resources:

Theorem 4. *Let* $\langle \sigma, h \rangle \in \mathcal{Q}_I$. *If* $\langle \sigma, h \rangle \rightarrow_0 \langle \sigma', h' \rangle$ *and* $\neg S(\sigma)$ *then* $O_s(\langle \sigma, h \rangle) = O_s(\langle \sigma', h' \rangle)$.

The *non-infiltration* property is a non-interference property guaranteeing that guest instructions and hypercalls executed on behalf of the guest do not depend on any information stored in resources not accessible by the guest.

Theorem 5. *Let* $\langle \sigma_1, h_1 \rangle, \langle \sigma_2, h_2 \rangle \in \mathcal{Q}_I$, $i \in \{0, 1\}$, *and assume that* $O_g(\langle \sigma_1, h_1 \rangle) = O_g(\langle \sigma_2, h_2 \rangle)$, $\neg S(\sigma_1)$ *and* $\neg S(\sigma_2)$. *If* $\langle \sigma_1, h_1 \rangle \rightarrow_i \langle \sigma_1', h_1' \rangle$ *and* $\langle \sigma_2, h_2 \rangle \rightarrow_i \langle \sigma_2', h_2' \rangle$ *then* $O_g(\langle \sigma_1', h_1' \rangle) = O_g(\langle \sigma_2', h_2' \rangle)$.

5.2   The Implementation Model

A critical problem of verifying low level platforms is that intermediate states of the MMU configuration can break the semantics of the high level language (e.g. C). This is the reason we introduced the implementation model, that is sufficiently detailed to expose misbehavior of the hypervisor accesses to the observable part of the memory (i.e. page tables, guest memory and internal data structure). The implementation interleaves standard non-privileged transitions and hypervisor functionalities. In contrast to the TLS, these functionalities now store their internal data in system memory, accessed by means of virtual addresses. In practice, in the implementation model the hypervisor functionalities are expressed as executable specifications that are, however, very to close the actions executed by an actual machine at instruction semantics level. We demonstrate these differences by comparing two fragments of the TLS and the implementation specifications.

The TLS models the update of a guest page table descriptor as $\sigma'.mem = write_{32}(\sigma.mem, pa, desc)$, where pa is the physical address of the entry, $desc$ is a word representing the new descriptor and $write_{32}$ is a function that yields a new memory having four consecutive bytes updated. At the implementation level the same operation is represented as

```
if ¬ mmu(σ, PL1, Gpa2va(pa)).wt
  then ⊥
  else write₃₂(σ.mem,mmu(σ,PL1,Gpa2va(pa)).pa,desc)
```

where `Gpa2va` is the function used by the hypervisor to compute the virtual address of a physical address that resides in guest memory. This function is statically defined and is the inverse of the injective translation established by the hypervisor master page table. The implementation can fail to match the TLS for two reasons: (i) the current page table can prevent the hypervisor from accessing the computed virtual address, and then the implementation terminates in a failing state (denoted by $\perp$), (ii) the current address translation does not respect the expected injective mapping, thus $mmu(\sigma, PL1, Gpa2va(pa)).pa \neq pa$ and the implementation writes in an address that differs from the one updated by the TLS.

The next example shows the difference between access of the reference counter in the TLS and at implementation level. The TLS models this operation as $h.refs(b)$, where b is the physical block. The implementation models the same operation using memory offsets as follows:

```
if ¬ mmu(σ, PL1, tbl_va + 4*b).rd )
  then ⊥
  else read_32(σ.mem,mmu(σ, PL1, tbl_va + 4*b).pa) & 0xCFFFFFFF
```

This representation is directly reflected in the hypervisor code. For each block, the page type (two bits) and the reference counter (30 bits) are placed contiguously in a word. These words form an array, whose initial virtual address is tbl_{va}.

The concrete handlers are represented by a HOL4 function H_r from concrete ARMv7 states to concrete ARMv7 states. The function is the executable specification of the various exception handlers including the MMU functionalities.

Then, implementation behavior is determined by the state transition relation $\rightarrow_{i \in \{0,1\}} \subseteq \Sigma \times (\Sigma \cup \{\perp\})$ as follows:

– If $\sigma \rightarrow_{PL0} \sigma'$ then $\sigma \rightarrow_0 \sigma'$; instructions executed in non-privileged mode that do not raise exceptions behave according to the standard ARMv7 semantics.
– If $\sigma \rightarrow_{PL1} \sigma'$ and $mode(\sigma) = PL0$ then $\sigma \rightarrow_1 H_r(\sigma')$; whenever an exception is raised, the hypervisor is executed and its behavior is modeled by the function H_r.

5.3   The Refinement

To show implementation soundness we exhibit a refinement property relating abstract states $\langle \sigma_1, h \rangle$ to concrete states σ_2. The refinement relation $\mathcal{R}$ requires that: (i) the registers and coprocessors contain the same value in both states, (ii) the guest memory contains the same values in both states, (iii) part of the memory of the implementation state contains a mapping of the hypervisor data structures of the TLS state and (iv) the reserved virtual addresses are always mapped equivalently to the master page table. Observations of the guest O_g are defined on concrete states using the hypervisor data structure mapping in analogy with the corresponding observations on abstract states defined above.

Theorem 6. *Let $\langle \sigma_1, h \rangle \in Q_I$ and $\sigma_2 \in \Sigma$ such that $\langle \sigma_1, h \rangle \mathcal{R} \sigma_2$. Let $i \in \{0, 1\}$. Then $\sigma_2 \rightarrow_i \sigma_2'$ if and only if $\langle \sigma_1, h \rangle \rightarrow_i \langle \sigma_1', h' \rangle$ and $\langle \sigma_1', h' \rangle \mathcal{R} \sigma_2'$.*

Finally we show that the security property of the TLS and the refinement relation directly transfer the mmu-integrity/non-exfiltration/non-infiltration to the implementation. We use Σ_I to represent the space of consistent concrete states: States σ_2 such that if $\langle \sigma_1, h \rangle \mathcal{R} \sigma_2$ then $I(\langle \sigma_1, h \rangle)$.

Corollary 1. *Let $\sigma_1, \sigma_2 \in \Sigma_I$, $i \in \{0, 1\}$ $O_g(\sigma_1) = O_g(\sigma_2)$:*

– *if $\sigma_1 \rightarrow_0 \sigma_1'$ then $\sigma_1 \equiv_{mmu} \sigma_1'$*
– *if $\sigma_1 \rightarrow_0 \sigma_1'$ and $\neg S(\sigma_1)$ then $O_s(\sigma_1) = O_s(\sigma_1')$*
– *if $\sigma_1 \rightarrow_i \sigma_1'$, $\sigma_2 \rightarrow_i \sigma_2'$, and $\neg S(\sigma_1)$ and $\neg S(\sigma_2)$ then $O_g(\sigma_1') = O_g(\sigma_2')$*

6 Linux Support

To evaluate the real-world feasibility of our approach we examine a virtualized Linux guest. The Linux kernel v2.6.34 has been modified to run on top of the hypervisor. This task required modification of architecture-dependent parts of the Linux kernel like (i) execution modes, (ii) low-level exception routines and (iii) page table management. High-level OS functions such as process, resource and memory manager, file system and networking did not require any modifications.

CPU Privilege Modes. The target CPU includes only two execution modes: privileged and unprivileged (user). Like for other approaches based on paravirtualization, since the hypervisor executes as privileged, then the Linux kernel has been modified to execute as unprivileged. To separate kernel and user applications, the hypervisor manages two separate unprivileged execution contexts: virtual user and virtual kernel modes. In x86 these virtual modes can be implemented by segmentation limits. This approach is not possible for CPUs that do not provide this feature (e.g. x86 64-bits and ARM). Instead, for kernel-user space isolation we use ARM domains, that implement an access control regime orthogonal to the CPU execution modes. Notice that the main security goal here is not to guarantee this OS-internal isolation, but to maintain the separation between the virtualized components.

CPU Exceptions. CPU exceptions such as aborts and interrupts change the processor mode to privileged. These exceptions must therefore be handled in the hypervisor, which after validation can forward them to the unprivileged exception handlers of the Linux kernel. The hypervisor supplies the kernel exception handlers with some privileged data needed to correctly service an on-going exception (i.e. for pre-fetch abort, the privileged fault address and fault status registers are forwarded to the guest). The exception handlers in the Linux kernel have thus been slightly modified to support this.

Memory Management. Within the Linux kernel, virtual memory is handled in two layers. The first is platform independent and provides a number of high-level functions to the rest of the kernel. The second layer provides a number of platform dependent functions to the first layer. To allow virtualization, we modified the second layer to perform a hypercall instead of performing privileged access to the hardware.

7 Benchmark and Evaluation

Runtime Overhead. To analyze runtime overhead we use LMBench [18] (of which the fork benchmarks stress the MMU virtualization) running on Linux 2.6.34[1] with and without virtualization. The outcome, measured on an

---

[1] The virtualization API is independent of the hosted OS, thus porting and running a different Linux kernel or BSD does not affect the security properties described in this paper.

ARMv7-A Cortex-A8 powered embedded system (BeagleBoard-xM), is presented in Table 1. Additionaly, we use the creation (tar) and compression (gzip) of archives as macrobenchmarks. The significant virtualization overhead for the fork benchmarks is due to a large number of simple operations (in this case, write access to a page-table) being replaced with a large number of expensive hypercalls. It may be possible to reduce this overhead with minimal optimization (e.g. batching).

In Table 1 we also report the overheads measured in [15] of several existing hypervisors for ARM. We point out that these performance numbers have been obtained from different sources, testing different ARM cores, boards and hosted Linux kernels. Moreover, the numbers presented here use a completely unoptimized version of the hypervisor that we believe can be significantly improved.

Table 1. Benchmarks

Benchmark	Our Hypervisor	L4Linux	Xen	OKL4	Processes	DP 256MB	DP 1GB	SPT
null syscall	342%	2955%	150%	60%	32	56	224	608
read	155%	836%	90%	15%	64	64	256	1216
write	181%	874%	84%	24%	128	72	288	2432
stat	93%	553%		60%	Memory usage (KB) of			
open/close	146%	433%		-10%	direct paging (mem_{size}) and			
select (10)	41%	363%		14%	shadow page tables			
pipe	115%	449%	73%	31%				
fork+exit	164%	949%	246%	8%				
fork+execve	166%	591%	238%	5%				
fork+bin/sh-c	60%	415%						
targz 500KB	1%							
targz 1MB	-4%							
targz 2MB	-1%							

Latency benchmarks

Footprint. The main difference between our proposal and the existing verified hypervisors is the MMU virtualization mechanism. The direct paging approach requires a table which contains at most $mem_{size}/block_{size}$ entries, where mem_{size} is the total available physical memory and $block_{size}$ is the minimum page size (here, $4KB$). Each entry in this table uses $2 + \log_2 max_{ref}$ bits, with the first two bits used to record entry type and max_{ref} being the maximum number of references pointing to the same page. Assuming this number is bound by the number of processes, Table 1 indicates the memory overhead introduced by direct paging. It should be noted that on ARMv7, most operating systems including Linux dedicate one L1 page to each process and at least three L2 pages to map the stack, the executable code and the heap. Then the OS itself has a minimum footprint of $16KB + 3 * 1KB$ per process. This footprint is doubled if the underlying hypervisor uses shadow page tables.

Implementation and Verification Effort. The hypervisor is implemented in C (and some assembly) and consists of 4529 lines of code (LOC). Excluding platform dependent parts, the hypervisor core is no larger than 2066 LOC. The memory virtualization subsystem consists of 1200 LOC. To paravirtualize Linux we changed 1025 LOC of its kernel, 950 in the ARM specific architecture folder and 75 in init/main.c. The paravirtuation is binary compatible with existing userland applications. For comparison, the only other hypervisor that implements direct paging is the Xen hypervisor, which consists of 100KLOC and its design is not suitable for verification. Instead, the small code base of our hypervisor makes it easier to experiment with different virtualization paradigms and enables formal verification of its correctness. The formal specification consists of 1500 LOC of HOL4 and intentionally avoids any high level construct, in order to make the model as similar as possible to the implementation, at the price of increasing the verification cost. The proof consists of 18700 LOC of HOL4.

The verification highlighted a number of bugs in the initial design of the APIs: (i) arithmetic overflow when updating the reference counter, caused by not preventing the guest to create an unbounded number of references to a physical block, (ii) bit field and offset mismatch, (iii) missing check that a newly allocated page table prevents the guest to overwrite the page table itself, (iv) usage of signed shift operator where the unsigned one was necessary and (v) approval of guest requests that cause unpredictable MMU behavior. The verification of the implementation model identified three additional bugs exploitable by the guest by requesting the validation of page tables outside the guest memory.

The project was conducted in three steps. The design, modeling and verification of the APIs for memory virtualization required nine person months. Here, the most expensive tasks have been the verification of Theorems 1 [20] and 6. The C implementation of the APIs and the Linux port has been accomplished in three months. While the implementation team was completing the Linux port the verification team started the verification of the refinement, which has taken three months so far. This work is continuing, in order to complete the verification from the HOL4 implementation level down to assembly.

8   Concluding Remarks

We presented the first hypervisor (i) for a COTS application processor architecture (ARMv7), (ii) whose spatial separation properties have been formally verified, (iii) capable of hosting a Linux system. As example application, in [6] we used the virtualization mechanism to support a tamper-proof run-time monitor that prevents code injection in an untrusted Linux guest.

The only verified hypervisor in the literature capable of hosting a commodity OS is Microsoft's Hyper-V [17]. However, little detailed information about the Hyper-V internal structure or the Hyper-V verification exercise is publicly available. As part of the Hyper-V verification project, a hypervisor for a simplified, MIPS-like architecture including memory virtualization is described in [3,21]. However, the relation of the simplified hypervisor to Hyper-V itself is not clear. As other, unverified, hypervisors for ARM such as the OKL4 microvisor [12] the Hyper-V precursor of Paul et al. uses shadow page tables for MMU virtualization. Our result demonstrates that secure isolation of a commodity OS can be achieved with highly promising performance without requiring either specialized hardware support or shadow data structures. This applies even before assembly level and cache related optimizations are performed. This represents the first trustworthy virtualization mechanism based on "direct paging", an approach inspired by the paravirtualization mechanism of Xen.

The implementation model takes into account low-level details (i.e. virtual address translation, bit field manipulation, finite integer arithmetic, accesses to the hypervisor data not mediated by high level data structures) and represent an executable specification. The model is sufficiently detailed to spot possible errors that arise when the hypervisor uses virtual addresses and exactly reflects the control flow of the C-implementation. Part of our ongoing research efforts is to adapt existing techniques [23] to verify the hypervisor binary code.

Acknowledgement. Work supported by framework grant "IT 2010" from the Swedish Foundation for Strategic Research.

References

1. ARMv7-AR Architecture Reference Manual: Technical documentation ARM DDI 0406B. ARM Limited (2008)
2. Alkassar, E., Cohen, E., Kovalev, M., Paul, W.J.: Verification of tlb virtualization implemented in c. In: Joshi, R., Müller, P., Podelski, A. (eds.) VSTTE 2012. LNCS, vol. 7152, pp. 209–224. Springer, Heidelberg (2012)
3. Alkassar, E., Hillebrand, M.A., Paul, W., Petrova, E.: Automated verification of a small hypervisor. In: Leavens, G.T., O'Hearn, P., Rajamani, S.K. (eds.) VSTTE 2010. LNCS, vol. 6217, pp. 40–54. Springer, Heidelberg (2010)
4. Barham, P., Dragovic, B., Fraser, K., Hand, S., Harris, T., Ho, A., Neugebauer, R., Pratt, I., Warfield, A.: Xen and the art of virtualization. ACM SIGOPS Operating Syst. Rev. **37**(5), 164–177 (2003)
5. Chen, X., Garfinkel, T., Lewis, E.C., Subrahmanyam, P., Waldspurger, C.A., Boneh, D., Dwoskin, J., Ports, D.R.: Overshadow: a virtualization-based approach to retrofitting protection in commodity operating systems. In: ACM SIGOPS Operating Systems Review, vol. 42, pp. 2–13. ACM (2008)
6. Chfouka, H., Nemati, H., Guanciale, R., Dam, M., Ekdahl, P.: Trustworthy prevention of code injection in linux on embedded devices. In: ESORICS (2015). Appear on 2015
7. Criswell, J., Dautenhahn, N., Kcofi, V.A.: Complete control-flow integrity for commodity operating system kernels. In: 2014 IEEE Symposium on Security and Privacy (SP), pp. 292–307. IEEE (2014)
8. Criswell, J., Dautenhahn, N., Adve, V.: Virtual ghost: protecting applications from hostile operating systems. In: SIGARCH Computer Architecture News, pp. 81–96. ACM (2014)
9. Criswell, J., Lenharth, A., Dhurjati, D., Adve, V.: Secure virtual architecture: a safe execution environment for commodity operating systems. In: ACM SIGOPS Operating Systems Review, vol. 41, pp. 351–366. ACM (2007)
10. Dam, M., Guanciale, R., Khakpour, N., Nemati, H., Schwarz, O.: Formal verification of information flow security for a simple arm-based separation kernel. In: Proceedings of the 2013 ACM SIGSAC Conference on Computer & Communications Security, pp. 223–234. ACM (2013)
11. Fox, A., Myreen, M.O.: A trustworthy monadic formalization of the armv7 instruction set architecture. In: Kaufmann, M., Paulson, L.C. (eds.) ITP 2010. LNCS, vol. 6172, pp. 243–258. Springer, Heidelberg (2010)

12. Heiser, G., Leslie, B.: The okl4 microvisor: convergence point of microkernels and hypervisors. In: Proceedings of the First ACM Asia-Pacific Workshop on Workshop on systems, pp. 19–24. ACM (2010)
13. Heitmeyer, C., Archer, M., Leonard, E., McLean, J.: Applying formal methods to a certifiably secure software system. IEEE Trans. Softw. Eng. **34**(1), 82–98 (2008)
14. Hofmann, O.S., Kim, S., Dunn, A.M., Lee, M.Z., Witchel, E.: Inktag: secure applications on an untrusted operating system. ACM SIGPLAN Not. **48**(4), 265–278 (2013)
15. Iqbal, A., Sadeque, N., Mutia, R.I.: An overview of microkernel, hypervisor and microvisor virtualization approaches for embedded systems. Report, Department of Electrical and Information Technology, **2110**. Lund University, Sweden (2009)
16. Klein, G., Elphinstone, K., Heiser, G., Andronick, J., Cock, D., Derrin, P., Elkaduwe, D., Engelhardt, K., Kolanski, R., Norrish, M., Sewell, T., Tuch, H., Winwood, S.: seL4: formal verification of an OS kernel. In: Proceedings SOSP 2009, pp. 207–220. ACM (2009)
17. Leinenbach, D., Santen, T.: Verifying the microsoft hyper-v hypervisor with vcc. In: Cavalcanti, A., Dams, D.R. (eds.) FM 2009. LNCS, vol. 5850, pp. 806–809. Springer, Heidelberg (2009)
18. McVoy, L., Staelin, C.: Lmbench: portable tools for performance analysis. In: Proceedings of the 1996 Annual Conference on USENIX Annual Technical Conference, ATEC 1996, Berkeley, CA, USA, pp. 23–23. USENIX Association (1996)
19. Murray, T., Matichuk, D., Brassil, M., Gammie, P., Bourke, T., Seefried, S., Lewis, C., Gao, X., Klein, G.: sel4: from general purpose to a proof of information flow enforcement. In: 2013 IEEE Symposium on Security and Privacy (SP), pp. 415–429. IEEE (2013)
20. Nemati, H., Guanciale, R., Dam, M.: Trustworthy virtualization of the armv7 memory subsystem. In: Italiano, G.F., Margaria-Steffen, T., Pokorný, J., Quisquater, J.-J., Wattenhofer, R. (eds.) SOFSEM 2015-Testing. LNCS, vol. 8939, pp. 578–589. Springer, Heidelberg (2015)
21. Paul, W., Schmaltz, S., Shadrin, A.: Completing the automated verification of a small hypervisor – assembler code verification. In: Eleftherakis, G., Hinchey, M., Holcombe, M. (eds.) SEFM 2012. LNCS, vol. 7504, pp. 188–202. Springer, Heidelberg (2012)
22. Richards, R.J.: Modeling and security analysis of a commercial real-time operating system kernel. In: Hardin, D.S. (ed.) Design and Verification of Microprocessor Systems for High-Assurance Applications, pp. 301–322. Springer, New York (2010)
23. Sewell, T.A.L., Myreen, M.O., Klein, G.: Translation validation for a verified os kernel. In: Proceedings of the 34th ACM SIGPLAN Conference on Programming Language Design and Implementation, pp. 471–482. ACM (2013)
24. Varanasi, P., Heiser, G.: Hardware-supported virtualization on arm. In: Proceedings of the Second Asia-Pacific Workshop on Systems, APSys 2011, pp. 11:1–11:5, New York, NY, USA, ACM (2011)

LookAhead: Augmenting Crowdsourced Website Reputation Systems with Predictive Modeling

Sourav Bhattacharya[1]($^\boxtimes$), Otto Huhta[2], and N. Asokan[2,3]

[1] Bell Laboratories, Dublin, Ireland
sourav.bhattacharya@bell-labs.com
[2] Aalto University, Espoo, Finland
otto.huhta@aalto.fi
[3] University of Helsinki, Helsinki, Finland
asokan@acm.org

Abstract. Unsafe websites consist of malicious as well as inappropriate sites, such as those hosting questionable or offensive content. Website reputation systems are intended to help ordinary users steer away from these unsafe sites. However, the process of assigning safety ratings for websites typically involves humans. Consequently it is time consuming, costly and not scalable. This has resulted in two major problems: (i) a significant proportion of the web space remains unrated and (ii) there is an unacceptable time lag before new websites are rated. In this paper, we show that by leveraging structural and content-based properties of websites, we can reliably and efficiently predict their safety ratings, thereby mitigating both problems. We demonstrate the effectiveness of our approach using four datasets of up to 90,000 websites. We use ratings from Web of Trust (WOT), a popular crowdsourced web reputation system, as ground truth. We propose a novel ensemble classification technique that makes opportunistic use of available structural and content properties of web pages to predict their eventual ratings in two dimensions used by WOT: trustworthiness and child safety. Ours is the first classification system to predict such subjective ratings. The same approach works equally well in identifying malicious websites. Across all datasets, our classification achieves average F_1-score in the 74–90 % range.

1 Introduction

Internet scammers set up various types of "unsafe" websites to lure their victims. These include *malicious* sites, intended for *phishing*, *drive-by-downloads* of malware and misusing private user data, as well as sites that are *inappropriate* in some sense, e.g., websites hosting offensive, objectionable, hateful or illegal content.

A variety of mechanisms have been developed for steering unsuspecting users away from unsafe websites. Popular browsers present interstitial security warnings when users attempt to navigate to a known malicious website [1]. Several anti-virus vendors maintain website reputation systems (e.g., TrustedSource[1]).

---

[1] http://www.trustedsource.org/

M. Conti et al. (Eds.): TRUST 2015, LNCS 9229, pp. 143–162, 2015.
DOI: 10.1007/978-3-319-22846-4_9

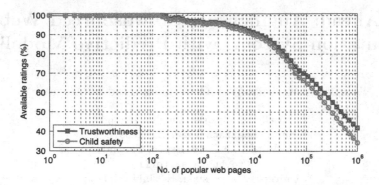

Fig. 1. Cumulative availability (%) of WOT ratings, trustworthiness and child safety, for the one million most popular webpages (as of July 2014).

These systems use a combination of machine learning techniques and manual expert evaluations to arrive at the rating for a given website. A popular sub-category of reputation systems use input ratings that are *crowdsourced* from the users of the system. *PhishTank*[2] and *Web of Trust* (WOT)[3] are examples of web reputation systems that rely fully or partly on crowdsourced ratings. An advantage of crowdsourced ratings is that the ratings can cover a broader class of unsafe websites, including those that are perceived to be inappropriate but not outright malicious [9].

All reputation systems, especially those that involve humans in the rating process, suffer from two major disadvantages: *insufficient coverage* and *time lag*. For example, Fig. 1, shows the cumulative availability of WOT reputation ratings (*trustworthiness* and *child-safety*) for one million most popular webpages (obtained from alexa.com) and indicates that the majority of the pages are unrated. The time gap between a new website coming online and the system assigning a rating can be often in the order of days to months.

A consequence of these drawbacks is that users, who rely on such reputation systems to protect them from unsafe websites, remain vulnerable when many unsafe websites are unrated. Although, machine learning techniques have been extensively used for detecting malicious websites based on the structure and content of web pages [8,10,27], in this work we address the following research question: *Can we reliably predict the eventual rating of an unrated website?*

We introduce *LookAhead*, a system that uses a combination of structural and content-based features to predict the eventual rating a website is likely to receive. In reality, the prediction task is non-trivial, as not all feature types are present on all webpages (see Sect. 4). To mitigate this feature unavailability problem, we propose an ensemble classification approach. We train different classifiers for each feature type and present different combination strategies to estimate the overall rating. For the structure of the websites, we consider HTML and JavaScript-based features. However, we show that structural features alone would not be

---

[2] http://www.phishtank.com/
[3] https://www.mywot.com/

sufficient for accurate predictions. Therefore, we introduce novel content-based feature sets, which are extracted from outgoing links with low ratings and the text present on a webpage. We make the following contributions:

(i) **Use of Content-Based Features** for effectively predicting future ratings of websites. In particular, we propose a novel use of the *empirical cumulative distribution function* (ECDF) as a feature set to extract clues about the content of a web page based on ratings of outgoing hyperlinks in it (Sect. 4.2). We also propose how *topic modeling* techniques can be used to extract features that capture the theme of a webpage (Sect. 4.2). (ii) **LookAhead**, an adaptive ensemble classification technique that effectively combines several individual classifiers by learning combination weights from the data (Sect. 4.3). (iii) **Systematic Comparative Evaluation** of LookAhead on several datasets with up to 90,000 web pages (Sect. 5). We show that the performance can be improved significantly (statistically) when utilizing content-based features in addition to the structural features of web pages (Sect. 6). In particular, this holds across both subjective dimensions (trustworthiness and child safety), as well as maliciousness.

2 Related Work

A typical approach for helping users avoid malicious websites is to use blacklists of known bad websites. For example, Microsoft's Internet Explorer and Mozilla Firefox warn users when they try to visit a page present on a blacklist. Unfortunately, blacklists suffer from a number of shortcomings, e.g., they are required to be updated periodically, are often slow to reflect new malicious websites, and have poor coverage of malicious web space. To mitigate problems with blacklists, Felegyhazi et al. [16] propose a system that, given an initial blacklist of domains, tries to predict potentially malicious domains based on nameserver features and registration information. Prakash et al. [26] propose five different heuristics that allow synthesizing new URLs from existing ones. The authors use this idea to enlarge the existing blacklist of malicious URLs.

Going beyond blacklists, application of machine learning techniques to successfully identify malicious websites has become popular. Ma et al. [21] explore the use of lexical features, including the length and number of dots in URLs, host-based features, such as IP address, domain name and other data returned by WHOIS queries [13] to identify malicious web links. Another popular approach is to analyze the structural properties of webpages, especially looking for known malicious patterns within the embedded JavaScript, to identify malicious sites [10,12,15,20,27]. JSAND by Cova et al. [10] combines anomaly detection with emulation and uses a naive Bayes classifier for malicious web page and script detection. Cujo by Rieck et al. [27] considers both static and dynamic JavaScript features and classifies websites using Support Vector Machines (SVM). ZOZZLE by Curtsinger et al. [12] considers over 1.2 million JavaScript samples and achieves FPR and TPR in the range of 1.2–5.1 %.

Closest to our work is Prophiler by Canali et al. [8], which identifies malicious websites by considering only static features related to the URL and the

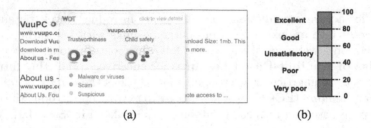

Fig. 2. (a) WOT user interface showing aggregated user ratings. (b) WOT divides the reputation rating range into five (color-coded) levels.

structure of a page. For example, they consider 37 URL-based, 20 HTML and 26 JavaScript features and train three different classifiers, one for each feature type. While systems like Prophiler [8] and JSAND [10] report good results for detecting malicious websites, we consider a much broader and non-trivial problem of predicting subjective rating dimensions like trustworthiness and child-safety of a website. In addition, we consider not only the structure and URL of a web page but also the content presented on that page.

3   Web Reputation System WOT

WOT provides reputation ratings of the domain of a given URL in two dimensions, trustworthiness and child safety as integers in the range [0–100]. WOT builds the reputation ratings of a web domain mainly based on crowdsourced input ratings from a large user base and then applying a proprietary aggregation algorithm. It also uses input from other *trusted sources*, but the identities of these sources are not public. WOT has seen well over 100 million downloads. It is also used by large scale services like *Facebook* and *Mail.ru*. It is reasonable to assume that the user base of WOT and similar rating systems runs into tens of millions.

The front-end of WOT is a browser extension that scans the page being rendered in the browser for URLs, looks up their reputation ratings in the WOT back-end, and shows the results as color-coded glyphs. For example, Fig. 2(a) shows a red glyph next to a website deemed unsafe by WOT. The rating space is divided into five levels, with a color code assigned to each level, see Fig. 2(b). WOT's confidence in a rating is also indicated by a set of dark figurines (up to five, Fig. 2(a)).

Our objective is to see if we can use information found on a hitherto unrated web page to predict what rating it will receive. In this paper we use WOT as the target reputation system. However, our proposed method is generic and would work with any web reputation system. We therefore use existing WOT ratings as the ground truth, and apply a supervised learning-based algorithm for model building. Instead of building a regression model, we formulate the web page reputation prediction as a binary classification task [4]. We divide reputation ratings into two (coarse) groups by applying a suitable threshold on the reputation ratings. This helps to minimize the effect of subjective variations among users in their ratings. Given a reputation rating $r \in [0, 100]$ of a URL, the class information of the URL is computed using the following simple rule:

$$class(r) = \begin{cases} bad & \text{if } r < \mathcal{T}_h \\ good & \text{otherwise} \end{cases} \qquad (1)$$

In our experiments (Sect. 6) we present results for $\mathcal{T}_h = 40$. Results for $\mathcal{T}_h = 60$ can be found in Appendix A.5 of the full version of this paper [2].

4 LookAhead: Predicting Safety Ratings

Our predictive approach utilizes existing reputation ratings of a large number of webpages to learn a mapping function from various webpage features to a set of target classes, in our case, either *good* or *bad* (see Eq. 1). Figure 3 illustrates an overview of our web safety prediction approach combined with WOT. The LookAhead part, highlighted in the figure, is composed of a web crawler, a database, and a predictive model. The web crawler extracts various features from webpages and stores them, along with reputation ratings in the two WOT dimensions[4], to a database. The predictive model learns a classification model and uses it for predicting web safety of unrated URLs. We consider two types of features to represent websites: (i) *structural* features, which are extracted from the HTML and embedded JavaScript code, and (ii) *content* features that capture ratings of outgoing web links and the thematic structure of page text.

4.1 Structural Features of Web Pages

For structural features, we mainly rely on past research that has identified and successfully validated a large set of features (extracted from HTML and embedded JavaScript code) to identify malicious webpages. Specifically, we adopt the handcrafted and domain specific features used by Canali et al. for their Prophiler system [8]. In the evaluation section (see Sect. 5.2), we consider Prophiler as our main baseline algorithm.

HTML-Based Features: We adopt the same 20 HTML features[5] used by the Prophiler. Examples of the features include the number of *iframe* tags, the number of hidden elements, the number of script elements, the percentage of unknown tags, and the number of malicious patterns, e.g., presence of the *meta* tag [8].

JavaScript-Based Features: We use the same 24 JavaScript-based features used by the Prophiler, which are extracted by analyzing either the JavaScript

---

[4] WOT ratings are obtained using their web API (https://www.mywot.com/wiki/API).

[5] See [8] for an exhaustive and in-depth description of all the HTML features.

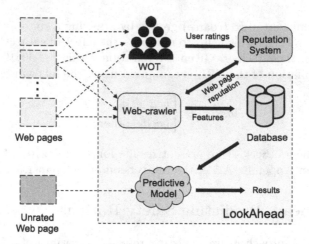

Fig. 3. An architectural overview of LookAhead in association with a crowdsourced web reputation system WOT.

file or the <script> element embedded within the HTML text. Examples of JavaScript-based features include the number of times the *eval()* function is used, the number of occurrence of the *setTimeout()* and *setInterval()* functions, the number of *DOM* modification functions, and the length of the script in characters [8].

4.2   Content Features of Web Pages

Contrary to the state-of-the-art approaches, in this paper we propose the use of a novel set of features based on (1) *empirical cumulative distribution function* (ECDF) of the reputation ratings of embedded outgoing links and (2) *topic modeling*. The main intuition behind using these features is that by learning (unsupervised) webpage content properties, we avoid the need for handcrafted features based on domain knowledge. In our evaluation, we show that the proposed novel features improve the recognition performance significantly (see Sect. 6).

Embedded Link-Based Features: To extract simple yet effective clues about the content of a web page, we hypothesize that the content of a page is related to the content of the pages it links to. In other words, we conjecture that the adage "*You are the company you keep*" is applicable here. This saying is based on the fact that often knowledge about an unknown person's friends provides some idea about the person's interests or personality. Similar ideas have been successfully applied in recommender systems [6] and in detecting susceptibility of mobile devices for malware infections [31].

Building on this idea, we propose a feature extraction scheme utilizing the available reputation ratings of embedded links. However, web pages may contain an arbitrary number of embedded links, ranging from none to several hundreds or more. Moreover, the range of the reputation ratings can be arbitrary. Thus we need a feature representation scheme that can compactly represent an arbitrary number of outgoing links, while remaining robust in the face of arbitrary ranges of ratings.

ECDF-based feature extraction has been previously explored in the field of ubiquitous computing and mobile sensing to represent human motion charac- teristics from continuous accelerometer data streams [3,18,25]. However, the method has attracted very little attention outside the sensing domain. The sim- plicity and fast computation time of the ECDF features make it a viable option for using it in static web page analysis. Contrary to mobile sensing, in this paper we primarily focus on discrete reputation ratings.

More formally, let $R = \{r_1, r_2, \ldots, r_n\}$ denote the set of available reputa- tion ratings of all the embedded web links on a page, where $r_i \in \mathbb{I}_{[0,100]}$, $\forall i \in \{1, \ldots, n\}$. The ECDF $\mathcal{P}_c(r)$ of R can be computed as:

$$\mathcal{P}_c(r) = p(X \leq r), \tag{2}$$

where, $p(X = r)$ is the probability of observing an embedded web link with a reputation rating of r, and X is a random variable that takes values from R (uniformly at random). For example, Fig. 4(a) shows an exemplary histogram of reputation ratings of web links found within a web page and Fig. 4(b) shows the corresponding ECDF computed using Eq. 2. Note that $\mathcal{P}_c(r)$ is defined on the entire range of the reputation ratings for embedded web links and is a monoton- ically increasing function.

Often the distribution of reputation ratings for embedded links is multimodal, e.g., as in our example shown in Fig. 4(a). In order to learn from such distrib- utions, a recognition system should extract descriptors that relate to the shape and spatial position of the modes [18]. The shape of the distribution is captured as $\mathcal{P}_c$ increases from 0 to 1 (see Fig. 4(b)). To extract a feature vector $f \in \mathbb{R}^k$ from the distribution, we first divide the range of $\mathcal{P}_c$, i.e., $[0, 1]$, into k equally sized bins with centers respectively at $[b_1, b_2, \ldots, b_k]$. The ith feature component $f_i \in \mathbb{R}$ is then computed as:

$$f_i = \mathcal{P}_c^{-1}(b_i) \tag{3}$$

Thus the feature vector f accurately captures the shape and positions from the underlying probability function $p(r)$, while the ECDF $\mathcal{P}_c$ can be computed efficiently using Kaplan-Meier estimator [11]. For completeness, Fig. 4(c) shows the extracted ECDF-based feature vector for $k = 75$. The only parameter for the ECDF-based feature extraction method is the number of bins k, which controls the granularity with which the shape of the underlying distribution is captured. In our experiments we also append the mean of ratings in R as a feature value to the extracted ECDF feature vector.

Adversarial Implications: If ECDF features were based on all outgoing links, a malicious website may attempt to evade detection by embedding a large num- ber of links to pages with high ratings. To deter such an attack, while con- structing the set R (see above), we only allow ratings $r \leq C_r$, where C_r is the

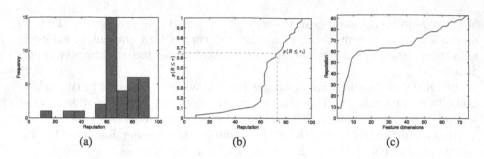

Fig. 4. Exemplary illustration of (a) the distribution of reputation ratings, (b) their Empirical Cumulative Distribution Function, and (c) ECDF-based features.

critical rating threshold. The choice of C_r can be application dependent and ideally should be adapted based on the overall costs of making false negative predictions.

Topic Model-Based Features: To gain further insight into the type of content on a web page, we analyze the text in the page and extract a set of features that captures the summary of the text as a distribution over a set of predefined topics. A topic is defined as a probability distribution over a fixed set of words. In order to learn the topics in an unsupervised manner, we employ the well established *Latent Dirichlet Allocation* (LDA) model [5]. The main objective of LDA, or in general in any topic modeling algorithm, is to extract short descriptions of documents, while preserving statistical relationships that are useful, e.g., for document summarization and classification. In this work, we only focus on text in English. As a significant portion of the webpages in our evaluation dataset (see Sect. 5.1) is non-english we use Google translation APIs, as part of the web crawler, to convert text into english. To avoid translation errors, we use an english dictionary to validate words before they are included in the *vocabulary* set V used by the LDA model.

The main objective of the LDA model is to learn model parameters, such as K topics $\beta_{1:K}$, the topic proportions θ_d in the document d, and topic assignments $z_{n,d}$ of observed word w_n in document d from the corpus of webpages. A brief overview of the topic model and the definitions of the parameters are given in Appendix A.1 of the full version [2]. Once the LDA parameters are learned, given the set of words w present on a webpage and the topics $\beta_{1:K}$, the topic model-based feature set for the webpage is computed as: $p(\theta_d|w, \beta_{1:K})$, i.e., the estimated topic proportions.

Adversarial Implications: Similarly to the ECDF-based features, the topic model-based features can be exploited by an adversary. As the topic proportion term, i.e., $p(\theta_d|w, \beta_{1:K})$ captures the relative weight of various topics being described within the text w, an attacker can simply add random words that can boost the probability of certain topics. In Sect. 7 we propose a possible solution to prevent this attack.

4.3   Ensemble Classification

One challenge in the feature extraction procedures, described above, is that often one or more feature types are missing from a web page. For example, in reality, not all web pages use JavaScript, contain embedded outgoing links, or use textual descriptions, although the HTML features are always available. Thus, a new classification technique is required that is able to overcome the problem of feature unavailability. Existing approaches such as [8,21,29,30], do not address this problem and therefore have limited generalizability.

According to Bayesian theory [19], given HTML (f_H), JavaScript (f_J), ECDF (f_E), and Topic (f_T) feature vectors, a URL should be assigned to the class $c_j \in \{bad, good\}$, if the posterior probability for class c_j is maximum, i.e.

$$assign \ \ URL \rightarrow c_j \ \ if$$
$$p(c_j|f_H, f_J, f_E, f_T) = \max_i \ p(c_i|f_H, f_J, f_E, f_T) \tag{4}$$

The computation of $p(c_j|f_H, f_J, f_E, f_T)$ depends on the joint probability functions (likelihood) $p(f_H, f_J, f_E, f_T|c_j)$ and the prior probability $p(c_j)$, i.e.:

$$p(c_j|f_H, f_J, f_E, f_T) \propto p(f_H, f_J, f_E, f_T|c_j) \, p(c_j) \tag{5}$$

The likelihoods are difficult to infer when one or more features are unavailable. The likelihood computation can be simplified by combining decision support of individual classifiers on different feature types [19]. Accordingly, we train four classifiers C_H, C_J, C_E, and C_T using valid f_H, f_J, f_E, and f_T features respectively, where each classifier returns a posterior probability distribution over the *bad* and *good* classes. However during prediction, if a feature type is unavailable, we do not include the corresponding classifier while computing the overall posterior probabilities.

A number of strategies can be adopted to combine the posterior probabilities of the classifiers to generate the overall belief. In this paper we propose a linear combination rule that determines the combination weights of individual classifiers using the Fukunaga class separability score [17]. Our adaptive weight selection method is based on the intuition that a classifier should be given more importance if it is easy to separate among the *bad* and *good* classes in the corresponding feature space. See Appendix A.2 of the full version [2] for the definition of class separability we use and other popular combination rules. For each classifier, we compute the separability score after correlation based feature subset selection. The separability scores, after normalization, are then used as the respective weight w_k for the classifier C_k. The final belief of the class c_j is estimated as:

$$p^*(c_j|f_H, f_J, f_E, f_T) = \sum_{k \in \{H,J,E,T\}} w_k \ p(c_j|f_k) \tag{6}$$

The final predicted class c_j is inferred by applying the decision rule given in Eq. 4 using the computed belief above. Figure 5 shows the data adaptive ensemble classification technique used by LookAhead.

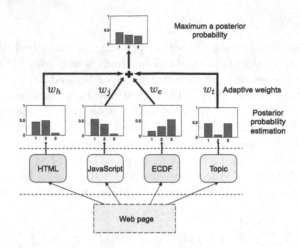

Fig. 5. Overview of the ensemble classification approach used by LookAhead.

5 Experimental Settings

5.1 Datasets

To perform an extensive and systematic study, we generated a pool of over 140,000 URLs and obtained their reputation ratings in both dimensions using the WOT API. Out of these, 80,000 URLs have positive reputation ratings, and 60,000 have negative ratings. For each URL we crawl the web page to extract HTML, JavaScript, ECDF and topic model features where available. Figure 6 illustrates the histograms of reputation ratings for all webpages in our dataset. The dataset, where at least HTML features and WOT ratings are available, is referred to as the *opportunistic* dataset. Out of 140,000 URLs, 89,220 web pages have trustworthiness ratings, and 84,714 have ratings for child safety. However, the number drops to 31,995, in case of trustworthiness, and to 38,118 for child safety, when validity of all feature types are considered (for $\mathcal{T}_h = 40$). We refer to this second dataset as the *all-valid* dataset. The significant drop in the size of the all-valid dataset further highlights that feature unavailability is intrinsic to web data analysis.

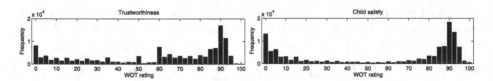

Fig. 6. Histograms of all webpages in our dataset in two reputation dimensions: trustworthiness (left) and child safety (right).

Existing research primarily focused on detecting if a webpage is malicious. However, the malware dataset used in [8] is no longer available, which makes exact replication of Prophiler results difficult. "Trustworthiness" in WOT does not directly correspond to malware. In addition to the reputation ratings, WOT provides category information, such as 'malware', 'scam', 'suspicious' and 'good site', of websites based on votes from users and third parties. From the all-valid dataset we generate a malware dataset consisting of 2,784 webpages that were categorized by WOT as 'malware or virus'. To generate a dataset containing both malware and benign webpages, we include an equal number of webpages that got very high trustworthiness ratings and have all feature types. We refer to this dataset as the *malware* dataset.

Lastly, we construct another dataset by considering only the URLs that fall either in the top most or the bottom most trustworthiness rating categories, see Fig. 2(b) for definitions of various rating categories used by WOT. As with malware dataset, we only consider webpages for which all feature types are available. Our *two-category* dataset consists of 10,118 sites with very poor ratings and 13,539 with excellent ratings.

5.2 Baseline Algorithms

In our experiments, we report comparison results against Prophier [8]. Prophiler relies on HTML, JavaScript, and URL/HOST features to detect if a webpage is malicious. However, it uses APIs to a proprietary WHOIS [14] system and uses a private database for blacklisted URLs to extract URL/HOST features. Neither of these are available openly, which makes the corresponding URL/HOST feature vectors invalid for our datasets. API inaccessibility and unavailability of suitable blacklisted database covering WOT URLs used in our dataset makes the majority of the URL/HOST feature vectors in our experiments invalid. Consequently, we do not use URL/HOST features in our ensemble classification system. Note that it is very easy to incorporate additional feature types in our classification system, e.g., training a classifier C using the new feature type and then considering the posterior probabilities in Eq. 6. Contrary to our approach, i.e., assigning data driven weighting of classifiers to compute the final belief (see Sect. 4.3), Prophiler uses the 'OR' combination rule (see Appendix A.3 of [2]). We systematically compare the performance of LookAhead with the ensemble classification methodology considering different subsets of feature types.

5.3 Evaluation Metric

We use 10-fold stratified random cross validations when presenting classification performance for all the approaches. As the primary performance metric, we use Avg. F_1-score, False Negative Rate (FNR), and False Positive Rate (FPR). The definitions of all the evaluation metrics can be found in Appendix A.4 of [2].

6   Evaluation

We begin our evaluation by first considering classification performance on the all-valid dataset using Random Forest as the basic classifier[6]. Note that, all URLs considered within this dataset have valid HTML (H), JavaScript (J), ECDF (E) and Topic-based (T) features. This dataset allows us to systematically study the influence of various feature combinations on the overall classification performance of LookAhead. Table 1 summarizes the performance of LookAhead in both reputation dimensions with the parametric settings $\mathcal{T}_h = 40$ (see Eq. 1), and $C_r = 40$ (see Sect. 4.2). The table also includes the performance of Prophiler.

For trustworthiness, LookAhead achieves the highest Avg. F_1-score of 81.3 %, when all feature types are considered (highlighted in gray), at the same time achieving the lowest FNR (19 %) and FPR (18.3 %). Similarly for child safety, LookAhead with all feature types achieves the best performance (86.4 %), lowest FNR (11.6 %) and lowest FPR (16.2 %). In both reputation dimensions, the performance using all features, is significantly better (statistically) than all other feature combinations, i.e., $p \ll 0.01$ in McNemar χ^2 test with Yates' correction [22].

Prophiler shows a statistically weaker classification performance in both reputation dimensions compared to LookAhead (employing all feature types). However, it achieves a better FNR in prediction than LookAhead. This is due to the use of a conservative 'OR' classifier combination rule (see full version [2]) that is more likely to report a URL as bad. This higher likelihood of predicting web pages as bad improves the overall recall of the bad class, which consequently pulls down the FNR for Prophiler, however, at the expense of a higher FPR. Prophiler focuses solely on reducing FNR. In contrast, in use cases where overall usability in prediction is important, both FNR and FPR should be reduced. For example, in predicting safety ratings, a low FPR is also needed to avoid showing frequent warnings to users for actually good websites.

In reality, not all feature types are available for all URLs. To evaluate the performance of LookAhead under real life situations we next present results on the opportunistic dataset. In these experiments, we only present the performance of LookAhead while considering all available feature types. Moreover, we study the performance of various classifier combination rules and present the results in Table 2 for both reputation dimensions. In contrast to the all-valid dataset, $\mathcal{T}_h = 40$, generates a high degree of class imbalance in our opportunistic dataset (see Fig. 6). During the training phase the prevalence of one class affects the process of learning, and the learned classifier is often biased towards the overrepresented class [23]. To mitigate class imbalances during training, we also report experimental results when a simple class balancing approach, i.e., reducing data from the prevalent class, is applied during classifier training. The data driven, adaptive classification combination rule of LookAhead generates the best classification performance, with a notable exception in the case of unbalanced dataset for trustworthiness, where the 'Product' rule achieves the highest Avg. F_1-Score.

---

[6] We also experimented using linear-SVM, SVM, KNN and C4.5 classifiers, and chose Random Forest for its superior performance.

Table 1. Performance of LookAhead (under various feature combinations H = HTML, J = JavaScript, E = ECDF, and T = Topic) and Prophiler on the all-valid dataset ($\mathcal{T}_h = 40$, $C_r = 40$, and **: Statistically significant with 99 % confidence).

All-valid dataset size: 31,995 URLs
Reputation dimension: Trustworthiness

H	J	E	T	Avg. F_1-Score (%)	FNR (%)	FPR (%)
✓				75.6 **	25.2	23.7
	✓			74.3 **	25.6	25.9
		✓		66.9 **	33.5	32.7
			✓	74.5 **	26.8	24.3
✓	✓			76.9 **	23.3	22.8
✓		✓		77.3 **	23.7	21.7
✓			✓	78.5 **	21.8	21.3
	✓	✓		72.1 **	28.9	26.9
	✓		✓	77.1 **	24.0	21.9
		✓	✓	77.5 **	23.9	21.2
✓	✓	✓		78.8 **	21.6	20.7
✓	✓		✓	79.5 **	20.9	20.1
✓		✓	✓	80.4 **	20.2	19.0
	✓	✓	✓	79.6 **	21.4	19.4
✓	✓	✓	✓	**81.3**	**19.0**	**18.3**
Prophiler				74.5 **	14.2	35.9

All-valid dataset size: 38,118 URLs
Reputation dimension: Child safety

H	J	E	T	Avg. F_1-Score (%)	FNR (%)	FPR (%)
✓				80.3 **	15.2	25.8
	✓			79.6 **	15.8	26.8
		✓		73.1 **	22.0	33.6
			✓	81.9 **	17.0	19.8
✓	✓			81.1 **	14.3	25.1
✓		✓		79.4 **	16.3	26.3
✓			✓	84.5 **	13.4	18.3
	✓	✓		77.3 **	18.1	29.1
	✓		✓	83.9 **	14.6	18.2
		✓	✓	83.9 **	14.9	17.7
✓	✓	✓		82.4 **	13.5	23.2
✓	✓		✓	85.2 **	12.2	18.4
✓		✓	✓	85.7 **	12.6	16.7
	✓	✓	✓	85.3 **	13.4	16.6
✓	✓	✓	✓	**86.4**	**11.6**	**16.2**
Prophiler				79.5 **	9.6	34.5

Table 2. Performance of LookAhead on the opportunistic dataset under various classifier combination rules ($\mathcal{T}_h = 40$ and $C_r = 40$, **: Significant with 99 % confidence, *: 95 % confidence).

Opportunistic dataset size: 89,220 URLs
Reputation dimension: Trustworthiness

Comb. Rule	Bal.	Avg. F_1-Score (%)	FNR (%)	FPR (%)
Adaptive		78.0	56.4	4.1
Sum		77.8	57.9	**3.5**
Product		**78.9 **	53.3	4.6
Or		32.4 **	**10.1**	84.2
Voting		71.4 **	38.8	25.2
Prophiler*		72.6 **	45.3	19.8
Adaptive	✓	**74.0**	22.3	29.1
Sum	✓	74.0	22.3	**29.0**
Product	✓	73.6 **	22.8	29.5
Or	✓	27.3 **	**2.3**	89.8
Voting	✓	57.3 **	11.1	57.0
Prophiler*	✓	62.0 **	14.4	49.8

Opportunistic dataset size: 84,714 URLs
Reputation dimension: Child safety

Comb. Rule	Bal.	Avg. F_1-Score (%)	FNR (%)	FPR (%)
Adaptive		**83.7**	29.8	7.2
Sum		83.4 *	31.2	**6.6**
Product		83.6	29.6	7.5
Or		40.7 **	**4.7**	82.3
Voting		73.9 **	19.7	30.7
Prophiler*		73.9 **	26.7	26.2
Adaptive	✓	81.5	25.3	**14.0**
Sum	✓	81.1 **	22.9	16.4
Product	✓	80.9 **	23.1	16.8
Or	✓	40.0 **	**3.0**	83.4
Voting	✓	68.1 **	12.3	44.3
Prophiler*	✓	69.4 **	15.6	40.5

Table 3. Performance of LookAhead and Prophiler on the malware and two-category datasets (**: Significant with 99 % confidence).

Malware dataset size: 5,568 URLs							Tow-category dataset size: 23,657 URLs						
Feature sets				Avg. F$_1$-Score	FNR	FPR	Feature sets				Avg. F$_1$-Score	FNR	FPR
H	J	E	T	(%)	(%)	(%)	H	J	E	T	(%)	(%)	(%)
✓	✓	✓	✓	89.0	10.3	11.6	✓	✓	✓	✓	89.8	13.9	7.4

Malware							Two-category						
Prophiler				80.7 **	11.1	27.3	Prophiler				79.3 **	16.2	24.3

Prophiler has previously been shown to perform well in detecting malicious websites. To show how LookAhead (with all features) perform in such scenarios, we repeated the experiments on the malware and two-category datasets and present the results in Table 3. LookAhead achieves average F$_1$-scores of 89 % for the malware dataset and 89.8 % for the two-category dataset, which are significantly better ($p \ll 0.01$) than Prophiler's performance of 80.7 % for the malware dataset and 79.3 % for the two-category dataset. LookAhead also generates better FNR and FPR than Prophiler on both datasets.

7   Discussion

7.1   Feature Importance in Reputation Prediction

Our results show that the structural and content related properties of a website can be effectively used to predict not only its maliciousness, but also the more challenging properties of trustworthiness and child safety. In order to understand the overall classification results, we study the importance of individual features as computed by a Random Forest classifier[7]. In Fig. 7 we plot the average importance for all (120) features used in this work when training a Random Forest classifier (using 100 trees) on the all-valid dataset. The higher the value, the more important is the feature. Figure 7 further highlights that different features are assigned different relative importances, while separating good websites from bad ones in each reputation dimension.

Interestingly, the importance scores of the HTML and JavaScript-based features look very similar for both trustworthiness and child safety predictions. The most important features, shown by the dotted region A in the figure, are related to script tags in HTML, direct assignments in JavaScript, and the total character count in both. Although, a few structural (i.e., HTML and JavaScript) features are found to be important, a majority of them have little or no significance. Contrary to the structural features, ECDF features show significant differences in importance scores for the two reputation dimensions. For trustworthiness, low ratings of the embedded links (region B) play an important role in prediction. In child safety, the mean value of the embedded ratings (region C) plays a significant role also. For trustworthiness, the three most important topics (region E)

---

[7] Feature importance is defined as the total decrease in node impurity averaged over all the trees [7].

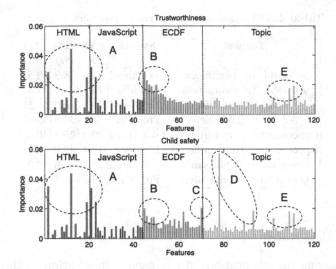

Fig. 7. Importance of individual features, while predicting trustworthiness and child safety, computed by the Random Forest classifier on the all-valid dataset.

are related to money-making, news, and weather. Among the rest of the topic features, none are significantly better or worse than the others. For child safety prediction there are three other topics (region D) that play a significant role and as expected, these topics correspond to adult content.

Although, we use the same feature set for predicting both reputation dimensions, the feature selection inherent to the Random Forest classifier learns very different mapping functions for each prediction task. Figure 7 provides evidence that our proposed ECDF and Topic-based features contribute consistently in predicting subjective ratings.

7.2   Tuning of Prediction Performance

Predictive performance of LookAhead can be primarily influenced by a number of factors: (i) the type of features considered (e.g., HTML and ECDF), (ii) the type of classifier used (e.g., Random Forest and SVM), (iii) strategies used to overcome class imbalances in the training data, and (iv) the combination rule used for computing the final posterior probability (e.g., Adaptive and Sum rule). Often, once the prediction pipeline is deployed, the factors (i)–(iii) are kept constant, as they are time consuming to re-build. However, the classifier combination strategy can be adapted in real time to control the overall performance of the LookAhead system. Based on the requirements, the system administrator can focus more on lowering the overall FNR by using the 'OR' combination rule, e.g., while predicting child safety a very low FNR is expected for parental filtering systems. As evident from Table 2, often emphasizing FNR inflates FPR. Our LookAhead system demonstrates a good balance of both FNR and FPR.

Table 4. Detection rates for various classifiers settings.

Dataset	System	FNR (%)	FPR (%)	$\mathcal{D}_r$ (%)
All-valid, Trustworthiness	LookAhead	19.0	18.3	52.5
All-valid, Trustworthiness	Prophiler	14.2	35.9	37.4
All-valid, Child safety	LookAhead	11.6	16.2	57.5
All-valid, Child safety	Prophiler	9.6	34.5	39.6
Opportunistic, Trustworthiness	LookAhead	22.3	29.1	40.0
Opportunistic, Trustworthiness	Prophiler	14.4	49.8	30.1
Opportunistic, Child safety	LookAhead	25.3	14.0	57.2
Opportunistic, Child safety	Prophiler	15.6	40.5	34.3

7.3 Detection Rate

When considering the implications of our results, in addition to the FNR and FPR, the proportion of good and bad websites in the wild should also be taken into account. In reality, this so-called base rate B_r, is biased towards good websites. Thus we look at the detection rate for bad websites, i.e., what percentage of web pages that our classifier predicts as bad are truly bad. From WOT statistics [28], we see that roughly 20 % of websites that have a rating are dangerous regarding either trustworthiness or child safety. We use this number as our estimate for B_r, and compute the detection rate as:

$$\mathcal{D}_r = \frac{(1 - FNR) \cdot B_r}{(1 - FNR) \cdot B_r + FPR \cdot (1 - B_r)}, \tag{7}$$

Table 4 presents detection rates of LookAhead and Prophiler on all-valid and opportunistic datasets for both reputation dimensions. We can see that due to the biased base rate, the detection rates are in the range of $30-40\%$ for Prophiler and $40-57\%$ for LookAhead, indicating better classification performances of LookAhead. For example, in case of a warning system for users, when all features are present, 52.5 % of possible warnings for untrustworthy web pages would be correct for LookAhead. The corresponding detection rate of 37.4 % for Prophiler is significantly lower. The results highlight that, while in general the problem of predicting reputation ratings is challenging, considering content-based features significantly improves the detection rate.

7.4 Applications

Fast-Tracking Publication of Ratings: Crowdsourced reputation rating services like WOT do not announce a rating for a web site until they have enough input ratings to reach a sufficient level of confidence. If a partially accumulated rating (that has not reached a sufficient level of confidence) matches the rating predicted by our classifier, the reputation service may choose to fast-track the publication of the rating.

Table 5. Time analysis for extracting various feature types.

Feature type	Average extraction time
HTML + JavaScript	3.1 s / link
ECDF	1.9 s / link
Topic + translation	3.4 s / link
Topic + without translation	1.3 s / link

Intermediate User Feedback: If a user attempts to navigate to an unrated page that is predicted by our classifier to have a potentially bad rating, the browser extension can warn the user accordingly. Earlier research [24] raised concerns about the usefulness of crowdsourcing for security and privacy applications. Nevertheless, given the popularity of systems like WOT, we argue that a tool like LookAhead is essential for the security of users who have chosen to rely on such systems. Also, note that although our analysis was done with WOT as the target rating system, the methodology is applicable to any website safety rating system, whether crowdsourced or expert-rated.

7.5   Performance Considerations

We summarize the performance of our various feature extraction techniques and report the average measured running time needed for computing them. For the purpose of computing the average extraction time we randomly selected $1,000$ URLs from our dataset and measured the time required to extract different classes of features on a standard Linux desktop computer (8 Gb RAM, 2.4 GHz processor). In case of Topic model features we also recorded the time for performing translation of non-english web pages. Table 5 summarizes the time analysis of our feature extraction methods. The time of 3.1 s that LookAhead needs for extracting structural features is comparable to that of 3.06 s reported by Prophiler. When including the content based features, in total, LookAhead needs 6.3 s to extract all features from an English-language web page (and 8.4 s if translation is needed). Moreover, caching and pre-fetching of features can be employed to further reduce the feature extraction time.

7.6   Limitations

Perhaps the most significant limitation of any system using machine learning to detect bad websites is the potential for adversaries to manipulate the system: either by modifying their website to avoid detection or by manipulating the classifier itself. While the use of the ECDF-function protects against manipulation of outgoing links, as we pointed out in Sect. 4.2, the simplistic approach of using topic modeling is vulnerable to an attacker who attempts to influence the inferred topic model for a page he controls. Instead of directly using the probability distribution of topics as we do in Sect. 4.2, we could convert to a boolean vector (indicating if the topic is present on the page). Such an approach will reduce false negatives (since an attacker can no longer gain by adding text to his page to make it appear to belong to an innocuous topic as the dominant topic), but will also raise false positives. We are currently investigating this avenue.

Another limitation is that, although the performance of LookAhead is comparable to previous solutions, real time use will require further speedup. One option here is to use server-side assisted feature extraction. Finally, an open question is how the use of predicted ratings will influence the actual rating. For example, if the predicted rating is used for intermediate user feedback as suggested above, it might sway future input ratings from the crowd towards the predicted rating.

7.7 Current Work

We are conducting a longitudinal study on a large number of websites that do not yet have a WOT rating. We plan to see (a) how well our predictions match those websites that do eventually get a rating and (b) how do our predictions as well as the actual ratings evolve over time.

Acknowledgments. This work was partially supported by the Intel Institute for Collaborative Research in Secure Computing (ICRI-SC) and the Academy of Finland project "Contextual Security" (Grant Number: 274951). We thank Web of Trust for giving access to their data which we used in this work. We also thank Timo Ala-Kleemola and Sergey Andryukhin for helping us understand the WOT data, Jian Liu and Swapnil Udar for helping to develop the web crawler. We would also like to thank Petteri Nurmi, Pekka Parviainen, and Nidhi Gupta for their feedback on an earlier version of this manuscript.

References

1. Akhawe, D., Felt, A.P.: Alice in warningland: a large-scale field study of browser security warning effectiveness. In: Proceedings of the 22Nd USENIX Conference on Security, SEC 2013, pp. 257–272. USENIX Association, Berkeley, CA, USA (2013)
2. Bhattacharya, S., Huhta, O., Asokan, N.: Lookahead: augmenting crowdsourced website reputation systems with predictive modeling (2015). http://www.arxiv.org/pdf/1504.04730.pdf
3. Bhattacharya, S., Nurmi, P., Hammerla, N., Plötz, T.: Using unlabeled data in a sparse-coding framework for human activity recognition. Pervasive and Mobile Computing, May 2014
4. Bishop, C.M.: Pattern Recognition and Machine Learning. Springer, Heidelberg (2007)
5. Blei, D.M., Ng, A.Y., Jordan, M.I.: Latent dirichlet allocation. J. Mach. Learn. Res. **3**, 993–1022 (2003)
6. Breese, J.S., Heckerman, D., Kadie, C.: Empirical analysis of predictive algorithms for collaborative filtering. In: Proceedings of the Fourteenth Conference on Uncertainty in Artificial Intelligence, pp. 43–52 (1998)
7. Breiman, L.: Random forests. Mach. Learn. **45**(1), 5–32 (2001)

8. Canali, D., Cova, M., Vigna, G., Kruegel, C.: Prophiler: a fast filter for the large-scale detection of malicious web pages. In: Proceedings of the 20th International Conference on World Wide Web, pp. 197–206. ACM (2011)

9. Chia, P.H., Knapskog, S.J.: Re-evaluating the wisdom of crowds in assessing web security. In: Danezis, G. (ed.) FC 2011. LNCS, vol. 7035, pp. 299–314. Springer, Heidelberg (2012)

10. Cova, M., Kruegel, C., Vigna, G.: Detection and analysis of drive-by-download attacks and malicious javascript code. In: Proceedings of the 19th International Conference on World Wide Web, pp. 281–290. ACM (2010)

11. Cox, D.R., Oakes, D.: Analysis of Survival Data. Champman and Hall, CRC (1984)

12. Curtsinger, C., Livshits, B., Zorn, B.G., Seifert, C.: Zozzle: fast and precise in-browser javascript malware detection. In: USENIX Security Symposium, pp. 33–48 (2011)

13. Daigle, L.: Whois protocol specification

14. Daigle, L.: Rfc 3912: Whois protocol specification, September 2014. http://www.tools.ietf.org/html/rfc3912

15. Feinstein, B., Peck, D.: Caffeine monkey: automated collection, detection and analysis of malicious javascript. In: Proceedings of the Black Hat Security Conference, **2007** (2007)

16. Felegyhazi, M., Kreibich, C., Paxson, V.: On the potential of proactive domain blacklisting. In: Proceedings of the 3rd USENIX Conference on Large-scale Exploits and Emergent Threats: Botnets, Spyware, Worms, and More, LEET 2010, p. 6. USENIX Association, Berkeley, CA, USA (2010)

17. Fukunaga, K.: Introduction to Statistical Pattern Recognition, 2nd edn. Academic Press, San Diego (1990)

18. Hammerla, N., Kirkham, R., Andras, P., Plötz, T.: On preserving statistical characteristics of accelerometry data using their empirical cumulative distribution. In: Proceeding of International Symposium on Wearable Computers (ISWC) (2013)

19. Kittler, J., Hatef, M., Duin, R., Matas, J.: On combining classifiers. IEEE Trans. Pattern Anal. Mach. Intell. **20**(3), 226–239 (1998)

20. Likarish, P., Jung, E., Jo, I.: Obfuscated malicious javascript detection using classification techniques. In: 4th International Conference on Malicious and Unwanted Software (MALWARE), pp. 47–54 (2009)

21. Ma, J., Saul, L.K., Savage, S., Voelker, G.M.: Beyond blacklists: learning to detect malicious web sites from suspicious URLs. In: Proceedings of the 15th ACM SIGKDD International Conference on Knowledge Discovery and Data Mining, KDD 2009, pp. 1245–1254. ACM, New York, NY, USA (2009)

22. McNemar, Q.: Note on the sampling error of the difference between correlated proportions or percentages. Psychometrika **12**, 153–157 (1947)

23. Menardi, G., Torelli, N.: Training and assessing classification rules with imbalanced data. Data Min. Knowl. Disc. **28**(1), 92–122 (2014)

24. Moore, T., Clayton, R.C.: Evaluating the wisdom of crowds in assessing phishing websites. In: Tsudik, G. (ed.) FC 2008. LNCS, vol. 5143, pp. 16–30. Springer, Heidelberg (2008)

25. Plötz, T., Hammerla, N.Y., Olivier, P.: Feature learning for activity recognition in ubiquitous computing. In: International Joint Conference on Artificial Intelligence (IJCAI), pp. 1729–1734 (2011)

26. Prakash, P., Kumar, M., Kompella, R., Gupta, M.: Phishnet: predictive blacklisting to detect phishing attacks. In: 2010 Proceedings IEEE INFOCOM, pp. 1–5, March 2010

27. Rieck, K., Krueger, T., Dewald, A.: Cujo: efficient detection and prevention of drive-by-download attacks. In: Proceedings of the 26th Annual Computer Security Applications Conference, pp. 31–39. ACM (2010)
28. Ruvolo, J.: WOT statistics, December 2014. https://www.mywot.com/en/community/statistics
29. Seifert, C., Welch, I., Komisarczuk, P.: Identification of malicious web pages with static heuristics. In: Telecommunication Networks and Applications Conference (ATNAC), pp. 91–96 (2008)
30. Seifert, C., Welch, I., Komisarczuk, P., Aval, C., Popovsky, B.: Identification of malicious web pages through analysis of underlying dns and web server relationships. In: 33rd IEEE Conference on Local Computer Networks (LCN), pp. 935–941 (2008)
31. Truong, H.T.T., Lagerspetz, E., Nurmi, P., Oliner, A.J., Tarkoma, S., Asokan, N., Bhattacharya, S.: The company you keep: mobile malware infection rates and inexpensive risk indicators. In: Proceedings of the 23rd International Conference on World Wide Web, pp. 39–50 (2014)

Ripple: Overview and Outlook

Frederik Armknecht[1], Ghassan O. Karame[2(✉)], Avikarsha Mandal[3],
Franck Youssef[2], and Erik Zenner[3]

[1] University of Mannheim, Mannheim, Germany
armknecht@uni-mannheim.de
[2] NEC Laboratories Europe, 69115 Heidelberg, Germany
{ghassan.karame,franck.youssef}@neclab.eu
[3] University of Applied Sciences, Offenburg, Germany
{avikarsha.mandal,erik.zenner}@hs-offenburg.de

Abstract. Ripple is a payment system and a digital currency which
evolved completely independently of Bitcoin. Although Ripple holds the
second highest market cap after Bitcoin, there are surprisingly no studies
which analyze the provisions of Ripple.

In this paper, we study the current deployment of the Ripple payment
system. For that purpose, we overview the Ripple protocol and outline
its security and privacy provisions in relation to the Bitcoin system. We
also discuss the consensus protocol of Ripple. Contrary to the statement
of the Ripple designers, we show that the current choice of parameters
does not prevent the occurrence of forks in the system. To remedy this
problem, we give a necessary and sufficient condition to prevent any fork
in the system. Finally, we analyze the current usage patterns and trade
dynamics in Ripple by extracting information from the Ripple global
ledger. As far as we are aware, this is the first contribution which sheds
light on the current deployment of the Ripple system.

Keywords: Ripple · Bitcoin · Security · Forks

1 Introduction

The wide success of Bitcoin has lead to a surge of a large number of alternative
crypto-currencies. These include Litecoin [1], Namecoin [2], Ripple [6,38], among
others. Most of these currencies are built atop the Bitcoin blockchain, and try to
address some of the shortcomings of Bitcoin. For example, Namecoin offers the
ability to store data within Bitcoin's blockchain in order to realize a decentralized
open source information registration based on Bitcoin, while Litecoin primarily
differs from Bitcoin by having a smaller block generation time, and a larger
number of coinbases, etc. While most of these digital currencies are based on
Bitcoin, Ripple has evolved almost completely independently of Bitcoin (and
of its various forks). Currently, Ripple holds the second highest market cap
after Bitcoin [4]. This corresponds to almost 20 % of the market cap held by
Bitcoin. Recently, Ripple Labs have additionally finalized the financing of an

© Springer International Publishing Switzerland 2015
M. Conti et al. (Eds.): TRUST 2015, LNCS 9229, pp. 163–180, 2015.
DOI: 10.1007/978-3-319-22846-4_10

additional 30 million USD funding round to support the growth and development of Ripple [5].

Ripple does not only offer an alternative currency, XRP, but also promises to facilitate the exchange between currencies within its network. Although Ripple is built upon an open source decentralized consensus protocol, the current deployment of Ripple is solely managed by Ripple Labs. Originally, the Ripple network was created with a limited supply of 100 billion XRP units; 20 % of those units are retained by Ripple founders, 25 % are held by Ripple Labs, while the remaining 55 % are set to be sold. This represents the largest holdback of any crypto-currency [4], but has not apparently stopped the adoption of Ripple by a considerable fraction of users. At the time of writing, Ripple claims to have a total network value of approximately 960 million USD with an average of almost 170 accounts created per day since the launch of the system [33]. Moreover, there are currently a number of businesses that are built around the Ripple system [14,20]. For instance, the International Ripple Business Association currently deploys a handful of Ripple gateways [22], market makers [23], exchangers [21], and merchants [24] located around the globe.

Although crypto-currencies are receiving considerable attention in the literature [11,16,28,31,37], there are surprisingly no studies—as far as we are aware—that investigate the Ripple system. In this paper, we remedy this problem and we analyze the deployment and security provisions of the Ripple payment system. More specifically, we overview the Ripple protocol and discuss the basic differences between the current deployments of Ripple and Bitcoin. Motivated by recent forks in the Ripple consensus protocol [25], we provide a new necessary and sufficient condition that provably prevent the realization of a fork in Ripple. Finally, we extract information on the current usage patterns and trade dynamics in Ripple from almost 4.5 million ledgers which were generated in the period between January 2013, and January 2015. Our findings suggest that—although it has been introduced almost 2 years ago—most Ripple users seem inactive and their trade volume is not increasing. As far as we are aware, this is the first contribution which investigates the current deployment of Ripple.

The remainder of this paper is structured as follows. In Sect. 2, we detail the Ripple protocol and the underlying consensus protocol. We also discuss the security and privacy provisions of Ripple in relation to the Bitcoin system. In Sect. 3, we analyze the conditions for forking in Ripple. In Sect. 4, we analyze the current usage patterns of Ripple by extracting information from the Ripple ledgers. In Sect. 5, we discuss related work in the area, and we conclude the paper in Sect. 6.

2   The Ripple Protocol

In what follows, we introduce and detail the Ripple system. We also analyze Ripple's consensus protocol and compare it to Bitcoin.

2.1   Overview of Ripple

Ripple [38] is a decentralized payment system based on credit networks [19,29]. The Ripple code is open source and available for the public; this means that anyone can deploy a Ripple instance. Nodes can take up to three different roles in Ripples: *users* which make/receive payments, *market makers* which act as trade enablers in the system, and *validating servers* which execute Ripple's *consensus* protocol in order to check and validate all transactions taking place in the system.

Ripple users are referenced by means of pseudonyms. Users are equipped with a public/private key pair; when a user wishes to send a payment to another user, it cryptographically signs the transfer of money denominated in Ripple's own currency, XRP, or using any other currency. For payments made in non-XRP currencies, Ripple has no way to enforce payments, and only records the amounts owed by one entity to the other. More specifically, in this case, Ripple implements a distributed credit network system.

A non-XRP payment from A to B is only possible if B is willing to accept an "I Owe You" (IOU) transaction from A, i.e., B trusts A and gives enough credit to A. Hence, A can only make a successful IOU payment to B if the payment value falls within the credit balance allocated by B to A. This may be the case, e.g., if the participants know each other, or if the involved amounts are rather marginal; typically however, such transactions require the involvement of "market makers" who act as intermediaries. In this case, enough credit should be available throughout the payment path for a successful payment.

For example, a trust line can be established between market maker $U1$ and A (cf. Fig. 1) by A depositing an amount at $U1$. In our example, A wants to issue a payment to B with the amount of 100 USD. Here, the payment is routed from $A \rightarrow U1 \rightarrow U2 \rightarrow U4 \rightarrow B$. This is possible because available credit lines are larger than the actual payment for every atomic transactions. Notice that we did not route through $U3$ as there is not enough credit available between $U1 \rightarrow U3$. However, we note that it is possible to break down the payment amount at $U1$, route a payment below 90 USD through $U1 \rightarrow U3 \rightarrow B$ and transfer the rest through $U1 \rightarrow U2 \rightarrow U4 \rightarrow B$ (extra fee at $U3$ required). In typical cases, Ripple relies on a path finding algorithm which finds the most suitable payment path from the source to the destination. By implementing credit networks, Ripple can act as an exchange/trade medium between currencies; in case of currency pairs that are traded rarely, XRP can act as a bridge between such currencies.

Ripple's Ledger: Ripple maintains a distributed ledger which keeps track of all the exchanged transactions in the system. Ledgers are created every few seconds, and contain a list of transactions to which the majority of *validating servers* have agreed to. This is achieved by means of Ripple's consensus protocol [38] which is executed amongst validating servers. A Ripple ledger consists of the following information: *(i)* a set of transactions, *(ii)* account-related information such as account settings, total balance, trust relation, *(ii)* a timestamp, *(iv)* a ledger number, and *(v)* a status bit indicating whether the ledger is validated or not. The most recent validated ledger is referred to as the *last closed ledger*. On the other hand, if the ledger is not validated yet, the ledger is deemed *open*.

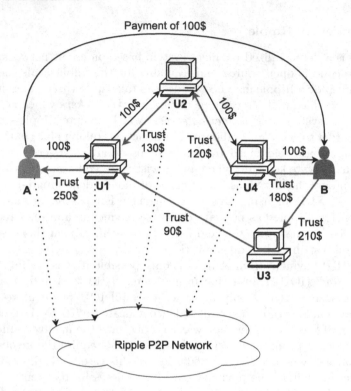

Fig. 1. Exemplary sketch of IOU payments in Ripple. Here, A wants to pay 100 USD to B.

Consensus and Validating Servers: Each validating server verifies the proposed changes to the last ledger; changes that are agreed by at least 50% of the servers are packaged into a new proposal which is sent to other servers in the network. This process is re-iterated with the vote requirements increasing to 60%, 70%, and 80% after which the server validates the changes and alerts the network of the closure of the last ledger. At this point, any transaction that has been performed but did not appear in the ledger is discarded and can be considered as invalid by Ripple users. Each validating server maintains a list of trusted servers known as Unique Node List (*UNL*); servers only trust the votes issued by other servers which are contained in their *UNL*. We detail and analyze Ripple's consensus protocol in Sect. 2.3.

Currently, 5 Ripple validating servers are run by Ripple Labs [7]; note however, that any entity can run its own server [34] (e.g., Snapswap [8]). By doing so, Ripple enables different institutions (e.g., banks which run their own servers) to reach a consensus with respect to the fate of financial transactions. For instance, in September 2014, Ripple Labs sealed a partnership agreement with two US banks which agreed to adopt Ripple's open-source distributed transaction infrastructure [9].

2.2   Ripple Transactions

Ripple currently supports six types of transactions [35], namely:

Payment: This is the most common type of transactions, and allows an entity to send funds from one account to another.

AccountSet: This transaction allows an entity to set options relevant for one's account. Notice that an `AccountSet` transaction enables the cancellation of a transaction with the same `SequenceNumber` provided that the transaction has not been incorporated yet in a validated ledger.

SetRegularKey: This transaction allows an entity to change/set the key used by the entity to sign future transactions.

OfferCreate: This transaction expresses an intent to exchange currencies.

OfferCancel: This transaction removes an offer from the ledger.

TrustSet: This transaction creates (or modifies) a trust link between two accounts.

As shown in Table 1, all six transaction types contain some common fields. Notice that for any entity to open an account in Ripple, it has to issue a payment with a value larger than the minimum XRP (i.e., 20 XRPs) to an account number which does not exist yet. Once this transaction is processed, a new `AccountRoot` node will be added to the global ledger to reflect the newly-created account.

2.3   The Consensus Protocol

As mentioned earlier, Ripple's consensus protocol is an asynchronous round-based protocol which is executed by the network's validating servers. At the end of every round, a new last closed ledger is published by all involved servers. The consensus protocol comprises three phases: the collection phase, the consensus phase, and the ledger closing phase.

In the collection phase, the validating servers collect the transactions that they receive from the network. Recall that transactions are typically broadcasted in the network. Upon receiving a transaction, validating servers check its authenticity; for that purpose, they verify the issuer's public key (from the ledger), and they check the validity of the corresponding signature. Transactions which come equipped with valid signatures are temporarily stored in the *candidate set CS* for subsequent validation. The validating servers then check the correctness of transactions stored in *CS*; this includes verifying that enough credit is available in the issuing account by going over the history of all transactions pertaining to that account (in case of an XRP transactions), or the existence of a trust path between the sender and receiver (in case of an IOU payment), etc. Each validating server packages validated transactions in an (authenticated) proposal and broadcasts its proposal in the network. In Ripple, this is achieved by constructing a hash tree of all validated transactions, and subsequently signing the root of the tree.

When validating server v receives a new proposal from the network, it checks that the proposal's issuer is a server which appears in its *UNL* and verifies the

Table 1. Common fields contained in all Ripple transaction types.

Field	Internal Type	Description
Account	Account	The unique address of the account that initiated the transaction
AccountTxnID	Hash256	(Optional) Hash value identifying another transaction. This field allows the chaining of two transactions together, so that a current transaction is only valid unless the previous one (by Sequence Number) is also valid and matches the hash
Fee	Amount	(Required) Integer amount of XRP, in drops, to be destroyed as a fee for distributing this transaction to the network
Flags	UInt32	(Optional) Set of bit-flags for this transaction
LastLedgerSeq	UInt32	(Optional) Highest ledger sequence number that a transaction can appear in
Memos	Array	(Optional) Additional information used to identify this transaction
Sequence	UInt32	(Required) A transaction is only valid if the sequence number is exactly 1 greater than the last-validated transaction from the same account
SigningPubKey	PubKey	(Required) ASCII representation of the public key that corresponds to the private key used to sign this transaction
SourceTag	UInt32	(Optional) Arbitrary integer used to identify the reason for this payment
TransactionType	UInt16	The type of transaction
TxnSignature	VariableLength	(Required) Transaction signature

correctness of the transactions included in the received proposal. In the positive case, these transactions are included into the locally managed transactions list TL_v. Moreover, the server maintains a vote list $Vote_t$ for every transaction t. This list is updated according to the received proposal. That is, if the transaction t is part of the proposal received from a server w ($t \in TL_v$ and $w \in UNL_v$), v will register t in $Vote_t$.

During the consensus phase, a validating server continuously processes and sends proposals. Here, the validating server only sends proposals which are agreed by more than θ percent of the servers in its UNL. This threshold value θ is initially set to 50 % and is gradually increased in each iteration by 10 % – until a proposal reaches consensus from 80 % of the servers in the UNL. Iterations are triggered by a local timer maintained by each validating server.

As shown in Algorithm 1, once a transaction t reaches 80 % acceptance, it will be removed from the candidate set, checked for double-spending (i.e., by checking

---

$L \leftarrow PreviousLedger$
foreach $t \in TL_v$ **do**
    if $\left(\frac{|Vote_t|}{|UNL_v|} \geq 0.8 \right)$ **then**
        if $t \notin L$ **then**
            | $L.\text{apply}(t)$
        $CS_v \leftarrow CS_v \setminus \{t\}$

    $TL_v \leftarrow TL_v \setminus \{t\}$
    $Vote_t \leftarrow \theta$
end
$\sigma_L \leftarrow Sign(H(L))$
Broadcast (L, σ_L)
foreach $u \in UNL_v$ **do**
    | Receive (L_u, σ_{L_u})
end
Find the ledger L' among L_u's with valid signature which has clear majority
(more than 80 %)
$CurrentLedger \leftarrow L'$

Algorithm 1. Closing the ledger

---

against the transactions included in the ledger). This transaction will be then
appended to the ledger ($L.\text{apply}(t)$), and the balance of the sender/recipient will
be appropriately updated. Each validating server v will forward a signed hash
of its version of L in the network. A ledger is considered validated (and closed)
by server v when a clear majority 80 % of validating servers which are contained
in v's UNL also sign the same ledger L. After closing the ledger, transactions
which have been received during the consensus phase will be processed, and the
next round will start.

2.4   Ripple Vs. Bitcoin

In what follows, we briefly discuss the security and privacy provisions of Ripple
in relation to the well-investigated Bitcoin system.

Security: Similar to Bitcoin, Ripple relies on ECDSA signatures to ensure the
authenticity and non-repudiation of transactions in the system. Furthermore,
since Ripple is an open payment system (like Bitcoin), all transactions and their
orders of execution are publicly available. This ensures the detection of any
double-spending attempt (and of malformed transactions). In Ripple, validating
servers check the log of all transactions in order to select and vote for the correct
transactions in the system. In this way, Ripple adopts a voting scheme across
all validating servers (one vote per each validating server); the transactions for
which (80 % of) the validators agree upon are considered to be valid [36]. Ripple
Labs claim it is easy to identify colluding validators and recommend users to
choose a set of heterogenous validators which are unlikely to be coerced as a
group and are unlikely to collude.

Notice that if validators refuse to come to a consensus with each other, this is detectable by other validators, which then pronounce the network broken. In this case, the only way to resolve the problem would be to manually analyze the signed validations and proposals to see which validators were being unreasonable and for all honest participants to remove those validators from the *UNLs* (i.e., from the lists of validators they try to come to a consensus with). As far as we are aware, there is no formal security treatment of the correctness of Ripple's consensus protocol; this protocol has recently received some criticism [13,25]. In Sect. 3, we show that the current choice of parameters does not prevent the occurrence of forks in the system, and we give a necessary and sufficient condition to prevent any fork in the system.

In contrast, Bitcoin security has been thoroughly investigated in numerous studies, and as such is better understood than Ripple. In Bitcoin, transaction security is guaranteed by means of Proof of Work (PoW) which replaces the vote per validating server notion of Ripple, with a vote per computing power of the miners that are solving the PoW. Unlike Ripple, once transactions are confirmed in the global ledger (i.e., once transactions receive six confirmation blocks), it is computationally infeasible to modify these transactions [30]. In contrast, in Ripple, if at any instant in time the majority of the validating servers becomes malicious, then they can rewrite the entire history of transactions in the system. Recall that, at the time of writing, there are only a handful of Ripple validating servers which are mostly maintained by the Ripple Labs; if these servers are compromised, then the security of Ripple is at risk.

Fast Payments: In Bitcoin, payments are confirmed by means of PoW in Bitcoin blocks every 10 min on average. A study in [26] has shown that the generation of Bitcoin blocks follows a geometric distribution with parameter 0.19. This means that, since transactions are only confirmed after the generation of six consecutive blocks, then a payment is only confirmed after 1 hour on average. Although Bitcoin still recommends merchants to accept fast payments—where the time between the exchange of currency and goods is short (i.e., in the order of few seconds), several attacks have been reported against fast payments in Bitcoin [26]; a best-effort countermeasure has also been included in the Bitcoin client [26].

Unlike Bitcoin, Ripple inherently supports fast payments. As shown in Fig. 3(a), almost all ledgers are closed within few seconds; this also suggests that payments in Ripple can be verified after few seconds from being executed.

Privacy and Anonymity: Ripple and Bitcoin are instances of open payment systems. In an open payment system, *all* transactions that occur in the system are publicly announced. Here, user anonymity is ensured through the reliance on pseudonyms and/or anonymizing networks, such as TOR [15]. Users are also expected to have several accounts (corresponding to different pseudonyms) in order to prevent the leakage of their total account balance. Notice that, in Bitcoin, transactions can take different inputs, which originate from different accounts. This is not the case in Ripple, in which payments typically have a single account as input.

Although user identities are protected in Ripple and Bitcoin, the transactional behavior of users (i.e., time and amount of transactions) is leaked in the process—since transactions are publicly announced in the system. In this respect, several recent studies have shown the limits of privacy in open payment systems [11,31,37]. There are also several proposals for enhancing user privacy in these systems; most proposals leverage zero-knowledge proofs of knowledge and cryptographic accumulators in order to prevent tracking of expenditure in the network [10,28]. Although most of these studies focus on the Bitcoin system, we argue that they equally apply to Ripple. Recently, a secure privacy-preserving payment protocol for credit networks which provides transaction obliviousness has been proposed [29].

Clients, Protocol Update, and Maintenance: Both Ripple and Bitcoin are currently open source, which allows any entity to build and release its own software client to interface with either systems. The official clients for Bitcoin and Ripple are however maintained and regularly updated by the Bitcoin foundation, and Ripple Labs respectively. Bitcoin clients can also run on resource-constrained devices such as mobile phones—owing to the simple payment verification of Bitcoin [30]. As far as we are aware, there exists no secure lightweight version of Ripple.

Notice that all changes to the official Bitcoin client are publicly discussed in online forums, well justified, and voted on amongst Bitcoin developers [18]. This process is however less transparent in Ripple.

((De-)Centralized Deployment: Ripple and Bitcoin leverage completely decentralized protocols. Nevertheless, a recent study has shown the limits of decentralization in the current deployment of Bitcoin; here, it was shown that only a handful of entities can control the security of all Bitcoin transactions [18].

We argue that the current deployment of Ripple is also centralized. At the time of writing, most validating servers are run by Ripple Labs. Although there are few other servers that are run by external entities, the default list of validating servers for all clients point to the ones maintained by Ripple Labs. This also suggests that Ripple Labs can control the security of all transactions that occur in the Ripple system. Moreover, Ripple Labs and its founders retain a considerable fraction of XRPs; this represents the largest holdback of any crypto-currency [4] and suggests that Ripple Labs can currently effectively control Ripple's economy. We contrast this to Bitcoin, where the current system deployment is not entirely decentralized, yet the entities which control the security of transactions, the protocol maintenance and update, and the creation of new coins are distinct [18]. In Ripple, the same entity, *Ripple Labs*, controls the fate of the entire system.

3   Analysis of Forking in Ripple

The security of Ripple relies on the fact that the majority of the validating servers are honest and correctly verify all the received transactions. Here, ledgers fork constitute a major threat to the correct operations of the system. Forks can occur if two conflicting ledgers get clear majority votes, and could lead to double-spending attacks [26].

Ripple claims that forks cannot occur if the UNL of any two servers u and v intersect in at least 20 % of the remaining validating servers ID [38]:

$$|UNL_u \cap UNL_v| \geq \frac{1}{5} \max\{|UNL_u|, |UNL_v|\} \forall u, v. \tag{1}$$

Recently, several forks [13,25] however lead to serious concerns about the correctness of the Ripple consensus protocol and the requirements for forks in the system. In what follows, we take a second look at the conditions for which a fork can occur in Ripple. More precisely, we investigate the values $w_{u,v}$, such that:

$$|UNL_u \cap UNL_v| \geq w_{u,v}(\max\{|UNL_u|, |UNL_v|\}) \forall u, v. \tag{2}$$

Notice that in the current specification of Ripple, $w_{u,v} = 0.2$ is required. We now show that this threshold is not sufficient to prevent forks in the system by means of a counter-example. Namely, consider the situation where $|UNL_u| = |UNL_v| = 5$ and $|UNL_u \cap UNL_v| = 2$. Obviously, it holds that $|UNL_u \cap UNL_v| = 0.4 \cdot \max\{|UNL_u|, |UNL_v|\}$. Assume now that one server in $UNL_u \cap UNL_v$ votes for L_1 and the other for (conflicting ledger) L_2. Moreover, assume that all servers in $UNL_u \setminus UNL_v$ vote for L_1 and similarly all servers in $UNL_v \setminus UNL_u$ vote for L_2. This means that a majority of 80 % in UNL_u vote for L_1 and likewise a majority of 80 % in UNL_v vote for L_2. This clearly results in a fork in the system.

As this example shows, the condition displayed in Eq. 2 cannot prevent forks in general for values $w_{u,v} \leq 0.4$. In the following, we will prove that if the intersection set size between the UNL of any two servers is more than 40 % of size of the largest UNL, that is $w_{u,v} > 0.4$, then forks in Ripple are impossible. The consequence is that forks in Ripple are impossible *if and only if*

$$|UNL_u \cap UNL_v| > 0.4 \cdot \max\{|UNL_u|, |UNL_v|\} \forall u, v. \tag{3}$$

For the sake of readability, we denote the threshold value for any transaction to get clear majority votes by ρ where $0.5 < \rho \leq 1$. We then prove that forks are not possible if $w_{u,v} > \rho/2$ for any servers u and v.

Recall that a fork refers to the situation that two different validating servers u and v agree on conflicting ledgers $L_1 \neq L_2$. This means that at least a fraction ρ of servers in UNL_u agree on ledger L_1 and at least a fraction ρ of servers in UNL_v agree on ledger L_2. We consider the following sets:

$$A := UNL_u \setminus UNL_v, \quad B := UNL_u \cap UNL_v, \quad C := UNL_v \setminus UNL_u. \tag{4}$$

For each server contained in $UNL_u \cup UNL_v$, three possible cases my occur:

Case 1: The server publishes ledger L_1.
Case 2: The server publishes ledger L_2.
Case 3: The server does not reply or publishes any other ledger besides L_1 and L_2.

In the sequel, we denote by A_1 the subset of servers in set A publishing L_1, by A_2 the subset of servers in A publishing L_2, and by A_3 the subset of servers publishing neither L_1 nor L_2. Clearly, A_1, A_2 and A_3 are mutually exclusive, and $|A_1| + |A_2| + |A_3| = |A|$. Analogously, we define sets B_1, B_2, B_3, C_1, C_2, and C_3 (cf. Eq. 4).

Necessary Conditions for Forking: According to the specification of Ripple, it holds that if more than a fraction ρ of the servers present in any server's *UNL* publishes the same validation ledger hash, that ledger will be accepted by that server. Hence,

1. Ledger L_1 will be accepted by server u if and only if

$$|A_1| + |B_1| \geq \rho(|A_1| + |A_2| + |A_3| + |B_1| + |B_2| + |B_3|)$$
$$\Leftrightarrow (1 - \rho)(|A_1| + |B_1|) \geq \rho(|A_2| + |A_3| + |B_2| + |B_3|)$$
$$\Leftrightarrow |A_1| + |B_1| \geq \frac{\rho}{1 - \rho}(|A_2| + |A_3| + |B_2| + |B_3|) \tag{5}$$

2. Likewise, ledger L_2 will be accepted by server v if and only if

$$|B_2| + |C_2| \geq \frac{\rho}{1 - \rho}(|B_1| + |B_3| + |C_1| + |C_3|) \tag{6}$$

Minimum Intersection Size: Notice that a fork is only possible if both Eqs. 5 and 6 are satisfied. Assuming that $|UNL_u \cap UNL_v| > w_{u,v} \max\{|UNL_u|, |UNL_v|\} \forall u, v$, we show in what follows that $w_{u,v} \geq 0.4$ ensures that no fork can occur in Ripple.

Observe that:

$$|UNL_u \cap UNL_v| > w_{u,v} \cdot |UNL_u|$$
$$|B_1| + |B_2| + |B_3| > w_{u,v}(|A_1| + |A_2| + |A_3| + |B_1| + |B_2| + |B_3|)$$
$$(1 - w_{u,v})(|B_1| + |B_2| + |B_3|) > w_{u,v}(|A_1| + |A_2| + |A_3|)$$
$$(|B_1| + |B_2| + |B_3|) > \frac{w_{u,v}}{1 - w_{u,v}}(|A_1| + |A_2| + |A_3|) \tag{7}$$

Similarly, we have:

$$(|B_1| + |B_2| + |B_3|) > \frac{w_{u,v}}{1 - w_{u,v}}(|C_1| + |C_2| + |C_3|) \tag{8}$$

Now, adding Eqs. (7) and (8) we get,

$$(|B_1| + |B_2| + |B_3|) > \frac{w_{u,v}}{2(1 - w_{u,v})}(|A_1| + |A_2| + |A_3| + |C_1| + |C_2| + |C_3|) \tag{9}$$

Assuming that both Eqs. 5 and 6 are satisfied, it follows that:

$$|A_1| + |B_1| + |B_2| + |C_2| \geq \frac{\rho}{1 - \rho}(|A_2| + |B_2| + |B_1| + |C_1| + |A_3| + |C_3|)$$
$$+ \frac{2\rho}{1 - \rho}|B_3|$$
$$|A_1| + |C_2| \geq \frac{\rho}{1 - \rho}(|A_2| + |C_1| + |A_3| + |C_3|)$$
$$+ \frac{2\rho - 1}{1 - \rho}(|B_1| + |B_2| + |B_3|) + \frac{1}{1 - \rho}|B_3|. \tag{10}$$

Combining Eqs. 9 and 10, we get the following strict inequality:

$$|A_1| + |C_2| > \frac{\rho}{1 - \rho}(|A_2| + |C_1| + |A_3| + |C_3|)$$

$$+ \frac{(2\rho - 1)w_{u,v}}{2(1 - \rho)(1 - w_{u,v})}(|A_1| + |A_2| + |A_3| + |C_1| + |C_2| + |C_3|)$$

$$+ \frac{1}{1 - \rho}|B_3|$$

This can be rephrased to:

$$(1 - \frac{(2\rho - 1)w_{u,v}}{2(1 - \rho)(1 - w_{u,v})}) >$$

$$\underbrace{\frac{1}{(|A_1| + |C_2|)}}_{\geq 0} \cdot \left[(\underbrace{\frac{\rho}{1 - \rho}}_{\geq 0} + \underbrace{\frac{(2\rho - 1)w_{u,v}}{2(1 - \rho)(1 - w_{u,v})}}_{\geq 0}) \underbrace{(|A_2| + |A_3| + |C_1| + |C_3|)}_{\geq 0} + \underbrace{\frac{1}{1 - \rho}|B_3|}_{\geq 0} \right]$$

As already marked, the right-hand side is ≥ 0. Hence, this cannot hold if:

$$(1 - \frac{(2\rho - 1)w_{u,v}}{2(1 - \rho)(1 - w_{u,v})}) \leq 0$$

$$(2 - 2\rho)(1 - w_{u,v}) - (2\rho - 1)w_{u,v} \leq 0$$

$$(2 - 2\rho - w_{u,v}) \leq 0$$

$$w_{u,v} \geq 2(1 - \rho)$$

In consequence, if $|UNL_i \cap UNL_j| > 2(1 - \rho)\max\{|UNL_i|, |UNL_j|\}\forall i, j$, then no fork can occur in Ripple for sure. Since $\rho = 0.8$ in the current Ripple system, a sufficient condition for preventing forks is to ensure $w_{u,v} > 0.4$ for all servers u and v.

4   Ripple Under the Hood

In this section, we study the current deployment of Ripple. For that purpose, we extract relevant statistics about the use of Ripple in the period from January 2013 till January 2015.

At the time of writing, there are more than 12 million ledgers starting from January 2013 [33]. Ripple also claims to have little above 150,000 accounts with an average of almost 170 accounts created per day since the launch of the system.

To better understand the current usage and dynamics in Ripple, we built a parser using Java, which uses the Websocket protocol to download and parse ledgers created in the period between January 2013 and January 2015 from the main Ripple server[1], and from three auxiliary servers[2]. Our parser leverages the

---

[1] Available from s1.ripple.com.
[2] Available from s-east.ripple.com, and s-west.ripple.com.

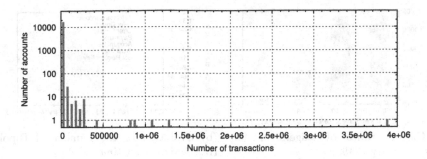

Fig. 2. Distribution of the number of transactions per address in Ripple in January/February 2015.

Tyrus library [3] and a connection pool to access a local MySQL database which stores information acquired from the downloaded ledgers. For ease of presentation, we divide the period of study into 5 different time intervals comprising of 2 months each. In total, we parsed a total of 4,645,799 ledgers comprising over 33,304,766 transactions, and 153,637 total accounts.

Transactions per account: Figure 2 depicts the distribution of transactions per Ripple account in the parsed ledgers. Our results show that most ($> 99\,\%$) Ripple accounts have performed very few transactions in the system. Notice that this does not necessarily provide evidence that Ripple users are inactive; for example, privacy-aware users could set up, in theory, different accounts for each transaction they perform in order to prevent the leakage of their total balance in the system [11].

Ledger closing time: In Fig. 3(a), we measure the time elapsed between the creation of two successive ledgers in the time interval spanning across January and February 2015. Our results show that indeed most ledgers are finalized in few seconds; while we observe that some ledgers take around 30–40 s to close, almost 99 % of the ledgers created in the first two months of 2015 were closed in less than 20 s.

Transactions dynamics over time: In Fig. 3(b), we compute the number of performed Ripple transactions over time. Our findings show that the number of transactions performed in the Ripple system has been steadily increasing over time. For instance, in the first two months of 2015, more than 20,000,000 Ripple transactions have been executed. Our findings however indicate that more than 60 % of these transactions correspond to Offers in the system—and not to actual payments—while OfferCancel transactions correspond to 20 % of the total transactions in the system. Payment transactions comprise less than 15 % of the total transactions in the system, and are only increasing marginally over time. For example, there are almost 33,000 payment transactions per day, on average, starting from March 2014 and until February 2015. Our results also show that there were a total of 6765 distinct accounts whose trust had been extended to using TrustSet transactions.

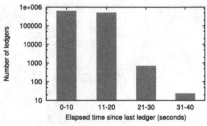

(a) Closure times of ledgers in January/February 2015.

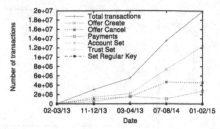

(b) Evolution of the number of Ripple transactions over time.

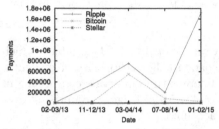

(c) Evolution of the number of XRP payments and trade of digital currencies over time.

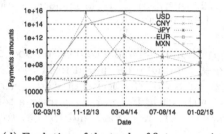

(d) Evolution of the trade of fiat currencies over time.

Fig. 3. Characterization of the Ripple system in the period between January 2013 and January 2015.

In Fig. 3(c) and (d), we further analyze the payment transactions performed in the Ripple system; our findings show that direct XRP to XRP transactions comprise the majority of transactions performed in Ripple. For example, in the first two months of 2015, there were almost 2 million payments in Ripple (cf. Fig. 3(b)); as shown in Fig. 3(c), almost 1.8 million of those correspond to direct XRP transactions.

Although Ripple was used as a medium to exchange BTCs in March/April 2014, we further remark that Bitcoin trade in Ripple has considerably shrunk in the first two months of 2015 to less than 1 % of the performed payments. Moreover, in July/August 2014, our findings suggest that the Ripple system has witnessed a considerable setback in the number of direct XRP transactions, and in the trade of digital currencies, such as Bitcoin. We also remark that other digital currencies, such as Stellar, are rarely traded in the Ripple system.

In terms of the trade of fiat currencies, our results show that trading of fiat currencies represents almost 10 % of the actual payments in Ripple in the start of 2015. However, as shown in Fig. 3(d), our findings suggest that extremely large amounts of fiat currencies are being traded in Ripple. For instance, we measure the trading of almost $1 \cdot 10^{16}$ USD in March/April 2014. Our results show that only a handful of payments trade such obscene amounts; we believe that these payments are not actual payments, but could result from testing/debugging in the system[3].

---

[3] Recall that Ripple has no means to enforce the execution of payments.

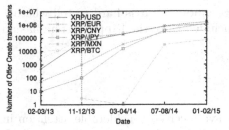
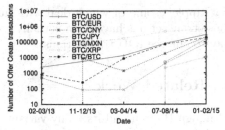

(a) Evolution of XRP-based trade over time.

(b) Evolution of BTC-based trade over time.

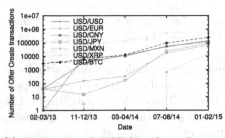
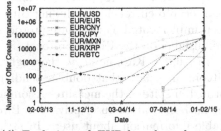

(c) Evolution of USD-based trade over time.

(d) Evolution of EUR-based trade over time.

Fig. 4. Characterization of IOU payments in the Ripple system over time starting from February 2013.

OfferCreate evolution: Figure 4(a), (b), (c), and (d) depict the distribution of OfferCreate transactions in the system. Recall that these transactions comprise almost 60 % of Ripple transactions, and are mainly performed by the market makers that populate the system. Our findings suggest that, as expected, the biggest market makers offer the trading of XRP to BTCs, USD, and EUR. Additional market makers offering the trade of XRP to CNY and JPY emerged starting from November 2013, and March 2014, respectively. There are also a considerable number of Offers for trading major fiat currencies such as USD and EUR. Although the total number of offers is growing over time, we do not find evidence for growth of the corresponding Ripple payments.

Summary of findings: In summary, our results suggest that—although it has been introduced almost 2 years ago—Ripple is still far from being used as a trade platform. Ripple advertises a large number of active accounts [33]. However, we do not find strong evidence that users are active in Ripple; most accounts contain a small number of XRPs—which users e.g., could have received from the one of the many giveaways organized by Ripple Labs [32]. Moreover, although the number of transactions in Ripple seems to be considerably increasing over time, most of the transactions in the system (>70 %) correspond to OfferCreate and OfferCancel transaction types. The number of actual payments in the system is only marginally increasing over time, and is dominated by direct XRP payments. Finally, although there are a number of currency exchanges performed via Ripple—some of which deal with huge amounts—it is hard to tell whether those transactions have been actually concluded since the Ripple system has no way to enforce IOU transactions.

5 Related Work

Although Bitcoin and its many variants have received considerable attention in the literature, there are surprisingly no studies—as far as we are aware—which analyze Ripple.

Bonneau *et al.* [12] provide a comprehensive exposition of the second generation crypto-currencies, including Bitcoin and the many alternatives that have been implemented as alternate protocols. However, this work does not provide any insights on the Ripple protocol.

In [26,27], Karame *et al.* thoroughly investigate double-spending attacks in Bitcoin and show that double-spending fast payments in Bitcoin can be performed in spite of the measures recommended by Bitcoin developers. In [11,17], the authors evaluate user privacy in Bitcoin and show that Bitcoin leaks considerable information about users. In [31], Ober *et al.* studied the time-evolution properties of Bitcoin. In [29], Moreno-Sanchez *et al.* propose a provably secure privacy-preserving payment protocol for credit networks, such as Ripple.

6 Conclusion

In this paper, we studied the current deployment of the Ripple payment system. We showed that although Ripple leverages a decentralized consensus protocol, the current deployment of Ripple is not decentralized, and offers unconditional power for Ripple Labs to control the fate and security of all Ripple transactions.

We also showed that the currently adopted assumptions to prevent the occurrence of forks in the system are insufficient. Namely, our findings show that the intersection set size between the *UNL* of any two validating servers needs to be more than 40 % of the maximum *UNL* set size in order to ensure the absence of any fork in the system. Finally, we analyzed the current usage of the Ripple system; our results show that most users in Ripple seem inactive, and that Ripple is still not being widely used as a trade platform.

Our results motivate the need for a rigorous analysis of the Ripple system prior to any large scale deployment. We therefore hope that our findings solicit further research in this area.

Acknowledgements. The authors would like to thank Ludovic Barman for the help in extracting the relevant statistics from the Ripple ledgers.

References

1. Litecoin: Open source P2P internet currency. https://litecoin.org/
2. Namecoin: A trust anchor for the internet. https://namecoin.info/
3. Project tyrus. https://tyrus.java.net/
4. Ripple. http://en.wikipedia.org/wiki/Ripple_%28payment_protocol%29
5. Ripple labs circling 30m$ in funding. http://www.pymnts.com/news/2015/ripple-labs-circling-30m-in-funding/#.VRLnJfnF98F
6. Ripple: Opening access to finance. https://ripple.com/
7. Ripple validating servers. https://ripple.com/ripple.txt
8. Snapswap Ripple gateway. https://snapswap.us/#/
9. US banks announce Ripple protocol integration. http://www.coindesk.com/us-banks-announce-ripple-protocol-integration/
10. Androulaki, E., Karame, G.O.: Hiding transaction amounts and balances in Bitcoin. In: Trust and Trustworthy Computing - 7th International Conference, TRUST 2014, Heraklion, Crete, Greece, 30 June – 2 July, 2014. Proceedings, pp. 161–178 (2014)
11. Androulaki, E., Karame, G.O., Roeschlin, M., Scherer, T., Capkun, S.: Evaluating user privacy in bitcoin. In: Sadeghi, A.-R. (ed.) FC 2013. LNCS, vol. 7859, pp. 34–51. Springer, Heidelberg (2013)
12. Bonneau, J., Miller, A., Clark, J., Narayanan, A., Kroll, J.A., Felten, E.W.: Research perspectives and challenges for Bitcoin and cryptocurrencies. In: 2015 IEEE Symposium on Security and Privacy, May 2015
13. Buterin, V.: Bitcoin network shaken by blockchain fork. https://bitcoinmagazine.com/3668/bitcoin-network-shaken-by-blockchain-fork/
14. Coinist Inc., Ripple gateways. https://coinist.co/ripple/gateways
15. Dingledine, R., Mathewson, N., Syverson, P.: Tor: The second-generation onion router. In: Proceedings of the 13th Conference on USENIX Security Symposium, SSYM 2004, Berkeley, CA, USA, vol. 13, p. 21. USENIX Association (2004)
16. Elias, M.: Bitcoin: Tempering the digital ring of gyges or implausible pecuniary privacy (2011). http://ssrn.com/abstract=1937769
17. Gervais, A., Capkun, S., Karame, G.O., Gruber, D.: On the privacy provisions of bloom filters in lightweight bitcoin clients. In: Proceedings of the 30th Annual Computer Security Applications Conference, ACSAC 2014, 8–12 December, 2014, New Orleans, LA, USA, pp. 326–335 (2014)
18. Gervais, A., Karame, G.O., Capkun, V., Capkun, S.: Is Bitcoin a decentralized currency? IEEE Secur. Priv. 12(3), 54–60 (2014)
19. Ghosh, A., Mahdian, M., Reeves, D.M., Pennock, D.M., Fugger, R.: Mechanism design on trust networks. In: Deng, X., Graham, F.C. (eds.) WINE 2007. LNCS, vol. 4858, pp. 257–268. Springer, Heidelberg (2007)
20. International Ripple Business Association. Listed businesses. http://www.xrpga.org/listed-businesses.html
21. International Ripple Business Association. Ripple exchangers. http://www.xrpga.org/exchangers.html
22. International Ripple Business Association. Ripple gateways. http://www.xrpga.org/gateways.html
23. International Ripple Business Association. Ripple market makers. http://www.xrpga.org/market-makers.html
24. International Ripple Business Association. Ripple merchants. http://www.xrpga.org/merchants.html

25. Joyes, K.: Safety, liveness and fault tolerance - the consensus choices. https://www. stellar.org/blog/safety_liveness_and_fault_tolerance_consensus_choice/
26. Karame, G.O., Androulaki, E., Capkun, S.: Double-spending fast payments in Bitcoin. In: Proceedings of the 2012 ACM Conference on Computer and Communications Security, CCS 2012, New York, NY, USA, pp. 906–917. ACM (2012)
27. Karame, G.O., Androulaki, E., Roeschlin, M., Gervais, A., Čapkun, S.: Misbehavior in Bitcoin: a study of double-spending and accountability. ACM Trans. Inf. Syst. Secur., 18(1), 2:1–2:32 (2015)
28. Miers, I., Garman, C., Green, M., Rubin, A.D.: Zerocoin: anonymous distributed e-cash from Bitcoin. In: Proceedings of the 2013 IEEE Symposium on Security and Privacy, SP 2013, Washington, DC, USA, pp. 397–411. IEEE Computer Society (2013)
29. Moreno-Sanchez, P., Kate, A., Maffei, M., Pecina, K.: Privacy preserving payments in credit networks: Enabling trust with privacy in online marketplaces. In: Network and Distributed System Security (NDSS) Symposium (2015)
30. Nakamoto, S.: Bitcoin: A peer-to-peer electronic cash system (2009). http://bitcoin.org/bitcoin.pdf
31. Ober, M., Katzenbeisser, S., Hamacher, K.: Structure and anonymity of the Bitcoin transaction graph. Future Internet 5(2), 237–250 (2013)
32. Ripple Labs Inc., Giveaways - XRPtalk. https://xrptalk.org/forum/105-giveaways/
33. Ripple Labs Inc., Ripple charts. https://www.ripplecharts.com
34. Ripple Labs Inc., Setup a validating server. https://wiki.ripple.com/Setup_a_validating_server
35. Ripple Labs Inc., Transactions. https://ripple.com/build/transactions/
36. Ripple Labs Inc., Why is Ripple not vulnerable to Bitcoin's 51 % attack?
37. Ron, D., Shamir, A.: Quantitative analysis of the full bitcoin transaction graph. In: Sadeghi, A.-R. (ed.) FC 2013. LNCS, vol. 7859, pp. 6–24. Springer, Heidelberg (2013)
38. Schwartz, D., Youngs, N., Britto, A.: The Ripple protocol consensus algorithm (2014). https://ripple.com/files/ripple_consensus_whitepaper.pdf

Time to Rethink: Trust Brokerage Using Trusted Execution Environments

Patrick Koeberl[1], Vinay Phegade[2], Anand Rajan[2], Thomas Schneider[3],
Steffen Schulz[1]([✉]), and Maria Zhdanova[4]

[1] Intel Labs, Darmstadt, Germany
{patrick.koeberl,steffen.schulz}@intel.com
[2] Intel Labs, Portland, ON, USA
{vinay.phegade,anand.rajan}@intel.com
[3] TU Darmstadt, Darmstadt, Germany
thomas.schneider@ec-spride.de
[4] Fraunhofer SIT, Darmstadt, Germany
maria.zhdanova@sit.fraunhofer.de

Abstract. Mining and analysis of digital data has the potential to provide improved quality of life and offer even life-saving insights. However, loss of privacy or secret information would be detrimental to these goals and inhibit widespread application. Traditional data protection measures tend to result in the formation of data silos, severely limiting the scope and yield of "Big Data". Technology such as privacy-preserving multiparty computation (MPC) and data de-identification can break these silos enabling privacy-preserving computation. However, currently available de-identification schemes tend to suffer from privacy/utility trade-offs, and MPC has found deployment only in niche applications.

As the assurance and availability of hardware-based Trusted Execution Environments (TEEs) is increasing, we propose an alternative direction of using TEEs as "neutral" environments for efficient yet secure multi-party computation. To this end, we survey the current state of the art, propose a generic initial solution architecture and identify remaining challenges.

1 Introduction

Large amounts of data are created and accumulated all around us. This trend is increasing and data is commonly named the digital fuel of the 21st century. In fact, analyzing such "big data" has huge expected business value. Already today, many applications in all areas of life benefit from such big data analysis ranging

Thomas Schneider—This work has been co-funded by the European Union (EU FP7/2007-2013) grant agreement n. 609611 (PRACTICE), by the DFG project E3 within the CRC 1119 CROSSING, by the BMBF within EC SPRIDE, and by the Hessian LOEWE excellence initiative within CASED.
Maria Zhdanova—This work has been co-funded by the EU project PRIPARE ID 610613.

© Springer International Publishing Switzerland 2015
M. Conti et al. (Eds.): TRUST 2015, LNCS 9229, pp. 181–190, 2015.
DOI: 10.1007/978-3-319-22846-4_11

from "people you might know" in social networks, over rating and reputation systems on eBay, to product recommendations on Amazon. However, privacy and security of data is increasingly critical to these applications as consumers become aware of the risks associated with aggregating digital identities, payment information and personal profiles in the cloud. Similarly, companies are hesitant to make their data assets available for external analysis due to the risk of losing control or violating their clients' privacy. As a result, vast amounts of data remain locked in data silos, unavailable to use for business and research.

Breaking the Data Silos. A solution to privacy-preserving multiparty computation must assure that data owners retain control of the data during transfer, storage and processing. In addition to data confidentiality, it must be assured that privacy is maintained even when results of different computations are combined or correlated with public information. Privacy-preserving filtering schemes must be applied to prevent such attacks, and the system must allow the data owners to flexibly negotiate and enforce such policies. Finally, data owners must obtain assurances that the requested policies are enforced and able to revoke access on violation. However, even if a solution meets all these security and privacy requirements, which have been the focus of much prior work, it must also meet some key ecosystem requirements in order to qualify as a practical solution:

1. **Solution Cost:** This includes cost to design the solution, and total cost to run and maintain the solution during deployment. The cost will increase if the system is complex to design, maintain or requires frequent re-design for different usages. Enabling existing developer skill sets, leveraging tools and automation are important factors for broad ecosystem acceptance.
2. **Data Utility:** In order to assure the privacy and confidentiality of the computation, implementations may demand sacrifices on the extent and accuracy of data sets. An ideal implementation should not limit the available privacy/utility trade-offs.
3. **Performance & Scalability:** Computational performance is important for the overall cloud analytics scenario to be economically viable. For interactive applications, users require acceptable application responsiveness. Additionally, as data size grows from terabytes to petabytes, the computation should be able to scale to distributed storage and computation networks.

Our Contributions. This position paper proposes a TEE-based "trust brokerage" approach that enables multiple parties to compute under previously agreed security assurances. We review current approaches based on Secure Multi-Party Computation (MPC) and Data De-Identification (DDI) in Sect. 2, pointing to the significant recent advances in Trusted Execution Environments (TEEs). We then describe a generic TEE-based solution architecture in Sect. 3 and compare it with previous approaches. As expected, a TEE-based solution is more efficient than MPC and enables better data utility and flexibility than DDI. We conclude with a call to action in Sect. 4, detailing the major research challenges that must still be resolved to achieve a secure and scalable solution.

2   Research Developments and State of the Art

In the following we review the state of the art in secure multi-party computation (Sect. 2.1), data de-identification (Sect. 2.2), and trusted execution environments (Sect. 2.3).

2.1   Secure Multi-party Computation

Secure Multi-party Computation (MPC) was invented in the late 1980s [12,27]. It allows two or multiple parties to jointly evaluate a function on their joint inputs without revealing anything but the result of the computation.

During the first twenty years after its invention, MPC was perceived as a feasibility result of theoretical interest. However, the situation changed in 2004 where the Fairplay project presented the first MPC implementation [16]. Since then, MPC has received renewed interest and many tools have been

The first real-world deployment of MPC was the Danish sugar beets auction in 2009 [3]. Since then, some small companies have developed the first MPC products, e.g., Cybernetica's Sharemind[1] to analyze confidential data, The Alexandra Institute's Partisia[2] for auctions and exchanges, or Dyadic Security[3] to protect against server breaches. However, some major roadblocks remain for large-scale deployment of MPC, mainly due to its low performance and high design costs that do not yet meet RoI expectations.

The drawback of MPC is that protocols often represent the computation function as a Boolean circuit, which results in of billions of gates for realistic applications. The runtime and communication of today's most efficient MPC protocols is linear in the size of this circuit.

MPC is designed for a world without trusted third parties, which would otherwise be able to retrieve all necessary inputs, compute the function and return the output to participants. In fact, MPC literature often argues that such trusted third parties do not exist or point to the poor computation and I/O capabilities of smartcards. However, some researchers also suggested to improve MPC performance by extending it with trusted hardware, e.g., [7,13].

2.2   Data De-Identification (DDI)

Data De-identification (DDI) is a procedure where personally identifying information is removed from a data set to ensure that distinct data items cannot be linked to individuals. It is different from anonymization and pseudonymization in that some identifying information may be retained in the data or remain accessible to trusted parties. Depending on the context, various types of information may be considered personally identifying, for example, it was shown that 87 % of US citizens can be uniquely identified by the combination of ZIP code, date of birth, and sex [25]. Unlike direct identifiers which are easily masked or deleted,

---

[1] https://sharemind.cyber.ee.

[2] http://alexandra.dk/uk/expertise/products/partisia.

[3] https://www.dyadicsec.com.

such quasi-identifiers tend to be valuable for analytics and are often retained, leaving a risk of re-identification.

Methods for mitigating the risk of re-identification were presented as early as 1974 as part of Statistical Disclosure Control (SDC) [4]. SDC methods include (1) non-perturbative techniques that re-encode attributes without modifying initial values, (2) perturbative techniques which add noise, randomize or aggregate attributes, and (3) generation of synthetic data such that the initial relationships and characteristics are preserved. However, depending on the computation to be performed, such modifications can destroy the integrity of data, reduce their quality and change overall statistics, rendering them useless for analytics. Moreover, SDC does not consider the problem of combining results of multiple carefully crafted queries to extract private information [25].

The first formalized privacy protection model which considers the challenge of outsourcing data for processing by remote parties was introduced as k-anonymity in 2002 [25]. Generally, k-anonymity can be achieved, e.g., by generalizing or suppressing identifying attributes until the data item does not differ anymore from the other $k - 1$ items. However, neither k-anonymity nor its various variations achieve reasonable data utility while ensuring complete privacy [8].

Besides respondents privacy, two additional dimensions are distinguished when outsourcing sensitive data for external analytics today: the privacy of data owners and that of data users [5]. Owner privacy aims to protect both the data and associated knowledge, for example, data mining rules. This is the focus of privacy-preserving data mining which comprises a variety of methods from statistics and database theory to cryptography to allow sharing of data for analysis and publish the results without jeopardizing owner privacy [26]. Among these, differential privacy emerged to achieve strong privacy guarantees for statistical databases which does not depend on the background knowledge of an adversary (data linkage attacks) or her ability to perform series of random queries (database reconstruction attacks) [9]. Differential privacy considers the setting where a trusted database curator processes statistical queries of the users, using a randomized mechanism to ensure that the published results do not reveal if any single data item is part of the computation or not [10]. Several implementations have been proposed recently [10], e.g., Fuzz[4] and GUPT[5], however, the balance between data utility and privacy assurance remains a problem.

User privacy deals with hiding user access patterns to a remote data source, such as which particular item the user wanted to retrieve with the query. Private Information Retrieval (PIR) solves this problem with reasonable efficiency[6], though it does not scale well with the number of accessible records [5].

2.3   Advancements in Trusted Execution

Trusted Execution Environments (TEEs) allow the execution of software in such a way that the main operating system and other "untrusted" software outside the

---

[4] http://privacy.cis.upenn.edu/software.html.
[5] https://github.com/prashmohan/GUPT.
[6] http://percy.sourceforge.net/.

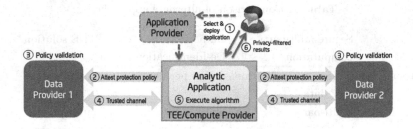

Fig. 1. Generic architecture of a Trust Brokerage solution.

TEE and its Trusted Computing Base (TCB) can neither violate the integrity of the performed computation nor the secrecy of processed data [1,11].

Considering this conservative definition, variations of TEE technology have been available and in fact widely deployed for many years in the form of secure co-processors, remote management interfaces and smartcards. However, these implementations are typically presented as fixed-function devices without an option for user programming.

With the rise of modern Trusted Computing technology, the benefits of controlled environments for verifiable (attested) code execution became more and more apparent. A significant body of research investigated the design and implementation of execution environments which would remain unaffected by security bugs in the "untrusted" or "non-secure" world and whose correct deployment, execution and outputs could be cryptographically confirmed by the underlying security infrastructure [17,21,24]). A variety of compelling usages have been examined under this model including secure online banking, credential storage, digital rights management and trusted virtual domains [2,18,24].

Today, we may be at the brink of a revolution in computer security as TEE technology becomes a wide-spread feature of computing platforms. Products such as ARM TrustZone and Texas Instruments M-Shield, which partition hardware in a simple secure/non-secure world view, are starting to embrace the concept of user-defined "trusted apps" which may be owned by different stakeholders and managed through a platform-independent API [11].

The Intel® Software Guard Extensions (SGX) [14,19] represent the next major step in this development. Intel® SGX enables users to run a large number of independent TEEs with only minor performance overhead [22]. It provides strong protection against software attacks including compromised hypervisors and platform firmware, and also defeats some common hardware attacks [1]. Application developers are offered a single TEE API across large segments of the computing spectrum, enabling modern software development and deployment practices such as "trusted app markets".

Following the trends in recent TEE research and attestation [6,15,20], we expect this development to continue down to low-end, resource-constrained devices, enabling an expansion of the trusted computing and TEE continuum across the whole IoT spectrum.

Table 1. Comparison of alternate approaches

	Secure multiparty computation	Data De-Identification	TEE solution
Solution Cost	design per application & data	design per data	design per application
Scalability	multi-party	multi-party	multi-party & interconnected
Data Utility	filters applied after computation	computation can be obstructed by filters	filters applied after computation
Performance	low	good	good
Assurance	high	good	good
Maturity	deployed in niches	widely deployed	new approach

3   TEE-based Trust Brokerage and Computation

We propose to leverage modern TEEs and attestation for trust brokerage and computing. As illustrated in Fig. 1, an analytics application running in a TEE would perform computation on data sourced from multiple, mutually untrusting data providers. The analytics application can be sourced from external software providers and executes in a neutral environment with strong protection against hardware and software attacks, while attestation and trusted channels enable negotiation and commit to security and privacy policies.

In more detail, we envision the following generic flow: (1) The user selects an analytics application, possibly from external application providers, and submits it for processing into the TEE of the compute provider. The application is bundled with one or more supported security and privacy policy options to be selected by the user. (2) The analytics application contacts the data providers, attesting to the application identity, and security and privacy configuration which were loaded into the TEE. (3) Before sourcing data to the analytics application, the data providers verify the information provided in the attestation report against the security and privacy policy associated with the requested data set. (4) If the request complies with the respective policies, the data is provided to the analytics application using a trusted channel. The data or channel may be subject to additional privacy protection filters depending on data protection policy. (5) The analytics application leverages TEE assurances to enforce the security and privacy policies while computing the result. Data providers may employ additional monitoring of requested data in order to validate the enforced protection policy. (6) On completion, the analytics application may apply additional privacy-filters as determined by the data protection policy before returning the results to the user.

Comparison of Approaches. Table 1 compares our TEE-based solution and previously pursued MPC and DDI approaches with regard to the requirements

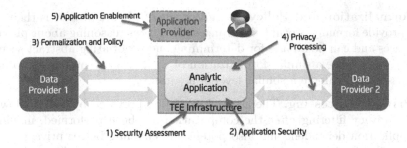

Fig. 2. Major challenges in TEE-based Trust Brokerage.

outlined in Sect. 1. As can be seen, MPC achieves high assurance by using well-established cryptographic techniques. Privacy filters can be applied after computation to provide privacy and confidentiality while maintaining high data utility. Unfortunately, MPC solutions incur a high performance penalty and require re-design for each application and data set. On the other hand, DDI solutions achieve good performance, however, data utility is lowered as the computation results may be distorted from privacy filters and designs cannot be generalized across data sets. In comparison, our TEE-based solution exhibits good performance as well as data utility. A lower solution cost is expected as applications and privacy filters can be ported once and re-used as enforced by TEE policy. Depending on the implementation, TEEs can deliver good assurance, however, additional research is required to analyze the security of TEEs in this scenario and mitigate possible attacks (see Sect. 4).

4 Research Challenges in TEE-based Trust Brokerage

While TEEs offer a scalable and efficient approach to trust brokerage, Fig. 2 points to a number of challenges which need to be addressed before a comprehensive solution can be achieved.

(1) Security Assessment. A number of TEE solutions have been proposed, and it can be expected that more products with different security properties will push into this market to cover the complete range of the computing spectrum. To maximize the use of this technology, it is necessary to investigate and assess their security properties and determine shortcomings based on the various possible usages, such as the resistance to side-channel attacks, malicious cloud providers and the level of isolation between multiple TEEs on the same platform.

(2) Application Security. While TEEs enable a major reduction of the trusted computing base, it must be expected that TEE applications will have their share of security vulnerabilities. Attackers will continue trying to trick users into installing trojan horses and making wrong decisions. Hence we must revisit known problems and solutions w.r.t. TEE applications, adopt modern defenses such as control-flow integrity and investigate the role that new deployment and attestation protocols might play.

(3) Formalization and Policy. An advantage of MPC and DDI is their ability to provide formally provable assurances. This helps reasoning about provided assurances and can be a basis for determining and negotiating abstract security policies. We require a similar formalization of TEE security properties to negotiate, assess and enforce a similar level of assurance.

(4) Privacy Processing. The assured execution provided by TEEs allows to enforce privacy filtering *after* the computation has been performed, making it less application dependent and also potentially enabling better privacy / data utility trade-offs. Processing larger data chunks or streams may also enable more efficient PIR schemes.

(5) Application Enablement. While prior work was focused on local TEE usages such as secure credential storage (see Sect. 2.3), we envision multi-party compute and collaboration services to enable a new secure cloud experience. Some applications may only require a generic TEE compatibility layer, while others will uniquely benefit from the deployment and policy negotiation technology supported by TEEs. Examples in this direction are the Contractual Anonymity System [23] and Verifiable Confidential Cloud Computing [22].

5   Conclusion

In this paper we propose TEE-based trust brokerage as a practical alternative to privacy-preserving multi-party computation. Recent advances in TEEs move us closer to a generic solution architecture that compares favorably with previous approaches in terms of efficiency, data utility and flexibility. A number of research challenges remain to be solved in order to meet security and scalability requirements; we detail these and suggest a path towards a comprehensive solution.

References

1. Asokan, N., Ekberg, J.E., Kostiainen, K., Rajan, A., Rozas, C., Sadeghi, A.R., Schulz, S., Wachsmann, C.: Mobile trusted computing. Proceedings of the IEEE **102**(8), 1189–1206 (2014)
2. Berger, S., Cáceres, R., Pendarakis, D.E., Sailer, R., Valdez, E., Perez, R., Schildhauer, W., Srinivasan, D.: TVDc: Managing security in the trusted virtual datacenter. Operating Syst. Rev. **42**(1), 40–47 (2008)
3. Bogetoft, P., Christensen, D.L., Damgård, I., Geisler, M., Jakobsen, T., Krøigaard, M., Nielsen, J.D., Nielsen, J.B., Nielsen, K., Pagter, J., Schwartzbach, M., Toft, T.: Secure multiparty computation goes live. In: Dingledine, R., Golle, P. (eds.) FC 2009. LNCS, vol. 5628, pp. 325–343. Springer, Heidelberg (2009)
4. Dalenius, T.: The invasion of privacy problem and statistics production. an overview. Statistik Tidskrift **12**, 213–225 (1974)
5. Danezis, G., Domingo-Ferrer, J., Hansen, M., Hoepman, J.H., Métayer, D.L., Tirtea, R., Schiffner, S.: Privacy and data protection by design - from policy to engineering. Technical report, ENISA (2015)

6. Defrawy, K.E., Francillon, A., Perito, D., Tsudik, G.: SMART: Secure and minimal architecture for (establishing a dynamic) root of trust. In: Network and Distributed System Security Symposium (NDSS 2012). The Internet Society (2012)
7. Demmler, D., Schneider, T., Zohner, M.: Ad-hoc secure two-party computation on mobile devices using hardware tokens. In: USENIX Security Symposium, pp. 893–908. USENIX (2014)
8. Domingo-Ferrer, J., Torra, V.: A critique of k-anonymity and some of its enhancements. In: Conference on Availability, Reliability and Security (ARES 2008) (2008)
9. Dwork, C.: Differential privacy. In: Bugliesi, M., Preneel, B., Sassone, V., Wegener, I. (eds.) ICALP 2006. LNCS, vol. 4052, pp. 1–12. Springer, Heidelberg (2006)
10. Dwork, C.: A firm foundation for private data analysis. Commun. ACM **54**(1), 86–95 (2011)
11. Global Platform: TEE system architecture v1.0 (2011). http://www.globalplatform.org/specificationsdevice.asp
12. Goldreich, O., Micali, S., Wigderson, A.: How to play any mental game or a completeness theorem for protocols with honest majority. In: Symposium on Theory of Computing (STOC 1987), pp. 218–229. ACM (1987)
13. Hazay, C., Lindell, Y.: Constructions of truly practical secure protocols using standard smartcards. In: ACM CCS 2008, pp. 491–500. ACM (2008)
14. Hoekstra, M., Lal, R., Pappachan, P., Phegade, V., Del Cuvillo, J.: Using innovative instructions to create trustworthy software solutions. In: Hardware and Architectural Support for Security and Privacy (HASP). ACM (2013)
15. Koeberl, P., Schulz, S., Sadeghi, A.R., Varadharajan, V.: Trustlite: A security architecture for tiny embedded devices. In: European Conference on Computer Systems (EuroSys). ACM (2014)
16. Malkhi, D., Nisan, N., Pinkas, B., Sella, Y.: Fairplay – a secure two-party computation system. In: USENIX Security Symposium, pp. 287–302. USENIX (2004)
17. McCune, J.M., Li, Y., Qu, N., Zhou, Z., Datta, A., Gligor, V., Perrig, A.: TrustVisor: Efficient TCB reduction and attestation. In: Security and Privacy (S&P), pp. 143–158. IEEE (2010)
18. McCune, J.M., Parno, B.J., Perrig, A., Reiter, M.K., Isozaki, H.: Flicker: An execution infrastructure for TCB minimization. In: European Conference on Computer Systems (EuroSys), pp. 315–328. ACM (2008)
19. McKeen, F., Alexandrovich, I., Berenzon, A., Rozas, C.V., Shafi, H., Shanbhogue, V., Savagaonkar, U.R.: Innovative instructions and software model for isolated execution. In: Hardware and Architectural Support for Security and Privacy (HASP). ACM (2013)
20. Noorman, J., Agten, P., Daniels, W., Strackx, R., Van Herrewege, A., Huygens, C., Preneel, B., Verbauwhede, I., Piessens, F.: Sancus: Low-cost trustworthy extensible networked devices with a zero-software trusted computing base. In; USENIX Security Symposium. USENIX (2013)
21. Pfitzmann, B., Riordan, J., Stüble, C., Waidner, M., Weber, A.: The PERSEUS system architecture. Technical report, RZ 3335 (#93381), IBM Research (2001)
22. Schuster, F., Costa, M., Fournet, C., Gkantsidis, C., Peinado, M., Mainar-Ruiz, G., Russinovich, M.: VC3: Trustworthy data analytics in the cloud using SGX. In: IEEE Security and Privacy (S&P 2015). IEEE (2015)
23. Schwartz, E.J., Brumley, D., McCune, J.M.: A contractual anonymity system. In: Network and Distributed System Security (NDSS). The Internet Society (2010)
24. Singaravelu, L., Pu, C., Haertig, H., Helmuth, C.: Reducing TCB complexity for security-sensitive applications: three case studies. In: European Conference on Computer Systems (EuroSys). ACM SIGOPS (2006)

25. Sweeney, L.: k-anonymity: A model for protecting privacy. Int. J. Uncertainty, Fuzziness Knowl.-Based Syst. **10**(05), 557–570 (2002)
26. Verykios, V.S., Bertino, E., Fovino, I.N., Provenza, L.P., Saygin, Y., Theodoridis, Y.: State-of-the-art in privacy preserving data mining. SIGMOD Rec. **33**(1), 50–57 (2004)
27. Yao, A.C.: How to generate and exchange secrets. In; Foundations of Computer Science (FOCS 1986). pp. 162–167. IEEE (1986)

Trust and Privacy

REWIRE – Revocation Without Resolution: A Privacy-Friendly Revocation Mechanism for Vehicular Ad-Hoc Networks

David Förster[1]([⊠]), Hans Löhr[1], Jan Zibuschka[1], and Frank Kargl[2,3]

[1] Robert Bosch GmbH, Stuttgart, Germany
{david.foerster,hans.loehr,jan.zibuschka}@de.bosch.com
[2] Ulm University, Ulm, Germany
[3] University of Twente, Enschede, The Netherlands
frank.kargl@uni-ulm.de

Abstract. We propose a novel mechanism for excluding misbehaving participants from a vehicular ad-hoc network (V2X system) that does not require resolution of pseudonyms. Our approach enables a revocation authority to exclude the sender of a given message from pseudonymous communication without resolving (or otherwise learning) his long-term identity. This is achieved by broadcasting (or geocasting) a request for self-revocation to which only the holder of the pseudonym in question will respond by revoking all relevant pseudonyms. Compliance to the request is enforced by a trusted component in each vehicle that ensures the integrity and correct operation of its V2X on-board unit.

With our revocation mechanism the deployment of privacy-friendly pseudonym schemes that do not implement pseudonym resolution becomes practical.

1 Introduction

Vehicular ad-hoc networks (VANET) based on Vehicle-to-X (V2X) communication will be deployed in the next years [6,12]. In the US the National Highway Traffic Safety Administration (NHTSA) has initiated an effort to make V2X support a mandatory requirement for all passenger cars in the near future [17]. V2X systems are expected to deliver new safety and comfort functions as well as improvements in traffic efficiency. Examples for envisioned V2X functions are "intersection collision warning", "emergency electronic brake lights" or "traffic light optimized speed advisory" [8]. These functions are based on messages that are exchanged between vehicles in an ad-hoc manner using short-range radios, as currently being standardized by ETSI [10] and IEEE [1]. Authentication is required in order to restrict communication to legitimate participants of the V2X network, as forged messages could cause confusion or even accidents. For privacy-friendly message authentication a scheme of short-lived *pseudonym certificates* (short: *pseudonyms*) is employed [18,19,21]. The pseudonyms are usually obtained from a certificate authority (CA) after authentication with a *long-term credential* [18] (we call this scheme the *basic pseudonym scheme*).

© Springer International Publishing Switzerland 2015
M. Conti et al. (Eds.): TRUST 2015, LNCS 9229, pp. 193–208, 2015.
DOI: 10.1007/978-3-319-22846-4_12

Revocation is needed to remove misbehaving nodes from the network. There are two main scenarios in which revocation is required. *Technical defect:* A vehicle is sending invalid messages (e.g. with incorrect data about its speed, position, etc.) due to a malfunctioning sensor or a technical problem in the V2X component. *Malicious attacker:* An attacker is intentionally sending manipulated messages with valid authentication data, e.g. by manipulating sensor inputs to the V2X component. Regardless of the cause, the misbehaving entities must be barred from communication as soon as possible (or rather, other participants should be able detect such messages as invalid and discard them) in order to avoid confusion and disruption of the network operation. The detection of misbehavior is a research area of its own (cf. Bißmeyer [2]) and is not in the scope of this work.

In most approaches to revocation, first, the misbehaving sender's long-term identity is resolved from a message he sent and that constitutes the misbehavior. Second, information about the revocation of the sender's long-term credentials (sometimes also about his pseudonyms) is disseminated to the other participants through certificate revocation lists (CRL) or other means. For instance, the approach proposed for the V2X network in Europe does not distribute pseudonym CRLs to vehicles, but allows revocation of a vehicle's long-term credential on a CA level [9], i.e., a revoked vehicle would not be able to obtain new pseudonyms.

These revocation mechanisms only work if the pseudonym scheme that is used in the V2X system supports resolution of participants' long-term identities from their pseudonyms. However, this is detrimental to the protection of their privacy. Even though resolution can typically only be performed by a dedicated (possibly distributed) authority, it still poses a threat to drivers' privacy, e.g. when the resolution authority is compromised or in countries where the authorities are not fully trusted.

A privacy-friendly V2X system, where pseudonym resolution is not possible, can be be set up in several ways. Trivially, the *basic pseudonym scheme* [18] can be implement such that the CA does not keep any logs about the pseudonyms it issues. Verifiable privacy can be achieved using advanced cryptography. The PUCA scheme by Förster et al. does not implement resolution of pseudonyms and employs anonymous credentials to offer strong privacy-guarantees [11]. Calandriello et al. propose a scheme, where vehicles generate pseudonyms for themselves using group signatures [5]. While their proposal includes pseudonym resolution, this property could be removed to strengthen privacy by using a different group signature scheme. Unfortunately, until now it has been unclear how revocation of misbehaving participants can be implemented in systems where resolution of pseudonym is not possible.

In this paper, we propose to leverage trusted hardware components (which are increasingly used in the automotive domain) to support revocation without identification. Security hardware for automotive electronic control units has been introduced some time ago (see, e.g., [4] for an example) – in particular, for V2X on-board units [13] – and recently, the Trusted Computing Group (TCG) has also released a specification for an automotive Trusted Platform Module [25].

Our Contribution

We propose a novel mechanism for excluding participants from a communication system that does not require resolution of pseudonyms. Instead, it is based on revocation orders broadcasted into the network and self-identification of participants. To ensure nodes follow self-revocation orders our solution leverages a trusted component in devices held by participants of the communication system. This allows for privacy-friendly solutions, where participants cannot be identified by the messages they send. It is still possible to revoke participants' authorization to participate in the system, without requiring any link to their identifiers or pseudonyms.

We apply our proposed solution to a V2X system. This allows the deployment of very privacy-friendly pseudonym schemes in this application field, while still making sure that malfunctioning or manipulated vehicles can be removed from the system quickly. In contrast to approaches where revocation information must be delivered to all network participants, our scheme scales very well as revocation information is only sent to a limited region via geocast.

The rest of the paper is organized as follows. We discuss related work in Sect. 2 and provide our system model and the attacker model in Sect. 3. In Sect. 4 we put forward our requirements. Our solution REWIRE (Revocation without resolution) is described in Sect. 5 and evaluated against the requirements in Sect. 6. We conclude the paper in Sect. 7.

2   Related Work

Petit et al. survey pseudonym systems in vehicular networks, including resolution and revocation mechanisms [21]. Papadimitratos et al. give an overview over security in vehicular communication systems in general [18]. They also describe several revocation mechanisms, all of which are based on pseudonym resolution. Several contributions describe the distribution of certificate revocation lists (CRL) in VANETs, e.g. via road-site infrastructure [20], car-to-car epidemic dissemination [15] or the radio data system (RDS) [18]. The V-Token scheme by Schaub et al. implements revocation by embedding the holder's encrypted identity in his pseudonym certificates [23]. Based on the encrypted identity, they implement resolution of pseudonyms by a distributed resolution authority. Our approach, in contrast, does not require resolution at all, but uses the encrypted identity for self-identification of vehicles.

Raya et al. propose RTC [22], a protocol for remote wiping of key material from a V2X component that is equipped with a trusted component. While their general approach is similar to ours, they require the vehicle's identity to be known for revocation, whereas we specifically implement revocation of vehicles whose identity is not known and cannot be resolved. Stumpf et al. use a trusted platform module (TPM) for generating privacy-friendly T-IVC certificates [24]. In their suggestion the users' privacy can be revoked by the authorities for revocation, whereas our revocation mechanism is designed to work without revocation of privacy (i.e. resolution of pseudonyms).

196   D. Förster et al.

Trusted hardware extensions have been proposed for the automotive domain in the past – see, e.g., [4,14] – and recently, the Trusted Computing Group has also introduced a profile of its Trusted Platform Module (TPM) for automotive use [25]. The EVITA project explored the use of a trusted component to secure in-vehicle communication [13]. The "Evita HSM Full Version" would be a good candidate for implementing our proposal. Recent European projects (EU or national) in the area of V2X communication, such as CONVERGE[1] or PRESERVE[2], typically rely on hardware security modules as a trust anchor.

Li and Wang survey geocast routing protocols for VANETs [16], which are an essential building block for our scheme. The CONVERGE project proposes a geomessaging protocol for a hybrid communication scenario with a combination of V2X short-range radio and cellular LTE connectivity [7].

3   System Model and Scenario

We assume a V2X system with the following participants:

- Participating vehicles V_i. Each vehicle is equipped with a V2X on-board unit (OBU), that contains a *long-term credential* which constitutes the vehicle's authorization to participate in the V2X system. Furthermore, each vehicles has some kind of *identity* associated, that may allow inference of its owner, e.g. its vehicles identification number (VIN) or the fingerprint of its long-term credential.
- The certificate authority (CA) issues long-term credentials and pseudonym certificates.[3]
- The revocation authority (RA) receives reports about misbehavior and takes decision about revocation of participants.

3.1   System Operation

Based on the established abstract pseudonym lifecycle for V2X systems as described by Petit et al. [21], the system's operation can be split into the following phases.

Pseudonym issuance. Vehicles obtain pseudonyms from the CA after authentication with their long-term credential. We assume that a privacy-preserving protocol is used to obtain the pseudonyms and that resolution, i.e. resolving the holder's identity from a pseudonym, is not possible. (Therefore, we omit the *pseudonym resolution* phase.)

Pseudonym use. The participating vehicles communicate using ad-hoc radio communication in order to execute V2X-based safety and comfort functions. All messages are signed using pseudonym certificates.

---

[1] See http://www.converge-online.de/.
[2] See http://preserve-project.eu/.
[3] Some schemes require dedicate long-term and pseudonym certificate authorities. We assume one single CA, without loss of generality, as this has no impact on our scheme.

Pseudonym change. In order to prevent long-term tracking, vehicles change their active pseudonym certificate every once in a while.

(Pseudonym) revocation. When vehicle is detected to send invalid messages its credentials (both pseudonyms and long-term) must be revoked in order to prevent further disruption of the network's operation.

We assume that a misbehavior detection mechanism is in place that allows vehicles to detect messages with implausible or invalid content (cf. Bißmeyer [2]). Furthermore, we assume the availability of a geocast mechanism, such as the one proposed by the CONVERGE project [7]. Figure 1 gives an overview of our system model.

3.2   Attacker Model

We consider three types of attackers that threaten the operation of the V2X system.

A.1 The *unintentional insider attacker* is sending messages with invalid content due to a malfunctioning sensor or a technical problem in the V2X component. The messages are properly authenticated and the driver of vehicle is most likely not aware of the problem.

A.2 The *malicious insider attacker* actively and intentionally manipulates message contents. The manipulation could be done by plugging into the vehicles OBD bus or by feeding manipulated sensor inputs directly into the V2X box. The attacker might even remove the V2X component and operate it outside of the car. His motive could be personal advantage in traffic, to manipulate

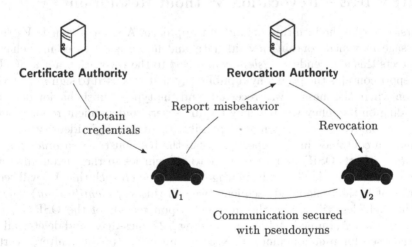

Fig. 1. The vehicle V_1 obtaines pseudonym certificates from the certificate authority (CA) and uses them to secure its communication with V_2. In case it detects any misbehavior it reports it to the revocation authority (RA), which may decide to revoke the reported vehicle.

traffic flow, or simply to cause confusion for other drivers. The messages this attacker sends contain valid authentication data.

A.3 The *outsider attacker* tries to disrupt the V2X system's operation from the outside. In contrast to A.1 and A.2 he is not in possession of any credentials and is unable to produce properly authenticated messages.

4   Requirements

We put forward the following requirements for revocation schemes in V2X systems.

R.1 *Revocation based on messages.* It must be possible to exclude the sender of a given message from the V2X system.

R.2 *Effectiveness of revocation.* It must not be possible for a vehicle that is subject to revocation to prevent the revocation to become effective.

R.3 *Short delay.* Revocation must take effect as soon as possible.

R.4 *Scalability.* The revocation mechanism must be applicable in a V2X system with a large number of participants.

R.5 *DoS-resistance.* It must not be possible to trigger revocation of a participant that was behaving correctly, as this would constitute a denial-of-service attack.

R.6 *No resolution required.* Revocation must be possible in a system without pseudonym resolution, i.e. where the holder of a given pseudonym (or the sender of a given signed message) cannot be identified.

Note that identifying the sender of invalid messages is not a requirement.

5   REWIRE – Revocation Without Resolution

We first describe the intuition behind our approach. Assume a vehicle V_A sends a message m which contains invalid data and hence constitutes misbehavior. V_B detects this and sends a *misbehavior report* to the revocation authority RA. The report contains the pseudonym public key that was used to sign m, the GPS location where the mesage was received, and the type of misbehavior detected. Depending on its policy the RA may require several independent reports before taking action. We recall that it is impossible to resolve V_A's identity from the information contained in the report. Instead the RA constructs a *order for self-revocation* (short: OSR) and geocasts it to all vehicles in the surrounding area where m was received. The OSR message is constructed such that V_A will recognize that it is the designated recipient (we call this *self-identification*) whereas all other vehicles will ignore the message. Upon receipt of the OSR V_A confirms it to the RA, immediately stops sending V2X messages, and deletes all key material used for pseudonymous V2X communication (possibly after a certain delay). Compliance to the request is enforced by a trusted component (TC) that is contained in every vehicle's OBU and that ensures that its behavior cannot be altered, at least with regard to V2X communications. Figure 2 shows a high level sketch of the revocation procedure.

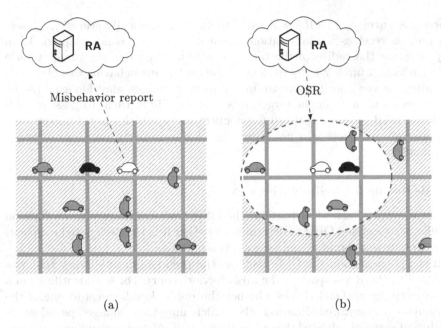

Fig. 2. The white vehicle reports the black vehicle for sending invalid messages to the RA (a). After checking its revocation policy, the RA geocasts an OSR (order for self-revocation) to the surrounding area where the misbehavior occurred (b). The order is ignore by all except the designated vehicle, which complies by ceasing communication and deleting its key material.

Self-revocation. When a participant receives an OSR directed to him he must stop sending V2X messages immediately. He sends a signed confirmation message to the RA. He deletes all his key material after the time T_{keep} has elapsed. Keeping the key material for some time is necessary as the RA may send more OSR messages that are directed to one of his other pseudonyms.[4] Those must be confirmed with a signed message, too.

When a vehicle's V2X unit is disabled, the driver should be informed that the vehicle requires maintenance. Once the reason for revocation (e.g. a malfunctioning sensor) has been identified and fixed the V2X unit can be equipped with new key material and resume its operation.

Revocation Policy. The RA's revocation policy determines its reaction to misbehavior reports. We refrain from suggesting a specific policy as it may depend on the misbehavior strategy employed. The policy is always a trade-off between avoiding false negatives (discard valid reports) and preventing denial-of-service attacks (someone deliberately files incorrect reports).

---

[4] Pseudonyms are unlinkable, hence the RA needs to send out separate OSRs for each pseudonym that was reported for misbehavior.

Geocast Strategy. The RA will send out OSRs periodically every T_{repeat} seconds until it receives a confirmation message or T_{send} seconds elapsed. With every iteration the radius of the target area is increased as the target vehicle may have moved further away from the location the misbehavior was observed. Depending on the specific geocast mechanism, messages may for example be sent to road-side units in the target area that distribute them to passing vehicles, using DAB, or via direct cellular connection to vehicles in the target area. Some geocast protocols also use forwarding between participants for message dissemination.

5.1   R-Tokens for Self-identification

For our concept of self-identification, the OSR must contain some information that allows a receiving OBU to determine, whether it is the designated recipient. We propose two variants of our revocation scheme.

In the *plain* version the OSR contains the pseudonym public key that was submitted to the RA as part as the misbehavior report. For self-identification a vehicle receiving an OSR checks whether the public key belongs to one of the pseudonyms it has stored. However, the vehicle may have changed pseudonyms already and may have deleted the old pseudonym, if submission and processing of the misbehavior report takes some time. Note that in this version, other vehicles can observe which vehicles are misbehaving.

To address this we propose *R-Tokens*, an adaptation of the *V-Token* pseudonym scheme by Schaub et al. [23]. In their scheme, prior to requesting pseudonyms, a vehicle obtains a number of V-Tokens from the CA that contain the vehicle's encrypted identity and are signed by the CA. By using a blind signature scheme, the CA does not learn their actual values, hence, it cannot link them to the vehicle's identity later on. At the same time it ensures their correct value using a "cut and choose protocol" (asking the requester to unveil some of the submitted tokens). Pseudonyms are requested in a second step (which the CA cannot link to the first one). Each pseudonym that is submitted to the CA for signing must contain a valid V-Token. In case of misbehavior the (distributed) revocation authority can resolve the owner of a pseudonym by decrypting the contained V-Token.

For our R-Token approach, we modify the encryption such that only the owner can decrypt the R-Token (thus removing the option for resolution). This is achieved by using a randomized asymmetric encryption scheme, e.g. ElGamal. In the cut and choose protocol the CA can verify the correctness of some of the R-Tokens by reproducing the encryption with the random input provided by the vehicle. If all verifications succeeds, the CA generates a blind signature on the R-Token. Furthermore, the pseudonym issuance protocol must be extended by requiring a valid R-Token to be included in each pseudonym to be signed by the CA. As R-Tokens are not linkable to its owners identity, this does not affect the privacy properties of the pseudonym scheme in use. The modification can be made for any pseudonym scheme, where vehicles obtain pseudonyms from a CA, e.g. the PUCA scheme [11]. In the R-Token variant of our scheme, the RA includes the R-Token extracted from the reported pseudonym instead of

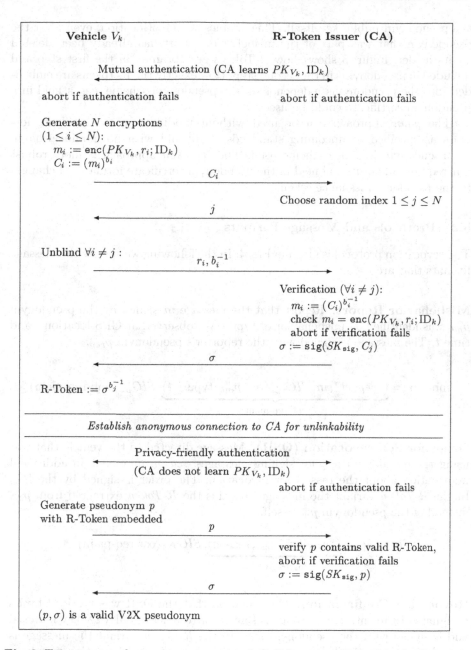

Fig. 3. Two step pseudonym issuance protocol: R-Tokens are obtained in the first step using blind signatures and a "cut and choose" approach, similarly to the original V-Token proposal [23]. The CA learns the vehicle's public key and identity, and makes sure it is contained in the R-Token before signing it. V2X pseudonyms with R-Tokens embedded are submitted for signature in the second step. The CA does not learn the vehicle's identity as it cannot decrypt the R-Tokens. For unlinkability of pseudonyms the second step must be executed independently for each pseudonym to be requested.

the pseudonym public key itself. This enables self-identification, even after the pseudonym that was part of the misbehavior report has already been deleted by its holder. Figure 3 shows how R-Tokens are obtained in the first step and included in pseudonyms in the second step. How exactly the R-Tokens are embedded into the pseudonyms p depends on the pseudonym scheme, e.g. a field in a pseudonym certificate could be used.

The *plain* approach can be used without modification to certificate formats as specified in upcoming standards [1,10] and with no modification to the pseudonym issuance scheme used. The *R-Token* approach is more robust but requires an additional field in the pseudonym certificate format and changes to the pseudonym issuance scheme.

5.2 Protocols and Message Formats

The revocation protocol is given in Fig. 4. In the following we specify the message formats that are used.

Misbehavior Report. Report that the message m signed by the pseudonym p_{mb} was identified as misbehavior of type *type*, observed at GPS location l and time t. The message is signed with the reporter's pseudonym p_{rep}.

$$\text{mb-rep} := \underbrace{(\text{``}report\text{''}, m, SIG_{p_{mb}}(m), p_{mb}, \text{type}, l, t)}_{\text{mb-rep-plain}}, SIG_{p_{rep}}(\text{mb-rep-plain})$$

Order for Self-revocation (OSR). Message directed to the vehicle that was using the pseudonym p_{mb} for signing messages. *reason* may contain additional information about the reason for revocation. The order is signed by the RA. In the *R-Token* variant the message contains the *R-Token* extracted from p_{mb} instead of the pseudonym p_{mb} itself.

$$\text{osr-req} := \underbrace{(\text{``}revoke\text{''}, p_{mb}, \text{reason})}_{\text{osr-req-plain}}, SIG_{RA}(\text{osr-req-plain})$$

Revocation Confirmation. Confirmation that the OSR was received by its designated recipient. The message is sent prior to deleting all V2X key material and is signed with the pseudonym p_{mb}. In the *R-Token* variant the message is signed with the vehicle's long-term key, as the pseudonym in question may have been deleted already.

$$\text{osr-conf} := \underbrace{(\text{``}confirm\text{''}, p_{mb})}_{\text{osr-conf-plain}}, SIG_{p_{mb}}(\text{osr-conf-plain})$$

5.3   Trusted Computing Integration

To provide adequate protection against malicious attackers, the mandated reaction to an OSR must be enforced via a trusted component (TC) that is contained in each vehicle's OBU. Figure 5 displays the architecture of a typical V2X OBU including a trusted component, similar to proposals from the automotive industry (e.g. the EVITA project [13]).

The TC protects all private keys by storing them in internal secure storage (or at least protected by a Root of Trust for Storage (RTS)) and performs all cryptographic operations that involve those keys. Moreover, it contains a Root of Trust for Measurement (RTM) to enable secure boot or runtime integrity verification on the V2X OBU. It may also include a Root of Trust for Reporting (RTR) for remote attestation, i.e. the possibility to prove the integrity of the software on the V2X OBU to a remote verifier.

We envision different levels of protection. In the *basic protection* level, the TC is only used for key storage, for cryptographic operations that require private keys, and for processing OSRs. This approach enables self-revocation because the TC controls the private keys and deletes them upon authorized request. However, a compromised software stack on the V2X OBU might be able to prevent the TC from receiving OSRs by recognizing OSRs for this vehicle and filtering them. The *full protection* level also includes checks of the OBU's integrity by the TC, either at boot time (using secure boot) or at run-time (with run-time integrity verification). Secure boot prevents the execution of modified or unauthorized software, because the TC checks hash values and signatures on the code before running it. For run-time integrity verification, the TC verifies the software during execution and aborts if manipulations are discovered. Optionally, the TC may also allow for remote attestation of integrity during pseudonym issuance, to make sure new pseudonyms are only issued to vehicles whose on-board unit has not been tampered with. In this case, the TC records hash values of the running software, signs them with an attestation key, and sends the result to the certificate authority together with the request for pseudonyms. Thus, the CA can verify that a V2X OBU with an authorized TC executing only authorized software is requesting the certificates. For this, an anonymous attestation scheme must be used to avoid revealing the OBU's identity, such as direct anonymous attestation (DAA, see [3]). Trusted Platform Modules (TPMs), for instance, support DAA since version 1.2.

5.4   Prevent Blocking of OSR Messages

It is crucial that an attacker cannot prevent OSR from reaching the trusted component. We propose several countermeasures.

Ensure Software Integrity. To prevent any software-level manipulations we can use the integrity checks for the *full protection* profile (see Sect. 5.3) to establish a *secure I/O path* from the radio transceiver to the trusted component. When a vehicle requests new pseudonym certificates, the RA can require it to

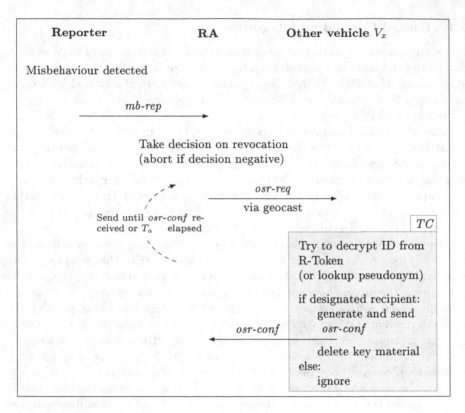

Fig. 4. Revocation protocol. A vehicle sends a misbehavior report to the RA which handles it according to its revocation policy. If revocation is required it sends an OSR (order for self-revocation) to all vehicles in the surrounding area where the misbehavior occurred. Only the designated recipient reacts to the message by confirming the receipt and deleting his key material, all other recipients ignore the message. All critical processing is done inside the TC.

prove the integrity of its systems using remote attestation. Then, before any new pseudonyms are granted, the RA can ensure that the requesting vehicle is exposed to all unresolved OSRs (for which the RA has not received confirmation). This countermeasure is most effective in combination with short pseudonym lifetimes.

Detect Blocking Using Keep-Alive Messages. To detect malicious vehicles, that manage to block revocation orders, the RA regularly sends *dummy keep-alive OSR messages*, that do not entail a revocation action, but also require confirmation by the TC on the vehicle. To make the dummy OSR messages indistinguishable from real OSR messages, all OSR messages can be encrypted with keys stored in the TC. The RA can identify vehicles that filter messages by keeping track of rate of answered dummy OSRs or unanswered dummy OSRs

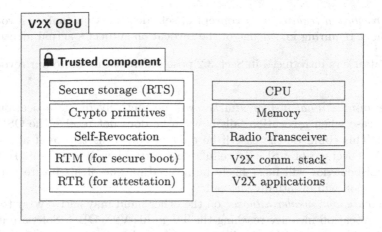

Fig. 5. A typical V2X on-board unit (OBU) that includes a trusted component

during a specific timeframe. Alternatively, the TC itself can detect filtering by the lack of keep-alive messages and act accordingly, e.g. by suspending its operation.

6 Evaluation and Discussion

We evaluate our proposal against the requirements from Sect. 4.

R.1 *Revocation based on messages* is achieved with our concept of *self-identification*. This alleviates the need for resolution of pseudonyms.

R.2 *Effectiveness of revocation* is ensured by the trusted component (TC) contained in each vehicle. Secure boot ensures that only authorized software can be executed on the V2X OBU, hence, software cannot prevent the TC from processing self-revocation orders. To block messages successfully, an advanced attacker would have to introduce additional hardware unless secure boot is not implemented properly or authorized software can be exploited.

R.3 *Short delay* is achieved by a vehicle's immediate reaction of ceasing V2X communication upon receipt of an OSR.

R.4 *Scalability* is maintained by geocasting the OSR to a limited region only (whose size is independent of the total system size), depending on the location of misbehavior. This prevents flooding of the network with a large number of OSR messages. Confirmation from revoked vehicles makes sure that an OSR messages is only sent until it has reached the target vehicle. The timeout T_{keep} ensures that a vehicle can still confirm additional OSRs (addressed to its other pseudonyms) after having been revoked, while T_{send} prevents that unanswered messages are sent indefinitely.

R.5 *DoS-resistance* is implemented by requiring all misbehavior reports to be signed by the reporter. Sending unjustified misbehavior reports would constitute misbehavior in itself and can be handled by revoking the misbehaving reporter.

R.6 *No resolution required.* Our concept of self-identification enables revocation without requiring knowledge of the revocation subject's actual identity.

The attackers introduced in Sect. 3.2 pose different threats to our revocation scheme.

A.1 The *unintentional insider attacker* will not actively resist revocation. The only case when revocation fails is when he does not receive the OSR message. This could be the case if he already ended his trip or if he was not in the coverage of RSUs or cellular network when it was sent. However, his misbehavior will most likely be noticed on one of his future trips and revocation will eventually succeed.

A.2 The *malicious insider attacker* on the other hand may actively try to block the revocation message reaching the TC in his V2X OBU. Software manipulation is prevented by the integrity checks described in Sect. 5.3. Due to the *secure I/O path*, revocation cannot be avoided, once the messages has been received successfully.

This leaves attacks on the wireless transmission level. Radio jamming or otherwise modifying the input to the V2X OBU requires an advanced attacker with additional hardware. This attack can be countered using the *dummy OSR keep-alive messages*.

An attacker may choose to come online exclusively to perform malicious actions, and evade the OSRs by simply not being available for communication. This is addressed by requiring remote attestation of software integrity, whenever a participant requests new pseudonym certificates, and exposing him to all OSRs that have not been confirmed yet.

Obviously, an attacker might try to extract the V2X key material from the TC. We assume that the TC provides adequate protection against this type of attack, e.g., by using state-of-the-art smartcard technology.

A.3 The *outsider attacker* cannot interfere with our revocation scheme in any meaningful way as he does not process any valid credentials and is unable to produce properly authenticated messages. For this protection to be effective, it is crucial that participants discard all messages that are not properly signed without further processing.

7   Conclusion

Vehicular ad-hoc networks are on the brink of deployment, and privacy is a crucial success factor for their acceptance by the general public. The REWIRE revocation protocol can complement proposals for privacy-friendly authentication in V2X systems. It does not require resolution of pseudonyms to exclude misbehaving entities and therefore avoids the negative privacy implications of previously suggested revocation schemes. To achieve this, we propose a novel self-revocation mechanisms, where we leverage a trusted hardware component (as they are currently proposed for V2X on-board units) for enforcement. Our proposal is well suited for systems that have a large number of participants.

As revocation information is only sent to the affected region via geocast, the communication overhead is independent of the total system size.

The *basic* variant of our solution is compatible with existing standards from the US [1] and Europe [10]. It requires no modifications to certificate or message formats and could also be deployed in parallel with other revocation mechanisms. The *R-Token* variant has additional advantages and requires the addition of one field in the format for pseudonym certificates.

Overall, we have shown that strong anonymity in vehicular networks can be achieved, despite the need for revocation of misbehaving entities.

Acknowledgments. This work was partially funded within the project CONVERGE by the German Federal Ministries of Education and Research as well as Economic Affairs and Energy.

References

1. WG - Dedicated Short Range Communication Working Group: 1609.0-2013 - IEEE guide for wireless access in vehicular environments (WAVE) - architecture (2013)
2. Bißmeyer, N.: Misbehavior detection and attacker identification in vehicular ad-hoc networks. Ph.D. thesis, TU Darmstadt, Germany, December 2014
3. Brickell, E.F., Camenisch, J., Chen, L.: Direct anonymous attestation. In: Atluri, V., Pfitzmann, B., McDaniel, P.D. (eds.) Proceedings of the 11th ACM Conference on Computer and Communications Security, CCS 2004, 25–29 October, 2004, Washington, DC, USA, pp. 132–145. ACM (2004)
4. Bubeck, O., Gramm, J., Ihle, M., Shokrollahi, J., Szerwinski, R., Emele, M.: A hardware security module for engine control units. In: Proceedings of the 10th ESCAR Conference (2011)
5. Calandriello, G., Papadimitratos, P., Hubaux, J.P., Lioy, A.: Efficient and robust pseudonymous authentication in vanet. In: Proceedings of the Fourth ACM International Workshop on Vehicular Ad Hoc Networks, pp. 19–28. ACM (2007)
6. CAR 2 CAR Communication Consortium: Memorandum of understanding on deployment strategy for cooperative ITS in europe, June 2011
7. CONVERGE: Deliverable D4.3 "Architecture of the car2x systems network", section 4.1.2, January 2015
8. ETSI Technical Committee Intelligent Transport Systems (ITS): Intelligent Transport Systems (ITS); Vehicular Communications; Basic Set of Applications; Definitions. Technical report, 102 638 V1.1.1, European Telecommunications Standards Institute, June 2009
9. ETSI Technical Committee Intelligent Transport Systems (ITS): Intelligent Transport Systems (ITS); Security; Security Services and Architecture. Technical report, TS 102 731 V1.1.1, European Telecommunications Standards Institute, September 2010
10. ETSI Technical Committee Intelligent Transport Systems (ITS): Intelligent Transport Systems (ITS); Cooperative ITS (C-ITS); Release 1. Technical report, 101 607 V1.1.1, European Telecommunications Standards Institute, May 2013
11. Föster, D., Kargl, F., Löhr, H.: PUCA: A pseudonym scheme with user-controlled anonymity for vehicular ad-hoc networks (VANET). In: Proceedings of the IEEE Vehicular Networking Conference 2014 (VNC 2014). IEEE (2014)

12. General Motors: Cadillac to introduce advanced 'intelligent and connected' vehicle technologies on select 2017 models, September 2014. http://media.gm. com/media/us/en/gm/news.detail.html/content/Pages/news/us/en/2014/Sep/ 0907-its-overview.html

13. Henniger, O., Ruddle, A., Seudié, H., Weyl, B., Wolf, M., Wollinger, T.: Securing vehicular on-board it systems: The EVITA project. In: VDI/VW Automotive Security Conference (2009)

14. Herstellerinitiative Software (HIS): SHE secure hardware extension version 1.1. (2009). http://portal.automotive-his.de

15. Laberteaux, K.P., Haas, J.J., Hu, Y.C.: Security certificate revocation list distribution for vanet. In: Proceedings of the Fifth ACM International Workshop on Vehicular Inter-Networking, VANET 2008, pp. 88–89. ACM (2008)

16. Li, F., Wang, Y.: Routing in vehicular ad hoc networks: a survey. IEEE Veh. Technol. Mag. **2**(2), 12–22 (2007)

17. National Highway Traffic Safety Administration (NHTSA): Federal motor vehicle safety standards: Vehicle-to-vehicle (V2V) communications. Advance notice of proposed rulemaking (ANPRM) (2014). http://www.nhtsa.gov/About+ NHTSA/Press+Releases/NHTSA-issues-advanced-notice-of-proposed-rulemaking -on-V2V-communications

18. Papadimitratos, P., Buttyan, L., Holczer, T., Schoch, E., Freudiger, J., Raya, M., Ma, Z., Kargl, F., Kung, A., Hubaux, J.P.: Secure vehicular communication systems: design and architecture. IEEE Commun. Mag. **46**(11), 100–109 (2008)

19. Papadimitratos, P., Buttyan, L., Hubaux, J.P., Kargl, F., Kung, A., Raya, M.: Architecture for secure and private vehicular communications. In: 7th International Conference on ITS Telecommunications, ITST 2007, pp. 1–6. IEEE (2007)

20. Papadimitratos, P., Mezzour, G., Hubaux, J.P.: Certificate revocation list distribution in vehicular communication systems. In: Proceedings of the Fifth ACM International Workshop on Vehicular Inter-Networking, VANET 2008, pp. 86–87. ACM (2008)

21. Petit, J., Schaub, F., Feiri, M., Kargl, F.: Pseudonym schemes in vehicular networks: a survey. IEEE Commun. Surv. Tutorials **17**(1), 228–255 (2015)

22. Raya, M., Papadimitratos, P., Aad, I., Jungels, D., Hubaux, J.P.: Eviction of misbehaving and faulty nodes in vehicular networks. IEEE J. Selected Areas Commun. **25**(8), 1557–1568 (2007)

23. Schaub, F., Kargl, F., Ma, Z., Weber, M.: V-tokens for conditional pseudonymity in VANETs. In: Wireless Communications and Networking Conference (WCNC), pp. 1–6. IEEE (2010)

24. Stumpf, F., Fischer, L., Eckert, C.: Trust, security and privacy in VANETs - a multilayered security architecture for C2C-communication. In: VDI BERICHTE 2016, 23. VDI/VW-Gemeinschaftstagung Automotive Security, Wolfsburg, p. 55, November 2007

25. Trusted Computing Group: TCG TPM 2.0 Library profile for automotive thin specification, version 1.0. TCG Specification, 2015. http://www.trusted computinggroup.org/resources/tcg_tpm_20_library_profile_for_automotivethin

DAA-TZ: An Efficient DAA Scheme for Mobile Devices Using ARM TrustZone

Bo Yang[1]([✉]), Kang Yang[1], Yu Qin[1], Zhenfeng Zhang[1],
and Dengguo Feng[1,2]

[1] Trusted Computing and Information Assurance Laboratory,
Institute of Software, Chinese Academy of Sciences, Beijing, China
{yangbo,yangkang,qin_yu,zfzhang,feng}@tca.iscas.ac.cn
[2] State Key Laboratory of Computer Science, Institute of Software
Chinese Academy of Sciences, Beijing, China

Abstract. Direct Anonymous Attestation (DAA) has been studied for
applying to mobile devices based on ARM TrustZone. However, current
solutions bring in extra performance overheads and security risks when
adapting existing DAA schemes originally designed for PC platform. In
this paper, we propose a complete and efficient DAA scheme (DAA-TZ)
specifically designed for mobile devices using TrustZone. By considering
the application scenarios, DAA-TZ extends the interactive model of original DAA and provides anonymity for a device and its user against remote
service providers. The proposed scheme requires only one-time switch of
TrustZone for signing phase and elaborately takes pre-computation into
account. Consequently, the frequent on-line signing just needs at most
three exponentiations on elliptic curve. Moreover, we present the architecture for trusted mobile devices. The issues about key derivation and
sensitive data management relying on a root of trust from SRAM Physical Unclonable Function (PUF) are discussed. We implement a prototype
system and execute DAA-TZ using MNT and BN curves with different
security levels. The comparison result and performance evaluation indicate that our scheme meets the demanding requirement of mobile users
in respects of both security and efficiency.

Keywords: DAA · Privacy · Mobile devices · ARM TrustZone · PUF

1 Introduction

With the development of wireless communication network as well as modern
mobile devices, a variety of mobile applications have been realized to provide
users convenient and comprehensive services. Depending on these achievements,
online interactive applications such as mobile payment, mobile ticketing, mobile
shopping and mobile voting, are benefiting people's daily lives. However, with the
widespread use of mobile services, users are faced with the risk of privacy disclosure. Generally, authenticating the users' legitimate identity is regarded as one
prerequisite for access to those remote application services. This authentication

© Springer International Publishing Switzerland 2015
M. Conti et al. (Eds.): TRUST 2015, LNCS 9229, pp. 209–227, 2015.
DOI: 10.1007/978-3-319-22846-4_13

is associated with an individual mobile device, a SIM card or a service account. As a result, when a user logins to enjoy services, his personal information, perhaps involving his real identity, locations, bank accounts or records of network behaviors etc., is potentially linked to each other and leaked to service providers [28]. And what is worse, the personal information could be further shared with some third parties, for example, to send consumers behaviorally targeted advertisements [8]. Thus, the issue of information leakage is seriously threatening mobile users' personal privacy and information security.

On PC platform, the analogous problem can be effectively solved by DAA [2], which is standardized by the Trusted Computing Group (TCG). DAA allows an embedded processor on a motherboard, called Trusted Platform Module (TPM), to anonymously attest the certain statements about the configuration of the host machine as well as its legitimate status to remote third parties [1]. The key requirement behind DAA is that this attestation is done in a way that maintains the privacy of the machine (i.e., the user). On the other hand, DAA is an anonymous credential system designed specifically to encapsulate security-critical operations within TPM, and the sensitive data including secret signing key and parameters are well protected by TPM. An adversary hardly shares a legitimate user's credential by just stealing related data on the host to gain unauthorized access to remote services. The DAA [2] is originally proposed based on strong RSA assumption. For better computing efficiency and shorter signature length, researches constructs several DAA schemes based on elliptic curves and bilinear maps [3,4,6,7], which we call ECC-DAA. Moreover, Bernhard et al. [1] give a new security model and a generic DAA protocol on it. Xi et al. [27] first add the property of forward anonymity. To date, DAA has gained lots of favor with industry and standard bodies [5,22,23], which renders it better prospects for practical applications than other anonymous credential systems [30].

For mobile platform, DAA is still attractive as an alternative anonymous authentication solution. Unfortunately, previous DAA schemes are exclusively designed for the model of TPM inside a host. The prevalent mobile devices are rarely equipped with special-purpose chip like TPM, so that the direct use of DAA on mobile platform would cause trouble. Opaak [12] is a simplified DAA scheme for mobile devices, but its executable codes and sensitive data are easily compromised or stolen by malwares.

The technique of Trusted Execution Environment (TEE) on mobile devices could lend us a helping hand. Isolated from a Rich Execution Environment (REE) where the Guest OS runs, TEE aims to protect sensitive code execution and assets. As an example of providing TEE for embedded devices, ARM Trust-Zone [26] has been used to execute security-critical services [20,21]. By Trust-Zone, TEE's resources are physically isolated from REE, such that adversaries in REE hardly access them directly [11]. As a hardware-based security extension of ARM architecture, TrustZone is widely supported and applied by many mobile manufacturers. Leveraging TrustZone, some solutions are proposed to construct software-based ECC-DAA with security-critical codes running within TEE, and treat REE as the role of "host". Wachsmann et al. [25] put forward an authentication scheme based on DAA and TLS but without user-controlled linkability. Yang et al. [28] present LAMS for anonymous mobile shopping, which is compatible with four unmodified ECC-DAA schemes. Given by Zhang et al. [30], Mdaak provides a general and flexible DAA framework for mobile devices. Nevertheless, these solutions neither implement pre-computation for anonymous signing nor consider comprehensive protection for DAA sensitive data. Furthermore, in these solutions, implementing unmodified or simply modified DAA in TrustZone brings much extra meaningless overhead and security issues. First, DAA does not concern the number of interactions between TPM chip and the host, while it is a problem for mobile devices using TrustZone. Each switching the context between TEE and REE carries both performance overhead and power consumption. In practice, these cannot be neglected, especially if the system or software is complicated, or the switch action needs to be triggered frequently [16]. When many switch actions occur, data transmission and protection for DAA procedure are also cumbersome, memory-consuming and time-consuming. Second, extra operations are demanded in original DAA for the sake of the limited bandwidth of TPM, which seems superfluous for TrustZone. Last but not least, TPM itself is hardware-based root of trust with inside root key for sensitive data management, while TrustZone does not definitely provide this root. To the best of our knowledge, there is no DAA scheme specially designed to adapt for mobile devices using TrustZone.

Our Contributions. In this paper, based on elliptic curves and bilinear maps, we propose an efficient DAA scheme (DAA-TZ) for mobile devices who are resource-constrained as compared with PC platform. DAA-TZ enables remote service providers to authenticate mobile users' trusted status or legitimate information without disclosing users' identity. DAA-TZ makes full use of ARM TrustZone and modifies the traditional interactive model as well as procedure of original DAA. The main signing efficiency for users is improved without the expense of security. Our work is summarized as follows.

- This is the first complete work that designs an efficient DAA scheme deeply integrated with TrustZone and expressly for mobile devices. In order to reduce the time delay and space overhead, the scheme minimizes the switch times of TrustZone for the frequent signing phase.
- According to the ecosystem of mobile devices, DAA-TZ supports manufacturers to acquire a batch of credentials through cooperative and trusted channels, and then embed them into devices before they leave factory. Users could immediately execute anonymous signing after getting devices.
- The pre-computation is carefully added into DAA-TZ, so that the on-line anonymous signing at most needs only three exponentiations on elliptic curve which is thought of as quite expensive computation.
- DAA-TZ utilizes the on-chip SRAM PUF to reproduce a root key seed and further create keys serving different purposes. The mechanism for sensitive data management using related keys is presented in detail.
- We implement a prototype system with full functions of DAA-TZ. The evaluation on it with two types of curves is performed. Both theoretical comparison and testing results show the high efficiency of our scheme.

2   Preliminaries

2.1   Notation

Throughout this paper, λ denotes the security parameter. We use $a \leftarrow S$ to denote sampling a from a set S uniformly at random. We also use $1_{\mathbb{G}}$ to denote the identity element of a group $\mathbb{G}$. For any group $\mathbb{G}$, $\mathbb{G}^*$ denotes $\mathbb{G} \backslash \{1_{\mathbb{G}}\}$. $\mathsf{MAC}_k(m)$ denotes the message authentication code for a message m computed with the secret key k, and $\mathsf{Enc}_k(m)$ denotes a ciphertext of a message m produced with the symmetric key k. Let $\Lambda = (p, \mathbb{G}_1, \mathbb{G}_2, \mathbb{G}_T, e, g_1, g_2)$ to be a description of bilinear groups which consist of three (multiplicatively written) groups $\mathbb{G}_1$, $\mathbb{G}_2$ and $\mathbb{G}_T$ of prime order p equipped with a bilinear map $e : \mathbb{G}_1 \times \mathbb{G}_2 \to \mathbb{G}_T$, where g_1 and g_2 be generators of $\mathbb{G}_1$ and $\mathbb{G}_2$ respectively. In this paper, we only consider the Type-3 pairings [9], thus $\mathbb{G}_1 \neq \mathbb{G}_2$ and there is no known efficiently computable isomorphism between $\mathbb{G}_1$ and $\mathbb{G}_2$.

2.2   ARM TrustZone

ARM TrustZone [15] is a hardware-based security extension technology incorporated into ARM processors. It enables a single physical processor to execute codes in one of two possible operating worlds: the normal world and the secure world. Accordingly, the system is separated into two domains to run the domain-dedicated OS and software. The isolation mechanisms of TrustZone are well defined. Access permissions are strictly under the control of the secure world that normal world components cannot access the secure world resources. As the processor only runs in one world at a time, to run in the other world requires context switch. A secure monitor mode controls the switch and migration between the two worlds. To date, TrustZone has been popularized and applied by many mainstream mobile manufacturers to achieving secure applications [28].

2.3   Physical Unclonable Functions

Physical Unclonable Functions (PUFs) [18] are functions where the relationship between input (or challenge) and output (or response) is decided by a physical system. Randomness and unclonability are two significant properties of PUFs. The unclonability originates from random variations in a device's manufacturing process. With the help of a fuzzy extractor that eliminates the noise from the response, PUFs are able to implicitly "store" a piece of secret data. PUFs provide much higher physical security by extracting the secret data from complex physical systems rather than directly reading them from non-volatile memory. Additionally, PUFs are cost-effective, since they take the advantage of the results from a preexisting manufacturing process [30].

Strictly speaking, TrustZone just provides an isolated environment. Only equipped with a root of trust, it becomes a real "trusted" execution environment (TEE) [31]. Because TrustZone almost does not internally install an available root key, it loses the capability to offer a root of trust. To cover this shortage, a PUF can be employed to properly act as the root of trust. In this paper, DAA-TZ takes the secret data extracted from the PUF as a root key seed to generate other keys. We adopt SRAM PUF [10] that leverages the relationship between an SRAM cell's address for the challenge and its power up value for the response.

3 System Model and Assumptions

3.1 System Model

The system model of DAA-TZ is composed of four kinds of entities: mobile device $\mathcal{D}$, manufacturer $\mathcal{M}$, issuer $\mathcal{I}$ and verifier $\mathcal{V}$. In practice, there could be a number of $\mathcal{D}$ and $\mathcal{V}$, thus we use $\mathcal{D}_i$ and $\mathcal{V}_j$ to represent an individual unite respectively. $\mathcal{D}_i$ is directly accessed by a user and equipped with ARM processor having TrustZone extension technology. $\mathcal{M}$, who produces $\mathcal{D}_i$, performs embedding some credentials to each $\mathcal{D}_i$ in advance before it leaves factory. $\mathcal{I}$ is responsible for issuing credentials to legitimate (or trusted) $\mathcal{D}_i$. $\mathcal{I}$ could be an independent trusted authority or a part of mobile network provider. The procedure of issuing could be executed with either $\mathcal{M}$ or $\mathcal{D}_i$ respectively. Service providers play the role of $\mathcal{V}$ in this interactive model. $\mathcal{V}_j$ outsources some verification strategies to $\mathcal{I}$ for confirming the legitimacy of $\mathcal{D}_i$. The verification strategies may involves $\mathcal{D}_i$'s configuration, user's membership status or the accounting and billing (e.g., $\mathcal{V}_j$'s subscription fees accounted with user's mobile phone bill). With these strategies, $\mathcal{V}_j$ authorizes $\mathcal{I}$ to distribute service-related credentials to $\mathcal{D}_i$. When requesting $\mathcal{V}_j$ for a service, the user generates an anonymous signature based on the corresponding credential to attests his legitimacy with other necessary information, such as the integrity measurement values of executing applications on $\mathcal{D}_i$, the amounts of e-cash or the content of e-ticket. The specific information structure and content are particularly defined by the service protocol. $\mathcal{V}_j$ authenticates the user's request by verifying his signature without revealing his identity. In some scenarios, $\mathcal{I}$ and $\mathcal{V}$ could be one entity. Figure 1 illustrates the system model for our proposed scheme.

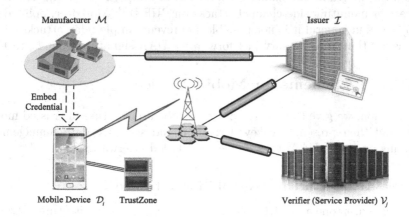

Manufacturer $\mathcal{M}$ Issuer $\mathcal{I}$

Embed Credential

Mobile Device $\mathcal{D}_i$ TrustZone   Verifier (Service Provider) $\mathcal{V}_j$

Fig. 1. System model of DAA-TZ.

3.2   Assumptions and Threat Model

In the system model, there is a dedicated channel between $\mathcal{M}$ and $\mathcal{I}$, which could be either physical connection or other forms of out-of-band communication, for $\mathcal{I}$ issuing credentials via $\mathcal{M}$. To simplify our design, we assume that data communications between $\mathcal{M}$ and $\mathcal{I}$, and between $\mathcal{D}_i$ and $\mathcal{V}_j$ build on secure transport protocols, like TLS/SSL, which can provide confidentiality, authenticity and integrity protection. Note that the secure channel between $\mathcal{D}_i$ and $\mathcal{V}_j$ is only verifier-authentication (i.e., unilateral authentication) in case $\mathcal{D}_i$'s identity is revealed. Additionally, Public Key Infrastructure (PKI) is also assumed to realize authenticating $\mathcal{I}$. As a consequence, $\mathcal{M}$, $\mathcal{V}_j$ and $\mathcal{D}_i$ can accurately obtain public keys, public parameters and revocation list from $\mathcal{I}$ who displays the public information with certificate for being downloaded.

Actually, the establishment of the whole system requires some premised trust relationships. First, the cooperation is assumed to be credible between $\mathcal{I}$ and each $\mathcal{M}$ who ensures not to embed credentials to illegal $\mathcal{D}_i$ or the $\mathcal{D}_i$ without available TrustZone. Second, $\mathcal{V}_j$ trusts that, before issuing credentials, $\mathcal{I}$ always checks $\mathcal{D}_i$'s legitimacy by using verification strategies provided by $\mathcal{V}_j$. As a result, $\mathcal{V}_j$ would believe that the right credentials are in the right users' hands. Another accepted fact is that the user trusts $\mathcal{M}$ not to deliberately damage his $\mathcal{D}_i$'s security. Constrained by the market supervision and the force of law, the above-mentioned trust relationships are easily established and maintained.

Based on the assumptions, DAA-TZ protects against the following adversary:

- The adversary can attack the scheme itself by attempting to pretend entities, manipulate data transmission between entities and forge data.
- The adversary can perform any software-based attacks which compromise the mobile Rich OS or existing applications running in REE. DAA-TZ interfaces in REE are also available for the adversary.
- The adversary can physically access the mobile device. He can reboot the device and gain access to data residing on persistent storage.

However, we ignore the malicious behaviors of tampering with the TrustZone hardware or mounting side-channel attacks on PUF [14]. Moreover, pointed out by [25], since in general it is not possible to prevent simple relay attacks, we do not consider that an adversary just forwards a DAA signature from $\mathcal{D}_i$ to $\mathcal{V}_j$.

4   DAA-TZ Scheme for Mobile Device

In this section, we give the specific design for the architecture of trusted mobile device, and then present the key derivation and sensitive data management. Depending on these, DAA-TZ scheme are detailed afterwards.

4.1   The Architecture of Trusted Mobile Device

Leveraging TrustZone and PUF technology, we design the architecture of trusted mobile device specifically for DAA-TZ. The software-based implementation of

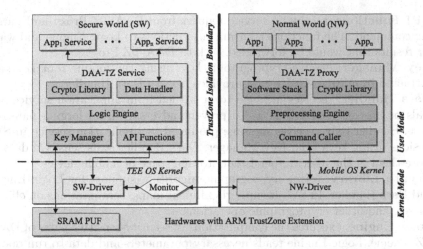

Fig. 2. Architecture of trusted mobile device for DAA-TZ.

DAA-TZ functionality on existing hardwares targets at economy, flexibility and extensibility. Figure 2 shows the detailed architecture with the way components interact with each other.

DAA-TZ functionality in the architecture contains two components: untrusted DAA-TZ Proxy in *normal world* (NW) and security-sensitive DAA-TZ Service in *secure world* (SW). In reality, SW instantiates TEE, while NW implements REE. DAA-TZ Service is isolated via TrustZone from other codes running in NW. The components are formally described as follows.

DAA-TZ Proxy. It is the component visible for mobile applications in NW. Waiting for their DAA-TZ service requests, the proxy handles the parameters and preprocesses them. According to the request type, the proxy would call DAA-TZ Service for substantive computations of the scheme and finally return the results. DAA-TZ Proxy consists of the following four subcomponents:

– **Software Stack**: provides top DAA-TZ interfaces for mobile applications. It parses the service requests and gives back service response results.
– **Crypto Library**: offers cryptographic algorithm support for Preprocessing Engine. In NW, this library only supports exponentiations on elliptic curves.
– **Preprocessing Engine**: executes pre-computation for DAA-TZ when one of two conditions is satisfied: a new credential is generated successfully, or a pre-computed result is consumed correctly.
– **Command Caller**: formats calling command and interacts with DAA-TZ Service. It sends the command through the GP TEE Client API [17], requests to switch NW to SW via NW-Driver and waits for the returned values.

DAA-TZ Service. It is the core component to perform DAA-TZ critical computations and operations. The execution of the component codes is under the well protection of TrustZone isolation mechanism. Five following subcomponents constitute DAA-TZ Service component:

- **API Functions**: receives a service request from DAA-TZ Proxy and parses the command. The functions transmit instructions to Logic Engine and waits for results that would be forwarded back to DAA-TZ Proxy.
- **Key Manager**: creates cryptographic keys using the unique root key seed extracted from SRAM PUF and provides keys to Data Handler.
- **Data Handler**: receives message to be signed from application service and seals or unseals sensitive data. To prevent adversary from forging message, Data Handler only receives message produced by application service in SW. Besides, using keys from Key Manager, Data Handler seals sensitive data to store them in the insecure persistent storage space of mobile device.
- **Crypto Library**: offers cryptographic algorithm support for Logic Engine and Data Handler. In SW, it supports bilinear maps, computations on elliptic curves, and other cryptographic operations.
- **Logic Engine**: executes the computations of security-sensitive parts of DAA-TZ scheme. Logic Engine reads necessary parameters and data to run operations relying on scheme specification.

Application and Application Service. The corresponding application should be launched if the user wants to enjoy a remote service from $\mathcal{V}_j$. The secure application released by $\mathcal{V}_j$ consists of two parts: App for NW and App Service for SW. App provides the GUI and basic functions. When App has the need to execute DAA-TZ procedures for remote service authenticating user's legitimacy with the message as service input, it calls DAA-TZ Proxy using its Software Stack. App could notify App Service in SW to prepare message to be signed through inter-domain communication mechanism supported by TrustZone [11]. App Service is trusted for processing security-sensitive data. It is sometimes non-existent if the remote service does not require secure computation or signed message as input.

Components in Kernels. SW-Driver in TEE OS Kernel and NW-Driver in Mobile OS Kernel handle the communication requests and responses with respect to switching the worlds. Implemented as Secure Monitor defined by TrustZone, the Monitor controls hardwares to fulfill the switching action.

Components in Hardwares. The hardware of mobile device support ARM TrustZone extension technology. Protected by TrustZone mechanism, SRAM PUF component is only accessible for SW.

4.2   Key Derivation and Sensitive Data Management

Prior to describing the concrete construction of our DAA scheme, we show how to derive various keys for different purposes using the root key seed extracted from SRAM PUF and how to utilize the derived keys to protect sensitive data.

Root Key Seed Extraction. We use the technique of SRAM PUF in [31] to extract the secret root key seed s, which is a unique bit string picked randomly by $\mathcal{M}$ who "stores" it in $\mathcal{D}_i$ through the physical features of one SRAM inside $\mathcal{D}_i$. From SRAM PUF component, s is only reproduced and securely cached by

Key Manager when $\mathcal{D}_i$ starts up every time in normal use. The confidentiality of s is rigidly guaranteed by TrustZone.

Key Derivation. Key Manager has the deterministic key derivation function $\mathsf{KDF} : \widetilde{\mathcal{S}} \times \widetilde{\mathcal{D}} \to \widetilde{\mathcal{K}}$, where $\widetilde{\mathcal{S}}$ is the key seed space, $\widetilde{\mathcal{D}}$ is a set of strings for statement of purposes with possible variables, and $\widetilde{\mathcal{K}}$ is the derived key space. Using the KDF, the device key pair which is analogous to the endorsement key pair in [22,23] and the storage root key for generating specific storage keys can be derived as $(dsk, dpk) \leftarrow \mathsf{KDF}_s(\text{'identity'})$ and $srk \leftarrow \mathsf{KDF}_s(\text{'storage\_root'})$ respectively, where s is the root key seed. Whereafter, we also use the storage keys derived from KDF with the storage root key srk to preserve sensitive data. The hierarchical structure of storage keys enhances the security for key usage. Note that all the derived keys are never stored permanently. Instead, they are regained via KDF with s at the same way when needed.

Sensitive Data Management. We can utilize the storage keys derived from the storage root key srk to seal the DAA-TZ's public parameters $params$, some mobile device $\mathcal{D}_i$'s credential $cred$ and a pair (f, T), where f is $\mathcal{D}_i$'s secret key and $T = g_1^f$ for some fixed basis g_1. The sealed results of these data can be stored in the insecure positions of NW.

- Protect integrity for $params$: $mk_{params} \leftarrow \mathsf{KDF}_{srk}(\text{'storage\_key'}, \text{'MAC'}, 0)$, $blob_{params} \leftarrow \mathsf{Data\_Seal}(\text{'MAC'}, mk_{params}, params)$, where

$$blob_{params} := params || \mathsf{MAC}_{mk_{params}}(params).$$

- Protect integrity for $cred$: $mk_{cred} \leftarrow \mathsf{KDF}_{srk}(\text{'storage\_key'}, \text{'MAC'}, T)$ and $blob_{cred} \leftarrow \mathsf{Data\_Seal}(\text{'MAC'}, mk_{cred}, cred)$, where

$$blob_{cred} := cred || \mathsf{MAC}_{mk_{cred}}(cred).$$

- Protect both confidentiality and integrity for (f, T): generate two kinds of keys by $(sk_f, mk_f) \leftarrow \mathsf{KDF}_{srk}(\text{'storage\_key'}, \text{'Enc+MAC'}, T)$, and then $blob_f \leftarrow \mathsf{Data\_Seal}(\text{'Enc+MAC'}, sk_f, mk_f, f, T)$, where

$$blob_f := \mathsf{Enc}_{sk_f}(f) || T || \mathsf{MAC}_{mk_f}(\mathsf{Enc}_{sk_f}(f) || T).$$

Data Handler can use $\mathsf{Data\_Unseal}()$ to recover and verify the sensitive data from blobs with the related keys regained by Key Manager.

4.3   The Details of DAA-TZ Scheme

Some preliminary work needs to be done as premise to start the normal procedures of the scheme. Specifically, when $\mathcal{M}$ initializes $\mathcal{D}_i$ in the factory, $\mathcal{M}$ guides $\mathcal{D}_i$ in SW to use its root key seed to generate the unique device key (dsk, dpk) which could uniquely identity $\mathcal{D}_i$. Then, $\mathcal{M}$ issues a certificate $cert$ for the public key dpk to indicate $\mathcal{M}$'s recognition for $\mathcal{D}_i$. The certificate $cert$ contains the configuration information (e.g., whether TrustZone is available) of $\mathcal{D}_i$.

For $\mathcal{D}_i$-centered design, DAA-TZ scheme consists of seven phases: **Setup**, **KeyGen**, **Embed**, **Sign**, **Verify**, **Revoke** and **Rejoin**. First of all, **Setup** is executed to create the public parameters. After that, the issuer $\mathcal{I}$ can execute **KeyGen** to generate its public/private key pair according to the public parameters. In addition, **KeyGen** and **Embed** are compelled to execute sequentially before $\mathcal{D}_i$ leaves the factory. Then, other phases are able to execute correctly according to application requirements. We adopt the techniques in [1,6,27] to build DAA-TZ scheme. The phases of DAA-TZ scheme are presented in detail as follows.

Setup. Given a security parameter λ, pick the suitable bilinear groups para-
meters $\Lambda = (p, \mathbb{G}_1, \mathbb{G}_2, \mathbb{G}_T, e, g_1, g_2)$ such that the bit-length of p is 2λ. In
addition, choose three independent collision-resistant hash functions:

$$\mathsf{H}_1 : \{0,1\}^* \to \mathbb{Z}_p, \ \mathsf{H}_2 : \{0,1\}^* \to \mathbb{G}_1, \ \mathsf{H}_3 : \{0,1\}^* \to \mathbb{Z}_p.$$

Finally, publish $(p, \mathbb{G}_1, \mathbb{G}_2, \mathbb{G}_T, e, g_1, g_2, \mathsf{H}_1, \mathsf{H}_2, \mathsf{H}_3)$ as the public parameters
params. For each mobile device $\mathcal{D}_i$, $\mathcal{M}$ imports *params* to $\mathcal{D}_i$ and calls
Data_Seal() to seal the *params*. The resulting blob $blob_{params}$ is stored in $\mathcal{D}_i$.

KeyGen. This phase initializes the public/private key pair for the issuer $\mathcal{I}$ and
generates a mobile device $\mathcal{D}_i$'s key.

–*Key Generation for Issuer.* Given *params* as input, $\mathcal{I}$ picks $x, y \leftarrow \mathbb{Z}_p^*$,
and computes $X := g_2^x$ and $Y := g_2^y$. $\mathcal{I}$ sets (x, y) as the private key $sk_{\mathcal{I}}$
and publishes (X, Y) as the public key $pk_{\mathcal{I}}$. We assume that some mobile
device $\mathcal{D}_i$ and verifier $\mathcal{V}_j$ could get the correct $pk_{\mathcal{I}}$ from $\mathcal{I}$ via verifying the
certificate[1] for $pk_{\mathcal{I}}$. Besides, $\mathcal{I}$ initializes a revocation list RL as empty.

–*Key Generation for Mobile Device.* In SW of a mobile device $\mathcal{D}_i$, Logic
Engine calls DAATZ_SW_Create() to generate key blob $blob_f$ that seals the
$\mathcal{D}_i$'s secret key f and public information T. It runs as:

$$blob_f \leftarrow \mathsf{DAATZ\_SW\_Create}(blob_{params}),$$

where the API mainly has the following four operations:
(1) Unseal the blob $blob_{params}$ to get *params* by calling Data_Unseal().
(2) Pick $f \leftarrow \mathbb{Z}_p^*$ and compute $T := g_1^f$.
(3) Call Data_Seal() to seal the pair (f, T) to obtain the key blob $blob_f$.
(4) Output $blob_f$.

$\mathcal{D}_i$ switches back to NW and stores $blob_f$ in its non-volatile memory.

Embed. In this phase, a credential *cred* for each mobile device $\mathcal{D}_i$ is produced
and embedded into the device before $\mathcal{D}_i$ leaves the factory as follows.
1. $\mathcal{M}$ obtains T from the key blob $blob_f$ and sends T to $\mathcal{I}$ through the
dedicated channel. Because of the cooperative relationship, $\mathcal{I}$ trusts $\mathcal{M}$
is asking for producing credential to embed into a $\mathcal{D}_i$ with legitimate
configurations. Thus, $\mathcal{I}$ does not check the validity of $\mathcal{D}_i$ any more. But
in this phase, only the credentials that do not require other more strict
verification strategies from $\mathcal{V}_j$ are permitted to issue.

---

[1] Utilizing PKI solution, a Certificate Authority (CA) issues a public key certificate
for $pk_{\mathcal{I}}$ to the issuer $\mathcal{I}$.

2. On input of a group element T, $\mathcal{I}$ runs the following signature algorithm to generate a credential $cred$ for T.

$$(A, B, C, D, c_\mathcal{I}, s_\mathcal{I}) \leftarrow \mathsf{SIG\_Cred}(params, sk_\mathcal{I}, T)$$

The signature algorithm has the following four steps:
(1) Choose $a \leftarrow \mathbb{Z}_p^*$ and compute $A := g_1^a$, $B := g_1^{a \cdot y}$, $C := g_1^{a \cdot x} \cdot T^{a \cdot x \cdot y}$, $D := T^{a \cdot y}$ and $t := a \cdot y$.
(2) Choose $r_\mathcal{I} \leftarrow \mathbb{Z}_p$ and compute $R_{\mathcal{I}1} := g_1^{r_\mathcal{I}}$, $R_{\mathcal{I}2} := T^{r_\mathcal{I}}$.
(3) Compute $c_\mathcal{I} := \mathsf{H}_1(B\|D\|g_1\|T\|R_{\mathcal{I}1}\|R_{\mathcal{I}2})$.
(4) Compute $s_\mathcal{I} := r_\mathcal{I} + c_\mathcal{I} \cdot t \pmod{p}$.
Then, $\mathcal{I}$ sends $(A, B, C, D, c_\mathcal{I}, s_\mathcal{I})$ to $\mathcal{M}$.
3. $\mathcal{M}$ imports the tuple $(A, B, C, D, c_\mathcal{I}, s_\mathcal{I})$ into SW of $\mathcal{D}_i$. Logic Engine calls the API DAATZ_SW_Join() to check the elements from $\mathcal{I}$ and generate a credential blob $blob_{cred}$ to store:

$$blob_{cred} \leftarrow \mathsf{DAATZ\_SW\_Join}(blob_{params}, pk_\mathcal{I}, T, A, B, C, D, c_\mathcal{I}, s_\mathcal{I}),$$

where the API executes the following operations:
(1) Call Data_Unseal() to unseal the blob $blob_{params}$ to obtain $params$.
(2) Compute $R'_{\mathcal{I}1} := g_1^{s_\mathcal{I}} \cdot B^{-c_\mathcal{I}}$ and $R'_{\mathcal{I}2} := T^{s_\mathcal{I}} \cdot D^{-c_\mathcal{I}}$.
(3) Compute $c'_\mathcal{I} := \mathsf{H}_1(B\|D\|g_1\|T\|R'_{\mathcal{I}1}\|R'_{\mathcal{I}2})$.
(4) Check whether the relations $A \neq 1_{\mathbb{G}_1}$, $e(A, Y) = e(B, g_2)$, $e(C, g_2) = e(A \cdot D, X)$ and $c_\mathcal{I} = c'_\mathcal{I}$ hold.
(5) If all the relations hold, set $cred := (A, B, C, D)$.
(6) Call Data_Seal() to seal $cred$, and output the resulting blob $blob_{cred}$.
Note that $\mathcal{M}$ could send simultaneously a set of $\{T_i\}_{i=1}^n$ to $\mathcal{I}$ by a single interaction, and obtain the corresponding credential set $\{cred_i\}_{i=1}^n$.
4. After a credential $cred$ is successfully obtained by $\mathcal{D}_i$, TrustZone switches to NW and DAA-TZ Proxy executes pre-computation in the background to prepare for user's fast anonymous signing operation in the following **Sign** phase. Preprocessing Engine calls DAATZ_NW_PreCmpt() to generate a blinded credential:

$$(l, S, U, V, W) \leftarrow \mathsf{DAATZ\_NW\_PreCmpt}(blob_{params}, blob_{cred}),$$

where the algorithm consists of the following steps.
(1) Get the prime p and credential $cred$ by directly reading the plaintext part of $blob_{params}$ and $blob_{cred}$ respectively.
(2) Parse $cred$ as (A, B, C, D).
(3) Choose $l \leftarrow \mathbb{Z}_p^*$ and compute $(S, U, V, W) := (A^l, B^l, C^l, D^l)$.
(4) Output (l, S, U, V, W).
Preprocessing Engine stores the output (l, S, U, V, W). Now that operations in $\mathcal{M}$ have been done, $\mathcal{D}_i$ is going to be delivered to the hand of a user.

Sign. This phase enables a user to anonymously attest the legitimacy of both his status and his mobile device.

1. App of a mobile device $\mathcal{D}_i$ connects a remote verifier $\mathcal{V}_j$. Then, $\mathcal{V}_j$ negotiates with $\mathcal{D}_i$ to decide a basename $bsn \in \{0,1\}^*$. If bsn is empty (i.e., $bsn = \bot$), it means that the signatures created by $\mathcal{D}_i$ are unlinkable. If bsn is a non-empty basename (i.e., $bsn \neq \bot$), the signatures produced by $\mathcal{D}_i$ are pseudonymous, i.e., signatures under the same basename could be linked and signatures under different basenames are unlinkable. In addition, $\mathcal{V}_j$ chooses a nonce $n_{\mathcal{V}_j} \leftarrow \{0,1\}^{2\lambda}$ and sends it to $\mathcal{D}_i$.

2. In NW, it is optional for App to notify App Service to prepare authentication information as message m to be signed. The notification is combined with the command for DAA-TZ Proxy to request generating signature.

3. On account of the request, the environment is switched into SW. App Service may need its user to securely input some information, such as password, to generate m. Then, Logic Engine calls DAATZ_SW_Sign() to create a DAA signature σ using the related pre-computation result as:

$$\sigma \leftarrow \mathsf{DAATZ\_SW\_Sign}(blob_{params}, blob_f, blob_{cred}, bsn, n_{\mathcal{V}_j}, m, l, S, U, V, W),$$

where the detailed process is presented as follows:
   (1) Unseal the blobs to get $params$, f, T and $cred$ by calling Data_Unseal().
   (2) If $bsn \neq \bot$, compute $J := \mathsf{H}_2(bsn)$ and $K := J^f$, else set $J, K := 1_{\mathbb{G}_1}$.
   (3) Choose $r_{\mathcal{D}_i} \leftarrow \mathbb{Z}_p$ and compute $R_{\mathcal{D}_i 1} := J^{r_{\mathcal{D}_i}}$ and $R_{\mathcal{D}_i 2} := B^{l \cdot r_{\mathcal{D}_i}}$.
   (4) Compute $c_{\mathcal{D}_i} := \mathsf{H}_3(J\|K\|S\|U\|V\|W\|R_{\mathcal{D}_i 1}\|R_{\mathcal{D}_i 2}\|bsn\|n_{\mathcal{V}_j}\|m)$.
   (5) Compute $s_{\mathcal{D}_i} := r_{\mathcal{D}_i} + c_{\mathcal{D}_i} \cdot f \pmod{p}$.
   (6) Output a signature $\sigma := (K, S, U, V, W, c_{\mathcal{D}_i}, s_{\mathcal{D}_i})$.
   After σ is generated successfully, the environment is switched back to NW with the returned outputs m and σ that are eventually sent to $\mathcal{V}_j$.

4. Through the above step, a pre-computation result (l, S, U, V, W) is consumed. Preprocessing Engine deletes the previous pre-computation result, then calls DAATZ_NW_PreCmpt() again to get a new pre-computation tuple (l', S', U', V', W') for the next use. This pre-computation process is executed parallelly in the background of NW without causing obvious time delays felt by the user.

Verify. In this phase, a verifier $\mathcal{V}_j$ checks whether or not a signature σ on a message m is valid.

1. $\mathcal{V}_j$ verifies (m, σ) by the means of calling verification algorithm Verify() as:

$$res \leftarrow \mathsf{Verify}(params, pk_{\mathcal{I}}, bsn, n_{\mathcal{V}_j}, m, \sigma),$$

where the algorithm runs in detail as follows:
   (1) Parse σ as $(K, S, U, V, W, c_{\mathcal{D}_i}, s_{\mathcal{D}_i})$.
   (2) For each $f_{rvk} \in RL$, if $W = U^{f_{rvk}}$, then set $res := false$ and abort.
   (3) If $bsn \neq \bot$, compute $J' := \mathsf{H}_2(bsn)$, else set $J' := 1_{\mathbb{G}_1}$.
   (4) Compute $R'_{\mathcal{D}_i 1} := J'^{s_{\mathcal{D}_i}} \cdot K^{-c_{\mathcal{D}_i}}$ and $R'_{\mathcal{D}_i 2} := U^{s_{\mathcal{D}_i}} \cdot W^{-c_{\mathcal{D}_i}}$.
   (5) Compute $c'_{\mathcal{D}_i} := \mathsf{H}_3(J'\|K\|S\|U\|V\|W\|R'_{\mathcal{D}_i 1}\|R'_{\mathcal{D}_i 2}\|bsn\|n_{\mathcal{V}_j}\|m)$.
   (6) Check whether the relations $S \neq 1_{\mathbb{G}_1}$, $e(S, Y) = e(U, g_2)$, $e(V, g_2) = e(S \cdot W, X)$ and $c_{\mathcal{D}_i} = c'_{\mathcal{D}_i}$ hold.

(7) If all the relations hold, then $res := true$, else $res := false$.

According to the verification result res, $\mathcal{V}_j$ decides whether to accept the message/signature pair (m, σ) and provide service for the owner of $\mathcal{D}_i$.

Revoke. In this phase, if a secrete key f has been revealed, it could be revoked.

1. $\mathcal{I}$ has the duty to censor the Internet. By collecting and analyzing daily logs, $\mathcal{I}$ tries to find the clue indicating the leakage of f and its declared valid credential $cred$. If the pair $(f, cred)$ is found, $\mathcal{I}$ checks whether $cred$ is a valid credential on the f with $params$ and $pk_{\mathcal{I}}$. For valid one, $\mathcal{I}$ adds f into RL, i.e., $RL := RL \cup \{f\}$.

2. $\mathcal{V}_j$ maintains locally a revocation list RL which is regularly updated from the revocation list published by $\mathcal{I}$.

Rejoin. This phase enables $\mathcal{D}_i$ to recreate a new secret key f' and obtain a related new credential $cred'$, when an old key f of $\mathcal{D}_i$ has already been revoked, or $\mathcal{D}_i$ intends to apply for a membership credential under a new public key created by either a new or an existing issuer[2]. We choose an IND-CCA secure public key encryption scheme (ENC, DEC) for the following usage with the device key pair (dpk, dsk). In particular, $C \leftarrow \mathsf{ENC}_{dpk}(M)$ and $M \leftarrow \mathsf{DEC}_{dsk}(C)$ denote that encrypting the message M with the public key dpk to obtain a ciphertext C, and decrypting the ciphertext C with the secret key dsk to recover a message M respectively. This phase is executed as follows.

1. DAA-TZ Proxy sends $\mathcal{D}_i$'s dpk and its certificate $cert$ to $\mathcal{I}$.

2. $\mathcal{I}$ checks whether dpk is valid with $cert$ for confirming $\mathcal{D}_i$'s configurations. Utilizing the verification policy from $\mathcal{V}_j$, $\mathcal{I}$ checks other properties of $\mathcal{D}_i$ and its owner. If all the checks are passed, $\mathcal{I}$ randomly chooses a key k for MAC operation, and a nonce $n_{\mathcal{I}} \leftarrow \{0,1\}^{2\lambda}$. $\mathcal{I}$ then adds $n_{\mathcal{I}}$ into a nonce list NL which is initially empty, i.e., $NL := NL \cup \{n_{\mathcal{I}}\}$. Next, $\mathcal{I}$ generates a commitment request by encrypting k and $n_{\mathcal{I}}$ with dpk, i.e., $comm_{req} \leftarrow \mathsf{ENC}_{dpk}(k\|n_{\mathcal{I}})$. Finally, $\mathcal{I}$ sends $comm_{req}$ to $\mathcal{D}_i$.

3. DAA-TZ Proxy invokes DAA-TZ Service with inputting $comm_{req}$. In SW, DAATZ_SW_Commit() is called to generate a commitment response:

$$comm_{res} \leftarrow \mathsf{DAATZ\_SW\_Commit}(comm_{req}),$$

where the process is executed as follows:

(1) Recover the device private key dsk using the root key seed s, i.e., $(dsk, dpk) \leftarrow \mathsf{KDF}_s(\text{'identity'})$.

(2) Use the secret key dsk to decrypt $comm_{req}$: $k\|n_{\mathcal{I}} \leftarrow \mathsf{DEC}_{dsk}(comm_{req})$.

(3) Call DAATZ_SW_Create() to generate a blob $blob_{f'}$ associated with a new secret key f' and the corresponding $T' = g_1^{f'}$.

(4) Compute $\tau \leftarrow \mathsf{MAC}_k(T'\|n_{\mathcal{I}})$ and $comm_{res} := (\tau, n_{\mathcal{I}}, T')$.

Finally, $\mathcal{D}_i$ switches back to NW and sends $comm_{res}$ to $\mathcal{I}$.

---

[2] If the public key of an existing issuer has expired, it should refresh its public key by creating a new one and obtaining the corresponding certificate.

4. $\mathcal{I}$ first verifies whether $comm_{res}$ is valid by computing $\tau' \leftarrow \mathsf{MAC}_k(T'||n_{\mathcal{I}})$ and checking if the relations $n_{\mathcal{I}} \in NL$ and $\tau = \tau'$ hold. If hold, as in the **Embed** phase, $\mathcal{I}$ runs the $\mathsf{SIG\_Cred}()$ algorithm with the public parameters $params$, its secret key $sk'_{\mathcal{I}}$ and the T' contained in $comm_{res}$ as the input to obtain a tuple $comm_{cred} := (A', B', C', D', c'_{\mathcal{I}}, s'_{\mathcal{I}})$, i.e.,

$$(A', B', C', D', c'_{\mathcal{I}}, s'_{\mathcal{I}}) \leftarrow \mathsf{SIG\_Cred}(params, sk'_{\mathcal{I}}, T').$$

Finally, $\mathcal{I}$ sends the above tuple $comm_{cred}$ to $\mathcal{D}_i$.

5. As in the **Embed** phase, DAA-TZ Service in SW calls $\mathsf{DAATZ\_SW\_Join}()$ with the tuple $comm_{cred}$ to generate a credential blob $blob'_{cred}$, i.e.,

$$blob'_{cred} \leftarrow \mathsf{DAATZ\_SW\_Join}(blob_{params}, pk'_{\mathcal{I}}, T', A', B', C', D', c'_{\mathcal{I}}, s'_{\mathcal{I}}),$$

where $pk'_{\mathcal{I}}$ is the public key of $\mathcal{I}$.

6. Back to NW, Preprocessing Engine invokes $\mathsf{DAATZ\_NW\_PreCmpt}()$ to obtain a pre-computation tuple, i.e.,

$$(l', S', U', V', W') \leftarrow \mathsf{DAATZ\_NW\_PreCmpt}(blob_{params}, blob'_{cred}).$$

4.4   Security Analysis

DAA-TZ satisfies the desired security properties for mobile devices, such as anonymity (including forward anonymity and pseudonymity), traceability and non-frameability. The detailed description of these properties and the analysis can be found in the full paper [29].

5   Implementation and Evaluation

In this section, we first present the prototype system of DAA-TZ from both aspects of hardware and software. Afterwards, we show the comparison of the proposed scheme to other four solutions. Finally, we give the performance evaluation and analysis based on our prototype system.

5.1   Implementation

Hardware Platform. To simulate real environment, we implement the role of manufacturer on one PC platform. Issuer and verifier are together implemented on another PC platform. For simulating mobile device, we leverage a development board Zynq-7000 AP Soc Evaluation Kit [24] to implement functions of DAA-TZ. It is TrustZone-enabled and equipped with ARM Cortex-A9 MPCore, 1GB DDR3 memory and On-Chip Memory (OCM) module including 256 KB SRAM. However, this SRAM is initialized by BootROM once the board is powered on, which prevents us from reading its initial data. Then we utilize an SRAM chip that is the type IS61LV6416-10TL [18] to act as our SRAM PUF. SRAM initial data is transferred to the Zynq development board by an FPGA implementation of Universal Asynchronous Receiver/Transmitter (UART) in Verilog hardware description language. A UART receiver in the Zynq board receives and stores the SRAM data in a RAM cache. Then the processor can fetch the SRAM data in the RAM cache via the bus.

Software Implementation. The software implementation on the development board for mobile device is divided into two parts. In secure world, we use Open Virtualization SierraTEE as the basic TEE OS which is compliant with GP's TEE Specifications [17]. For Key Manager of DAA-TZ Service, the fuzzy extractor of PUF is constructed on an open source BCH code [13]. For Crypto Library, we use OpenSSL-0.9.8y for general cryptographic algorithms, and Pairing-Based Cryptography (PBC) 0.5.14 library for computations of elliptic curves and pairings. We choose SHA256 for $H_2()$, 1280-bit RSA key pair for the device key and 128-bit AES encryption with HMAC-SHA256 for sealing and unsealing operations. 2315 lines of code (LOC) in C language totally make up our components and auxiliary functions in secure world. In normal world, we run a Linux as REE OS with kernel 3.8.6. The SieraTEE project provides the Linux with NW-Driver and GP TEE Client API., DAA-TZ Proxy totally comprises 1651 LOC. Besides we program one test application that could request executing DAA-TZ scheme. It contains 1068 LOC running in NW. In addition, there are several tens of thousands of LOC for implementing manufacturer, issuer and verifier.

5.2 Comparison

Dedicated for TrustZone security extension, DAA-TZ achieves some valuable and meaningful properties. In Table 1, we show how our scheme compares to existing solutions from the latest literature. These are ISC10 [25], BCL08 in LAMS [28], BL10 and CPS10 in Mdaak [30]. Likewise building on ECC-DAA and TrustZone technology, these solutions are all designed for mobile platform. The comparison focuses on the items related to mobile device, involving the most time-consuming computation amount of on-line anonymous signing (that leads user to wait for its instant result) depending on whether bsn is null, the switch times between SW and NW when executing signing, and other properties including realized pre-computation, user-controlled pseudonym, forward anonymity and sensitive data management using a root of trust. The notations used in the table are as follows: when we write $E_{\mathbb{G}_1}$ or $E_{\mathbb{G}_T}$, we mean the exponentiation is in group $\mathbb{G}_1$ or $\mathbb{G}_T$; $E_{\mathbb{G}_1}^2$ denotes 2 simultaneous exponentiations on $\mathbb{G}_1$, i.e. computing $a_1^{b_1} \cdot a_2^{b_2}$; P is short for pairing computation; the check mark ($\checkmark$) denotes the solution considers or has this property while the X mark ($\times$) denotes not; the slash (/) indicates it does not support pseudonym.

From the table, it is clear that the proposed scheme not only has the least on-line computation amount and switch times for mobile devices in signing phase, but also provides all other listed properties. The signing phase is the most frequent execution and deeply influences the whole scheme's efficiency. Overall, the combination of these advantages endows DAA-TZ with a good user experience as well as high security.

Table 1. Comparison of DAA-TZ to other related solutions

	Computation Amount of On-line Signing		Switch Times of Signing	Pre-Compute	Controllable Pseudonym	Forward Anonymity	Data Management
	$bsn = \perp$	$bsn \neq \perp$					
ISC10	$4E_{\mathbb{G}_1}$	/	$\geqslant 1$	✗	✗	✗	✗
BCL08 (LAMS)	$3E_{\mathbb{G}_1} + 4E_{\mathbb{G}_T} + 3P$	/	2	✗	✗	✗	✗
BL10 (Mdaak)	$4E_{\mathbb{G}_1} + E^2_{\mathbb{G}_1} + E_{\mathbb{G}_T} + P$		2	✗	✔	✗	✔
CPS10 (Mdaak)	$7E_{\mathbb{G}_1}$		1	✗	✔	✗	✔
DAA-TZ	$E_{\mathbb{G}_1}$	$3E_{\mathbb{G}_1}$	1	✔	✔	✔	✔

5.3 Performance Evaluation

We measure the performance of DAA-TZ on the prototype system revolving around mobile device through a series of experiments with different parameters. Referring to ISO/IEC 15946-5 standard [19], we select two kinds of elliptic curves that are suitable for realizing Type-3 pairings. These curves are MNT curve with embedding degree 6 and BN curve with embedding degree 12. For testing various security levels of curves, we totally conduct 6 experiments respectively using MNT160, MNT224, BN160, BN192, BN224 and BN256, where each number denotes the approximate number of bits to optimally represent an element of the group $\mathbb{G}_1$. More precisely, MNT160 and BN160 provide 80-bit security level; MNT224 and BN192 provide 96-bit; BN224 and BN256 respectively provide 112-bit and 128-bit. Our experiments simulate the whole DAA-TZ running process covering instantiated protocol, TrustZone switch and sensitive data management. Each average experimental result is taken over 20 test-runs.

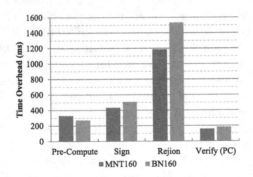

Fig. 3. Time overheads of the critical processes with 80-bit security level.

On MNT and BN curves with 80-bit security level, Fig. 3 illustrates the average time overheads of critical processes including the computations of pre-compute, **Sign** (excluding pre-computation) and **Rejoin** on mobile device and **Verify** on PC for verifier. The results indicate that using both curves the frequent computations about either pre-compute or **Sign** only take less than 500 milliseconds (ms), while infrequent and time-consuming **Rejoin** spends less than 1550 ms. Even if the computation amount of **Verify** is quite large, the time overhead is indeed low on PC platform.

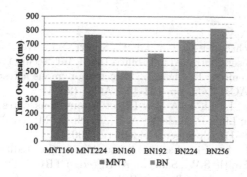

Fig. 4. On-line time overheads of **Sign** phase with different security levels.

Figure 4 shows the average on-line time overheads of single **Sign** phase (excluding pre-computation) on mobile device using two curves with different security levels. From the figure, we can see that as the security levels increase, the time overheads of **Sign** phase have evident growth. Encouragingly, all the resulting overheads spend less than 820 ms, which is completely acceptable for a mobile user.

Actually, a direct performance comparison of our competitive scheme to others is difficult because of four inevitable differences: the hardware platforms, the algorithm libraries, the selections of elliptic curves, and the completeness degrees of programming. Anyhow, according to our comparison and experimental results, DAA-TZ can be considered as a reasonably efficient scheme for mobile device. In regard to adopting modern mobile devices that are much more powerful than our development board and a more optimal library to implement elliptic curves and parings, the time overhead of our scheme could be further decreased.

6 Conclusion

In this paper, we propose DAA-TZ, a complete and efficient DAA scheme using TrustZone, to deal with the security and privacy issues specially for mobile users. DAA-TZ enables manufacture to embed credentials into devices and guarantees the minimal switch times of TrustZone during signing phase. Pre-computation is also carefully taken into consideration to raise scheme's efficiency. The root of trust provided by SRAM PUF, key derivation and sensitive data management collectively enhance the security of our scheme. The implementation and evaluation convince that DAA-TZ is quite practical for mobile users. Our next step is to design the concrete secure applications based on DAA-TZ.

Acknowledgment. We thank Shijun Zhao and the anonymous reviewers for their valuable comments. This work was supported in part by grants from the National Natural Science Foundation of China (No. 91118006, No. 61202414 and No. 61402455) and the National 973 Program of China (No. 2013CB338003).

References

1. Bernhard, D., Fuchsbauer, G., Ghadafi, E., Smart, N.P., Warinschi, B.: Anonymous attestation with user-controlled linkability. Int. J. Inf. Secur. **12**(3), 219–249 (2013)
2. Brickell, E., Camenisch, J., Chen, L.: Direct anonymous attestation. In: Proceedings of the 11th ACM CCS, pp. 132–145. ACM (2004)
3. Brickell, E., Chen, L., Li, J.: A New Direct Anonymous Attestation Scheme from Bilinear Maps. In: Lipp, P., Sadeghi, A.-R., Koch, K.-M. (eds.) Trust 2008. LNCS, vol. 4968, pp. 166–178. Springer, Heidelberg (2008)
4. Brickell, E., Li, J.: A pairing-based DAA scheme further reducing TPM resources. In: Acquisti, A., Smith, S.W., Sadeghi, A.-R. (eds.) TRUST 2010. LNCS, vol. 6101, pp. 181–195. Springer, Heidelberg (2010)
5. Chen, L., Li, J.: Flexible and scalable digital signatures in tpm 2.0. In: Proceedings of the 20th ACM CCS, pp. 37–48. ACM (2013)
6. Chen, L., Page, D., Smart, N.P.: On the design and implementation of an efficient DAA scheme. In: Gollmann, D., Lanet, J.-L., Iguchi-Cartigny, J. (eds.) CARDIS 2010. LNCS, vol. 6035, pp. 223–237. Springer, Heidelberg (2010)
7. Chen, X., Feng, D.: Direct anonymous attestation for next generation tpm. J. Comput. **3**(12), 43–50 (2008)
8. Commission, F.T., et al.: Mobile privacy disclosures: Building trust through transparency. Federal Trade Commission Staff Report (2013)
9. Galbraith, S., Paterson, K., Smart, N.: Pairings for cryptographers. Discrete Appl. Math. **156**(16), 3113–3121 (2008)
10. Guajardo, J., Kumar, S.S., Schrijen, G.-J., Tuyls, P.: FPGA intrinsic PUFs and their use for IP protection. In: Paillier, P., Verbauwhede, I. (eds.) CHES 2007. LNCS, vol. 4727, pp. 63–80. Springer, Heidelberg (2007)
11. Jang, J., Kong, S., Kim, M., Kim, D., Kang, B.B.: Secret: Secure channel between rich execution environment and trusted execution environment. In: NDSS 2015 (2015)
12. Maganis, G., Shi, E., Chen, H., Song, D.: Opaak: using mobile phones to limit anonymous identities online. In: Proceedings of the 10th International Conference on Mobile Systems, Applications, and Services, pp. 295–308. ACM (2012)
13. Morelos-Zaragoza, R.: Encoder/decoder for binary bch codes in c (version 3.1)
14. Oren, Y., Sadeghi, A.-R., Wachsmann, C.: On the effectiveness of the remanence decay side-channel to clone memory-based PUFs. In: Bertoni, G., Coron, J.-S. (eds.) CHES 2013. LNCS, vol. 8086, pp. 107–125. Springer, Heidelberg (2013)
15. ARM: Trustzone. http://www.arm.com/products/processors/technologies/trustzone. Last accessed 5 May 2015
16. GENODE: An exploration of arm trustzone technology. http://genode.org/documentation/articles/trustzone. Last accessed 1 May 2015
17. GlobalPlatform: Tee client api specification version 1.0 (2010)
18. Integrated Silicon Solution Inc: IS61LV6416-10TL. http://www.alldatasheet.com/datasheet-pdf/pdf/505020/ISSI/IS61LV6416-10TL.html
19. ISO/IEC: 15946–5: 2009 information technology-security techniques: Cryptographic techniques based on elliptic curves: Part 5: Elliptic curve generation (2009)
20. Proxama (2015). http://www.proxama.com/platform/
21. Sansa Security: Discretix (2014). https://www.sansasecurity.com/blog/discretix-becomes-sansa-security/. Last accessed 22 June 2014
22. Trusted Computing Group: TPM main specification version1.2, revision 116 (2011). http://www.trustedcomputinggroup.org. Last accessed 25 October 2014

23. Trusted Computing Group: Trusted platform module library, family 2.0 (2013). http://www.trustedcomputinggroup.org. Last accessed 10 March 2015
24. Xilinx: Zynq-7000 all programmable soc zc702 evaluation kit. http://www.xilinx.com/products/boards-and-kits/EK-Z7-ZC702-G.htm
25. Wachsmann, C., Chen, L., Dietrich, K., Löhr, H., Sadeghi, A.-R., Winter, J.: Lightweight anonymous authentication with TLS and DAA for embedded mobile devices. In: Burmester, M., Tsudik, G., Magliveras, S., Ilić, I. (eds.) ISC 2010. LNCS, vol. 6531, pp. 84–98. Springer, Heidelberg (2011)
26. Wilson, P., Frey, A., Mihm, T., Kershaw, D., Alves, T.: Implementing embedded security on dual-virtual-cpu systems. IEEE Des. Test **24**(6), 582–591 (2007)
27. Xi, L., Yang, K., Zhang, Z., Feng, D.: DAA-related APIs in TPM 2.0 revisited. In: Holz, T., Ioannidis, S. (eds.) Trust 2014. LNCS, vol. 8564, pp. 1–18. Springer, Heidelberg (2014)
28. Yang, B., Feng, D., Qin, Y.: A lightweight anonymous mobile shopping scheme based on daa for trusted mobile platform. In: 2014 IEEE 13th International Conference on TrustCom, pp. 9–17. IEEE (2014)
29. Yang, B., Yang, K., Qin, Y., Zhang, Z., Feng, D.: DAA-TZ: An effcient DAA scheme for mobile devices using ARM Trust Zone (full version) (2015) (ePrint)
30. Zhang, Q., Zhao, S., Xi, L., Feng, W., Feng, D.: Mdaak: A flexible and efficient framework for direct anonymous attestation on mobile devices. In: Information and Communications Security. Springer (2014)
31. Zhao, S., Zhang, Q., Hu, G., Qin, Y., Feng, D.: Providing root of trust for arm trustzone using on-chip sram. In: Proceedings of the 4th International Workshop on Trustworthy Embedded Devices, pp. 25–36. ACM (2014)

DAA-A: Direct Anonymous Attestation with Attributes

Liqun Chen[1] and Rainer Urian[2]([✉])

[1] Hewlett-Packard Laboratories, Bristol, UK
liqun.chen@hp.com
[2] Infineon Technologies AG, Neubiberg, Germany
rainer.urian@infineon.com

Abstract. The TPM 2.0 specification has been designed to support a new family of Elliptic Curve (EC) based Direct Anonymous Attestation (DAA) protocols. DAA protocols are limited to anonymous or pseudonymous attestations. But often a more flexible attestation would be needed. For instance, attesting that the platform is a certain model from a certain vendor. Such an attestation would require to bind the attributes "model" and "vendor" to the TPM.

This paper shows how the DAA protocols can be augmented with an arbitrary number of attributes. This gives a new family of protocols called DAA-A, which means DAA with attributes. In a DAA-A protocol, the user of the TPM/platform can select which attributes he will show to the verifier and which attributes he will hide. The authenticity of the hidden attributes will be proved by a zero knowledge protocol. The DAA-A protocols have user controlled linkability in the same way as the DAA protocols. We show explicitly, how the two most prominent EC based DAA protocols for TPM 2.0 can be extended to DAA-A protocols.

Keywords: Direct anonymous attestation · Attributes · Trusted platform module

1 Introduction

Direct Anonymous Attestation (DAA) is a cryptographic protocol used to provide verifiable attestation for a computer platform with a TPM chip. The attestation is done by showing a signed authentication token to the verifier (e.g. service provider). The TPM chip and the host processor of the platform share the calculation of the authentication token. The TPM chip performs only a minor part of the calculations. Advanced arithmetic, like pairing calculations, will be done by the host processor. Since privacy protection is very important, the DAA protocol has two modes of user controlled linkability.

- Full anonymous attestation mode. This means, if two attestations to the same or to different service providers have been performed it is not possible for anyone to decide if both attestations have been done by the same platform or by two different ones.

© Springer International Publishing Switzerland 2015
M. Conti et al. (Eds.): TRUST 2015, LNCS 9229, pp. 228–245, 2015.
DOI: 10.1007/978-3-319-22846-4_14

– Pseudonymous attestation mode. In this mode a service provider can recognize a platform by its pseudonym. But different service providers get different pseudonyms for the same platform. This implies that nobody can correlate two pseudonymous attestations.

The current TPM 2.0 specification [14] supports two different DAA protocols which are based on pairings over elliptic curves. The first [4] is based on Camenisch-Lysyanskana (CL) credentials [7] and the second one [5] is based on sDH credentials [2]. The paper from Chen and Li [9] shows how both DAA protocols can be used with a TPM 2.0 chip.

In some circumstances neither anonymous nor pseudonymous attestation is ideally suited. For instance, consider the following use-case. The platform manufacturer wants to provide the customers of its premium models a free cloud account. Instead of requiring a cumbersome registration procedure from the customer, he uses the TPM chip to attest the cloud service the manufacturer and model version of the platform. In order for this to work, the platform manufacturer must somehow bind the attributes 'manufacturer' and 'model' to the TPM. Privacy is also an important issue here. Therefore, the user must always be in control what attributes he will show to the service provider and what attributes he will hide from him. On the other hand, the service provider shall only get the attributes he really needs for the attestation process. In data privacy this is called the minimum disclosure principle.

The purpose of this paper is to show how the DAA protocols can be extended with attributes. Instead of representing the possession of a single secret in a DAA signed token, the signed authentication token in DAA-A represents the possession of a set of attributes. The platform user can select which attributes he will disclose to the service provider and which attributes he will hide from him. The authenticity of the hidden attributes will then be proved by a zero knowledge protocol. This new protocol family is therefore called DAA-A, which means DAA with Attributes. Each attribute can optionally be associated to a pseudonym and can be protected by the TPM chip. Protecting the attribute in a TPM chip provides much greater security. In addition to that, it has also a further benefit. The TPM 2.0 specification contains so called policy authorizations. One can associate to each TPM protected attribute an authorization policy which constraints the usage of the attribute. This makes the following use-cases possible:

– Binding a user password authentication to the token.
– Providing the token with an expiration date.
– Providing the token with a limited number of authentication uses.

We show DAA-A extensions for the CL- and sDH-based DAA protocols. In summary, our proposed DAA-A protocols have the following features:

– They are based on CL or sDH DAA protocols with user controlled linkability.
– They can have an arbitrary number of additional attributes.
– Each attribute can be associated with a pseudonym.
– Each attribute can be stored in TPM shielded location.
– Each attribute can be selectively disclosed under control of the user.

From a high level view, our DAA-A construction consists of an underlying DAA scheme with an anonymous credential of a public key. But in contrast to a DAA scheme, the public key does not correspond to a single secret key, but is the result of a discrete logarithm representation of multiple attributes. A DAA protocol is a special case of the DAA-A protocol. By using a single attribute, one gets a protocol which is mathematically identical to the DAA protocol. By hiding all attributes one gets a protocol which is equivalent to the DAA protocol, i.e. it has the same security and privacy properties.

Although the DAA-A protocols have been primarily designed for use with a TPM chip they can also be used in other contexts, for instance as an identity smart card. In this case, the complete signing operation of the protocol has to be performed on the smart card. The CL based DAA-A protocol is especially well suited for this, because it uses only standard elliptic curve calculations. The whole protocol can therefore effectively be implemented on a standard Java card.

2   Related Work

The first RSA DAA protocol was introduced by Brickell, Camenisch and Chen [3] for the TPM 1.2 specification [13]. The Idemix protocol uses the same RSA based anonymous credential scheme as that DAA protocol and adds attributes with selective disclosure [6]. But Idemix can neither be used with a TPM 1.2 nor with a TPM 2.0.

The U-Prove protocol [11] from Microsoft is an attribute based protocol with user controlled selective disclosure. The paper of Chen and Li [9] shows how U-Prove can be integrated with a TPM 2.0 chip. But the U-Prove protocol has the severe drawback that it is not multi-show unlinkable. The reason for this is that the authentication token of the U-Prove protocol is signed by a Schnorr-like signature and the signature value can be used as a correlation handle. To be unlinkable, a U-Prove token may only be used once. Our DAA-A protocols use similar tokens like the U-Prove protocol. One can therefore interpret our DAA-A protocols as U-Prove with anonymous credentials.

Bangerter et al. [1] show a cryptographic framework for multi-show and selective disclosure protocols. But their framework does not support the integration of a TPM. They show the BM-CL protocol as an application for their framework. This protocol is also based on CL credentials. But it uses a symmetric type I pairing, while our CL-DAA proposal uses a type III pairing, which is more efficient. In order to get comparable cryptographic strength to a 256 bit type III curve, the finite field of the type I curve must have approximately 1536 bit. Also, a BM-CL authentication token needs two curve points per attribute, while our CL-DAA protocol needs only one point per attribute. This implies that our protocol is much more efficient. Finally, type I pairings cannot be integrated with TPM 2.0 chips, based on the current TPM 2.0 specification [14].

3 Two DAA-A Schemes

3.1 A General View of Them

Preliminaries. Let $\mathbb{F}$ be a finite base field and $\tilde{\mathbb{F}}$ be a finite extension field of $\mathbb{F}$. Let $\mathbb{E}$ be an elliptic curve defined over $\mathbb{F}$ with a base point G. Let $\tilde{\mathbb{E}}$ denote the points of $\mathbb{E}$ over the extension field $\tilde{\mathbb{F}}$ and $\tilde{G}$ be a base point of $\tilde{\mathbb{E}}$. The curve $\mathbb{E}$ shall be equipped with a type III pairing $\tau : \mathbb{E} \times \tilde{\mathbb{E}} \to \tilde{\mathbb{F}}$. Uppercase Latin or Greek letters always indicate elliptic curve points on the curve $\mathbb{E}$. Uppercase Latin or Greek letters with a tilde on top will denote elements on the curve $\tilde{\mathbb{E}}$. The operation on $\mathbb{E}$ (resp. $\tilde{\mathbb{E}}$) is written with additive notation. Multiplication by scalars is always written on left. Scalars are always defined on $\mathbb{Z}_q$, where q is the group order of the subgroup $\langle G \rangle$ in $\mathbb{E}$. Arithmetic has to be understood in the respective finite fields. Two hash functions: $H_1 : \{0,1\}^* \to \mathbb{Z}_q$ and $H_2 : \{0,1\}^* \to \mathbb{E}$, are used in these two schemes.

The public system parameters consist of the additional group elements G_1, ..., $G_n \in \mathbb{E}$. As the same as in a DAA scheme, players in a DAA-A scheme include signers, verifiers and a certificate issuer. The issuer has a secret signature key isk and its corresponding public verification key ipk.

A signer generates its authentication token denoted by Γ. Let $x_1, \ldots, x_n$ be elements from $\mathbb{Z}_q$ which encodes attributes belonging to the signer. The authentication token is then a discrete logarithm representation:

$$\Gamma := \sum_{k=1}^{n} x_k G_k.$$

Without losing generality, the first attribute x_1 is used as the signer identity key. When the signer is separated into the TPM and host, as discussed in Sect. 6.1, this attribute is the TPM DAA-A secret key tsk, and the corresponding public key is tpk $= x_1 G_1$. All the other attributes can be either held by the TPM or by the host. Each attribute can be associated with a pseudonym. For user-controlled linkability, we need a pseudonym associated to the signer identity key.

In a DAA-A scheme, the issuer will calculate a certificate for the token Γ. How the issuer gets the token and checks its authenticity is out of scope for this paper. The issuer may know all attributes of the token, i.e. the whole discrete logarithm representation of the token. But it may also be the case that the issuer knows only some or none of the attributes of the token; particularly with a TPM involvement the issuer should never know the TPM identity key. In this case, the issuer must probably get some assurance that the token is authentic. One way to do this is to use the Sign/Verify protocol of an already established token. We understand that this is an application and implementation decision.

The Join Protocol. The Join protocol is performed by the issuer and signer and the later can be split between the TPM and host.

1. The issuer gets the token value Γ. The method to achieve this is dependent on implementations for specific applications. As an example, this can be done in any of the following cases.

- The signer sends only the value tpk to the issuer. For each of the other attributes $x_k : k = 2 \ldots n$, the issuer must get either the attribute x_k itself or the corresponding public key $P_k := x_k G_k$. The issuer calculates Γ from tpk and $x_2(\text{resp. } P_2), \ldots, x_n(\text{resp. } P_n)$.
   - The signer directly sends the value Γ to the issuer.
   - The signer sends part of the Γ value and the issuer finds the remaining part from other resources.
2. The issuer calculates a signature on Γ under its isk, denoted by cre, and returns cre back to the signer.
3. The signer verifies cre. This step is optional. If there is a perfect trust relationship between issuer and signer, then this step can be omitted.

When the TPM is involved, this means that the issuer will authenticate the TPM. The details of this implementation will be discussed in Sect. 4.

The Sign/Verify Protocol. The Sign/Verify protocol is performed by the signer and verifier. Let $D \subseteq \{2 \ldots n\}$ denote the indices of the disclosed attributes and $U = \{1 \ldots n\} \backslash D$ the set of non disclosed attributes. Note that the first index is the signer ID attribute which is never disclosed. Let $T \subseteq U$ be the attributes held by the TPM and $P \subseteq U$ be the attributes which are associated with a pseudonym. Without loss of generality, let $U = \{1 \ldots u\}$ and $P = \{1 \ldots p\}$ where $p \leq u$.

1. The verifier sends a challenge m to the signer. The challenge usually includes a message to be signed and the verifier's nonce in order to guarantee that the signature is fresh. In order to link the signer identity key x_1 to a particular base name, denoted by bsn_1, both the signer and verifier should be aware of this value. If two signatures by the same signer using the same bsn_1 value, they should be linked. In reality, any hidden attribute with associated pseudonym can be used to check if tokens are linked or not. Pseudonyms must not be unique; they can also be associated to groups. By combining several pseudonyms, arbitrary linking policies can be defined. For simplicity, we only consider linking or not linking by the signer identity key.
2. The signer randomizes cre to obtain cre′ in such a way that given cre′ one cannot connect it to the original cre. This is done by the host. The signer computes a DAA-A signature σ on m under $\forall x_k \in U$. The signature includes the pseudonym $J_k = H_2(\mathsf{bsn}_k)$ and $K_k = x_k J_k$ associated to attribute x_k if $k \in P$. The special attribute x_1 with associated pseudonym is used for two purposes:
   (a) if x_1 is in RogueList, a verifier can reject any signature under this signer;
   (b) if two signatures signed by the same signer and using the same bsn_1, they can be linked.
3. The signer sends the signature to the verifier.
4. The verifier first check if the signer identity key has been revoked or not:

$$\forall \hat{x}_1 \in \mathsf{RogueList}, \text{ if } K_1 = \hat{x}_1 J_1, \text{ reject } \sigma \text{ and abort.}$$

If x_1 is not in RogueList, the verifier verifies the signature.

5. If required, the verifier checks the linkability: Given two valid signatures $\sigma = (\ldots, K_1, \ldots)$ and $\bar{\sigma} = (\ldots, \bar{K}_1, \ldots)$ with the same bsn_1 value, if $K_1 = \bar{K}_1$, output *linked*; otherwise output *not linked*.

In the next two subsections, we will introduce two concrete DAA-A schemes. These two DAA-A schemes can be seen as an extension of their corresponding underlying DAA schemes [4,5]. The difference between them is only the way to generate a credential cre, which will naturally affect the way to generate a DAA-A signature. In the first scheme, cre is a modified CL signature [7], and in the second scheme, cre is an sDH based signature [2]. We call these two schemes the CL-based scheme and the sDH-based scheme, respectively. We only explain the credentials and DAA-A signatures in these two schemes and omit the other parts, since they follow the general view we have just talked about.

3.2   The CL-Based Scheme

Issuer Parameters. The Issuer parameters consist of the following elements:

- The public group elements $G, G_1, \ldots, G_n \in \mathbb{E}$ and $\tilde{G}, \tilde{G}_1, \ldots, \tilde{G}_n \in \tilde{\mathbb{E}}$ corresponding to the token attributes, where $G_k = r_k G$ and $\tilde{G}_k = r_k \tilde{G}$ for $k = 1 \ldots n$ and $r_k \in_R \mathbb{Z}_q$.

  It is required that the values r_k for $k = 1 \ldots n$ are generated by the setup system and erased after the setup process, such that there is no known discrete logarithm relation between any G_k and G_j and between any G_k and G.
- The secret signature keys $x, y \in \mathbb{Z}_q$.
- The public signature group elements $\tilde{X} = x\tilde{G}, \tilde{Y} = y\tilde{G}$.

Generate and Verify cre. The issuer generates cre by performing the following steps:

1. Calculate a modified Camenisch-Lysyanskaya (CL) signature for the signer's authentication token Γ, denoted by (A, B, C, D, E_k) with $r \in_R \mathbb{Z}_q$:

$$A = rG; \quad B = yA; \quad C = xA + rxy\Gamma; \quad D = ry\Gamma; \quad E_k = ryG_k, k = 1 \ldots n.$$

2. Perform a Schnorr ZK proof written as $(\hat{c}, \hat{s})$, which shows that the discrete logarithms to the base G of B, to the base G_k of E_k and to the base Γ of D are equivalent:

$$w \in_R \mathbb{Z}; \quad \hat{c} = \mathsf{H}_1(wG \| wG_1 \| \ldots \| wG_n \| w\Gamma \| m); \quad \hat{s} = w - \hat{c}ry,$$

where m is a message for freshness agreed by the issuer and signer. This step is optional. If the issuer and signer have a trust relationship, these steps can be skipped.
3. Form the certificate $cre = (A, B, C, D, E_1, \ldots, E_n, \hat{c}, \hat{s})$.

Given the credential cre, the signer verifies it as follows. This step is also optional. If the issuer and signer have a trust relationship, these steps can be skipped.

1. Verify the certificate cre:

$$\tau(A, \tilde{Y}) \stackrel{?}{=} \tau(B, \tilde{G}); \quad \tau(A + D, \tilde{X}) \stackrel{?}{=} \tau(C, \tilde{G}).$$

2. Verify the discrete logarithm equivalence via $(\hat{c}, \hat{s})$:

$$\hat{c} \stackrel{?}{=} \mathsf{H}_1(\hat{c}B + \hat{s}G \| \hat{c}E_1 + \hat{s}G_1 \| \ldots \| \hat{c}E_n + \hat{s}G_n \| \hat{c}D + \hat{s}\Gamma \| m).$$

3. Accept cre if both the above verification pass; otherwise reject it.

Generate and Verify σ. To generate a DAA-A signature σ, the signer performs as follows:

1. **Blind:** Choose blinding factors: $a \in_R \mathbb{Z}_q$, and blind the modified CL certificate:

$$A' = aA; \quad B' = aB; \quad C' = aC; \quad D' = aD; \quad E'_k = aE_k, k = 1 \ldots n.$$

2. **Commit:** For $k \in U$ compute the commit values. If $k \in T$ then this calculation is done by the TPM, else by the host.
   (a) If $k \in T$, the TPM returns R_k to the host and store w_k in a protected place.
   (b) if $k \in P$ then calculate $J_k = \mathsf{H}_2(bsn_k); \quad K_k = x_k J_k; \quad L_k = w_k J_k;$

3. **Hash:** The host calculates the Hash value.

$$c = \mathsf{H}_1\left(A'\|B'\|C'\|D'\|E'_1\|\ldots\|E'_n\| \sum_{k \in U} R_k \, \|J_1\|K_1\|L_1\|\ldots\|J_p\|K_p\|L_p\| \, m\right)$$

4. **Sign:** For $k \in U$ compute the sign values. If $k \in T$ then this calculation is done by the TPM, else by the host.

$$s_k = w_k - c x_k$$

5. **Form a Signature:**

$$\sigma = (A', B', C', D', E'_1, \ldots, E'_n, c, s_{k \in U}, x_{k \in D}, J_1, K_1, \ldots, J_p, K_p).$$

Given a signature σ, the verifier performs as follows to verify its validation.

1. Verify the modified CL certificate,

$$\tau(A', \tilde{Y}) \stackrel{?}{=} \tau(B', \tilde{G}); \quad \tau(A' + D', \tilde{X}) \stackrel{?}{=} \tau(C', \tilde{G}).$$

2. Verify the discrete logarithm equivalence by the batch proof trick:

$$t_1, \ldots t_n \in_R \mathbb{Z}; \quad \tau\left(\sum_{k=1\ldots n} t_k E'_k, \tilde{G}\right) \stackrel{?}{=} \tau\left(B', \sum_{k=1\ldots n} t_k \tilde{G}_k\right).$$

3. Verify the Schnorr ZK proof of knowledge of the hidden attributes:

$$\mu := c\left(D' - \sum_{k \in D} x_k E'_k\right) + \sum_{k \in U} s_k E'_k$$

$$c \stackrel{?}{=} \mathsf{H}_1\left(A'\|B'\|C'\|D'\|E'_1\|\ldots\|E'_n\|\mu\|J_1\|K_1\|cK_1 + s_1 J_1\|\ldots\|J_p\|K_p\|cK_p + s_p J_p\| m\right).$$

4. Accept the signature σ if all the above verifications pass; otherwise reject it.

3.3 The sDH-Based Scheme

Issuer Parameters. The Issuer parameters consist of the following elements:

- The public group elements $G, G_0, G_1, \ldots, G_n, H \in \mathbb{E}$ and $\tilde{G} \in \tilde{\mathbb{E}}$. It is required that the elements are generated randomly, such that there is no known discrete logarithm relation between any two elements.
- The secret signature key $x \in \mathbb{Z}_q$.
- The public signature verification key $\tilde{X} := x\tilde{G}$.

Generate and Verify cre. The issuer generates cre by calculating a sDH signature cre for the authentication token Γ:

$$\xi \in_R \mathbb{Z}_q; \quad A := (x + \xi)^{-1}(G_0 + \Gamma); \quad \mathsf{cre} = (A, \xi).$$

The signer verifies $\mathsf{cre} = (A, \xi)$. This step is optional. If the issuer and signer have a trust relationship, this step may be skipped.

$$\tau(A, \tilde{X} + \xi\tilde{G}) \stackrel{?}{=} \tau(G_0 + \Gamma, \tilde{G}).$$

Remark 1. The additional group element G_0 is necessary here. Otherwise the signer could chosen an arbitrary integer α and create a second valid token $\Gamma' := \alpha\Gamma$; $A' := \alpha A$

Generate and Verify σ. To generate a DAA-A signature σ, the signer performs as follows:

1. **Blind:** Randomize the group element A.

$$\eta \in_R \mathbb{Z}_q; \quad A' := A + \eta H.$$

2. **Commit:** For $k \in U$ compute the commit values, $R_k = w_k G_k$ where $w_k \in_R \mathbb{Z}_q$. If $k \in T$ then this calculation is done by the TPM, else by the host.
   (a) compute c. If $k \in T$ the TPM returns R_k to the host and store w_k in a protected place.
   (b) if $k \in P$ then calculate $J_k = \mathsf{H}_2(\mathsf{bsn}_k); \quad K_k = x_k J_k; \quad L_k = w_k J_k;$
3. **Hash:** The host calculates the Hash value.

$$w_\alpha, w_\beta, w_\gamma \in_R \mathbb{Z}_q; \quad \mu := \tau\left(w_\alpha H, \tilde{X}\right); \quad \omega := \tau\left(w_\beta A' + w_\gamma H + \sum_{k \in U} R_k, \tilde{G}\right)$$

$$c := \mathsf{H}_1\left(\mu\omega \| J_1 \| K_1 \| L_1 \| \ldots \| J_p \| K_p \| L_p \| m\right)$$

$$s_\alpha := w_\alpha - c\eta; \quad s_\beta := w_\beta + c\xi; \quad s_\gamma := w_\gamma - c\eta\xi;$$

4. **Sign:** For all $k \in U$ compute the sign values. If $k \in T$ then this calculation is done by the TPM, else by the host.

$$s_k := w_k - cx_k$$

5. **Form a Signature:**

$$\sigma = (A', c, s_\alpha, s_\beta, s_\gamma, s_{k \in U}, x_{k \in D}, J_1, K_1, \ldots, J_p, K_p).$$

Given a signature σ, the verifier performs as follows to verify its validation.

1. Verify the signature:

$$\mu := \tau \left(cA' + s_\alpha H, \tilde{X} \right)$$

$$\omega := \tau \left(s_\beta A' + s_\gamma H + \sum_{k \in U} s_k G_k - cG_0 - c \sum_{k \in D} x_k G_k, \tilde{G} \right)$$

$$c \overset{?}{=} \mathsf{H}_1 \left(\mu \cdot \omega \, \| J_1 \| K_1 \| cK_1 + s_1 J_1 \| \ldots \| J_p \| K_p \| cK_p + s_p J_p \| \, m \right).$$

2. Accept the signature σ if the above verification passes; otherwise reject it.

4   Implementation of DAA-A with TPM 2.0

In this section, we present how the TPM operations in the DAA-A scheme can be implemented by using a TPM 2.0 chip. Most of the TPM commands have multiple options, regarding to different types of keys and applications. For simplicity, we only explain these options that are related to the DAA-A implementation, and we also omit some input and output information if they are not relevant to our purposes.

4.1   TPM 2.0 Hosted Attributes

When attributes are stored in a TPM, they can be treated as ECDAA signing keys. Each attribute value is the private key part. Let $attr_k$ denote the handle of the TPM signing key which is associated to the TPM hosted attribute. Although the public key part will not be used by the ECDAA protocol, the TPM needs it for security reasons. There are two different ways how the attributes will be bound to a TPM. The attribute can be generated by the TPM itself or it can be generated by a third party and then imported by the TPM. The TPM generates a key by using the TPM2_Create() command. The command returns the public key part and an encrypted key blob containing the private key. The host will then send the public part of the generated key to the issuer. Before the TPM can use the key, the private key blob must be loaded with the TPM2_Load() command.

    The attribute may also be provided by a third party, which is normally the issuer. For instance, this could be an issuer chosen identifier which is used for a revocation check. The TPM will import such a key with the TPM2_LoadExternal() command.

    The TPM has restricted resources and can only host a few keys at the same time. One strategy is that the TPM creates for each key $attr_k$ a context blob ctx_k with the TPM2_ContextSave($attr_k$) command. This returns an encrypted context blob which can be stored on the host. If the key is needed it can be reloaded to the TPM with the TPM2_ContextLoad(ctx_k) command, which returns the key handle $attr_k$. The procedure for using a TPM hosted key is then as follows:

1. Load the key blob with $attr_k$ = TPM2_ContextLoad(ctx_k).
2. Execute TPM2_Commit($attr_k$,...) or TPM2_Sign($attr_k$,...).
3. Unload the key with TPM2_FlushContext($attr_k$), to make room for the next one.

4.2   The TPM 2.0 DAA-A Join Process

The Join process is basically an agreement of the token Γ between the issuer and the prover (i.e. host/TPM). It is not necessary that the issuer knows all the attributes x_k of Γ. The issuer must only get enough information form the prover that the issuer can reconstruct the token $\Gamma := \sum_{k=1}^{n} x_k G_k$. It is equally well possible that the prover sends only the public part $H_k = x_k G_k$ of some attributes x_k. More generally, the prover may also send some linear combination of attributes, i.e. the sub-token $\Gamma' := H_{k_1} + H_{k_2} + \cdots + H_{k_l}$. This could be useful in the following situation: The prover wants to keep an attribute x_k hidden from the issuer. But if that attribute has low entropy, sending the public part $H_k = x_k G_k$ reveals the same information then sending the private value x_k, because the issuer can simply calculate x_k by exhaustive search. To mitigate this threat, the prover chooses a second attribute x_r with high entropy, e.g. a random value, and calculates $H_r = x_r G_r$. He then builds the sub-token $\Gamma' = H_k + H_r$ and sends it to the issuer.

There are numerous other methods, how the issuer and prover can share information of the token. Here are two further examples:

- Host and issuer have pre-agreed on some attributes by some out-of-band process.
- Host and issuer perform a Diffie-Hellman key agreement to build a shared secret attribute.

How the issuer, host and TPM get assurance that the attributes are correct and from the correct party is depending on the particular situation. One typical use-case would be the following adaption from the standard DAA scheme as described in [12], ch. 12.4: The TPM master private key $sDAAkey$ is assigned to the first attribute x_1. The host and issuer agree on the other attributes $x_2, \ldots, x_n$. The host then sends the TPM public key $pDAAkey$ to the issuer. The issuer calculates the token $\Gamma = pDAAKey + \sum_{k=2}^{n} x_k G_k$. The further issuance steps go in the same way as described in [12], ch. 12.4. The only difference is that the issuer creates a credential for Γ instead of for $pDAAKey$.

4.3   The TPM 2.0 DAA-A Sign/Verify Process

The verification process does not involve a TPM. Therefore we describe here the sign process only. We assume that in advance the verifier and host have agreed upon the basename values bsn_k for each $k \in P$ and a message msg, which primary use is to proof freshness of the signature. The TPM is only involved in the *Commit* and *Sign* substeps of the Sign/Verify protocols. We describe the process for the sDH scheme only. This can be easily adapted to the CL based scheme by replacing the points G_k with E'_k.

Commit: The TPM command TPM2_Commit() has two modes, one for attributes with assigned pseudonyms and the other one for attributes without associated pseudonyms. Both variants get a handle of the loaded TPM key $attr_k$ and the base point G_k as input parameter and return the commitment point R_k and an integer value $count_k$, i.e. $(R_k, count_k) = $ TPM2_Commit($attr_k, G_k$). This counter value is incremented for each call to the TPM2_Commit() command. The counter is used as an index to the committed value. It will be given as a parameter for the corresponding TPM2_Sign() command, such that both commands can be correctly associated.

The variant with pseudonym gets the additional parameter bsn_k and y_k as input parameter. The reason for the parameter y_k is the following. The TPM must calculate a point J_k on the elliptic curve from bsn_k. To do that, it first hashes the bsn_k value by the hash function which has been associated to the key $attr_k$ beforehand. That results in the x-coordinate of the elliptic curve point J_k. Since the related y coordinate is not unique, it will be given as a further parameter. The commit function returns the additional points K_k and L_k, which are used for the pseudonym calculation: $(R_k, K_k, L_k, count_k) = $ TPM2_Commit($attr_k, G_k, bsn_k, y_k$).

Sign: The sign step will be performed by the TPM2_Sign() command. This command gets the key handle $attr_k$, the counter value cnt_k from the related TPM2_Commit() command and the hash value c which has been calculated by the host in the *Hash* step. The Sign command returns the integer sign value: $s_k = $ TPM2_Sign($attr_k, count_k$).

5   Performance Comparison

Here we compare the performance of both proposed DAA-A schemes. Token issuance will be done very rarely compared to signing and verification of the token. Therefore we only analyze sign and verification step of the DAA-A protocol. We will also not make performance estimations of TPM hosted attributes and pseudonyms. In this chapter we use the following assumptions: Let λ be the bit size of the prime field. We are working with a Barreto-Naehrig curve over this prime field with cofactor 1. Therefore the extension field will have degree 12 and the bit size of the group order will be λ. Let n denote the number of attributes, u the number of hidden attributes and p the number of pseudonyms.

5.1   Token Size

First we analyze the token size. We assume that elliptic curve points are encoded in compressed form. That means, an elliptic curve point over the base field will need λ bits of space. We further assume that the attribute values are encoded in λ bits. Then we get the following table

Scheme	Token size
sDH DAA-A	$(5 + n + 2p) \cdot \lambda$
CL DAA-A	$(5 + 2n + 2p) \cdot \lambda$

5.2 Computational Cost

By using Karatsuba multiplication we get the time complexity $m(\lambda) := O(\lambda^{log_2 3})$ for multiplication in a finite prime field of size λ bits. We make the simplifying assumption that field multiplication and squaring operations are of the same time complexity. An elliptic curve addition uses 14 finite field multiplications and an elliptic curve doubling operation uses 10 multiplications in projective coordinates. We assume the standard "double and add" algorithm for scalar multiplication in the elliptic curve. Assuming that half of the bits of the scalar multiplicand will require an addition operation, a scalar multiplication in the elliptic curve will cost:

$$\epsilon(\lambda) := (10 + 14/2) \cdot \lambda \cdot m(\lambda)$$

In the extension field of degree 12, a multiplication costs 45 base field multiplications (see [10], ch. 5). Scalar multiplication in the elliptic curve over the extension field of degree 12 will cost

$$\tilde{\epsilon}(\lambda) := 17 \cdot \lambda \cdot 45m(\lambda)$$

According to ([10], ch. 8.5), a type III Tate pairing over an elliptic curve with embedding degree 12 will cost

$$\tau(\lambda) := 203 \cdot \lambda \cdot m(\lambda)$$

We will only count elliptic curve scalar multiplication and pairing operations, as they dominate the execution time. This gives us the following time complexity table:

Scheme	Sign cost	Verify cost
sDH DAA-A	$(3 + u + p) \cdot \epsilon(\lambda) + 2 \cdot \tau(\lambda)$	$(5 + u + 2p) \cdot \epsilon(\lambda) + 2 \cdot \tau(\lambda)$
CL DAA-A	$(4 + u + 2p) \cdot \epsilon(\lambda)$	$(2n + 2p) \cdot \epsilon(\lambda) + n \cdot \tilde{\epsilon}(\lambda) + 6 \cdot \tau(\lambda)$

The table shows that the CL DAA-A scheme is more efficient for the signer, while the sDH DAA-A scheme is more efficient for the verifier.

Measurements of a typical TPM 2.0 chip showed the following timings for a 256 bit elliptic curve:

A typical host computer with optimised big number arithmetic will perform a 256 bit elliptic curve exponentiation in less than 1 ms.

Command	Timing
TPM2_Commit (with pseudonym)	$\approx 400\ ms$
TPM2_Sign	$\approx 90\ ms$
TPM2_ContextLoad/FlushContext	$< 50\ ms$

6   Security Analysis of the DAA-A Schemes

6.1   Formal Security Definition of DAA-A

In this section, we discuss the security definition of *DAA with Attributes* (DAA-A). We modify the DAA security model described in [8] by adding the concept of attributes to get the security model of a DAA-A scheme. In a DAA scheme a signer has a single DAA secret which is usually used as the signer's identity. In a DAA-A scheme, except the secret identity a signer also has a set of attributes. Some attributes may be kept at secret (i.e., given a DAA-A signature one can't tell the values of these attributes) and others may appear in a DAA-A signature; in this paper, we call them *"hidden attributes"* and *"open attributes"*. In reality, a signer has a single identity but can have multiple sets of attributes. For simplicity, we assume that each signer will only have one set of attributes. We also consider only the most important case that the first attribute is held by the TPM and has an associated pseudonym. All other attributes are held by the host and have no associated pseudonym. Some attributes might not be known to any adversary, but in this security model we assume that any attribute value is not a secret although it might be a hidden attribute. We believe that this will not make the security model weaker than it should be against common real life threats.

The same as a DAA scheme, a DAA-A scheme involves four types of players: a DAA-A issuer i, a set of TPM $\mathfrak{m}_i \in \mathfrak{M}$, host $\mathfrak{h}_i \in \mathfrak{H}$ and verifier $\mathfrak{v}_j \in \mathfrak{V}$. Throughout the paper, for the purpose of simplicity, we may omit some of the index values if it does not occur any confusion. There might be more than one issuer involved in a system but we assume that they are independent to each other.

The players $\mathfrak{m}_i$ and $\mathfrak{h}_i$ form a computer platform in the trusted computing environment and share the role of a DAA-A signer. More specifically, $\mathfrak{m}_i$ plays a major role of the signer by holding a secret key tsk_i that is cryptographically bounded with the signer's identification (denoted as ID_i in the security model); $\mathfrak{h}_i$ plays a helper role of the signer by holding a set of attributes att_i and the credential cre_i associated with tsk_i att_i. The set att_i means here only the additional attributes, i.e. not including the first attribute, which is the signer's secret identity key tsk_i. A DAA scheme can be seen as a special case of a DAA-A scheme with $|\mathsf{att}_i| = 0$.

Like in the DAA security model, the following three cases are considered in the DAA-A security model: (1) neither $\mathfrak{m}_i$ nor $\mathfrak{h}_i$ is corrupted by an adversary, (2) both of them are corrupted, and (3) $\mathfrak{h}_i$ is corrupted but not $\mathfrak{m}_i$. We do not consider the case that $\mathfrak{m}_i$ is corrupted but not $\mathfrak{h}_i$.

A DAA-A scheme DAA-A = (Setup, Join, Sign, Verify, Link) consists of the following five polynomial-time algorithms and protocols:

- Setup: On input of a security parameter 1^t, i uses this randomized algorithm to produce a pair (isk, pp), where isk is the issuer's secret key, and pp is the global public parameters for the system, including the issuer's public key ipk, a description of a DAA-A credential space C, a description of a finite message space M and a description of a finite signature space Σ. We will assume that pp are publicly known so that we do not need to explicitly provide them as input to other algorithms.
- Join: This protocol is performed between a signer $(\mathfrak{m}_i, \mathfrak{h}_i)$ and an issuer i. $\mathfrak{m}_i$ inputs a secret key tsk_i, $\mathfrak{h}_i$ and i jointly select a set of attributes att_i, and i with the input of isk produces cre_i that is a DAA-A credential associated with tsk_i and att_i. As a result, $\mathfrak{m}_i$ saves tsk_i, $\mathfrak{h}_i$ holds att_i and cre_i, and i records cre_i.
- Sign: On input of tsk_i, att_i (with an indication of hidden/open attributes), cre_i, a basename bsn_j (the name string of $\mathfrak{v}_j$ or a special symbol $\perp$), and a message m that includes the data to be signed and optionally the verifier's nonce n_V for freshness, $\mathfrak{m}_i$ and $\mathfrak{h}_i$ run this protocol to produce a randomized signature σ on m under $(\mathsf{tsk}_i, \mathsf{att}_i, \mathsf{cre}_i)$ associated with bsn_j. The basename bsn_j is used for controlling the linkability.
- Verify: On input of m, bsn_j, a candidate signature σ for m, and a set of rogue signers' secret keys RogueList, $\mathfrak{v}_j$ uses this deterministic algorithm to return either 1 (accept) or 0 (reject). Note that how to build the set of RogueList is out the scope of the DAA-A scheme.
- Link: On input of two signatures σ_0 and σ_1, $\mathfrak{v}_j$ uses this deterministic algorithm to return 1 (linked), 0 (unlinked) or $\perp$ (invalid signatures). The algorithm will output $\perp$ if, by using an empty RogueList (which means to ignore the rogue TPM check), either $\mathsf{Verify}(\sigma_0) = 0$ or $\mathsf{Verify}(\sigma_1) = 0$ holds. Otherwise, the algorithm will output 1 if signatures can be linked or 0 if the signatures cannot be linked. Note that, unlike Verify, the result of Link is not relied on whether the corresponding $\mathsf{tsk} \in$ RogueList or not.

In this security model, a DAA-A scheme must hold the notions of *correctness*, *user-controlled-anonymity* and *user-controlled-traceability*. They are defined as follows.

Correctness. If both the signer and verifier are honest, that implies $\mathsf{tsk}_i \notin$ RogueList, the signatures and their links generated by the signer will be accepted by the verifier with overwhelming probability. This means that the above DAA-A algorithms must meet the following consistency requirement.

If $(\mathsf{isk}, \mathsf{pp}) \leftarrow \mathsf{Setup}(1^t)$,

$(\mathsf{tsk}_i, \mathsf{att}_i, \mathsf{cre}_i) \leftarrow \mathsf{Join}(\mathsf{isk}, \mathsf{pp})$, and

$(m_b, \sigma_b) \leftarrow \mathsf{Sign}(m_b, \mathsf{bsn}_l, \mathsf{tsk}_i, \mathsf{att}_i, \mathsf{cre}_i, \mathsf{pp})|_{b=\{0,1\}}$, then

$1 \leftarrow \mathsf{Verify}(m_b, \mathsf{bsn}_l, \sigma_b, \mathsf{pp}, \mathsf{RogueList})|_{b=\{0,1\}}$, and

$1 \leftarrow \mathsf{Link}(\sigma_0, \sigma_1, \mathsf{pp})|_{\mathsf{bsn}_l \neq \perp}$.

Further if $(\mathsf{tsk}_j, \mathsf{att}_j, \mathsf{cre}_j) \leftarrow \mathsf{Join}(\mathsf{isk}, \mathsf{pp}), i \neq j$;
$(m_3, \sigma_3) \leftarrow \mathsf{Sign}(m_3, \mathsf{bsn}_l, \mathsf{tsk}_j, \mathsf{att}_j, \mathsf{cre}_j, \mathsf{pp})$, then
$0 \leftarrow \mathsf{Link}(\sigma_b, \sigma_3, \mathsf{pp})|_{\mathsf{bsn}_l \neq \perp}$.

User-Controlled-Anonymity. The notion of user-controlled-anonymity is defined via the following game played by a challenger $\mathcal{C}$ and an adversary $\mathcal{A}$, in which except for an arbitrary pair of legitimate signers the adversary $\mathcal{A}$ could be any player (including the issuer, verifiers or other legitimate signers):

- *Initial:* $\mathcal{C}$ runs $\mathsf{Setup}(1^t)$ and gives the resulting isk and pp to $\mathcal{A}$. Alternatively, $\mathcal{C}$ receives pp from $\mathcal{A}$ with a request for initiating the game, and then verifies the validation of the pp by checking whether each element of the pp is in the right groups or not.
- *Phase 1:* $\mathcal{C}$ is probed by $\mathcal{A}$ who makes the following queries:
  - Corrupt. $\mathcal{A}$ submits a signer's identity ID of his choice to $\mathcal{C}$, who responds with the values tsk and att of the signer.
  - Join. $\mathcal{A}$ submits a signer's identity ID and a set of attributes of his choice to $\mathcal{C}$. They run the protocol Join, in which $\mathcal{C}$ plays as the signer and $\mathcal{A}$ plays as the issuer. As a result the values tsk, att and cre are created. $\mathcal{C}$ verifies the validation of cre and keeps tsk and att.
  - Sign. $\mathcal{A}$ submits a signer's identity ID, a set of attributes att (with the hidden/open indication), a base name bsn (either $\perp$ or a data string) and a message m of his choice to $\mathcal{C}$, who runs Sign to get a signature σ and responds with σ.
- *Challenge:* At the end of Phase 1, $\mathcal{A}$ chooses two signers' identities ID_0 and ID_1, two sets of attributes att_0 and att_1 each for one signer, a message m and a base name bsn of his choice to $\mathcal{C}$. $\mathcal{A}$ must not have made any Corrupt query on either ID_0 or ID_1, and not have made the Sign query with the same bsn if $\mathsf{bsn} \neq \perp$ with either ID_0 or ID_1. One more condition, the attribute sets att_0 and att_1 must include the same number of attributes and the same open attribute values. Note that their hidden attributes could be different to each other. To make the challenge, $\mathcal{C}$ chooses a bit b uniformly at random, signs m associated with bsn under $(\mathsf{tsk}_b, \mathsf{att}_b, \mathsf{cre}_b)$ to get a signature σ and returns σ to $\mathcal{A}$.
- *Phase 2:* $\mathcal{A}$ continues to probe $\mathcal{C}$ with the same type of queries that it made in Phase 1. Again, it is not allowed to corrupt any signer with the identity either ID_0 or ID_1, and not allowed to make any Sign query with bsn if $\mathsf{bsn} \neq \perp$ with either ID_0 or ID_1.
- *Response:* $\mathcal{A}$ returns a bit b'. We say that the adversary wins the game if $b = b'$.

Definition 1. *Let $\mathcal{A}$ denote an adversary that plays the game above. We denote by $\mathbf{Adv}[\mathcal{A}_{\mathsf{DAA-A}}^{anon}] = |\mathbf{Pr}[b' = b] - 1/2|$ the advantage of $\mathcal{A}$ in breaking the user-controlled-anonymity of $\mathsf{DAA-A}$. We say that a DAA scheme is user-controlled-anonymous if for any probabilistic polynomial-time adversary $\mathcal{A}$, the quantity $\mathbf{Adv}[\mathcal{A}_{\mathsf{DAA-A}}^{anon}]$ is negligible.*

Note that a value is *negligible* means this value is a function $\epsilon(t)$, which is said to be *negligible* in the parameter t if $\forall c \geq \mathbb{Z}_{>0} \exists t_c \in \mathbb{R}_{>0}$ such that $\forall t > t_c, \epsilon(t) < t^{-c}$.

User-Controlled-Traceability. The notion of User-Controlled-Traceability is defined via a game played by a challenger C and an adversary A as follows:

- *Initial:* There are two initial cases. In Initial Case 1. C executes $\mathsf{Setup}(1^t)$ and gives the resulting pp to A, and C keeps isk secret. This indicates that A does not corrupt the issuer i. In Initial Case 2. C receives pp from A and does not know the value of isk. This indicates that A is i. In both the cases, C setups a list of RogueList starting with empty.
- *Probing:* C is probed by A who makes the following queries:
  - Corrupt. This is the same as in the game of user-controlled-anonymity, except that at the end C puts the revealed tsk into the list of RogueList.
  - Join. There are three join cases of this query; the first two are used associated with the Initial Case 1, and the last one is used associated with the Initial Case 2. Suppose that A does not use a single ID for more than one join case or more than one time; this means that each signer will only have a triple (tsk, att, cre).
    * Join Case 1: A submits a signer's identity ID and attributes att of his choice to C, who runs Join to create tsk and cre for the signer, and then C sends cre to A and keeps tsk secret. This case indicates that A is the host $\mathfrak{h}$.
    * Join Case 2: A submits a signer's identity ID with a tsk value and attributes att of his choice to C, who runs Join to create cre for the signer and puts the given tsk into the list of RogueList. C responds A with cre. This case indicates that A is the signer $(\mathfrak{m}, \mathfrak{h})$.
    * Join Case 3: A submits a signer's identity ID and attributes att of his choice to C, who runs Join with A to create tsk and to obtain cre from A. C verifies the validation of cre and keeps tsk secret. This case indicates that A is the issuer i and the host $\mathfrak{h}$.
  - Sign. The same as in the game of user-controlled-anonymity.
  - Semi-sign. A submits a signer's identity ID along with the data transmitted from $\mathfrak{h}$ to $\mathfrak{m}$ in Sign of his choice to C, who acts as $\mathfrak{m}$ in Sign and responds with the data transmitted from $\mathfrak{m}$ to $\mathfrak{h}$ in Sign. Here A is the host $\mathfrak{h}$ and makes use of C as $\mathfrak{m}$.
- *Forge:* A returns a signer's identity ID, a signature σ, its signed message m and the associated basename bsn. We say that the adversary wins the game if either of the following two situations is true:
  1. With the Initial Case 1 (A does not have access to isk),
     (a) $\mathsf{Verify}(m, \mathsf{bsn}, \sigma, \mathsf{RogueList}) = 1$ (accepted), but σ is neither a response of the existing Sign queries nor a response of the existing Semi-sign queries (partially);
     (b) In the case of bsn $\neq \perp$, there exists another signature σ' associated with the same identity and bsn, and the output of $\mathsf{Link}(\sigma, \sigma')$ is 0 (unlinked); and/or
     (c) $\mathsf{Verify}(m, \mathsf{bsn}, \sigma, \mathsf{RogueList} = \mathsf{empty}) = 1$ (accepted without checking RogueList), but att in σ is different from the attributes in Join Cases 1 or 2 associated with the same identity.

2. With the Initial Case 2 ($\mathcal{A}$ knows isk), the same as the item (a), in the condition that the secret key tsk used to create σ was generated in the Join Case 3 (i.e., $\mathcal{A}$ does not have access to tsk).

Definition 2. *Let $\mathcal{A}$ be an adversary that plays the game above. We denote* $\mathbf{Adv}[\mathcal{A}_{\mathsf{DAA-A}}^{trace}] = \mathbf{Pr}[\mathcal{A}\ wins]$ *as the advantage that $\mathcal{A}$ breaks the user-controlled-traceability of* DAA-A. *We say that a DAA scheme is user-controlled-traceable if for any probabilistic polynomial-time adversary $\mathcal{A}$, the quantity* $\mathbf{Adv}[\mathcal{A}_{\mathsf{DAA-A}}^{trace}]$ *is negligible.*

Note that if a DAA-A scheme is implemented with a single signer, e.g., a smartcard plays both the roles of m and $\mathfrak{h}$, the above security definition is still valid, and it only requires some minor modification by removing the cases that $\mathcal{A}$ corrupts $\mathfrak{h}$ but not m. In reality, if a DAA-A scheme can be proved secure under the security model above, a modified scheme with only merging m and $\mathfrak{h}$ should be secure as well.

6.2 Security Proofs

Due to the limited page space of each paper in the conference proceedings, the security proofs will be given in the full version of this paper.

References

1. Bangerter, E., Camenisch, J.L., Lysyanskaya, A.: A cryptographic framework for the controlled release of certified data. In: Christianson, B., Crispo, B., Malcolm, J.A., Roe, M. (eds.) Security Protocols 2004. LNCS, vol. 3957, pp. 20–42. Springer, Heidelberg (2006)
2. Boneh, D., Boyen, X.: Short signatures without random oracles. In: Cachin, C., Camenisch, J.L. (eds.) EUROCRYPT 2004. LNCS, vol. 3027, pp. 56–73. Springer, Heidelberg (2004)
3. Brickell, E.F., Camenisch, J., Chen, L.: Direct anonymous attestation. In: Proceedings of the 11th ACM Conference on Computer and Communications Security, CCS 2004, 25–29 October 2004, Washington, DC, USA, pp. 132–145 (2004)
4. Brickell, E., Chen, L., Li, J.: A (Corrected) DAA scheme using batch proof and verification. In: Chen, L., Yung, M., Zhu, L. (eds.) INTRUST 2011. LNCS, vol. 7222, pp. 304–337. Springer, Heidelberg (2012)
5. Brickell, E., Li, J.: A pairing-based DAA scheme further reducing TPM resources. IACR Cryptology ePrint Archive 2010, 67 (2010)
6. Camenisch, J., Van Herreweghen, E.: Design and implementation of the idemix anonymous credential system. In: Proceedings of the 9th ACM Conference on Computer and Communications Security, CCS 2002, 18–22 November 2002, Washington, DC, USA, pp. 21–30 (2002)
7. Camenisch, J.L., Lysyanskaya, A.: Signature schemes and anonymous credentials from bilinear maps. In: Franklin, M. (ed.) CRYPTO 2004. LNCS, vol. 3152, pp. 56–72. Springer, Heidelberg (2004)

8. Chen, L.: A DAA scheme requiring less TPM resources. In: Bao, F., Yung, M., Lin, D., Jing, J. (eds.) Inscrypt 2009. LNCS, vol. 6151, pp. 350–365. Springer, Heidelberg (2010)
9. Chen, L., Li, J.: Flexible and scalable digital signatures in TPM 2.0. In: 2013 ACM SIGSAC Conference on Computer and Communications Security, CCS 2013, 4–8 November 2013, Berlin, Germany, pp. 37–48 (2013)
10. Koblitz, N., Menezes, A.: Pairing-based cryptography at high security levels. In: Smart, N.P. (ed.) Cryptography and Coding 2005. LNCS, vol. 3796, pp. 13–36. Springer, Heidelberg (2005)
11. Microsoft. U-prove cryptographic specification v1.1 (revision 3) (2014). http://research.microsoft.com/en-us/projects/u-prove
12. Proudler, G., Chen, L., Dalton, C.: Trusted Computing Platforms - TPM2.0 in Context. Springer, Heidelberg (2014)
13. TCG. TPM main specification version 1.2 (2003). http://www.trustedcomputinggroup.org/resources/tpm_main_specification
14. TCG. Trusted platform module library specification family 2.0 (2013). http://www.trustedcomputinggroup.org/resources/tpm_library_specification

Building Blocks for Trust

Proposed Processor Extensions for Significant Speedup of Hypervisor Memory Introspection

Andrei Luțaș[1,2], Sándor Lukács[1,2]([✉]), Adrian Coleșa[2], and Dan Luțaș[1,2]

[1] Bitdefender, Cluj-Napoca, Romania
{alutas,slukacs,dlutas}@bitdefender.com
[2] Technical University of Cluj-Napoca, Cluj-Napoca, Romania
adrian.colesa@cs.utcluj.ro

Abstract. Hypervisor based memory introspection can greatly enhance the security and trustworthiness of endpoints. The memory introspection logic requires numerous memory address space translations. Those in turn, inevitably, impose a considerable performance penalty. We identified that a significant part of the overall overhead induced by introspection is generated by mappings of guest pages into the virtual memory space of the hypervisor. We show that even if we employ highly efficient software caching, the mapping overhead still remains significant. We propose several new x86 instructions, which can fully eliminate the mapping overhead from memory introspection techniques. We give performance estimates for and argue why we strongly believe the implementation of such instructions to be feasible. The introspection logic also relies on monitoring guest page tables. Here we identified a second important performance overhead source, showing that numerous VM-exits induced by EPT violations are caused by the CPU updating page table A/D bits. We propose a set of simple x86 architectural modifications, that can fully eliminate this overhead.

Keywords: Hypervisor · Memory introspection · Memory mappings · New x86 instructions · Access/dirty bits

1 Introduction

Memory Introspection (MI) can be roughly defined as the process of analyzing a guest VM's memory from the hypervisor level. MI can be used to enforce the integrity of in-guest components or to detect a wide range of attacks against the OS kernel or user mode applications. MI scores a growing number of research in academia [9,10,14,18,22] and widening adoption by industry [11,27].

While having numerous advantages over conventional in-guest security solutions, like isolation and transparency, MI needs to solve two key challenges. The first one is the *semantic gap* [6,10], briefly described in Sect. 2.2.

The second challenge arises from the fact that running MI logic outside the guest implicitly imposes running it inside a *separate virtual memory address space*, without direct access to the virtual memory space of the guest OS kernel

© Springer International Publishing Switzerland 2015
M. Conti et al. (Eds.): TRUST 2015, LNCS 9229, pp. 249–267, 2015.
DOI: 10.1007/978-3-319-22846-4_15

or user mode processes the MI is protecting. For each guest memory area that needs to be accessed and analyzed by the MI logic (e.g. an instruction, a simple DWORD operand, a guest OS kernel structure etc.) it needs to parse, interpret and create paging structures that allows it to access the in-guest data from the hypervisor's virtual memory address space. While creating translations and mappings across various memory address spaces is a frequent operation in widely used operating systems, such as creating shared memory between two processes or mapping memory pages from the kernel into user space, the problem and impact of address space translations is exacerbated in memory introspection scenarios. During a typical MI analysis process we need to frequently access numerous and usually small sized in-guest data structures, in most cases only for a very short period of time, like for instance, only for the time it takes to execute a couple of "*if*" instructions. We show that such a usage pattern imposes a considerable performance penalty on the overall memory introspection process.

Besides the two key challenges, there are limitations imposed by the architecture and implementation of the underlying platform's support for hardware accelerated virtualization (in our case Intel x86) and/or by the guest VM's OS. One such limitation appears when the MI logic decides to perform detailed monitoring of a guest VM's paging structures. Such monitoring can be achieved by write-protecting the guest page tables at EPT level, but doing so, numerous unwanted VM-exits will be generated when the processor regularly updates the accessed/dirty (A/D) bits of the guest page tables.

The main contributions of this paper are:

- we identify guest-to-hypervisor memory mappings as being responsible for a significant part of performance overhead induced by MI (Sect. 3.2);
- we show that even with very good software caching (Sect. 3.1) there is still significant room to improve performance of guest-to-hypervisor memory mappings, thus there is a valid reason to consider hardware based speedups;
- we show that A/D-bit update is a key source of overhead, limiting efficient MI on Intel x86 platforms (Sect. 3.3);
- we propose several new x86 instructions (Sect. 4.1) that can fully eliminate the memory mapping overhead from memory introspection, propose small architectural changes that can fully eliminate the A/D-bit update overhead (Sect. 4.2), argue why it should be feasible to implement them on future x86 platforms (Sect. 4.3) and present performance estimations based on synthetic tests (Sect. 4.4).

During our research we did not explicitly seek to propose new processor instructions. We were focused on the speed-up of the MI logic and the underlying hypervisor. The feasibility of new instructions came when we realized that during the effective analysis process the MI logic from the hypervisor repeatedly needs to do very complex steps in order to access guest memory, while for the processor (just a couple of instructions before, while running in the guest) accessing the very same memory was a simple and straightforward thing to do. We initially noticed the overhead induced by A/D-bit updates by basic profiling, and subsequent detailed analysis revealed its significant impact.

1.1   Our Use-Case Scenario

We performed our work on a production-grade proprietary thin-layer security hypervisor, built upon Intel x86 hardware virtualization acceleration technology. Our intended final use-case scenario imposed the MI logic to be capable of synchronously securing live Windows client endpoints (e.g. such as a typical office PC or home laptop running Windows), providing extensive protection for both the OS kernel and user-mode applications. We need to underline that such a use-case scenario requires both a very low overhead solution (the analysis is done on-the-fly for the running VMs) and not relying on in-guest modules at all (due to security reasons we assume the guest to be potentially malicious). Thus, our scenario excluded from the very beginning several traditional MI related approaches known in the prior art (such as, but not limited to, binary translation, shadow paging, asynchronous and/or snapshot based processing, source code level enlightenment of guest OS or that of the monitored applications, or relying on hardware memory acquisition).

While it is beyond the scope of this article to describe in details what our MI method covers, in order to place in context the measurements, we indicate some of the key capabilities. In kernel mode we mainly protect kernel and driver code sections and function tables (such as the IATs, SSDT, IRP dispatch tables and so on). In user mode we protect code sections, stacks, heaps, among others. Our method heavily relies on detailed monitoring of gust page tables with EPT interceptions on all 4 hierarchical levels. We use generic detection logic to identify events like code injections, function detouring or malicious code unpacking. We apply protection on the most critical user-mode applications, such as Adobe Acrobat, Microsoft Office or web-browsers, as those are key targets for the most prevalent malware and cyberattacks today.

2   Memory Introspection on X86 Platforms

2.1   Hardware Accelerated X86 Virtualization and Security

Although hardware accelerated x86 virtualization [16] was not specifically designed for security, because it provides strong isolation, it can be used to efficiently isolate a security solution from a possibly malicious environment or to isolate several execution environments from each other [20,21]. Virtualization can be used in numerous ways to enhance security, such as providing secure execution environments [8,30], do malware analysis [9,29], provide integrity protection or attestation, among others. Lately, beside academic and open source community research, also traditional security solution vendors [11,13,27,28] and security startups embraced virtualization based security [3].

Intel implements hardware accelerated second level address translation (SLAT) technology in their processors, termed Extended Page Table (Intel EPT), since 2008. Using it a hypervisor can efficiently control the physical memory seen by a virtual machine and specify read/write/execute permissions with 4KB page level granularity. The introduction of the EPT was essential to support efficient implementation of MI based security solutions.

2.2   Memory Introspection

Using Virtual Machine Introspection (VMI) [14] or hypervisor-based Memory Introspection (MI) we can analyze from the outside the contents of a guest VM, either suspended or in execution, observing not only objects inside the guest's memory space (like processes, modules, heaps, stacks, threads), but also events in real-time (such as the creation of a new process, allocation of memory or alteration of paging structures managed by the guest OS). While MI can have many other useful applications, the most widely researched area is to use MI to enhance security [9,10,18,19,22,25], which led to its adoption by industry [11,26,27]. The two key security supporting strengths of MI are *(1) isolation*, by which the security module can be isolated by hardware from the possibly malicious or under-attack guest (e.g. an attacker inside the guest does not have access to the MI module running outside the guest, see Fig. 1), and *(2) transparency*, which ensures that a MI solution can analyze the content of the guest without the need to alter it (e.g. without the need to use and rely on in-guest filter drivers, hooks or similar).

A key challenge that MI needs to solve is the so called semantic gap [6] between what the in-guest OS sees and what the MI running outside the guest, in the hypervisor, can see. In a rough approximation, we could say that an in-guest OS kernel and security solution, using well known OS provided APIs, can see and interpret the guest VM's memory as processes, threads, modules, heaps, stacks and various other, semantically rich and interconnected structures. In contrast with this, an out-of-guest, hypervisor level MI might see on the same VM only just a huge sequence (several gigabytes) of physical memory bytes, split into 4KB pages, plus some processor registers to start the analysis with.

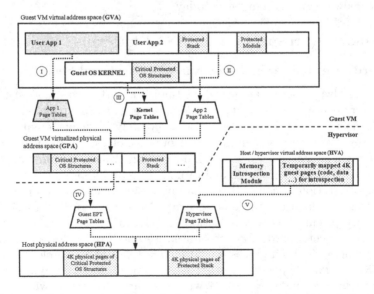

Fig. 1. Memory Introspection. General setup and memory address translations involved

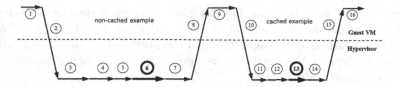

Fig. 2. Useful work steps (6 & 13) in the exemplary execution of two successive memory introspection related EPT violation events

In order to bridge the semantic gap, a MI solution needs to analyze the contents of the guests' memory and understand its contents. This way, data structures, code sections and other objects can be identified inside the guest OS. Figure 1 illustrates the place of the MI module, as well as all the guest and hypervisor elements involved in the introspection process. Eventually, using such analysis of the raw physical memory, the MI can reconstruct the entire image of the OS by determining where the kernel is loaded, where the drivers, heaps, stacks, processes and threads are. In addition, information about user-mode objects can be inferred and protection can be provided for user-mode code and data as well. Once the semantic gap has been bridged, the MI can provide protection for many objects that lie inside the guest memory. First of all, inside the kernel-space, objects such as the kernels and drivers code sections or function tables can be write protected using EPT page permissions (set in Fig. 1, item IV). To achieve this, the MI logic needs to determine their detailed GVA-to-GPA mappings (item III). Similarly, objects such as the stacks or heaps can be protected against execution using EPT, in both user and kernel memory space. To achieve this, the MI logic needs to analyze numerous GVA-to-GPA mappings (such as item I and II). Every time a violation of EPT access rights takes place (for example, the guest tries to write inside a page that is flagged as non-writable), the processor generates an EPT violation, which causes a VM-exit (a transition from the guest to the hypervisor). The hypervisor forwards the event to the MI module, which can analyze the attempt and decide whether it is legitimate or not. If it is legitimate, the instruction that triggered the violation can be either emulated or single-stepped. If the attempt is malicious, security measures can be taken. In its simplest form, the MI can decide to simply skip the instruction without doing any modification to the accessed page (e.g. this way could avoid setting a kernel hook). In another example, the MI logic can identify the process trying to do the illegal action and can terminate it.

Figure 2 illustrates, in a very simplified way, two typical guest ⇔ host transitions performed due to EPT violations, as a response to MI configured EPT access rights (item IV in Fig. 1). Initially, the guest is executing code during step *1*. An EPT violation takes place, which causes a transition from the guest to the hypervisor at step *2*. This may cause the MI to initially map the memory page containing the offending instruction at step *3* into MI accessible virtual memory (item V in Fig. 1). The analysis of the instruction takes place at step *4*, and it is followed by the mapping of the page that has been offended during step *5*.

The actual useful work performed by MI follows in step *6*, such as analyzing the write attempt and deciding whether to allow it or not based on its maliciousness. This is followed by the unmapping of the previously mapped pages during step *7*, after which a VM-entry can be performed during step *8*, resuming the execution of guest code.

As we will further describe in Sect. 3.1, we implemented software caches to speed-up many repetitive guest-to-hypervisor memory mappings. A simple example could be the execution of successive instructions from a page marked non-executable in the EPT tables. In such a case, it is useful to avoid remapping the same guest page for each successive instruction. In line with this, in another example, during guest code execution in step *9* another violation may take place that will cause a transition to hypervisor in step *10*. This time, mappings might be present in internal software caches, which can be used during step *11* to search for the offending instruction's RIP and similarly, to lookup already-mapped pages that contains the written page. The evaluation of the instruction takes place during step *12*, and it is followed by the useful MI logic during step *13*. It is important to point out, that using caches involves also maintaining them up-to-date, so, while mappings might take much less time compared to the previous example, we need an additional step *14* to handle software cache maintenance. Finally, a VM-entry can be done during step *15*, then the guest can resume its execution again in step *16*.

3   Problems and Limitations of Memory Introspection

3.1   Software Speedup of Guest-to-Hypervisor Memory Mappings

Employing software caching to speedup memory translation or instruction emulation is not new. Among others Zhang et al. use [36] per-VCPU software caching to reduce the overhead associated with privileged instruction emulation.

In order to improve guest-memory accesses, our HV also employs several software caching layers. The first one is a decoded-instructions cache, which stores information about instructions located at certain addresses inside the guest. The second cache is a guest-mapping cache which stores translations information for guest-virtual and guest-physical pages. The third one is a GPA-to-HVA translation cache, which stores HV mappings for the most used guest-physical pages. Instead of the third cache we could have used alternative mechanisms, such as mapping the entire GPA space into the HVA space. Though, such an approach would incur additional memory consumption and be more difficult to maintain in a many-guest-VM environment. Based on our measurements, our caching mechanisms had a hit rate of more than 99 %, offering a very significant performance improvement. Particularly, in the case of the third cache, the performance improvement obtained was over 400x.

3.2   Overhead of Guest-to-Hypervisor Memory Mappings

The total overhead of the steps the MI module performs when accessing the guest memory is illustrated in Fig. 3. The measurements were made on a DELL

Windows 7 x64					Windows 8.1 x64				
Action	Idle, caches	Usage, caches	Idle, no caches	Usage, no caches	Action	Idle, caches	Usage, caches	Idle, no caches	Usage, no caches
	Percent of total time spent in host					Percent of total time spent in host			
Map GPA	2.36	12.42	21.15	27.26	Map GPA	3.46	10.94	31.93	27.87
Map GVA	2.48	6.12	32.90	27.32	Map GVA	3.61	5.69	23.42	31.51
Unmap GPA	0.00	0.13	0.56	4.92	Unmap GPA	0.00	0.13	0.25	3.98
Unmap GVA	0.06	0.08	1.52	1.39	Unmap GVA	0.08	0.07	1.19	1.69
Translate GPA	2.15	11.09	3.55	3.64	Translate GPA	2.58	9.92	3.76	3.33
Translate GVA	3.12	9.57	26.12	22.65	Translate GVA	3.67	9.20	18.80	26.06

Fig. 3. Time consumed (percents of in-hypervisor time) by various phases during the handling of memory introspection related EPT violation events

Optiplex990, 8GB RAM, i7-2600 CPU system, using both Windows 7 SP1 × 64 and Windows 8.1 × 64 and four different testing scenarios. Firstly, the impact has been measured in *idle* conditions, with all software caches enabled. Then, the measurement has been made using typical *light usage* scenario, which included Internet browsing, opening PDF and MS Office documents. During the whole process, not only the guest OS kernel, but the browsers, Acrobat Reader and office applications were also protected by the MI module. The same two scenarios have been repeated, but this time without any software caches. The execution time has been accounted using the *RDTSC* instruction. We measured the total ticks spent inside VMXROOT (ring -1) and the total time spent inside the operations illustrated in Fig. 1 together with the total number of VM-exits. The average time spent inside the guest memory access functions was computed using the formula $\frac{100*t_f}{T}$, where t_f is the number of processor ticks spent in a measured function and T is the total number of processor ticks spent in VMXROOT. It is worth specifying that in our measurements a small part of the operations overlap. For example, translating guest-virtual memory also involves mapping guest-physical memory and mapping guest-virtual memory also involved translating guest-virtual memory and mapping guest-physical memory.

In the light usage scenario the performance impact may be easily over 15 % with caches and over 30 % without. Considering the workload involved, we believe the actual real impact may be even much higher in practice. We explicitly didn't try to obtain much finer grained or detailed measurements. On one hand this would have not been possible without extensive changes to the hypervisor, which in turn would generate biased results. On the other hand, it can be clearly seen from our analysis that the magnitude of the results is really significant.

Figure 4 illustrates the performance impact for two representative user-mode process operations: heap creation and destruction. Firstly, a scenario without any caches involved has been tested. The last two scenarios involves all the caches (as described in Sect. 3.1) and a special, application-specific cache. This special cache was created to maximize efficiency by keeping the heaps-array page mapped. However, this cache could not deal with the location of the newly created heap, which was rarely the same, and it still needed to map at least one guest-virtual page. We can see that software caches offer a significant improvement of about 3x.

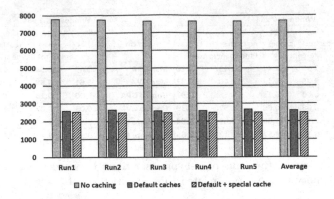

Fig. 4. Heap "create-destroy" software cache speedup of MI mappings (ms)

As the difference between the generic and the application-specific cache is very small, we conclude that it is very difficult to come up with any additional software optimizations, even if they are highly specific.

3.3 Overhead of A/D-Bit Update Induced VM-exits

Looking at Fig. 1, it is important to consider that GVA-to-GPA mappings are usually dynamic in time. The guest OS can arbitrarily alter them, such as by remapping a certain page to different GPAs due to the page swapping process. This imposes some important challenges for MI, as it needs to monitor not only the GPA addresses, but also the guest page tables that are used to perform GVA-to-GPA translations. This way, each time the guest OS performs a write to a page table, in order to update its content, the MI logic will be notified via an EPT violation, and thus, it can update its monitoring logic.

This process can impose a considerable penalty if numerous writes take place on guest page tables. While at first, intuitively, it might seem that this is not the case, we need to factor in that on x86 platforms the CPU updates accessed/dirty bits regularly on guest page tables and any such update will generate an EPT violation that needs to be processed by the MI module, if and only if the MI

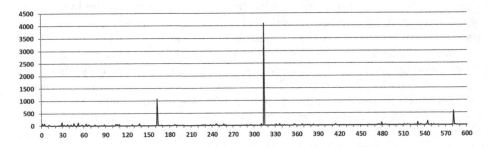

Fig. 5. Number of EPT violation VM-exits due to A/D bit updates (Idle)

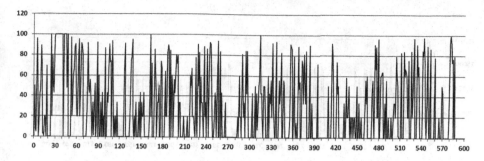

Fig. 6. Percentage of EPT violation VM-exits due to A/D bit updates (Idle)

logic is monitoring that particular page table. As the system load increases, so does the number of paging operations (e.g. allocation, mapping, swapping), and also the overhead induced by MI. While not exclusively so, this phenomenon is highly specific to user-mode introspection, where the GVA-to-GPA mappings (items I and II in Fig. 1) are more frequently changed than in the case of kernel mode introspection (item III in Fig. 1).

To analyze the impact of A/D bit updates done by the CPU page-walking on MI (we excluded the ones caused by the OS, which periodically clears those flags), we have carried out numerous tests on a Broadwell CPU based system, with 4 GB RAM and Windows 8.1 × 64. Each test was run for roughly 600 s, and we have done sampling of EPT violation events at each second. Protected user-mode applications included Opera, Firefox, IE, Acrobat Reader and one custom memory-intensive application. We activated all MI protection mechanisms, both for user-mode and kernel-mode. The page table structures were not monitored entirely, only portions of them associated with protected guest memory areas.

We analyzed the impact of A/D bit updates in several different scenarios. The first scenario, as shown in Figs. 5 and 6 corresponds to an idle system that was running no other tasks than the OS itself. We consider this to be a baseline scenario. The easily observable spikes in this scenario are most likely related to periodic background OS processing.

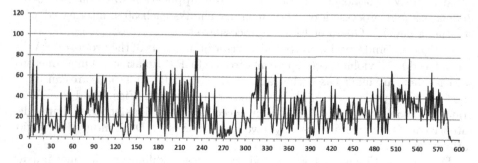

Fig. 7. Percentage of EPT violation VM-exits due to A/D bit updates (Light)

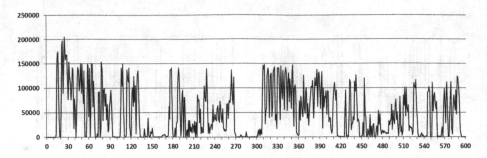

Fig. 8. Number of EPT violation VM-exits due to A/D bit updates (Intensive)

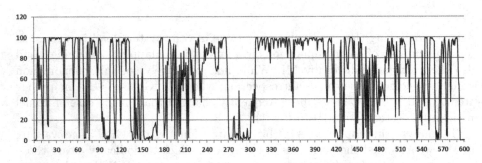

Fig. 9. Percentage of EPT violation VM-exits due to A/D bit updates (Intensive)

A second scenario is depicted in Fig. 7. This corresponds to a typical light office workload, including browsing the internet with IE, playing YouTube videos, downloading files and opening documents with Adobe Reader. The spikes in this scenario are correlated with the creation of new MI-protected user-mode processes. This test clearly confirmed us that process creation regularly induces much bigger performance overhead for user-mode MI, as each new process requires the setup of complete memory spaces, thus heavily page-table (and implicitly A/D bit update) related workloads.

In a third case, as shown in Figs. 8 and 9, we analyzed the impact in the case of an intensive workload scenario. Here a test application was doing repeated allocations and processing of 2 GB memory chunks each 30 s, interleaved with starting a new IE, Opera or Firefox process every 10 s.

In Figs. 6, 7 and 9 we illustrate the distribution in time of the proportion A/D-bit induced EPT violations (as percents from all EPT violations). One can easily see that there are many cases when almost all of the EPT violations are caused by the CPU page-walker setting the accessed or dirty bits. In Figs. 5 and 8 we illustrate the absolute numbers of A/D-bit induced EPT violations, showing that under intensive memory pressure, we may have up to 200,000 A/D-bit induced EPT violations per second.

Finally, Fig. 10 aggregates all previous results, highlighting the high impact of the A/D-bit induced EPT violations and making it clear that they can be

	Idle	Light	Intensive
Percent of A/D updated generated EPT violations (of all EPT violations)	65.14	17.51	90.04
Average no. of A/D update generated EPT violations per second	16.69	801.38	48067.31
Maximum no. of A/D update generated EPT violations per second	4086.00	13513.00	204749.00
Average estimated A/D update overhead of CPU time, percent	0.01	0.27	16.02
Maximum estimated A/D updated overtead of CPU time, percent	1.36	4.50	68.25

Fig. 10. Estimated total CPU time impact of VM-exits due to A/D bit update

a major bottleneck. The most important slowdown appears on the creation of protected processes and under heavy memory pressure, accounting for up to 90 % of all the EPT violations and up to over 60 % of the total CPU time. For the later one, we done our estimates normalizing the measurements to a 3 GHz clocked CPU and considering an average EPT violation handling time of 10000 clock ticks (without going into lengthy technical details, this includes the platforms round-trip, the HV context saving/restoring, handling software caches, decoding and emulation instructions, among others).

We underline that our results do not show that hypervisor based MI for user-mode applications would not be feasible at all, quite the contrary: for typical client endpoint doing everyday office work (as shown in the light workload scenario) the average overhead is acceptable. Our analysis confirmed our presumption that the biggest overhead is induced by workloads that put big pressure on the guest page table structures, indicating also the overhead's magnitude in unfavorable conditions. We plan to do more detailed analysis in the future, covering well standardized, server specific workloads also. We also point out for clarification that there is no relevant technical difference from the point of view of the MI logic between how user-mode and kernel-mode page tables are treated. What makes more costly for MI logic to monitor the page-tables of user-mode applications is the more dynamic nature of user-mode processes (e.g. start/stop, loading of modules) and much more dynamic virtual memory space allocation patterns, compared with kernel-mode code.

4 Proposed X86 Processor Extensions

4.1 New X86 Instructions for Direct Guest Memory Access

We propose the introduction of several new simple, yet very powerful x86 instructions, according to the following logic:

```
1. READGPAB/W/D/Q <dest-reg>, [<src-gpa-addr>]
2. READGVAB/W/D/Q <dest-reg>, [<src-gva-addr>]
3. WRITEGPAB/W/D/Q [<dest-gpa-addr>], <src-reg>
4. WRITEGVAB/W/D/Q [<dest-gva-addr>], <src-reg>
```

Those instructions differ in one essential way from a common MOV instruction: the translation of the operand's virtual address is to be performed in the virtual address space indicated by the *guest CR3 value* from the current VMCS (and not the current host CR3). The common step of GPA-to-HPA translation can be performed using the EPT pointer (EPTP) from the current VMCS, just as they are already performed by existing CPUs.

Handling of potential failures could be done easily. If the indicated GVA or GPA address is invalid or not present (or any other condition that would normally trigger a page-fault is encountered), the proposed instructions might simply set a common flag (e.g. carry flag) to indicate the error condition. This way, their usage should be very simple and straightforward.

4.2   Mechanism to Avoid VM-exits on A/D-Bit Updates

EPT violations caused by the MMU page-walker setting the A/D-bit are generally not needed by the MI logic, although they induce a significant performance penalty. We propose simple extensions that would eliminate the performance impact caused by these exits.

Firstly, the A/D-bit induced EPT violations could be globally disabled via a control field inside the VMCS. This should inhibit any EPT violation that would be generated by the CPU page-walker when setting the A/D-bit. Such a mechanism would not restrict or alter the guest's functionality at all (e.g. the guest will be able to use page swapping as usual), and any effects would be visible only at the level of the CPU and of the EPT violation handling MI logic.

Secondly, the mechanism may be made more fine-grained by selectively flagging certain guest-physical pages as being "guest page tables". One bit inside the EPT page table entries could be reserved for this purpose: whenever the CPU page-walker sets the A/D-bit in a guest-physical page that has the "is guest page-table" bit set inside the EPT, an EPT violation would not be triggered (in other cases the exception shall be generated as usual). Using such a mechanism, the HV would have greater flexibility to control exiting on A/D-bit updates.

4.3   About the Feasibility of the Proposed Extensions

While we are not CPU designers, observing a set of relevant facts, we can still meaningfully argue on weather the proposed extensions are reasonable or not to be implemented. We assume as a general rule of thumb, that implementation complexity increases proportionally with functional complexity.

– We can be sure that in many cases translation information is already present inside the processor TLB for GVA or GPA addresses that cause EPT violations. This become clear if we consider two aspects. On one hand, since 2008 Intel already supports a feature called virtual processor IDs (VPIDs). When activated, the TLBs tag each cached memory address translation with a guest specific unique ID, with the ID 0 being reserved for the hypervisor. Later on, when the HV asks the processor to invalidate cached translations, it can specify individual VPIDs to specify the target of the invalidation. Thus, while executing code inside the HV, all translation cached in the TLB on behalf of the guest OS remain valid and present, unless the HV explicitly requires their invalidation. On another hand, when dealing with MI related EPT violations, we can safely suppose that most of the in-guest memory addresses involved are already in the TLB, as they are from the last instruction being executed by the guest, the one that just triggered the EPT violation. We also note that if we need to access other different in-guest structures, not directly related to the last executed instruction, the processor might still need to perform a dedicated page walk and address translation, using the already available in-CPU page walking logic (but using a different root).

– ARM architecture processors [1] already include today control registers and instructions to perform translations from a GVA to either an intermediate physical address (GPA) or to a HPA.
– Regarding the proposed A/D-bit optimization, the CPU already knows during the EPT violation generation whether the fault was caused by the MMU page-walker setting the A/D-bit. This information is *already explicitly provided* in the exit-qualification field on EPT violations. Therefore, in our opinion, it would be simple and straightforward to just ignore the generation of the EPT violation for such cases.
– Intel delivered regularly new CPU enhancements during the last few years. Many of them are directly related to virtualization and security, such as EPT, #VE, nested-VMCS, very fast round-trip latency for VM-exits, APICv among others. From this, we conclude that they are actively looking into ways to enhance their platform. We can also easily realize that the complexity of any of those extensions is much greater than what we are proposing here.

4.4   Estimated Speed-Up

Initially we considered extending BOCHS [2] to simulate the functionality of the proposed instructions, but abandoned the idea after we analyzed its capabilities. First of all, its slow simulation speed would mostly prohibit running any serious workload to be executed on. Secondly, such a simulation would not provide us any accurate and representative time measurements. Obviously, we did not had the capability to implement the instructions in real silicon either. Therefore, we decided to simulate the existence of these instructions by forcibly keeping some guest pages mapped inside the hypervisor virtual address space.

To estimate the speed-up of guest-memory access instructions, we performed a simple synthetic test: we created a test application that generated 1 million EPT violations in a loop by writing to a write-protected page. Each write generated an EPT violation, which in turn triggered a VM-exit. The MI logic analyzed each faulty attempt, but both the page containing the faulty instruction and the written page were kept permanently mapped inside the HVA memory space. Therefore, only the core processing was made by the MI, the guest memory reads being replaced by simple comparisons to validate the violation's address, and redirections to the permanently mapped HVA addresses. We believe this to

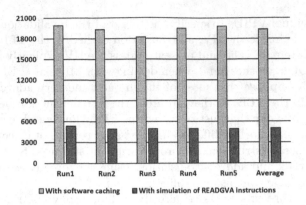

Fig. 11. EPT write violation speedup using the proposed new instructions (ms)

be an as close as possible software estimation for what a real, in-silicon implementation could provide, as we replaced each READGVA with a sequence of only a few other x86 instructions. Besides, both the throughput and latency values of comparable MOV instructions are very low, so we believe that the estimation's replacement sequence to use *at least as much time* as it would take for any in-silicon implementation of those instructions to execute.

As seen in the results from Fig. 11, with all our software caches, the total time needed to execute the test application was around 19.3 s. With the simulation of the fast instructions, this reduced to little over 5 s. While the performance boost is significant, it is important to point out that it would be infeasible to use this synthetic optimization on a larger scale. First of all, keeping guest pages mapped inside the hypervisor is not scalable because virtual addresses inside the guest may overlap with virtual addresses inside the hypervisor or in other guests, and they may be swapped in and out of the physical memory. Therefore, maintaining this kind of mappings can be done only for guest physical pages, and translation for guest virtual pages would still be needed. Even so, in the case of multi-guests, keeping these mappings synchronized would induce significant performance impact, not to mention the implementation complexity.

In the case of A/D-bit induced EPT violations we didn't need to do any further performance estimation. We argue that the performance impact would be eliminated entirely by our proposal, as no more EPT violations would be generated at all when the CPU updates the A/D bits. As we have shown already in Sect. 3.3, with an average processing time of about 10000 clock ticks inside the HV, the A/D-bit induced EPT violations processing may account for up to over 60 % of the entire CPU time in intensive workload scenarios. We believe this to be a significant result to support in-hardware optimizations.

5   Related Work

There are several in-silicon improvements introduced by Intel in the last years that greatly enhance the performance of memory introspection. As a first example, Intel is steadily working with each CPU generation to reduce the round-trip VM-exit/VM-entry time, from over 3000 cycles in the original VT-x implementation to around 500 cycles in the Haswell [15] and around 400 cycles in their latest Broadwell [7] architecture. As another example, most likely, Intel is also working towards providing finer-grained memory monitoring CPU primitives [29]. Yet another technology is Virtualization Exceptions #VE, introduced in the Broadwell CPUs, which sustains moving the MI module inside a guest VM in order to further eliminate many of the round-trip overhead [12]. However, #VE has several limitations. Currently only EPT violations are delivered using this mechanism, and other events important for MI (e.g. such as MSR or CR accesses) need to be handled inside the hypervisor – thus forcing the implementation of split MI logic: some parts inside the HV, others in a guest agent. Besides this, in the context of a #VE agent, memory-validations are still needed – for example, the agent still has to translate a GVA that points inside user-space before accessing it. While not the scope of this paper, we can mention that our preliminary in-lab analysis indicated that using #VE to handle A/D bit update induced EPT violations can eliminate roughly about 25 % of the overall overhead, compared with the results presented in Sect. 3.2. However it is important to point out, that such improvement would came mainly from the reduced round-trip latency of #VE and thus it would not be mutually exclusive with the A/D bit update speedup proposed by us, but instead, would lead to a cumulative improvement.

Memory introspection was introduced in [14] by Garfinkel and Rosenblum in 2003 as a way to implement an intrusion detection system that is well isolated from the host system. Jain et al. have done recently [17] a good survey of MI research. Jiang and Wang [18] implemented high-interaction honeypots based on memory introspection. Dinaburg et al. [9] uses virtualization to analyze malware. Among others, Dolan-Gavitt et al. [10] tries to overcome the semantic gap in automatic ways. Mohandas and Sahita [29] use virtualization and introspection to perform behavioral malware monitoring.

Originally VMware products [4] instrumented page table updates and other guest writes by the means of shadow page tables. However, on modern CPU with hardware accelerated SLAT, shadow paging mechanisms are not used anymore for efficiency reasons. Chang et al. [5] also describe a number of techniques to accelerate memory address translation, but their implementation is done in QEMU, based on binary translation, and thus is not applicable for our scenario. Somewhat similar to the #VE approach, Srinivasan et al. presents [32] a method to relocate the context of a monitored process so that it runs in the same context with the security agent (usually in a separate VM). This has significant implementation challenges on close-source operating systems. Sharif et al. proposes [31] the injection of an MI agent inside the monitored VM, to perform the most critical tasks. While protected by the hypervisor, any in-guest code can still be attacked through numerous vectors (e.g. such as via stack or shared data).

There are several noteworthy results on using MI in an asynchronous way, both for malware analysis [22,23] and for on-premise security solutions [13]. We must however note, that our live VM protection scenario imposes very fast processing, thus we can't afford using tools like Volatility or relying on PDB metadata as Lengyel et al. does.

Vasudevan et al. performed a great work on identifying the requirements for trustworthy hypervisors on x86 platforms [35], and presented the implementation and formal verification of a module hypervisor framework [33]. They also present tamper-resistant execution environments for x86 platforms [34].

Well known, mainstream hypervisors, such as Xen, have been extended to support MI [24], and several traditional security solution vendors, such as McAffee/Intel [27] or Bitdefender [11], developed MI-based security technologies.

6   Conclusions

We analyzed some of the main performance overhead sources of EPT-level monitoring based synchronous live memory introspection, with focus on introspection of user-mode applications on x86 Windows platforms. Our research clearly indicates that a significant part of the overall overhead of user-mode introspection is induced by mappings of guest pages into the virtual memory space of the hypervisor. Our analysis shows, that even if we employ several software caches that reduce the mapping overhead by a factor of three, significant room remains for speedup. We believe the ultimate solution would be the introduction of new x86 instructions to allow reading/writing the guest virtual memory space from introspection logic executing inside the hypervisor's context. We strongly believe, that the proposed changes could fully eliminate both the memory mapping overhead and the overhead induced by numerous unnecessary VM-exits due to guest page table A/D bit updates incurred by memory introspection techniques. The overall speeding up of MI can be conservatively estimated to be at least 25 %.

In the last few years Intel was continuously improving both the virtualization and security related in-silicon capabilities of the x86 processors, regularly introducing new instructions and technologies with every new processor generation. We argue that the proposed instructions could be rather easily incorporated into future x86 processors, as their functional complexity is much smaller than that of numerous recently introduced extensions and all required building blocks are known to be already present inside the processor.

Although simple in essence, the value and usability of the proposed extensions go far beyond the realms of MI based security. They could be used to speedup numerous other virtualization tasks, unrelated to security or introspection. Beside their presented form, the instructions themselves could be enhanced in several ways. For instance, they could be extended to support reading-writing memory not only inside the guest context of the active VMCS, but inside the guest context of an arbitrary VMCS, selected by a third operand.

Acknowledgments. Adrian Colesa's work on this paper was supported by the Post-Doctoral Programme POSDRU/159/1.5/S/137516, project co-funded from European Social Fund through the Human Resources Sectorial Operational Program 2007-2013.

References

1. ARM: ARM Architecture Reference Manual ARMv7-A and ARMv7-R (2014)
2. BOCHS: The cross-platform IA-32 emulator. http://bochs.sourceforge.net/. Accessed on 24–11–2014
3. BROMIUM: Bromium vSentry and LAVA products (2014–11–24). http://www.bromium.com/products.html. Accessed on 24–11–2014
4. Bugnion, E., Devine, S., Rosenblum, M., Sugerman, J., Wang, E.Y.: Bringing virtualization to the x86 architecture with the original vmware workstation. ACM Trans. Comput. Syst **30**(4), 12:1–12:51 (2012)
5. Chang, C.J., Wu, J.J., Hsu, W.C., Liu, P., Yew, P.C.: Efficient memory virtualization for cross-ISA system mode emulation. In: Proceedings of the 10th ACM SIGPLAN/SIGOPS International Conference on Virtual Execution Environments (VEE 2014), pp. 117–128. ACM, New York (2014)
6. Chen, P.M., Noble, B.D.: When virtual is better than real. In: Proceedings of the Eighth Workshop on Hot Topics in Operating Systems (HOTOS 2001), IEEE Computer Society, Washington, DC (2001)
7. Chennupaty, S., Jiang, H., Sreenivas, A.: Technology Insight: Intel's Next Generation 14nm Microarchitecture for Client and Server (2014)
8. Citrix: XenClient XT. The ultimate in multi-level secure local virtual desktops. http://www.citrix.com/products/xenclient/features/editions/xt.html. Accessed on 24–11–2014
9. Dinaburg, A., Royal, P., Sharif, M., Lee, W.: Ether: Malware analysis via hardware virtualization extensions. In: Proceedings of the 15th ACM Conference on Computer and Communications Security (CCS 2008), pp. 51–62. ACM, New York (2008)
10. Dolan-Gavitt, B., Leek, T., Zhivich, M., Giffin, J., Lee, W.: Virtuoso: narrowing the semantic gap in virtual machine introspection. In: IEEE Symposium on Security and Privacy (SP), pp. 297–312. IEEE (2011)
11. Dontu, M., Sahita, R.: Zero-Footprint Guest Memory Introspection from Xen. In: XenProject Developer Summit (2014)
12. Durham, D.: Mitigating exploits, rootkits and advanced persistent threats. In: Proceedings of the 2014 Symposium on High Performance Chips (Hot Chips 2014), IEEE Technical Committee on Microprocessors and Microcomputers in Cooperation with ACM SIGARCH (2014)
13. FireEye: Advantage FireEye. Debunking the Myth of Sandbox Security (2013)
14. Garfinkel, T., Rosenblum, M.: A Virtual Machine Introspection Based Architecture for Intrusion Detection. In: Proceedings of Network and Distributed Systems Security Symposium, pp. 191–206 (2003)
15. Hammarlund, P.: 4th Generation Intel Core Processor, codenamed Haswell. In: HotChips (2013)
16. Intel Corporation: intel® 64 and IA-32 Architectures Software Developer's Manual (2015). Accessed on 02 Feb 2015

17. Jain, B., Baig, M.B., Zhang, D., Porter, D.E., Sion, R.: SoK: Introspections on trust and the semantic gap. In: Proceedings of the 2014 IEEE Symposium on Security and Privacy (SP 2014), pp. 605–620. IEEE Computer Society, Washington, DC (2014)

18. Jiang, X., Wang, X.: "Out-of-the-box" monitoring of VM-based high-interaction honeypots. In: Kruegel, C., Lippmann, R., Clark, A. (eds.) RAID 2007. LNCS, vol. 4637, pp. 198–218. Springer, Heidelberg (2007)

19. Joshi, A., King, S.T., Dunlap, G.W., Chen, P.M.: Detecting past and present intrusions through vulnerability-specific predicates. In: Proceedings of the Twentieth ACM Symposium on Operating Systems Principles (SOSP 2005), pp. 91–104. ACM, New York (2005)

20. Lampson, B.: Accountability and freedom (2005)

21. Lampson, B.: Privacy and security: usable security: how to get it. Commun. ACM 52(11), 25–27 (2009)

22. Lengyel, T., Kittel, T., Webster, G., Torrey, J.: Pitfalls of virtual machine introspection on modern hardware. In: 1st Workshop on Malware Memory Forensics (MMF) (2014)

23. Lengyel, T.K., Neumann, J., Maresca, S.: Virtual machine introspection in a hybrid honeypot architecture. In: Presented as part of the 5th Workshop on Cyber Security Experimentation and Test. USENIX, Berkeley (2012)

24. LibVMI: Virtual machine introspection tools. http://libvmi.com/. Accessed on 20-06-2015

25. Ligh, M.H., Case, A., Levy, J., Walters, A.: The Art of Memory Forensics: Detecting Malware and Threats in Windows, Linux, and Mac Memory, 1st edn. Wiley, New York (2014)

26. Luțaș, A., Lukács, S., Luțaș, D., Coleșa, A.: U-HIPE: hypervisor-based protection of user-mode processes in windows. J. Comput. Virol. Hacking Tech. 9(1), 1–14 (2015)

27. McAfee: A New Paradigm Shift: Comprehensive Security Beyond the Operating System (2012)

28. McAfee: McAfee DeepSAFE and Deep Defender (2013)

29. Mohandas, R., Sahita, R.: Detecting Evasive Malware in Sandbox. In: Focus Security Conference (2014)

30. Rutkowska, J., Wojtczuk, R.: Qubes OS. http://www.qubes-os.org/. Accessed on 24-11-2014

31. Sharif, M.I., Lee, W., Cui, W., Lanzi, A.: Secure in-VM monitoring using hardware virtualization. In: Proceedings of the 16th ACM Conference on Computer and Communications Security (CCS 2009), pp. 477–487. ACM (2009)

32. Srinivasan, D., Wang, Z., Jiang, X., Xu, D.: Process out-grafting: an efficient "out-of-VM" approach for fine-grained process execution monitoring. In: Proceedings of the 18th ACM Conference on Computer and Communications Security (CCS 2011), pp. 363–374. ACM, New York (2011)

33. Vasudevan, A., Chaki, S., Jia, L., McCune, J., Newsome, J., Datta, A.: Design, implementation and verification of an eXtensible and modular hypervisor framework. In: Proceedings of the 2013 IEEE Symposium on Security and Privacy (SP 2013), pp. 430–444. IEEE Computer Society, Washington, DC (2013)

34. Vasudevan, A., McCune, J., Newsome, J., Perrig, A., van Doorn, L.: CARMA: a hardware tamper-resistant isolated execution environment on commodity x86 platforms. In: Proceedings of the 7th ACM Symposium on Information, Computer and Communications Security (ASIACCS 2012), pp. 48–49. ACM, New York (2012)

35. Vasudevan, A., McCune, J.M., Qu, N., van Doorn, L., Perrig, A.: Requirements for an integrity-protected hypervisor on the x86 hardware virtualized architecture. In: Acquisti, A., Smith, S.W., Sadeghi, A.-R. (eds.) TRUST 2010. LNCS, vol. 6101, pp. 141–165. Springer, Heidelberg (2010)
36. Zhang, F., Chen, J., Chen, H., Zang, B.: CloudVisor: retrofitting protection of virtual machines in multi-tenant cloud with nested virtualization. In: Proceedings of the Twenty-Third ACM Symposium on Operating Systems Principles (SOSP 2011), pp. 203–216. ACM, New York (2011)

MWA Skew SRAM Based SIMPL Systems
for Public-Key Physical Cryptography

Qingqing Chen[1(✉)], Ulrich Rührmair[2], Spoorthy Narayana[1],
Uzair Sharif[1], and Ulf Schlichtmann[1]

[1] Institute for Electronic Design Automation,
Technische Universität München, Munich, Germany
{qingqing.chen, spoorthy.narayana, uzair.sharif,
ulf.schlichtmann}@tum.de
[2] Horst Görtz Institute for IT Security,
University of Bochum, Bochum, Germany
ruehrmair@ilo.de

Abstract. SIMulation Possible, but Laborious (SIMPL) systems are a novel cryptographic concept for physical cryptography that have been suggested in recent years. They can potentially solve inherent vulnerabilities of conventional public-key cryptography that is based on unproven mathematical hypotheses. The security of SIMPL systems rests on their physical unclonability and on the runtime difference between the real-time behavior of the unique SIMPL system and any adversarial simulation or emulation of it. One first circuit-based realization of SIMPL systems via so-called skew SRAMs has previously been discussed in the literature. This paper presents an approach to enhance the security of skew SRAM based SIMPL systems by introducing more complicated and parallel computing behavior taking place in the skew SRAM, which we call multiple-wordline-activation (MWA) skew SRAM. Simulations of the MWA skew SRAM show expected behavior complexity that can be taken advantage of in SIMPL systems to amplify the speed advantage over emulators (functional physical clones) or simulators (digital clones), which plays a key role in the security of SIMPL systems.

Keywords: Security · Cryptography · Physical cryptography · Public-key physical cryptography · Physical unclonable function · Simulation possible, but laborious system · SIMPL system · Public physical unclonable function · Public PUF · Skew SRAM · MWA skew SRAM · Multiple wordline activation

1 Introduction

SIMulation Possible, but Laborious systems (SIMPL systems or just SIMPLs) [1, 2] are a novel cryptographic concept within so-called physical cryptography. Unlike physical unclonable functions (PUFs) [3–7], whose aim is to resolve inherent issues of conventional *private-key* cryptography, SIMPL systems and public PUFs [8] are new cryptographic primitives for typical *public-key* like scenarios.

A PUF is a physical function that maps challenges (inputs) to responses (outputs) depending on the physical phenomena taking place in the PUF structure. Based on the

M. Conti et al. (Eds.): TRUST 2015, LNCS 9229, pp. 268–282, 2015.
DOI: 10.1007/978-3-319-22846-4_16

challenge-response pairs (CRPs), a PUF is able to serve in various cryptographic protocols [9], e.g., challenge-response authentication. However, all these protocols require a piece of previously shared information that must be kept secret, restricting the application of PUFs as secret-key like primitives. Similar to a PUF, every SIMPL system also realizes an individual function that maps challenges to responses. Unlike PUFs, however, any SIMPL system possesses an individual public numeric simulation program. This allows everyone to simulate and calculate the responses of the SIMPL system, and therefore to verify the correctness of the responses received from the party who claims to be in possession of the original SIMPL system. As the SIMPL system is designed such that any adversarial simulation or hardware emulation of it is slower and more time consuming than the real-time behavior of the original SIMPL system, which means that only the person physically holding the original SIMPL system can compute the responses at a certain speed (equal to or faster than a threshold speed value that is publicly available, together with or given by the simulation program), everyone may verify the realness of the claimant's possession of the SIMPL system by checking the *quickness* (speed) of the responses with a timer and the *correctness* with the simulation program. It has been shown that the speed advantage or "speed gap" can be used for a number of different cryptographic protocols, including identification, key exchange, bit commitment, zero-knowledge protocols, and digital rights management applications [1].

1.1 SIMPL Systems and Public PUFs

SIMPL systems and public PUFs are actually equivalent cryptographic concepts. However, recent research on both primitives has shown a slightly different accentuation. Publications on public PUFs have mostly focused on nanoelectronic solutions, trying to achieve an *exponential* time gap between the public PUF hardware and any adversaries [10, 11]. While being scientifically highly interesting, such exponential time gaps between hardware and its simulation may be hard to achieve in practical, inexpensive, and stable implementations. Furthermore, an exponential time gap makes the simulation of the public PUF, which is one inherent protocol step, very time consuming, leading to practically inefficient schemes. For these reasons, recent investigations on SIMPL systems followed a different route [1, 2, 12, 13]: They examined practical, circuit-based implementations with a sufficiently large, but constant time gap. In order to avoid attacks, the SIMPL system implemented a non-parallelizable function, whose computation is closely tied to the maximal clock frequency of today's integrated circuits. It is well-known that this frequency cannot be raised indefinitely due to physical constraints imposed by semiconductor materials. This strategy promises to thwart many attacks while still maintaining practicality.

We follow and extend this route in this paper, attempting to achieve a substantial improvement over previous skew-SRAM-based designs of SIMPL systems: We try to lift the relative security margin from a small factor of around 2 to larger factors of $2n$ by a new, so-called multiple wordline activation (MWA) skew SRAM, in which n represents the number of wordlines that can possibly be activated simultaneously in skew SRAM write operations.

1.2   Implementation of SIMPL Systems via Skew SRAMs

A first implementation of SIMPL systems known as skew SRAM based SIMPL systems has been introduced in [2, 12, 13]. It uses specially designed ("skew") SRAM architectures to outperform their emulators/simulators when executing certain, specialized computing tasks that skew SRAMs are designed for. Figure 1 shows the structure of the skew SRAM based SIMPL system of [12, 13]. The system consists of four main blocks, namely a skew SRAM block (SS), a challenge control block (CC), a voltage control block (VC), and a feedback and output control block (FOC).

Similar to PUFs, SIMPL systems calculate responses R_i when fed with challenges C_i. The challenge control block CC "scrambles" the challenge and generates voltage select (*SEL*), read/write address (*ADR*), write data (*D$_{IN}$*) and other control (*CTRL*) signals, e.g., write enable, for the skew SRAM. References [12, 13] suggested realizing the challenge control block with a hash function. The skew SRAM block SS is designed similar to normal SRAMs, except that different types of cells (normal cells and skew cells, of which skew cells differ from normal, i.e., standard SRAM cells in the sizing of their transistors and therefore in their electrical characteristics, specifically their write behavior) are distributed in the array and write operations taking place in those specially designed skew cells may fail to modify their previously stored contents depending on the current supply voltage (controlled by voltage control block VC). To be specific, the skew cells discussed in [12, 13], which were designed for a 0.18-μm CMOS technology, will retain their previously stored values when the *VDD* to the skew SRAM block SS is 1.3 V, and the write operation will be successful (like in conventional SRAM cells) when the *VDD* is 1.8 V. Therefore, writing and reading successively in a cell of such a skew SRAM is effectively a computation process based on the *VDD* and *D$_{IN}$* signals, as well as the type and the current contents of the cell.

As the skew SRAM behavior cannot be outperformed by emulators or simulators [13], its speed advantage can be used to distinguish real SIMPL systems from faked ones. The speed advantage of the SIMPL system over emulators/simulators can be amplified if the data read out from the skew SRAM in a cycle is fed back into the challenge control, thus influencing the next cycle. This can of course be repeated multiple times. In [12, 13], the feedback loop is realized with a linear feedback shift register (LFSR) that XOR's the read-out data D_{OUT} of the skew SRAM block. More details of the operation and the design can be found in [12, 13].

By randomly allocating skew as well as normal cells in the skew SRAM array SS, a specific design is achieved. However, individualized SIMPL systems should not be realized by creating many different designs with different skew/normal cell distribution patterns, as it is too expensive to fabricate just one single or several chips out of one design for usual commercial applications. References [12, 13] suggested to randomly modify a portion of the skew and normal cells in the array to become fixed-"0" or fixed-"1" cells, which can be realized with laser fuses and "burn-in" fabrication steps. These fixed-"0" and fixed-"1" cells have their data nodes directly connected to *GND* and *VDD*, respectively. Their stored and read-out values will remain fixed no matter what operation is carried out. Depending on where the fixed-"0" and fixed-"1" cells are located, a practically infinite number of different SIMPL systems can be fabricated out of one design, with properly chosen parameters including the skew SRAM array sizes and the portions of skew and normal, as well as fixed cells.

In public-key applications, the public key, i.e., the simulator part, implements a function that calculates response R_i when fed with the description $D(S)$ of a SIMPL system S as well as the challenge C_i (the challenge C_i should be given by the verifier). The simulator should also be able to tell the response time limit t_{max} of the legal SIMPL system S, so that a verifier can check both the *quickness* and the *correctness* criteria discussed at the beginning of this section. To create such a public simulation program for a specific SIMPL system, one needs to know the accurate logic functionalities of each block of the system including the configurations of the skew SRAM block, i.e., allocations of normal, skew, as well as fixed cells. The simulation program just needs to implement the logic functionality of the SIMPL system in software, and, based on the specifications, calculate the response time limit t_{max} of the legal SIMPL system.

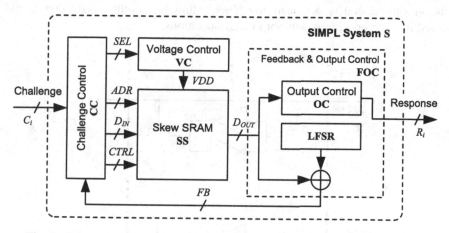

Fig. 1. Schematic illustration of the skew SRAM based SIMPL system [12, 13].

The security of SIMPL systems is determined by the speed/performance advantage which the systems have over all emulators or simulators of them. Specifically for skew SRAM based SIMPL systems, the security results from the speed advantage of skew SRAM write operations over emulators using conventional memories and logic, as well as simulators using standard computing systems [13], which can theoretically mimic each skew SRAM write operation in three sequential steps: (1) read out the contents and the type of addressed cells; (2) compute the result of the write operation; (3) write back the result into addressed cells. However, as technology develops, the speed advantage of a previously fabricated skew SRAM may decrease since emulators/simulators using new technologies become faster, making the secured service lifetime of a skew SRAM based SIMPL system shorter. To further enhance the security of skew SRAM based SIMPL systems and to ensure longer service lifetime, the concept of multiple wordline activation (MWA) skew SRAM is proposed in this paper. This concept attempts to write into multiple cells in each column of a skew SRAM array by activating multiple wordlines simultaneously in a write operation.

The rest of the paper is organized as follows: Section 2 proposes the security enhancement approach using MWA skew SRAM for SIMPL systems. Section 3 presents a design of MWA skew SRAM. Section 4 shows simulations of the design. Section 5 briefly assesses the security enhancement of the MWA skew SRAM and summarizes the paper.

2 MWA Skew SRAM Based SIMPL Systems

As discussed in Sect. 1, the long-term security of skew SRAM based SIMPL systems can be enhanced by increasing the speed advantage executing an operation in the skew SRAM over mimicking it through emulation/simulation. To enlarge the speed asymmetry, multiple wordline activation during write operations is introduced, which allows the attempt of writing the same data appearing on skew SRAM bitlines into multiple cells on simultaneously activated wordlines. Multiple wordline activation is only allowed in write operations, but not in read operations.

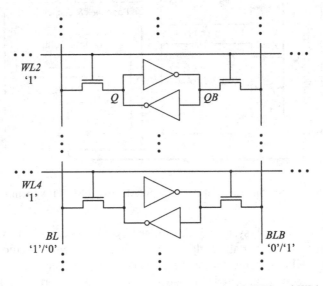

Fig. 2. Part of the schematic of an MWA skew SRAM array, with *WL2* and *WL4* activated at the same time. The two illustrated cells of the same column are activated simultaneously for write operations.

As an example, Fig. 2 shows when wordlines *WL2* and *WL4* are activated (become logic '1') at the same time in a write operation, the write data '1'/'0' appearing in bitline *BL/BLB* attempts to overwrite the internal data node *Q/QB*, respectively. Depending on the type of the addressed cells, the current supply voltage level, as well as their previously stored contents, the write operation may succeed or fail (i.e., previously stored contents stay unchanged, and are different from the write data). Since the activation of multiple wordlines connects the internal data nodes of multiple cells electrically through access transistors and bitlines, the operations of these cells influence each other (e.g., if a '1' is to be written, and one of the two activated cells already contains a '1', then writing '1' into the other cell becomes easier), making the computation taking place in write operations even more complicated. As any combination (defined by the challenge control module, see Fig. 1) of wordlines can be activated simultaneously, this parallel write operation can be emulated or simulated only by evaluating the type and the current contents of all the addressed cells together. That would require the emulator/simulator to read all needed information from different addresses, which cannot be done in a single read operation using normal memories or standard computing systems (resources available for attackers making functional physical clones or digital clones discussed in [13]). And the same also holds for the writing of the computed results back into those addresses, which cannot be done in a single write operation. While the SIMPL system can effectively perform *reading, computing,* and *writing-back* in one single cycle, an attacker will have to read the necessary data one by one in multiple cycles, compute the results based on all readout information, and write back again in multiple cycles. That would make the attacker's emulator/simulator many times slower, and the factor is dependent on the number of wordlines that can possibly be activated at the same time. Further discussions about the security assessment of the MWA skew SRAM are carried out in Sect. 5.

As the security of the skew SRAM based as well as the MWA skew SRAM based SIMPL system relies on the speed advantage of the skew SRAM block, other blocks described in Sect. 1 may stay unchanged. Section 3 presents a specific design of our MWA skew SRAM that enhances the security of the SIMPL system based on skew SRAM concepts.

3 Design of an MWA Skew SRAM

As a proof of concept, an MWA skew SRAM design using 45-nm PTM nano-CMOS models [14] is presented below, with up to two simultaneously activated wordlines (in each write cycle, one or two wordlines are activated simultaneously for writing) and two different supply voltages (1.0 V and 1.3 V). Two types of skew cells (Type 1 skew cell S_1, and Type 2 skew cell S_2) are designed, which differ in their transistor sizing and thus in their write behavior. They are randomly distributed in the skew SRAM array, with some of them configured to be fixed cells in post fabrication steps [13]. Therefore, four types of fixed cells exist (F_1: S_1 fixed to '0'; F_2: S_1 fixed to '1'; F_3: S_2 fixed to '0'; F_4: S_2 fixed to '1'). All types of cells work normally as conventional SRAM cells do in read operations, but show relatively complicated behavior when data is attempted to be written into them, depending on the combination of cell types activated in the write cycle, the current supply voltage, the previously stored data in the activated cells, as well as the data to be written into them. The defined write behavior is presented in Table 1.

The left-most column specifies the type(s) of the activated cell(s) in write operations, with previously stored data in the parentheses. The upper-most two rows give the operating conditions (supply voltage VDD during the write cycle, and the data WD to be written). Non-bold numbers in the rest of the table are the stored data (result) of corresponding activated cells after the write operation.

Compared to the behavior definition of the skew SRAM cells (normal/skew/fixed cells) described in [12, 13], we name the MWA skew SRAM cells differently, since no cell behaves the same as normal SRAM cells under all conditions. For the MWA skew SRAM, two types of skew cells, which behave differently in write operations, are defined. As described in Table 1, the "$S_2(0)$, $S_2(1)$" line defines that when a Type 2 skew cell (with previously stored data '0') and another Type 2 skew cell (with previously stored data '1') from the same column are activated simultaneously in a write cycle under the condition that VDD is 1.3 volt and the write data is '1', the first S_2 cell succeeds to store the new data '1', while the second S_2 cell remains storing the previously stored data '1', which is the same as the write data. Figure 3 shows the schematic and carefully chosen transistor sizes of Type 1 and Type 2 skew cells, which fulfill the behavior specification of Table 1.

Table 1. Write behavior of MWA skew cells

Cell type[a] (prev. stored data)	VDD = 1.0 V[b]		VDD = 1.3 V	
	WD = 0[b]	WD = 1	WD = 0	WD = 1
S_1	0	1	0	1
S_2	0	1	0	-[d]
S_1, S_1	0, 0	1, 1	0, 0	1, 1
S_1, S_2	0, 0	1, 1	-, -	-, -
$S_2(0), S_2(0)$	0, 0	0, 0	0, 0	0, 0
$S_2(0), S_2(1)$[c]	0, 0	1, 1	0, 0	1, 1[c]
$S_2(1), S_2(1)$	0, 0	1, 1	1, 1	1, 1
$F_x(0), S_x$	0, 0	0, 0	0, 0	0, 0
$F_x(1), S_x$	1, 1	1, 1	1, 1	1, 1
F_x, F_x	-, -	-, -	-, -	-, -

[a]The type(s) of cells that are activated simultaneously for write. For example, "S_1, S_2" means that a Type 1 skew cell and a Type 2 skew cell are activated simultaneously (both cells are from the same column, sharing the same bitline). "S_1" only means that one single Type 1 skew cell is activated. "F_x, S_x" stands for a fixed cell of any type and a skew cell of any type activated simultaneously. Data in the parentheses is the previously stored data in the corresponding cell, or the fixed value in case of a fixed cell. Without parentheses means that the previously stored data could be '1' or '0'.

[b]"VDD" is the supply voltage of the current write cycle. "WD" is the data to be written in that cycle.

[c] "1, 1" here means the stored data of the first S_2 (with previously stored data '0') and the second S_2 (with previously stored data '1') cells after the write operation, respectively: Under the condition of VDD=1.3V and WD=1, '1' is successfully written into the first S_2 cell, while the second S_2 cell retains its previously stored data '1', which is the same as the write data.

[d]"-" means that previously stored data remains unchanged after the write operation.

Fixed cells are simulated by adding connections between internal nodes Q to *VDD* (for Fixed '1' cells) or *GND* (for Fixed '0' cells) through resistors of 600 ohm (a typical value for antifuses using ONO, i.e., oxide-nitride-oxide technologies [15]).

As up to two wordlines need to be activated at the same time in write cycles, the challenge control block (see Fig. 1) and/or the address decoder of the skew SRAM need to be redesigned. A simple solution is to double the address (output of challenge control) bit width for the skew SRAM row decoder which controls the activation of wordlines, and duplicate the row decoder, with each taking half of the row address as input. The two row decoders may produce the same or different outputs, and each wordline is controlled by an "OR"-gate taking the corresponding output bits of the two row decoders as its inputs. Thus, one or two wordlines of the array will be activated simultaneously in each write cycle. In read cycles, the inputs of the two row decoders should be the same, so that only one wordline is activated in read cycles. This can be realized with simple logic based on the state of the R/W signal (read/write signal, which is part of the *CTRL* signal of Fig. 1).

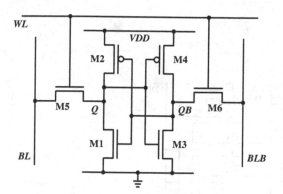

	Type 1	Type 2
M1, M3	180 / 45	145 / 45
M2, M4	50 / 90	115 / 45
M5, M6	85 / 45	54 / 45

Fig. 3. Schematic of skew cells and transistor sizing (W/L in nanometer) of Type 1 and Type 2 skew cells using 45-nm PTM nano-CMOS models [14].

Other modules, i.e., voltage control and feedback & output control modules, of the skew SRAM based SIMPL system do not require any modification.

4   Simulation

We simulate an MWA skew SRAM column as shown in Fig. 4 to verify the design. In the MWA skew SRAM column, S1 and S2 cells are randomly distributed. Several cells are chosen to be fixed cells. All combinations of situations described in Table 1 are simulated for verification. Figure 5 shows part of the simulation that verifies, e.g., the "S1(1), S2(0)" situation with VDD = 1.3 V and WD = 1 of Table 1 at simulation time 420 ns. It can be seen that the write operation of the S2 cell fails (to overwrite its previously stored value '0', see signal "qs22") as is desired, while the operation of the

S1 cell (see signal "qs12") can be regarded as successful although WD is the same as its previously stored value. Through simulations, all functionalities under different situations defined in the specification of Table 1 have been verified.

To approximately evaluate the yield of the design, simulations of the MWA skew SRAM column of Fig. 4 considering global process variations were carried out to verify the design further. Gaussian distributed variations (with three standard deviations of 30 millivolt, i.e., about 16.7 %) of the threshold voltages of PMOS and NMOS transistors were considered. However, since the simulated circuit is not small and there are a lot of different situations (Table 1) to check, it is time-consuming to run a large amount of Monte Carlo simulations. Our solution was to sweep the process variation parameters and find the parameter space boundary first. Within the boundary, all the specifications of Table 1 should be met. This greatly reduced the number of required simulations. After that, we just need to check if a Monte Carlo sample falls in the yield region or not. Out of all 1,000,000 Monte Carlo samples, 997,334 (over 99.7 %) totally meet the specification of Sect. 3 in all cases.

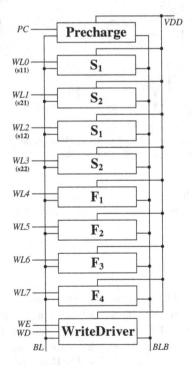

Fig. 4. MWA skew SRAM column design for simulation (PC: precharge; WLn: wordlines; WE: write enable; WD: write data; BL/BLB: bitlines; S1: Type 1 skew cell; S2: Type 2 skew cell; Fx: fixed cells).

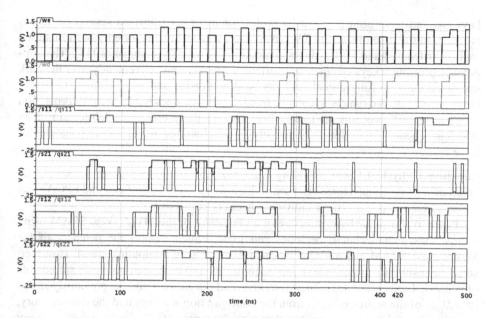

Fig. 5. Waveform of Type 1 and Type 2 skew cell operations. The voltage of logic '1' varies between 1.0 V and 1.3 V as VDD changes. Signals: we (write enable), wd (write data), s11/qs11 (WL/Q of an S1 cell), s21/qs21 (WL/Q of an S2 cell), s12 and qs12 (WL/Q of a second S1 cell), s22 and qs22 (WL/Q of a second S2 cell).

5   Discussion and Conclusion

This section briefly discusses the security improvement of the MWA skew SRAM based SIMPL system over the original described in [2, 12, 13] and concludes the paper.

5.1   Security Assessment

As in [12, 13], three basic possibilities for a faker to imitate the SIMPL system are discussed.

Exact Physical Clone. Similar to the conventional skew SRAM based SIMPL system, the MWA skew SRAM based SIMPL system is also refabricatable in a silicon foundry, if one-time costs of millions of US dollars are available for the faker [12]. However, if the value to be protected by the SIMPL system is much lower than that, which is the usual case for consumers or individual hackers and consumer application scenarios, fabricating an exact physical clone of the system is not only practically difficult, but also pointless from an economic perspective.

Furthermore, it is interesting to compare the attacker's need to fabricate a certain ASIC in silicon to the security level of secret binary keys, say, be they stored in classical memory or in alternative technologies like PUFs. In the past, such individual keys can and have been read out by professional hacker teams on several occasions [16, 17]. In the case of satellite TV boxes, such attacks have reportedly been mounted by hacker teams hired by the direct competitors of the TV companies [18]. The supposedly protective keys can then be distributed quickly and conveniently over the dark net, since they are fully digital, and can be downloaded and used even by relatively untrained private consumers to commit fraud. The same does not hold for IP protection based on SIMPL systems, as attacks here require the professional fabrication of an ASIC in silicon. This offers a potentially game-changing novel security feature for large consumer markets.

Functional Physical Clone. Building functional physical clones using resources like "normal" (mass-manufactured) memories, logic IC components, PLDs and FPGAs that are available for consumers or individual hackers is discussed.

Figure 6 shows the basic structure of an emulator of the MWA skew SRAM using normal mass-manufactured memories and logic, which mimics the behavior of the MWA skew SRAM and attempts to catch up with it in computing speed. However, since the result of a write cycle is dependent on the type and the previously stored data of addressed cells, the emulator needs to first read out *celltype* and the previously stored data D_{prev} of the addressed cells from the configuration memory and the data memory, respectively, and then calculate (together with the write data D_{IN} and the voltage select signal *SEL*) in the logic block the new data (result of the write cycle) to be written back into the data memory. For an MWA skew SRAM emulator, the data for *celltype* as well as for D_{prev} for different MWA wordlines come from multiple addresses, making it

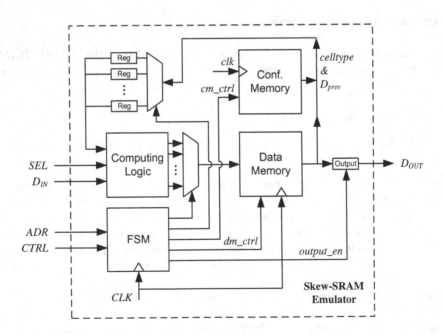

Fig. 6. Basic structure of an MWA skew SRAM emulator based on normal SRAMs and logic.

impossible to read in a single cycle. Therefore, *celltype* and D_{prev} must be read out with multiple read operations (to be specific, n read operations where n is the number of simultaneously activated wordlines) and stored at the input of the logic block until all needed information is collected for calculation. For writing back, a similar procedure must be done (to be specific, in n write operations where n is the number of simultaneously activated wordlines), since writing back into multiple addresses simultaneously is not possible. Thus, write back data must be present at the output of the logic block until all data are written back into the data memory cycle by cycle. And a finite state machine (FSM) needs to be implemented to control all the operations, e.g., the cycle-by-cycle read out and write back should be controlled by the FSM through *cm_ctrl* and *dm_ctrl* that contains the addresses and other control signals for each operation cycle. Since a write operation in the MWA skew SRAM has to be substituted with multiple read and multiple write operations in sequence, this emulator is at least a factor of $2 \times n$ slower in write operations where n is the number of wordlines activated, if the configuration and the data memories work at the same speed as our MWA skew SRAM, and if the delay of the computing logic of the emulator is ignored. Realizing the same structure of Fig. 6 with FPGAs wouldn't be dramatically different in speed since the multiple read and write operations have to be done in sequence.

Another possible FPGA-based emulation approach is to replicate the behavior of the MWA skew SRAM block cell by cell. Emulating the logic behavior of a single cell defined in Table 1 is not complicated. However, to be noted is that determining the result of MWA write operations in a Type 1 or Type 2 skew cell (S_1 or S_2) requires some knowledge about the other simultaneously activated cell in the same column (on the same bitline). An emulated S_1 cell needs to know the cell type of the other activated cell, while an emulated S_2 cell needs to know both the cell type and the cell contents (previously stored data) of the other activated cell. Since any two cells in the same column may be activated at the same time, there must be a path between a skew cell and all the other cells in the same column to communicate the cell type (for both S_1 and S_2 cells) and the cell contents (for S_2 cells). That indicates a large amount of connections between cells. Directly connecting all the cells would be impossible, since it quickly uses up the wiring resources of FPGAs. A crossbar-like implementation [19] based on multiplexers and demultiplexers may solve the wiring resource problem, if the array size is not too large. However, that causes more delays as many stages of multiplexing are required for a large MWA skew SRAM array. Although emulating a single cell with FPGA is possible, another issue arises when emulating a complete MWA skew SRAM array. As the logic behavior of MWA skew cells are much more complicated than the original skew cells described in [12, 13], the number of configurable cells (look-up-tables or LUTs, and Flip-flops) required for emulating their behavior increases a lot. To verify that, we implemented a 2 Kbit (with 32 bit word-width) MWA skew SRAM array with a Xilinx Virtex-6 FPGA (fabricated with a 40-nm technology). Even in such a highly simplified case with only 16.7 % S_1 and 16.7 % S_2 cells randomly distributed in the array, already 84 % LUT resources of the FPGA were used. Implementing a 512 Kbit (an optimal array size suggested in [13]) MWA skew SRAM array with commercially available FPGAs would be simply impossible. Even if an emulator can be built by connecting hundreds of FPGAs, the communication delay between FPGA chips would further widen the speed gap between the emulator and the "legal" monolithic SIMPL system. As the maximum operating frequency for MWA write operations achieved with the Xilinx Virtex-6 FPGA implementing a 2 Kbit array is only 21 MHz, implementing a full-size MWA skew SRAM array with hundreds of FPGA chips would end up with an even much slower emulator. By increasing the number of wordlines n that may be activated at the same time, the connections between skew cells and other cells in the same column will also at least linearly increase when implementing the emulator in the cell-by-cell way described above. And since the complexity of skew cell logic behavior also increases with n, emulating the MWA skew SRAM array will become even harder and slower as n increases.

Digital Clone. Building a digital clone using standard computing systems like PC and software could be the most cost-effective way to emulate the behavior of an MWA skew SRAM. However, due to the data dependency of a computing cycle on its previous cycles, parallelization of the computation taking place in the MWA skew SRAM is impossible. As discussed in [13], building a digital clone wouldn't produce a faster system compared to a functional physical clone. Even if the delay for computing logic (for calculating the new data to be stored) is ignored, just reading the data required for computing logic and writing back the new data already makes the emulator (implemented with an Intel Core 2 Quad CPU working at 2.5 GHz and a 3 GB RAM) at least 25 times slower [13]. By applying MWA designs, this speed gap will be further enlarged by at least a factor of n (where n is the number of simultaneously activated wordlines) in write operations, as the data bit-width of PCs is just comparable with that of skew SRAMs, and any combination of wordlines to be activated in a cycle may happen, today's memory architectures in standard computing systems are not able to parallelize or speed up the required cycle-by-cycle read out and write back procedure as described in building "functional physical clone(s)".

5.2   Conclusion and Future Scope

This paper presented a multiple wordline activation (MWA) skew SRAM design to improve the security of the original skew SRAM based SIMPL systems discussed in [12, 13]. By enabling parallel computations taking place in different cells controlled by multiple wordlines using the MWA skew SRAM design, the security of SIMPL systems based on that is enhanced by a factor linearly related to the number of simultaneously activated wordlines. Simulations of the enhanced skew SRAM show expected behavior complexity and satisfying yield considering manufacturing process variations. This makes our approach one of the first practically viable, circuit-based implementations of SIMPL system and public PUFs.

The security level can be further enhanced by increasing the number of supply voltages and/or the number of simultaneously activated wordlines. However, as the number of supply voltages and/or the number of simultaneously activated wordlines increase, the stability of the skew behavior against ambient noises, temperature changes, supply voltage ripples as well as process variations may decrease. A trade-off between security level and stability needs to be determined in future work.

References

1. Rührmair, U.: SIMPL systems: on a public key variant of physical unclonable functions. In: IACR Cryptology ePrint Archive, No. 2009/255 (2009)
2. Rührmair, U., Chen, Q., Stutzmann, M., Lugli, P., Schlichtmann, U., Csaba, G.: Towards electrical, integrated implementations of SIMPL systems. In: Samarati, P., Tunstall, M., Posegga, J., Markantonakis, K., Sauveron, D. (eds.) WISTP 2010. LNCS, vol. 6033, pp. 277–292. Springer, Heidelberg (2010)
3. Suh, E., Devadas, S.: Physical unclonable functions for device authentication and secret key generation. In: Proceedings of the 44th annual Design Automation Conference, DAC 2007, pp. 9–14. ACM Press (2007)
4. Chen, Q., Csaba, G., Lugli, P., Schlichtmann, U., Rührmair, U.: The bistable ring PUF: a new architecture for strong physical unclonable functions. In: Proceedings of the 2011 IEEE International Symposium on Hardware-Oriented Security and Trust, HOST 2011, pp. 134–141. IEEE Press (2011)
5. Kumar, S.S., Guajardo, J., Maes, R., Schrijen, G.J., Tuyls, P.: The butterfly PUF protecting IP on every FPGA. In: Proceedings of the 2008 IEEE International Workshop on Hardware-Oriented Security and Trust, HOST2008, pp. 67–70. IEEE Press (2008)
6. Maes, R., Tuyls, P., Verbauwhede, I.: Intrinsic PUFs from flip-flops on reconfigurable devices. In: 3rd Benelux workshop on information and system security, WISSec 2008, **17** (2008)
7. Chen, Q., Csaba, G., Lugli, P., Schlichtmann, U., Rührmair, U.: Characterization of the bistable ring PUF. In: Proceedings of the 2012 Design, Automation & Test in Europe Conference & Exhibition, DATE 2012, pp. 1459–1462. IEEE Press (2012)
8. Beckmann, N., Potkonjak, M.: Hardware-based public-key cryptography with public physically unclonable functions. In: Katzenbeisser, S., Sadeghi, A.-R. (eds.) IH 2009. LNCS, vol. 5806, pp. 206–220. Springer, Heidelberg (2009)
9. Rührmair, U., Sölter, J., Sehnke, F.: On the foundations of physical unclonable functions. In: IACR Cryptology ePrint Archive, No. 2009/277 (2009)
10. Potkonjak, M., Meguerdichian, S., Nahapetian, A., Wei, S.: Differential Public Physically Unclonable Functions: Architecture and Applications. In: Proceedings of the 48th annual Design Automation Conference, DAC 2011, pp. 242–247. ACM Press (2011)
11. Meguerdichian, S., Potkonjak, M.: Matched public PUF: ultra low energy security platform. In: Proceedings of International Symposium on Low Power Electronics and Design, ISLPED 2011, pp. 45–50 (2011)
12. Chen, Q., Csaba, G., Ju, X., Natarajan, S., Lugli, P., Stutzmann, M., Schlichtmann, U., Rührmair, U.: Analog circuits for physical cryptography. In: Proceedings of the 12th International Symposium on Integrated Circuits, ISIC 2009, pp. 121–124. IEEE Press (2009)
13. Chen, Q., Csaba, G., Lugli, P., Schlichtmann, U., Stutzmann, M., Rührmair, U.: Circuit-based approaches to SIMPL systems. J. Circuits Syst. Comput. **20**(01), 107–123 (2011)
14. Predictive technology model, Nanoscale Integration and Modeling (NIMO) Group, ASU. http://ptm.asu.edu/
15. Trimberger, S.: Field-Programmable Gate Array Technology, p. 100. Springer, New York (1994)
16. Anderson, R.: Security Engineering. John Wiley, New York (2008)
17. Helfmeier, C., Boit, C., Nedospasov, D., Seifert, J.: Cloning physically unclonable functions. In: Proceedings of the 2013 IEEE International Symposium on Hardware Oriented Security and Trust, HOST 2013, pp. 1–6. IEEE Press (2013)

18. Biddle, P., England, P., Peinado, M., Willman, B.: The darknet and the future of content protection. In: Feigenbaum, J. (ed.) DRM 2002. LNCS, vol. 2696, pp. 155–176. Springer, Heidelberg (2003)
19. Sonntag, S., Reinig, H., Linz, S., Pitter, F., Ruhwandl, M.; XB07: a highly reusable crossbar architecture for multiprocessor system on chip (MPSoC). In: IP Based Electronic System Conference, IP 2007, pp. 307–311 (2007)

Secure Erasure and Code Update
in Legacy Sensors

Ghassan O. Karame[✉] and Wenting Li

NEC Laboratories Europe, 69115 Heidelberg, Germany
{ghassan.karame,wenting.li}@neclab.eu

Abstract. Sensors require frequent over-the-air reprogramming to patch software errors, replace code, change sensor configuration, etc. Given their limited computational capability, one of the few workable techniques to secure code update in legacy sensors would be to execute Proofs of Secure Erasure (PoSE) which ensure that the sensor's memory is purged before sending the updated code. By doing so, the updated code can be loaded onto the sensor with the assurance that no other malicious code is being stored. Although current PoSE proposals rely on relatively simple cryptographic constructs, they still result in considerable energy and time overhead in existing legacy sensors.

In this paper, we propose a secure code update protocol which considerably reduces the overhead of existing proposals. Our proposal naturally combines PoSE with All or Nothing Transforms (AONT); we analyze the security of our scheme and evaluate its performance by means of implementation on MicaZ motes. Our prototype implementation only consumes 371 bytes of RAM in TinyOS2, and improves the time and energy overhead of existing proposals based on PoSE by almost 75 %.

Keywords: Secure code update · All or nothing transformations · Proofs of secure erasure

1 Introduction

Sensors and actuators require frequent over-the-air reprogramming to update their cryptographic credentials, patch software errors, change configuration, etc. Clearly, code update needs to be *securely* realized in order to ensure that the newly downloaded code is installed in its entirety and can be correctly executed in the installation environment with the assurance that no other malicious code is being stored.

The literature features a number of solutions based on device attestation to secure code execution in embedded devices [13,14,18,26,27]; however, recent studies show that existing (hardware and software-based) techniques are still far from being practical to be deployed in legacy sensors [22].

To remedy this, Perito and Tsudik [22] introduced the notion of Proofs of Secure Erasure (PoSE) in order to secure code update. PoSE enable a device to prove to a remote verifier that it has purged all of its memory. For example, in a

© Springer International Publishing Switzerland 2015
M. Conti et al. (Eds.): TRUST 2015, LNCS 9229, pp. 283–299, 2015.
DOI: 10.1007/978-3-319-22846-4_17

PoSE, the prover downloads large amounts of incompressible data which fills all of its writable memory contents, and then proves (e.g., using MACs, or Proofs of Data Possession schemes [5,15,29]) to a remote verifier that it has downloaded the data in its entirety. The main intuition here is that if the prover can attest that it is storing new data which covers all of its writable memory, then the prover must have purged its (old) memory contents. By doing so, PoSE can be used as a prelude to secure code update [22]; once all prior state has been erased, new code can be downloaded onto the device with the assurance that no other malware or malicious code is being stored.

Although existing PoSE schemes rely on relatively simple cryptographic constructs, such as MACs, these schemes still result in considerable energy and time overhead in existing low-cost sensors. For example, in MicaZ motes, the computation of HMACs based on SHA1 for 648 KB of data (which constitutes the total memory of a MicaZ mote) requires almost 90 s, and consumes $3.5 \mu J$ per byte [22]. This is mainly due to the fact that legacy sensors are still not optimized to execute cryptographic algorithms.

In this paper, we address this problem and we propose an efficient PoSE scheme which considerably improves the verification overhead of existing PoSE proposals in legacy sensors. Our construction makes use of basic operations such as XORing and cyclic bitwise shifting; we show that our solution incurs moderate computational costs when compared to existing PoSE proposals—while ensuring secure memory erasure. We then extend our proposal and present a secure code update protocol, SUANT (Secure code Update based on All or Nothing Transforms), which naturally combines PoSE with an efficient all or nothing transform; SUANT requires the same number of communication rounds as PoSE, and results in a considerably smaller computational overhead when compared to existing secure code update protocols based on PoSE. We evaluate the performance of SUANT by means of implementation on MicaZ sensor nodes [2]. Our evaluation results show that our scheme only consumes 371 bytes of RAM, and incurs approximately 75 % energy and time savings when compared to the optimized secure code update protocol of [22].

The remainder of this paper is organized as follows. In Sect. 2, we present PoSE, and describe the building blocks that we will use throughout the paper. In Sect. 3, we introduce our proposals aimed at efficiently proving memory erasure and secure code update. In Sect. 4, we implement and evaluate our secure code update protocol using MicaZ motes. In Sect. 5, we overview related work in the area, and we conclude the paper in Sect. 6.

2   Background and Preliminaries

We start by outlining our system and attacker model. We then discuss the shortcomings of device attestation for sensors, introduce PoSE, and the building blocks that we will use throughout this paper.

2.1   Model

Our system consists of a verifier V and a resource-constrained prover P. Here, V is interested in updating the code of P; for that purpose, V transmits over the air the required code to be updated. To ensure that P can correctly execute the new code update, V requires a proof that P has correctly downloaded the code update, and does not host any malware in its memory. By memory, we refer to the entirety of the writable storage available to P. We assume that V has a larger memory than P, and knows the exact memory size of P. This is a reasonable assumption since we consider the typical case where P is a sensor mote, whose total memory capacity is accurately reported in its datasheets.

We assume a computationally bounded adversary A which controls P. Here, A is a program or a malware executing on P, and has complete read/write access over the memory of P. We assume, nevertheless, that A does not have write access to a small part of the read-only memory (ROM) of the device. Read-only memory can be instantiated in most embedded devices by locking parts of the device's memory. Writing to this memory portion without physically accessing the device is not possible.

Similar to existing software attestation protocols [22,26,27], we assume that A cannot modify the hardware configuration of P, and can only communicate with the verifier (and no other external entity). Assuming wireless communication with the sensors, this can be practically enforced if the verifier actively jams the prover throughout their interaction phase. Jamming can be effectively realized by the verifier—without affecting the ability of the prover to interact with the verifier—by emitting signals with larger strength than the maximum threshold set at prover's side [20,22].

Notice that since A is restricted to P's running environment without any external help, then A is bounded by the computational and storage capabilities of the prover (i.e., by P's memory). Similar to existing protocols, we assume that the device authenticates the verifier prior to the start of the secure code update protocol. To this end, we assume, e.g., that the public key of the verifier and the authentication algorithm are stored in the ROM of the device. Throughout the rest of the paper, we do not focus on the overhead incurred by authenticating the verifier since this step is not particular to our protocols and applies to all similar protocols.

2.2   Remote Attestation

As mentioned earlier, device attestation constitutes one possible way to ensure that an embedded device is executing correct software. Device attestation can be categorized in two main branches: hardware-based attestation, and software-based attestation.

Hardware-based attestation leverages hardware support, such as TPM chips, ARM Trustzone [3], Intel SGX [4], to securely bootstrap a trusted measurement environment. Hardware-based attestation offers strong security guarantees but is unfortunately not yet supported on low-cost embedded devices [12]. On the other hand, software-based attestation [26,27] aims to verify the correctness of software executing on a device without the reliance on additional hardware support. Recently, several attacks have been reported against existing software-based attestation schemes [8,28,30].

In [13], Jakobsson and Johansson propose the reliance on a memory printing algorithm to practically enable software-based attestation. The proposed algorithm acquires a random seed from a secure source of (pseudo-)randomness located in the close proximity of the device (e.g., a SIM or a smart card), executes an expansion function using the seed as input to fill the RAM of the device, then mixes and shuffles the output of the expansion function. By doing so, if a malware is executing in the RAM of the device, then this will slow down the aforementioned process that requires all the RAM for fast computation—which would facilitate the detection of misbehavior. This solution is, however, unsuitable for legacy sensors which do not have any SIM/smart card slot and solely rely on the slow radio channel for communication. This renders the detection of delays originating from the execution in RAM a rather challenging task.

2.3   Proofs of Secure Erasure (PoSE)

In [22], Perito and Tsudik proposed proofs of secure erasure (PoSE) for resource-constrained sensor nodes. Their PoSE comprise two steps:

Step 1: Erase memory. The prover erasures all of its memory by downloading high entropy data (e.g., an encrypted stream of data) sent by the verifier. Here, the code must be large enough to fill all the writable memory of the prover.

Step 2: Proof of erasure. The prover attests to the verifier that it has stored all the downloaded code. This can be done e.g., by sending a MAC of the downloaded code to the verifier.

As shown in [22], the basic PoSE protocol described above can be transformed into a secure code update protocol by invoking an additional communication round between the prover $\mathcal{P}$ and the verifier $\mathcal{V}$. The resulting code update protocol is depicted in Fig. 1. Here, the verifier first chooses a random encryption key K' and encrypts the code[1] to be updated $P_1, \ldots, P_n$ using a semantically secure encryption function Enc. Upon reception of the ciphertext blocks $C_0, \ldots, C_n$, the prover uses the last m blocks as a MAC key K, constructs a MAC over the remaining ciphertext blocks $MAC(K, C_0, \ldots, C_{n-m})$, and sends the MAC to $\mathcal{V}$ who verifies it. If the verification passes, $\mathcal{V}$ sends to $\mathcal{P}$ key K' in order for $\mathcal{P}$ to decrypt $C_0, \ldots, C_n$ into the plaintext code.

The aforementioned PoSE protocol, and the corresponding secure code update protocol incur considerable communication and computational costs on the prover, namely:

---

[1] In case the code size to be updated is smaller than the total writable memory of the device, the verifier pads the code with zeros until it reaches the device's memory size.

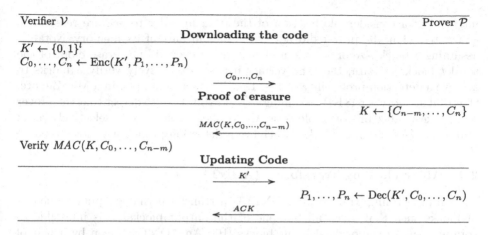

Fig. 1. Summary of the optimized secure code update protocol of [22].

1. The prover needs to download data which is as large as its own memory (e.g., 648 KB in MicaZ nodes).
2. The prover needs to compute a MAC over the entire data to verify that the prover has indeed stored the downloaded bytes[2].
3. The secure code update protocol results in an additional communication round for the verifier to send the encryption key K' in case the PoSE protocol successfully completes.

One possible alternative to reduce the downloaded data size would be to make use of a secure expansion function which fills the entire prover's memory with high entropy data (similar to [13]). By doing so, it might be possible to detect if a malware still resides in the memory of the device by timing the verification step (i.e., I/O access vs. heavy computations). In an experiment that we conducted, we measured the time and energy required by a MicaZ sensor to erase its total memory by *(i)* downloading code from an external verifier over the radio channel as in [22] or by *(ii)* adapting the memory printing algorithm of [13] to fill the prover's memory. Our findings show that the former approach consumes 8.64 μJ/B at 8.86 KB/s,[3] while the latter solution consumes 35.74 μJ/B with a throughput of 0.77 KB/s. Therefore, filling the prover's memory with data downloaded from an external verifier emerges as the most workable mechanism to purge the memory of legacy sensors.

On the other hand, to reduce the computational costs of the PoSE protocol in Fig. 1, one alterative would be to selectively verify a fraction of the downloaded data (e.g., similar to POR/PDP [5,15,29]). This approach considerably speeds up the verification stage in PoSE, but still requires that the verifier verifies the

---

[2] As shown in [22], computing an HMAC-SHA1 over 648 KB of data in a MicaZ mote requires almost 90 s.

[3] The maximum claimed transmission throughput of TI-CC2420 radio chip used in MicaZ motes is 250 kbps, which translates to 31250 bytes/sec. However, our experiments show that the effective throughput is around 8860 bytes/sec using TinyOS 2.0.

integrity of a considerable fraction of the data in order to acquire reasonable guarantees that the prover did not erase a small part of its memory. Notably, assuming a block size of m bits, and that the prover did not erase c out of the total t blocks of data, then the verifier needs to selectively verify d blocks to achieve a detection probability of $1 - (1 - \frac{c}{t})^d$. As an example, in a MicaZ mote, the total memory is 648 KB; assuming $m = 128$ bit, then to detect that the prover did not keep 1,000 bits of its old code, the verifier would have to selectively check almost 30 % of the data blocks to achieve a detection probability close to 90 %.

2.4   All or Nothing Transforms (AONT)

An All or Nothing Transform (AONT) is a transform that outputs sequences of blocks such that given all but one of the output blocks, it is infeasible to compute any of the original input blocks [16]. An AONT is given by a pair of p.p.t. algorithms $(\mathbb{E}, \mathbb{D})$ where [10, 16]:

$\mathbb{E}$ The encoding algorithm is a probabilistic algorithm which takes as input a message $x \in \{0, 1\}^*$, and outputs ciphertext y.

$\mathbb{D}$ The decoding algorithm is a deterministic algorithm which takes as input ciphertext y, and outputs either a message $x \in \{0, 1\}^*$ or $\perp$ to indicate that the input ciphertext is invalid.

To construct an AONT, Rivest [25] suggested the package transform which leverages a block cipher and maps m block strings to $m+1$ block strings. The first m output blocks are computed by encrypting the input blocks using a random key K. The last output block is computed by XORing K with the encryption of each of the previous output blocks, using a key K_0 that is publicly known.

Desai [10] proposed a faster version where the block cipher round which uses K_0 is skipped and the last output block is computed as the XOR of all the ciphertext blocks: That is, given block cipher F/F^{-1} and on input $x[1] \ldots x[m]$, Desai's transform outputs $y[1] \ldots y[n]$, with $n = m + 1$, where:

$$y[i] = x[i] \oplus F_K(i), \ 1 \leq i \leq n - 1,$$

$$y[n] = K \bigoplus_{i=1}^{n-1} y[i].$$

Notice that Desai's AONT leverages a block cipher to ensure that the output blocks have high entropy. In this paper, we leverage Desai's AONT to construct an efficient secure code update scheme for legacy sensors. By doing so, our construct requires that the prover fetches all the output code blocks in order to decode any part of the (plaintext) code; if the prover possesses all but one output block, then it is computationally infeasible for the prover to acquire any meaningful bit of information about any plaintext block. As we show later, this also removes the need for an additional communication round to transmit the code encryption key.

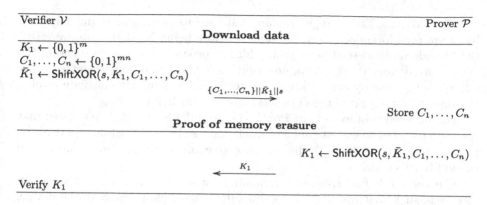

Fig. 2. Sketch of our lightweight PoSE scheme. Here, we assume that the code $C_1, \ldots, C_n$, of size mn, fills the total writable memory of $\mathcal{P}$ (with the exception of the minimum amount of volatile memory required to execute the PoSE scheme).

3   Lightweight Proofs of Secure Erasure and Code Update

In this section, we present and analyze our proposal for secure code update. We will do so incrementally, starting with an initial scheme which enables the construction of efficient proofs of secure memory erasure, and later extending it to construct our code update protocol, SUANT.

3.1   Lightweight Proofs of Secure Erasure

Our solution shares the same intuition with existing PoSE proposals [22]; namely, the prover fills its memory with high-entropy data acquired from the verifier and proves to the latter that it has stored all the downloaded data. As mentioned in Sect. 2.3, this alternative is more efficient than filling the memory of the prover using a local source of pseudo-randomness. The main difference between our proposal and the PoSE of [22] lies in the fact that, here, the data is specifically constructed in such a way that if the prover has stored that data in its entirety, then $\mathcal{P}$ can issue a compact proof of memory erasure—without the need to rely on MACs.

In our solution, this is achieved as follows: the verifier picks a random secret, divides the data into equal sized-blocks, and XORs the secret with (a function of) the data blocks which the prover is requested to download. The output of the XOR is appended and sent to the prover as the last data block. If the prover can correctly extract the secret inserted by the verifier, then this offers a strong proof that the prover has downloaded all the data sent by the verifier.

Notice that the straightforward XORing of the data blocks with the secret does not offer a proof of memory erasure, since a malicious prover can simply XOR all the downloaded blocks without the need to store them. Later on, after receiving the last block (which is the XOR of the secret with the remaining data blocks), the prover can correctly revert the secret without having to store all the downloaded data. Therefore, we require that the bits pertaining to different data block are pseudorandomly (cyclic) shifted before being XORed; here, we reveal the (pseudorandom) seed used in the shifting procedure at the very end of the data transmission. By doing so, our solution ensures that the advantage of an adversary in correctly computing the secret by performing intermediate results, or dropping a fraction of the data bits/blocks is negligible.

The detailed protocol of our PoSE scheme unfolds in Fig. 2. We stress that the code required to execute our PoSE scheme resides in a read-only part of the prover's memory (cf. Sect. 4); this does not give any advantage for the adversary to modify this code.

The verifier $\mathcal{V}$ first chooses n random data blocks $C_1, \ldots, C_n$ of length m bits each, such that mn fills the total *available* writable memory of the device. This corresponds to the total writable memory of the device excluding *(i)* the memory occupied by the code required to download and process the data, and *(ii)* the minimum amount of volatile memory necessary to execute the code of PoSE. $\mathcal{V}$ then chooses a random secret K_1 and a seed s of size m bits each, and executes the following ShiftXOR procedure:

1: **procedure** $\bar{K}_1 \leftarrow$ ShiftXOR$(s, K_1, C_1, \ldots, C_n)$
2:     $S \leftarrow G(s)$
3:     $l = \log_2 m$
4:     $\bar{K}_1 \leftarrow K_1$
5:     **for** $i = 0 \ldots n - 1$ **do**
6:         $c \leftarrow S_{il \to l(i+1)}$
7:         $\bar{K}_1 \leftarrow \bar{K}_1 \oplus \{C_{(i+1)}\}_{\gg c}$
8:     **end for**
9: **end procedure**

Here, $S_{x \to y}$ refers to the bit sequence of S indexed from position x to y, $X_{\gg y}$ refers to the bitwise cyclic shift of X by y positions, and $G : \{0,1\}^m \to \{0,1\}^{nl}$ is an expansion function. For example, G can be instantiated by iteratively applying a hash function using as input the seed and a counter until the required number of bits are reached. The verifier then sends $C_1, \ldots, C_n || \bar{K}_1 || s$ to the prover. Notice that the ShiftXOR procedure is symmetric. That is, K_1 can be obtained by computing ShiftXOR$(s, \bar{K}_1, C_1, \ldots, C_n)$.

Claim 1. *Assuming a secure cryptographic source of randomness on $\mathcal{V}$, the protocol of Fig. 2 enables the verifier to detect that an adversary has not erased any m bits in its memory with overwhelming probability.*

Proof Sketch. *Suppose that a malicious code of size $b > 0$ persists in the memory of $\mathcal{P}$ after the completion of our PoSE. Then, this means that the adversary was able to compute K_1 without storing all the downloaded data in its memory. Recall that we assume that $C_1, \ldots, C_n$ fill the total writable memory of the prover with the exception of the minimum amount of volatile memory required to run the PoSE code. Moreover, K_1 is generated from a cryptographically secure source of randomness and therefore cannot be easily guessed. Moreover, since s is*

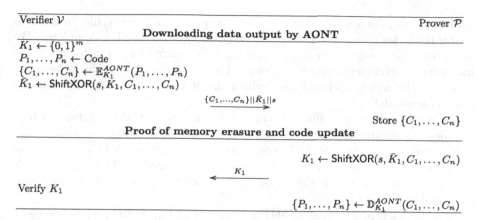

Fig. 3. Sketch of SUANT. Our construct combines PoSE with Desai's AONT in order to reduce the communication rounds required to prove secure code update.

communicated to $\mathcal{P}$ at the very end of the transmission, then this precludes any straightforward pre-computation of K_1. Since the data is also generated from a secure source of randomness on $\mathcal{V}$, then its entropy also rules out any possibility of compression. Recall also that the adversary cannot modify the code required to execute our PoSE scheme, since this code resides in a read-only part of $\mathcal{P}$'s memory.

Without knowledge of s, notice that each bit of each data block can affect the outcome of any bit of K_1 (due to the ShiftXOR routine). That is, any intermediate processing on the received bits (e.g., dropping some bits, XORing bits) can affect any of the m bits of the computed response. In other words, if the adversary stores $b > 0$ m-bits blocks of malicious code after the completion of the protocol (e.g., by dropping bm bits of the received data), then the adversary has to guess the correct shifting applied to at least b blocks of received data. This guessing probability is bounded by $\max(m^{-b}, 2^{-m})$.

Assuming $m = 128$ bits, the probability that a malicious code of size 1000 bits persists in the memory of $\mathcal{P}$ is bounded by 2^{-56}. We contrast this to existing PoSE schemes based on selective checking, where the probability that the verifier detects that the adversary did not erase 1,000 bits of its old memory contents after checking the integrity of 30 % of the downloaded blocks is approximately 90 %, when the prover's memory size is 648 KB.

3.2   SUANT: Secure Code Update Based on AONT

We now show how to extend our aforementioned PoSE scheme in order to construct an efficient secure code update protocol.

Notice that extending a PoSE into a secure code update protocol can be easily realized by (*i*) first padding the code to be updated to reach the total memory size of the prover, (*ii*) encrypting the padded code, and (*iii*) executing PoSE is over encrypted code. However, as shown in [22], this results in an additional communication round between the prover and the verifier in order to enable the latter to communicate the encryption key once PoSE is completed. We point out that the decryption key should only be shared with $\mathcal{P}$ after the PoSE has correctly completed since, otherwise, there is a risk that malware acquires access to the newly updated code which might contain sensitive information (e.g., credentials).

In what follows, we offer a natural extension to our PoSE scheme which satisfies this requirement without incurring an additional communication round. Our extension, dubbed SUANT, combines PoSE with an AONT in order to ensure that only if the prover has downloaded and stored all the encrypted code update, then it can acquire the necessary decryption key to revert the encrypted code and update its code.

The detailed protocol of SUANT is depicted in Fig. 3. Here, the code to be updated is first encrypted using key K_1, which will be subsequently used as the secret XORed with the data blocks in the ShiftXOR procedure. From that point on, SUANT unfolds similarly to our PoSE protocol in Fig. 2. Recall here that the code required to execute our scheme resides in a read-only part of the prover's memory (cf. Sect. 4).

Notice that by first encrypting the code and then XORing all the cipher-text blocks with the encryption key, this exactly yields the AONT transform of Desai (cf. Sect. 2.4). One major difference between SUANT and Desai's AONT lies in the fact that the last output block is replaced with $\bar{K}_1$, as outputted by ShiftXOR, which corresponds to the XOR of the pseudorandomly shifted cipher-text blocks with K_1. As mentioned earlier, this prevents the adversary from computing intermediate XOR on the fly, without the need to store the down-loaded blocks.

Claim 2. *Assuming a secure cryptographic source of randomness on $\mathcal{V}$, the protocol of Fig. 3 enables the verifier to detect that an adversary has not securely updated his code with overwhelming probability.*

Proof Sketch. *It is easy to see that, given our assumptions, (i) the prover has a fixed and known memory size, and (ii) the adversary cannot modify the hardware of the provers, the security of SUANT follows directly from Claim 1 (cf. Sect. 3.1) and from the security of Desai's transform [10].*

Namely, since the downloaded code has high entropy (recall that the code is encrypted), and fills the total memory of the prover, then this prevents any straightforward attack where the adversary e.g., compresses the code. Similarly, the adversary cannot hide malware in parts of the writable memory, since our code update fills the entire memory of the device, including the volatile mem-ory (with the exception of the minimum amount of RAM required to execute SUANT). Moreover, the use of Desai's AONT also ensures that the prover can-not acquire any meaningful bit of plaintext code unless it has processed all the output ciphertext blocks [10].

Since s is communicated at the very end of the transmission, then the prover has to store all the blocks, in order to subsequently revert $\bar{K}_1$, compute K_1, and decode the encrypted blocks to acquire the code update. As shown in Claim 1, *the probability that a malicious code of size bm bits resides in the memory of* $\mathcal{P}$ *after the successful completion of* SUANT *is given by* $\max(m^{-b}, 2^{-m})$, *which corresponds to the probability that the adversary guesses the correct shifting of all the b blocks or the key* K_1.

Reducing I/O Costs in SUANT: The ShiftXOR routine employed by SUANT incurs high I/O costs since it requires access to each and every data block. Notice that this overhead can be reduced if ShiftXOR only operates on a randomly chosen fraction f of the blocks. Such an alternative approach ensures that the secret is XORed (line 7 of ShiftXOR) with a randomly selected fraction f of the data blocks and thus requires the prover to only fetch those blocks from memory—thus tremendously reducing I/O costs. Here, the advantage of the adversary in computing the correct key K_1 without storing any given b ciphertext blocks of size m is bounded by $\max(m^{-b}, (1-f)^b)$. For example, when $f = 0.5$, if the adversary does not delete 1,000 bits of its old code (e.g., and selectively deletes 8 ciphertext blocks with size $m = 128$ bits each), then the probability that she can correctly compute K_1 is bounded by 0.004. We evaluate the comparative performance of this approach in Sect. 4.

4   Implementation and Evaluation

In this section, we implement and evaluate SUANT in MicaZ motes. For comparison purposes, we also evaluate the secure code update protocol of [22].

4.1   Implementation Setup

In order to evaluate the performance of our proposal in a realistic setting, we implemented SUANT on the ATMEGA128 micro-controller mounted on a MicaZ sensor. MicaZ [2] has a total memory of 648 KB, divided into 512 KB of external flash memory, 128 KB of internal flash, 4 KB of SRAM, and 4 KB of EEPROM. To access the on-chip memory, we made use of the *InternalFlashC* and *ProgFlashC*[4] modules from TinyOS bootloader (TOSBoot). The maximum transmission throughput of MicaZ is bounded by 250 kbps; however, our experiments suggest that only 30 % of this throughput can be effectively attained in a realistic scenario.

In addition to SUANT, we implemented f-SUANT, the optimized version of SUANT in which a fraction f of the data blocks are randomly processed by the ShiftXOR routine. In our implementation, we set $f = 0.5$; as mentioned earlier, this ensures the detection of a malicious prover which did not erase 1,000 bits (or more) of its old memory content with a probability of 0.996. For comparison purposes, we also implemented the optimized secure code update protocol of [22] (SCU) and a variant protocol adapted from [22] which replaces the verification of the entire downloaded code by a probabilistic verification (using MACs) of a fraction $p = 0.3$ of the downloaded data blocks[5]; we refer to this protocol by p-SCU.

---

[4] For that purpose, we extended the *ProgFlash* interface using AVR Libc.
[5] In this case, the probability to detect that a prover did not delete 1,000 bits of its old code is 0.9.

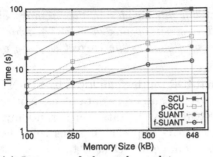
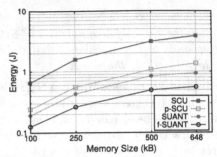

(a) Latency of the code update process w.r.t. the code size.

(b) Energy dissipated by MicaZ nodes during code update.

Fig. 4. Performance evaluation using MicaZ sensors. Each data point is averaged over 10 independent measurements; we do not include the corresponding 95 % confidence intervals due to their small size.

Table 1. Required code and volatile memory sizes.

	Total Memory (bytes)	RAM (bytes)	ROM (bytes)
SUANT	15,516	371	6822
f-**SUANT**	15,718	384	6960
SCU	19,256	610	8562
p-**SCU**	19,436	614	9722

Our implementation was integrated with TinyOS2. We relied on the TinySec and TinyECC libraries [17,19] to implement the cryptographic algorithms. We instantiated MACs using HMAC-SHA1, and made use of the Lehmer pseudo-random number generator [21]. In all the implemented schemes, we assume a fixed block size $m = 128$ bits.

Since all the implemented protocols require the initial transmission of a code of size mn bits and its decryption, we did not measure the overhead incurred by these processes. As shown in Sect. 2.3, our findings show that the code transmission to a MicaZ mote consumes $8.64\,\mu J/B$ at $8.86\,KB/s$.

In our experiments, we measured the time and energy that are consumed by the above mentioned four protocols, namely SUANT, f-SUANT, SCU, and p-SCU, in accessing and computing the memory blocks until the decryption key is obtained. To measure the energy consumption of the implemented protocols, we relied on the Avrora simulator [32] which provides an accurate cycle-based simulation of the ATMEGA128 micro-controller. All data points in our (latency) plots are averaged over 10 independent measurements; where appropriate, we also show the corresponding 95 % confidence intervals.

Ideally, the code update protocol should be stored in the ROM of the device to prevent tampering with the process. At present, many embedded devices support the use of mask ROM (e.g., the MSP430 micro-controller). In our case, we included the codes responsible for executing SUANT, f-SUANT, SCU, and p-SCU (respectively) in the internal flash of the MicaZ mote. Recall that ATmega128 allows part of its internal flash to be locked from writing—thus emulating a read-only memory. For instance, setting Boot Lock Bit 0 to '10' in ATmega128 and the BOOTSZ fuse to '00' on the bootloader section grants us an 8 KB equivalent of read-only memory in the internal flash [1]. Notice that, once locked, this memory can only be unlocked by means of physical access through the JTAG debugger.

4.2   Evaluation Results

Latency and Energy Overhead: In Fig. 4, we compare the latency and energy overhead incurred by SUANT and f-SUANT, when compared to SCU and p-SCU, with respect to the varied writable memory size of the device. Our results show that SUANT improves by more than 75 % the energy and time consumption of SCU, and results in more than 30 % energy and latency savings when compared to p-SCU. For example, to securely update code installed on MicaZ sensors whose total memory size is 648 KB, SUANT only requires 23.3 s and 0.94 joules, while SCU requires 96.6 s and 3.87 joules. f-SUANT further improves the performance of SUANT by reducing I/O costs by almost 50 %; our findings indicate that f-SUANT improves the latency and energy of p-SCU by almost 60 %. Recall that both SUANT and f-SUANT achieve higher detection probabilities when compared to p-SCU (which relies on selectively verifying 30 % of the downloaded code blocks).

Memory Usage: Table 1 summarizes the memory usage of SUANT and f-SUANT. Our results show that the total code size of SUANT (and f-SUANT) is almost 4 KB smaller than that of SCU and p-SCU. Moreover, SUANT almost halves the RAM consumption of SCU and only requires up to 371 bytes of RAM. These memory savings mainly originate from the fact that SUANT does not make use of cryptographic hashes and only relies on basic operations such as bitwise shifting and bitwise XORing—which consume less memory in legacy sensors. As shown in [22], HMAC-SHA1 alone occupies around 4500 bytes of ROM, and 120 bytes of RAM when loaded into memory. Since SUANT (and f-SUANT) leaves a smaller footprint in the RAM, this makes it harder for the attacker to compress the data and hide the malicious code—when compared to SCU.

Notice that since we integrated our implementation with TinyOS, the underlying code size for all protocols was larger than the maximum lockable memory in the bootloader section of the MicaZ mote. To remedy this, we can separate our codes into two parts: one part containing the memory accessing and computation routines (such as ShiftXOR) which we include in the bootloader section of the flash. The second part containing the necessary networking routines (such as the code required to send and receive bits) can be stored in the remaining part of the internal flash (i.e., in the application section). Recall that program code within the bootloader section has the capability to read/write to the entire internal flash memory through SPM (Store to Program Memory) instruction [1].

In Table 1, we show the minimum code size which should be included in read-only memory (labelled by "ROM") for all protocols; our results show that SUANT consumes a total of 6822 bytes of ROM—almost 2 KB less ROM than SCU. Recall that the bootloader section is limited to 8 KB in size; this suggests that SUANT and f-SUANT can be directly integrated into the MicaZ motes using this approach. The critical parts of SCU (and p-SCU) on the other hand cannot fit entirely in the bootloader section in MicaZ.

5   Related Work

In this section, we overview related work in the area.

Securing Code-Update in Embedded Devices: Deng *et al.* [9] propose the use of Merkle hash trees and hash chains in order to authenticate code distribution in wireless sensor networks. In [11], Dutta *et al.* leverage authenticated streams in order to secure code update in the TinyOS network programming system. In [33], Ugus *et al.* propose to authenticate code updates using an efficient stateful verifier T-time signature scheme based on Merkle's one-time signature. However, these proposals do not aim at proving to a remote party that the code has been securely distributed and installed within the embedded device.

In [26], Seshadri *et al.* propose indisputable code execution in order to dynamically establish a trusted code base on remote untrusted wireless sensor nodes. In [13,14], the authors propose the reliance on a novel memory printing algorithm to practically enable software-based attestation. However, the proposed scheme relies on a trusted proxy that executes secure cryptographic algorithms, such as SIM card, that needs to be located in the close proximity of the device; clearly, this assumption cannot be met in existing sensor nodes.

A number of contributions address the problem of secure data deletion [6,23,24]; however, as far as we are aware, only few works consider the problem of securely deleting data in resource-constrained devices [22] and proving to a third party that data was securely deleted from these devices. In [22], Perito and Tsudik propose the notion of Proofs of Secure Erasure (PoSE) as an enabler of secure code update in embedded devices. In this paper, we borrow the notion of PoSE, and we propose lightweight PoSE and secure code update protocols that considerably improve the performance and energy consumption of existing proposals.

All or Nothing Transforms: All-or-nothing transforms (AONTs) were first introduced in [25] and later studied in [7,10,16]. The majority of AONTs leverage a secret key that is embedded in the output blocks. Once all output blocks are available, the key can be recovered and single blocks can be inverted. As such, AONT is not an encryption scheme and does not require the decoder to have any key material.

In [31], Stinson proposed a fast linear all or nothing transform based on matrix multiplication. Karame *et al.* showed in [16] that by first encrypting the data then post-processing it using an efficient Stinson-like transform over the field $\mathbb{F}^2$, one can construct an encryption mode which ensures that any single block of data cannot be decrypted unless the adversary has acquired almost all the ciphertext blocks and the encryption key.

6 Conclusion

In this paper, we tackled the problem of securing code update in legacy sensors. Here, code update needs to be securely realized in order to ensure that the newly downloaded code is installed in its entirety and can be correctly executed in the installation environment with the assurance that no other malicious code is being stored.

To this end, we proposed an efficient secure code update scheme, SUANT, which naturally combines PoSE with an efficient all or nothing transform inspired by Desai's transform [10]. We analyzed the security of SUANT, and we evaluated its performance by means of implementation on MicaZ sensor nodes [2]. Our evaluation results show that our scheme consumes a small footprint in RAM, and considerably improves the time and energy overhead of existing secure code update protocols.

References

1. ATmega128 Datasheet: Available from http://www.atmel.com/images/doc2467. pdf
2. MicaZ: Wireless Measurement System. http://www.openautomation.net/ uploadsproductos/micaz_datasheet.pdf
3. Building a Secure System using TrustZone Technology (2009). http://infocenter. arm.com/help/topic/com.arm.doc.prd29-genc-009492c/PRD29-GENC-009492C_ trustzone_security_whitepaper.pdf
4. Software Guard Extensions Programming Reference (2013). https://software.intel. com/sites/default/files/329298-001.pdf
5. Ateniese, G., Di Pietro, R., Mancini, L.V., Tsudik, G.: Scalable and efficient provable data possession. In: Proceedings of the 4th International Conference on Security and Privacy in Communication Netowrks, SecureComm 2008, pp. 9:1–9:10. ACM, New York, NY, USA (2008)
6. Bauer, S., Priyantha, N.B.: Secure data deletion for linux file systems. In: Proceedings of the 10th Conference on USENIX Security Symposium - Volume 10, SSYM 2001. USENIX Association, Berkeley, CA, USA (2001)
7. Boyko, V.: On the security properties of OAEP as an all-or-nothing transform. In: Wiener, M. (ed.) CRYPTO 1999. LNCS, vol. 1666, pp. 503–518. Springer, Heidelberg (1999)
8. Castelluccia, C., Francillon, A., Perito, D., Soriente, C.: On the difficulty of software-based attestation of embedded devices. In: Proceedings of the 16th ACM Conference on Computer and Communications Security, CCS 2009, pp. 400–409. ACM, New York, NY, USA (2009)

9. Deng, J., Han, R., Mishra, S.: Secure code distribution in dynamically programmable wireless sensor networks. In: Proceedings of the 5th International Conference on Information Processing in Sensor Networks, IPSN 2006, pp. 292–300. ACM, New York, NY, USA (2006)

10. Desai, A.: The security of all-or-nothing encryption: protecting against exhaustive key search. In: Bellare, M. (ed.) CRYPTO 2000. LNCS, vol. 1880, pp. 359–375. Springer, Heidelberg (2000)

11. Dutta, P.K., Hui, J.W., Chu, D.C., Culler, D.E.: Securing the deluge network programming system. In: Proceedings of the 5th International Conference on Information Processing in Sensor Networks, IPSN 2006, pp. 326–333. ACM, New York, NY, USA (2006)

12. Eldefrawy, K., Francillon, A., Perito, D., Tsudik, G.: SMART: secure and minimal architecture for (establishing a dynamic) root of trust. In: NDSS 2012, 19th Annual Network and Distributed System Security Symposium, San Diego, USA, 5–8 February 2012

13. Jakobsson, M., Johansson, K.-A.: Practical and secure software-based attestation. In: LightSec (2011)

14. Jakobsson, M., Stewart, G.: Mobile malware: why the traditional AV paradigm is doomed, and how to use physics to detect undesirable routines. In: BlackHat (2013)

15. Juels, A., Jr., B.S.K.: PORs: proofs of retrievability for large files. In: ACM Conference on Computer and Communications Security, pp. 584–597 (2007)

16. Karame, G.O., Soriente, C., Lichota, K., Capkun, S.: Securing cloud data in the new attacker model. IACR Cryptology ePrint Archive 2014, p. 556 (2014)

17. Karlof, C., Sastry, N., Wagner, D.: Tinysec: a link layer security architecture for wireless sensor networks. In: Proceedings of the 2nd International Conference on Embedded Networked Sensor Systems, SenSys 2004, pp. 162–175. ACM, New York, NY, USA (2004)

18. Koeberl, P., Schulz, S., Sadeghi, A.-R., Varadharajan, V.: Trustlite: a security architecture for tiny embedded devices. In: Proceedings of the Ninth European Conference on Computer Systems, EuroSys 2014, pp. 10:1–10:14. ACM, New York, NY, USA (2014)

19. Liu, A., Ning, P.: Tinyecc: a configurable library for elliptic curve cryptography in wireless sensor networks. In: Proceedings of the 7th International Conference on Information Processing in Sensor Networks, IPSN 2008, IEEE Computer Society, Washington, DC, USA (2008)

20. Martinovic, I., Pichota, P., Schmitt, J.B.: Jamming for good: a fresh approach to authentic communication in wsns. In: Proceedings of the Second ACM Conference on Wireless Network Security, WiSec 2009, pp. 161–168. ACM, New York, NY, USA (2009)

21. Payne, W.H., Rabung, J.R., Bogyo, T.P.: Coding the lehmer pseudo-random number generator. Commun. ACM **12**(2), 85–86 (1969)

22. Perito, D., Tsudik, G.: Secure code update for embedded devices via proofs of secure erasure. In: Gritzalis, D., Preneel, B., Theoharidou, M. (eds.) ESORICS 2010. LNCS, vol. 6345, pp. 643–662. Springer, Heidelberg (2010)

23. Reardon, J., Basin, D., Capkun, S.: Sok: secure data deletion. In: Proceedings of the 2013 IEEE Symposium on Security and Privacy, SP 2013, pp. 301–315. IEEE Computer Society, Washington, DC, USA (2013)

24. Reardon, J., Ritzdorf, H., Basin, D., Capkun, S.: Secure data deletion from persistent media. In: Proceedings of the 2013 ACM SIGSAC Conference on Computer and Communications Security, CCS 2013, pp. 271–284. ACM, New York, NY, USA (2013)

25. Rivest, R.L.: All-or-nothing encryption and the package transform. In: Biham, E. (ed.) FSE 1997. LNCS, vol. 1267, pp. 210–218. Springer, Heidelberg (1997)

26. Seshadri, A., Luk, M., Perrig, A., van Doorn, L., Khosla, P.: Scuba: secure code update by attestation in sensor networks. In: Proceedings of the 5th ACM Workshop on Wireless Security, WiSe 2006, pp. 85–94. ACM, New York, NY, USA (2006)

27. Seshadri, A., Perrig, A., Doorn, L.V., Khosla, P.: Swatt: software-based attestation for embedded devices. In: Proceedings of the IEEE Symposium on Security and Privacy (2004)

28. Shacham, H.: The geometry of innocent flesh on the bone: return-into-libc without function calls (on the x86). In: Proceedings of the 14th ACM Conference on Computer and Communications Security, CCS 2007, pp. 552–561. ACM, New York, NY, USA (2007)

29. Shacham, H., Waters, B.: Compact proofs of retrievability. In: Pieprzyk, J. (ed.) ASIACRYPT 2008. LNCS, vol. 5350, pp. 90–107. Springer, Heidelberg (2008)

30. Shankar, U., Chew, M., Tygar, J.D.: Side effects are not sufficient to authenticate software. In: Proceedings of the 13th Conference on USENIX Security Symposium - Volume 13, SSYM 2004, pp. 7–7. USENIX Association, Berkeley, CA, USA (2004)

31. Stinson, D.R.: Something about all or nothing (transforms). Des. Codes Crypt. 22(2), 133–138 (2001)

32. Titzer, B.L., Lee, D.K., Palsberg, J.: Avrora: scalable sensor network simulation with precise timing. In: Proceedings of the 4th International Symposium on Information Processing in Sensor Networks, IPSN 2005. IEEE Press, Piscataway, NJ, USA (2005)

33. Ugus, O., Westhoff, D., Bohli, J.-M.: A rom-friendly secure code update mechanism for wsns using a stateful-verifier t-time signature scheme. In: Proceedings of the Second ACM Conference on Wireless Network Security, WiSec 2009, pp. 29–40. ACM, New York, NY, USA (2009)

Efficient Provisioning of a Trustworthy Environment for Security-Sensitive Applications

Adrian Coleşa[1]([✉]), Sándor Lukács[1,2], Vlad Topan[1,2],
Radu Ciocaş[1,2], and Adrian Pop[2]

[1] Technical University of Cluj-Napoca, Cluj-Napoca, Romania
adrian.colesa@cs.utcluj.ro
[2] Bitdefender, Bucharest, Romania
{slukacs,itopan,rciocas,apop}@bitdefender.com

Abstract. We propose a method to provide the users a trusted secure environment to run their security-sensitive applications within. Our solution runs user applications in different virtual machines (VMs): security-sensitive applications in a trusted green VM, while the others in an untrusted red VM. We isolate the two VMs using hardware virtualization mechanisms and run them alternatively. This contributes for a smaller hypervisor, a safer VM isolation and trusted I/O channels to the green VM. Switching between VMs is based on the ACPI S3 sleep events. The trustworthiness of the green VM is sustained by its reduced and restricted software stack and its launch-time integrity attestation. We focus on reducing the red-to-green VM switching time by applying a stateless strategy for the green VM: use a RAM-disk and start it in a pristine state any time a red-to-green VM switch is performed. We load the green VM's image in memory and reserve memory space for the green VM at boot time. This leads to a lower switching time of about 18 s.

Keywords: Virtualization · Red/green virtual machines · Isolation · Protection · Integrity · Trusted path · Fast switch

1 Introduction

We aim to protect security-sensitive user actions, like performing transactions on e-banking/e-commerce sites in an Internet browser. It is essential in such cases that the users trust their systems. Securing end-user systems is not an easy task. The traditional solutions that placed the security tool inside the user system proved to be ineffective due to the numerous vulnerabilities of the underling OS.

One of the most credited alternative approach relies on virtualization [4] to better isolate the security tool from the user system. The original user system is run in a virtual machine (VM) and the security tool is placed outside that VM, either in another dedicated VM or inside the virtualization system, i.e. the hypervisor (HV). The HV isolates and protects VMs from one another and provides the security tool mechanisms to transparently control the user VM.

© Springer International Publishing Switzerland 2015
M. Conti et al. (Eds.): TRUST 2015, LNCS 9229, pp. 300–309, 2015.
DOI: 10.1007/978-3-319-22846-4_18

One type of such virtualization-based security tool uses *introspection* [3] of the protected VM. The main problem the introspection faces is the *semantic gap*. Different solutions proposed lack either generality or precision. Introspection also induce performance penalties not acceptable for all types of user applications.

Another approach [6] separates user applications in different classes based on their security requirements and run them in separate VMs:

1. A *red VM*, which imposes no restriction on the user applications that can be run, actions that could be performed and remote services that could be accessed. The red VM exposes a large attack surface. It is therefore considered *untrustworthy* and used as the *untrusted environment* (though with a rich functionality) to run the *security-insensitive applications* in.
2. A *green VM*, which imposes high security restrictions on the user applications that could be run and the actions that could be perform. The green VM exposes a narrower attack surface. Furthermore, its integrity can be measured and attested at launch time and specialized security tools could protect it. All these measures make the green VM to be considered *trustworthy* and used as the *trusted environment* (though with a restricted, well-defined particular functionality) to run the *security-sensitive applications* in.

There are two different ways the red and green VMs could be used.

Running the two VMs *concurrently* [8] has the advantage of providing the user the possibility to simultaneously use both types of applications. This strategy increases the attack surface of the green VM: firstly, due to an increased complexity and size of the HV needed to virtualize the resources shared between the two VMs, and secondly, due to the difficulty to close all side-channels opened by resource sharing. It is also difficult to assure the privacy and security of I/O channels between the user and the green VM [11].

Running the two VMs *alternatively* [15] eliminates almost entirely side channel attacks and reduces considerably the HV complexity and size, while the hardware resources must not be virtualized, since they are given directly to the only running VM. It also makes straightforward providing trusted I/O channels between the user and the green VM as long as only the running VM is in control and use of the I/O devices. The main problem of such strategy, though, is the relatively large switching time between the VMs, usually in range of tens of seconds [15]. Notwithstanding, from the users' point of view that could be considered acceptable as long as they generally agree to trade time for security, especially when the security-sensitive applications are run infrequently.

We decided to develop a solution based on running the two VMs alternatively. Our HV uses hardware virtualization support for isolation and protection of the green VM. Like other solutions [9,14], we aimed for getting a light, security-dedicated HV. We used ACPI sleep events to switch between VMs, in a non-intrusive and transparent way.

The main contributions of our solution over the general approach are:

– a reduced switching time from the red VM to the green VM, obtained by
  (1) preparing a small image of the green VM, reducing its software stack to

a simplified OS and only the protected user application, (2) saving a partial system snapshot in the green VM's image, (3) loading the green VM's image in memory at HV's boot time (avoiding reading it from a HDD), (4) reserving the needed memory space for the green VM at boot time, which allowed us using the faster transition to the ACPI S3 sleep state instead of the S4 one [15], (5) configuring the green VM to use a RAM-based disk;
- an improved trustworthiness of the green VM, by (1) reducing its size (as mentioned before), (2) attesting both locally and remotely the green VM's integrity at launch time, (3) always switching to its pristine state.

2   Threat Model and Objectives

We consider that an attacker can compromise and control the entire software stack in the red VM. A malicious software in the compromised red VM could try to attack the HV and the green VM. Denial of service (DoS) attacks are out of scope of our solution. The user's physical system is inaccessible to the attacker.

We consider all the chipset hardware and I/O devices trusted. We also include in our Trusted Computing Base (TCB) the HV and the software stack in the green VM. The latter is large in general, though we reduce it at minimum and apply usage restrictions and security protection mechanisms. In case the protected user application accesses a remote service, we also consider it trusted. The privacy and security of the communication channel between the client user application and the remote server is done by cryptographic methods.

Our solution assumes existence on the protected user system of hardware virtualization support (e.g. Intel VT-x), including SLAT and IOMMU extensions (e.g. Intel EPT and VT-d), and platform-level enhancements for supporting trusted environments (e.g. TPM and Intel TXT).

3   "Alternative Red-Green VMs" Protection Method

Our HV schedules the two VMs *alternatively*, having just one VM running at one moment, with the other one suspended. A switch from the currently running VM to the suspended one is triggered when a dedicated ACPI sleep event is transparently generated in the running VM and intercepted by the HV.

The VM switching mechanism is built on the assumption that APCI events are handled in each VM by its OS, which deals with saving the entire machine state in order to be able to resume it later. The only task the HV is responsible for is to intercept the ACPI sleep request sent by the guest OS (at the end of its own internal sleep request handling) to power off the CPU. At that moment the HV could suppose that the current VM's state was completely saved by that VM's guest OS according to the generated sleep request. By interposing on the normal APCI sleep path, the HV avoids the final step (i.e. powering off the CPU), translating it instead in an ACPI wake-up signal sent to the suspended (sleeping) VM. Following that moment, the VM switching, i.e. loading and resuming the

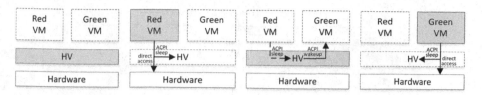

Fig. 1. Alternative execution of the red and green VMs and the way the VM switching is performed. The gray boxes indicate the running software component

new VM, is supposed to be performed entirely by its guest OS, based on the VM's state saved previously. Figure 1 illustrates the alternate execution strategy.

Having just one VM running at one moment allows our HV to give the currently running VM direct access and control over almost all host's hardware resources. This strategy drastically reduces the HV's size and complexity.

The HV's main responsibility is to isolate and protect the memory areas where itself and the green VM are loaded against accesses from the red VM. The memory protection is based on hardware virtualization support.

Another important security property is the trustworthiness of the I/O channels of the green VM. When the green VM is woken up it considers all host's I/O devices to be in an inconsistent state and re-initializes them. This way, an attacker in the compromised red VM cannot store malicious data in the I/O devices in an attempt to influence the green VM state and behavior.

4   Improve the Green VM's Trustworthy Properties

While trusted by design, the green VM can still be compromised due to its large software stack. We propose a few techniques to reduce such risks.

Integrity Attestation. One common method is to securely measure the state of the booted software on the user system (e.g. firmware, boot-loader, HV and green VM's software stack). This mechanism is called *secure boot* and could be used to attest both locally and remotely that the current system's state is trustworthy. The green VM is not launched if its image is corrupted. The remote service could also ask the user system to attest its integrity, not accepting a communication with a client that cannot prove its integrity.

Stateless Green VM. There are two mechanisms involved:

1. Start the green VM in its pristine state any time a switch is performed to it. That state is loaded in memory during the host system's boot. There is no state information saved by the HV, when the user switches from the green to the red VM. So, the user cannot resume a previous green "session". While such a strategy suffers from usability restrictions, it limits any possible control of the green VM an attacker obtained in a previous session.
2. Our green VM is configured to use a RAM-based disk. We eliminate thus any interference between the two VMs through a shared HDD.

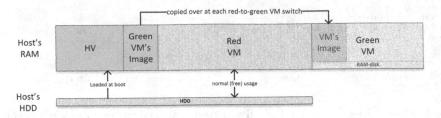

Fig. 2. Structure of the host system memory. The host's HDD is used just for the red VM. The green VM is configured to use a RAM-disk. The HV is the first one loaded and run to isolate and protect all memory domains from each other.

Reduced and Restricted Software Stack. We applied this method by:

1. Preparing the green VM to only contain just one particular security-sensitive application. Our strategy requires therefore a different green VM's image for each different security-sensitive application a user wants to run.
2. Reducing the green VM's OS configuration to the minimum required to run only the security-sensitive application, which could also be configured to include just the needed functionality.
3. Restricting the URLs that can be accessed from the green VM. The custom application (e.g. an Internet browser) could be changed to allow access to just one trusted URL, i.e. that of the service that application should access.

Runtime Protection. We used U-HIPE [7], a virtualization-based introspection module that runs in HV and protects both the guest OS and the custom application in the green VM. The protection mechanism imposes $W \oplus X$ (*write* XOR *execute*) permissions for all memory pages of the green VM. Initially, all pages are marked as read-only. When a page is firstly accessed, if an execution is tried, that page is permanently set for X but not W, while if a write is tried, the W but not X is set.

5 Reduce the Switching Time to the Green VM

Memory Boot. The green VM's image is loaded in memory at the host system's boot time (see its place in memory in Fig. 2) and protected as read-only by the HV. The green VM will boot faster from memory, the only operation performed is making a writable copy of the image in the green VM's reserved memory.

Standby-Based Switch. The ACPI sleep states that could be used to alternate the execution of the two VMs are S3 and S4. In both states all devices are powered-off, losing their state, excepting the memory in S3 state. As long as our HV reserves at boot-time memory for both VMs and the green VM's image (see Fig. 2), it can use the faster ACPI S3 transition, based on the fact that the memory's contents are not affected during the ACPI-based switch.

RAM-Disk Usage. Using a RAM-based HDD for the green VM not only makes it safer, but also reduces its boot time, as only the memory is accessed.

Reduced Memory Needs. This is a logical result of customizing the green VM for having a reduced software stack: the smaller the VM's image, the faster its boot time, so the faster the switch from red to green VM.

6   Implementation Technical Aspects

The green VM image consists of a custom built Linux kernel with an embedded minimal *initramfs*, which contains a *BusyBox*-based environment, a *X.Org* installation and a *Chromium* browser. The image has a size of around $130MB$.

The green VM image is loaded during the boot of the HV and its authenticity is validated. Hardware support for enforcing a secure boot process (e.g. Intel TXT) is used when available. After the image is loaded, the red and green VMs are created. The green VM is only partially initialized at this stage.

When the red VM requests the memory layout from the BIOS (using "*int $0 \times 15/E820$*"), the call is intercepted by the HV and the memory map is altered to mark the space used by the green VM as reserved. Additionally, the red VM is denied access to that area by the HV, using Intel EPT.

The switch from the red to the green VM occurs on a dedicated sleep event. The user presses a button which, after notifying via a VMCALL the HV to switch to the green VM, initiates the ACPI S3 state using the Windows API. The HV intercepts the I/O event that signals the CPU to enter S3 sleep. At this point all devices have been placed in S3 sleep by their OS drivers. The CPU is prevented from entering the sleep state and the green VM is woken up.

In order to provide the green VM with a "default" state of the hardware, ACPI methods are used to power on the entire PCI hierarchy. Each PCI configuration area is restored to a snapshot of the contents it had during the host boot or just before calling the Windows API S3 sleep request. Fine tuning to specific hardware situations may be required, but the alternative of embedding drivers for all possible network and video cards inside the HV for a proper initialization of each device is infeasible and would greatly increase the TCB size.

The memory map of the green VM is configured via the EPT to allow access to the range reserved for it on boot and to the memory ranges used by the devices for MMIO. The RAM address range it receives is compacted via remapping to a continuous space above the $1MB$ address and remapped through VT-d as well.

After the Linux kernel boots and runs BusyBox as the "*init*" process, the X.Org environment and then the Chromium browser are started, with the custom web site set as the homepage. Special *iptables* rules are in place, which restrict network access strictly to the requirements of the secured application.

After the user completes the secure operations inside the green VM, another ACPI sleep event is used to restore control to the red VM.

7   Performance Measurements

Our *host system* was a Dell Optiplex 990 with an Intel i7@3.4 GHz CPU, $4\,GB$ DDR3 RAM and a $500\,GB$ HDD. The *red VM* ran Windows 7/x64 and was allocated the host's memory minus what was needed for HV, green VM's image and running green VM, i.e. about 2.5 GB. The *green VM* was allocated $1\,GB$ RAM and configured to use a RAM-disk based on *initramfs*. It ran Linux 3.8.8, over which we configured a minimal user-space environment built from BusyBox 1.23, X.Org X11R7.6 package, and Chromium 31.0. We used a proprietary HV.

We estimated the minimum space needed for the green VM and got a compressed (LZO) image size of about $138\,MB$ from the uncompressed $8\,MB$ Linux kernel, $81\,MB$ X.org and $225\,MB$ Chromium. First column of Table 1 illustrates different sizes of the VM's image, based on different compression methods. The minimum memory needed to run such a distribution was about $1\,GB$.

Table 1. Green VM's Linux startup time without HV

Compression method	Size [MB]	Kernel startup time [s]	X.org & Chromium startup time [s]	Total time [s]
GZIP	125	6	1.92	7.92
BZIP2	112	15	1.97	16.97
LZMA	82	12	1.94	13.94
XZ	81	11	1.93	12.93
LZO	138	5	1.91	6.91

We measured the overhead induced by the HV functionality. It consists of two components: (1) *Boot time*, needed to load both the HV and green VM. Being an one-time operation, its overhead is attenuated over the system runtime. It depends on the sizes of HV and green VM's image and the read bandwidth of the booting device. In our tests we booted from PXE using a $1\,GB$ network link, which takes about 2 s for the given sizes. (2) *Protection overhead*, imposed by the HV operation. Our HV introduces practically no overhead, while it intercepts very few events: "int 0×15" and ACPI S3 sleep. Both are generated only in singular situations, i.e. VM's boot time and the user's switching request, respectively. Otherwise, the HV overhead is only that induced by the virtualization hardware, which is not relevant relative to what we can optimize.

For measuring the red-to-green VM *switching time* we considered the main three steps involved: (1) red VM's Windows sleep (internal handling of the sleep request), (2) HV ACPI S3 interception and preparation for waking-up the green VM, and (3) wake-up of the green VM's Linux. Table 2 illustrates the average of measured times. The total switching time was about 18 s on average, an approximately 2x reduction compared to Lockdown [15].

Table 2. Red-to-Green VM switching time with LZO/Linux in green VM

Red VM's windows sleep [s]	HV S3 handling [s]	Green VM's linux startup [s]	Total time [s]
4.10	4.60	9.30	18.00

We measured the *Linux startup time* on the bare hardware for different images we got. Table 1 illustrates the results. The difference of about 2*s* between the last line total time and the time in Table 2 column 3 is the HV's overhead due to I/O device preparation in order to consistently wake-up the green VM's.

8 Related Work

The most similar solution to ours is Lockdown [15]. Main differences consist in the methods we use to improve the trustworthy of the green VM and reduce the red-to-green VM switching time.

SecureSwitch [13] also uses a similar strategy, but they do not use virtualization to isolate the two environments, but the BIOS and SMM. Even if faster and based on a smaller TCB, their method is less flexible and general than ours.

Other low-level solutions like Oasis [12], HyperCheck [16], even if based on a smaller TCB due to usage of lower-level hardware mechanisms, are limited regarding the trusted (green) environment they provide or are based on custom hardware. Actually, newer processors [5] will include specialized hardware support (e.g. Intel SGX) to isolate parts of an application (enclaves) from the untrusted application's parts and environment, so they naturally provide a reduced TCB. Their main problem, compared to our strategy results from the fact that isolation alone is not enough to run real-life applications, which need to cooperate with the untrusted environment.

In this context, other solutions like Flicker [10], Wimpy-kernel [17], Overshadow [1], VirtualGhost [2] propose ways for the isolated enclaves to trustily communicate with the untrusted OS. There is however no general method to verify such a communication. Even if more heavyweight, our strategy allows running complex-functionality applications and also naturally provides trusted I/O channels between the user and that applications.

9 Conclusions

We proposed a method to provide the users a trustworthy environment to run their applications in. Our method runs alternatively two VMs: red (untrustworthy) and green (trustworthy). We developed methods to improve both the green VM's trustworthiness and the red-to-green VM switching time.

The alternative red-green VMs protection method suffers some limitations, which we want to deal with in the near future. One problem regards the usability of the method due to the still relatively large switching time and usage restrictions. Other problems refer to ways to convince the users to switch to the green VM when running security-sensitive applications, be aware of the VMs they interact with, attest visually the authenticity of the green VM etc.

Acknowledgments. Adrian Coleşa's work on this paper was supported by the Post-Doctoral Programme POSDRU/159/1.5/S/137516, project co-funded from European Social Fund through the Human Resources Sectorial Operational Program 2007–2013.

References

1. Chen, X., Garfinkel, T., Lewis, E.C., Subrahmanyam, P., Waldspurger, C.A., Boneh, D., Dwoskin, J., Ports, D.R.K.: Overshadow: a virtualization-based approach to retrofitting protection in commodity operating systems. SIGOPS Oper. Syst. Rev. **42**(2), 2–13 (2008)
2. Criswell, J., Dautenhahn, N., Adve, V.: Virtual ghost: protecting applications from hostile operating systems. SIGPLAN Not. **49**(4), 81–96 (2014)
3. Garfinkel, T., Rosenblum, M.: A virtual machine introspection based architecture for intrusion detection. In: Proceedings of the Network and Distributed Systems Security Symposium, pp. 191–206 (2003)
4. Garfinkel, T., Warfield, A.: What virtualization can do for security. Login: USENIX Mag. **32**(6), 28–34 (2007)
5. Hoekstra, M., Lal, R., Pappachan, P., Phegade, V., Del Cuvillo, J.: Using innovative instructions to create trustworthy software solutions. In: Proceedings of the 2nd International Workshop on Hardware and Architectural Support for Security and Privacy, HASP 2013, ACM (2013)
6. Lampson, B.: Privacy and security: usable security: how to get it. Commun. ACM **52**(11), 25–27 (2009)
7. Lutas, A., Lukács, S., Colesa, A., Lutas, D.: U-HIPE: hypervisor-based protection of user-mode processes in windows. J. Comput. Virol. Hacking Tech. pp. 1–14 (2015)
8. Lutas, D.H., Lukacs, S., Tosa, R.V., Lutas, A.V.: Towards secure network communications with clients having cryptographically attestable integrity. In: Proceedings of the Romanian Academy, **14**(Special issue), 338–356 (2013)
9. McCune, J.M., Li, Y., Qu, N., Zhou, Z., Datta, A., Gligor, V., Perrig, A.: TrustVisor: efficient TCB reduction and attestation. In: 2010 IEEE Symposium on Security and Privacy (SP), **0**, pp. 143–158. IEEE, May 2010
10. McCune, J.M., Parno, B.J., Perrig, A., Reiter, M.K., Isozaki, H.: Flicker: an execution infrastructure for TCB minimization. SIGOPS Oper. Syst. Rev. **42**(4), 315–328 (2008)
11. Newsome, J., McCune, J.M., Zhou, Z., Gligor, V.D.: Building verifiable trusted path on commodity x86 computers. In: 2012 IEEE Symposium on Security and Privacy, SP 2012, **0**, pp. 616–630. IEEE, May 2012
12. Owusu, E., Guajardo, J., McCune, J., Newsome, J., Perrig, A., Vasudevan, A.: OASIS: on achieving a sanctuary for integrity and secrecy on untrusted platforms. In: Proceedings of the 2013 ACM SIGSAC Conference on Computer and Communications Security, CCS 2013, pp. 13–24. ACM (2013)

13. Sun, K., Wang, J., Zhang, F., Stavrou, A.: SecureSwitch: BIOS-assisted isolation and switch between trusted and untrusted commodity OSes. In: Proceedings of the 19th Annual Network and Distributed System Security Symposium (2012)
14. Vasudevan, A., Chaki, S., Jia, L., McCune, J., Newsome, J., Datta, A.: Design, implementation and verification of an eXtensible and modular hypervisor framework. In: Proceedings of the 2013 IEEE Symposium on Security and Privacy, SP 2013. pp. 430–444. IEEE Computer Society (2013)
15. Vasudevan, A., Parno, B., Qu, N., Gligor, V.D., Perrig, A.: Lockdown: towards a safe and practical architecture for security applications on commodity platforms. In: Katzenbeisser, S., Weippl, E., Camp, L.J., Volkamer, M., Reiter, M., Zhang, X. (eds.) Trust 2012. LNCS, vol. 7344, pp. 34–54. Springer, Heidelberg (2012)
16. Zhang, F., Wang, J., Sun, K., Stavrou, A.: HyperCheck: a hardware-assisted integrity monitor. IEEE Trans. Dependable Secure Comput. 4, 332–344 (2014)
17. Zhou, Z., Yu, M., Gligor, V.D.: Dancing with giants: wimpy kernels for on-demand isolated I/O. In: 2014 IEEE Symposium on Security and Privacy (SP), pp. 308–323. IEEE, May 2014

Poster Session

Towards a Trust Model for Social Networks of Wireless Smart Objects Work-in-Progress

Jonathan Ouoba[1(✉)], Cyril Cassagnes[2], and Tegawendé F. Bissyandé[2]

[1] VTT Technical Research Center, Espoo, Finland
jonathan.ouoba@vtt.fi
[2] SnT - University of Luxembourg, Luxembourg, Luxembourg
cyril.cassagnes@vtt.fi, tegawende.bissyand@uni.lu

Abstract. Smart wireless objects are now pervasive in our lives. As these devices are increasingly used in chain to deliver rich services to users, the next trend will make them evolve in their own social network with the different challenges that it entails. In this paper, we focus on how trust can be modeled and managed in such a network to preserve user privacy and ensure the security of peer-to-peer interactions. We propose to rely on light-weight machine-learning mechanisms to allow these devices, which can be perceived as people's extensions, to mimic the human behavior of their owners regarding trust.

Keywords: IoT · Trust management · Wireless smart objects · Machine learning · Social network

An Adaptive Trust Model for Wireless Smart Objects

According to Cisco IBSG predictions, the number of smart connected objects is expected to reach billions of items by 2020 [5]. As such, a lot of effort has gone into the initiation of research projects in the field of Internet-of-Things (IoT).

At a very high level, IoT represents the conceptual framework for various systems designed to handle the interactions among smart wireless objects. The roadmap is then to pursue the development of more efficient and interoperable solutions regarding the interconnection of wireless objects with network infrastructures (e.g., High-Speed Internet or other future networks) and the direct interconnections among the objects themselves [1]. Transversal to those functional concerns, security and privacy challenges must be overcome to accelerate and strengthen public acceptance of IoT-based systems.

Security and privacy issues are becoming pressing as the paradigm of social-IoT is becoming commonplace [1]. In our work, we focus on the possible interactions among personal wireless smart objects [3] and the resulting trust issues. Indeed, such interactions increasingly threaten privacy as, in many cases, personal data, with different levels of sensitivity, is exchanged. There is still a need to investigate in a generic framework the notion of trust underlying the possible links between wireless objects to allow communications following the degree of sensitivity of the information [6].

© Springer International Publishing Switzerland 2015
M. Conti et al. (Eds.): TRUST 2015, LNCS 9229, pp. 313–314, 2015.
DOI: 10.1007/978-3-319-22846-4

Although initial approaches have been emerging recently for trust management in "social network" of smart objects, we take a different approach. Our analytical perspective is based on assumptions derived from the relationship that exists between the objects and their owners. As personal devices, wireless smart objects can be considered as "extensions" of their human owners. As such, these owners can expect that the interactions among their respective objects follow the "rules" of real life (e.g., requirements to recognize people, possibilities for direct exchanges to retrieve useful complementary information, etc.). Our approach is backed by the fact that it is now commonly accepted that to develop systems which are suitable for mobility contexts, a relevant option is to base the design on models mimicking the behavior of people in real life [2, 4].

The central question of our work is thus as follows: *how can one adequately build a trust scheme integrating the mechanisms of autonomous reasoning which makes it possible for personal smart objects to properly exchange information of different levels of sensitivity?*

We propose to answer this question as follows:

- By setting the basis for an adaptive trust model inspired by human behavior, in particular with regards to how trust is incrementally build and destroyed.
- By discussing with practical use cases how machine-learning mechanisms help to realize a trust engine for interactions of smart wireless objects.
- By proposing an empirical demonstration of the suitability of our approach to supporting a consistent behavior of wireless smart objects.

References

1. Atzori, L., Iera, A., Morabito, G.: From "smart objects" to "social objects": the next evolutionary step of the internet of things. IEEE Commun. Mag. 52(1), 97–105 (2014)
2. Chaumette, S., Ouoba, J.: Multilevel and secure services in a fleet of mobile phones: the multilevel secured messaging application (MuSMA). In: Uhler, D., Mehta, K., Wong, J.L. (eds.) MobiCASE 2012. LNICST, vol. 110, pp. 169–185. Springer, Heidelberg (2013)
3. Chaumette, S., Ouoba, J.: Direct transmission vs relay transmission for information dissemination in a manet: an analytical study. In: 10th IEEE International Conference on Collaborative Computing: Networking, Applications and Worksharing, CollaborateCom 2014, Miami, Florida, USA, 22-25 October 2014, pp. 442–446 (2014)
4. Chaumette, S., Ouoba, J.: A multilevel platform for secure communications in a fleet of mobile phones. In: In: 6th International Conference on Mobile Computing Applications and Services, MobiCASE 2014, Austin, TX, USA, 6–7 November 2014, pp. 173–174 (2014)
5. Evans, D.: The internet of things - how the next evolution of the internet is changing everything. Technical report, Cisco (2011)
6. Sicari, S., Rizzardi, A., Grieco, L., Coen-Porisini, A.: Security, privacy and trust in internet of things: the road ahead. Comput. Netw. 76, 146–164 (2015)

BYOD for Android — Just add Java

Jessica Buttigieg, Mark Vella$^{(\boxtimes)}$, and Christian Colombo

PEST Research Lab, University of Malta, Msida, Malta
{jessica.buttigieg.12,mark.vella,
christian.colombo}@um.edu.mt

Bring-Your-Own-Device (BYOD) implies that the same mobile device is used for both work and personal purposes. This poses a security concern where untrusted user-installed applications might interfere maliciously with corporate ones. Android has only limited support for dual work-personal contexts. Our proposition, *BYOD-RV*, uses Dynamic Binary Instrumentation (DBI) and Runtime Verification (RV). DBI (in-memory code patching) avoids Android source code changes as typically required by similar approaches, e.g. [3]. RV (runtime monitoring of program correctness properties) enables expressing dynamic policy rules in Java, e.g. [2].

Method. The architecture for the Dalvik runtime (**libdvm**) version is shown in Fig. 1 - left. The DBI component is loaded in process memory via **ptrace** and patches **libdvm** (G) to create in-line hooks that intercept (C) security-sensitive Android method calls by re-defining them as native. This is lightweight DBI that requires no code block copying. Device events e.g. low battery or incoming call events, are intercepted (D) with the inclusion of a **BroadcastReceiver** component. The DBI component is injected into every launched application by a system 'starter' application (requires a firmware update). It requires root privileges/SELinux re-configuration. Intercepted events are passed to the RV monitor, which is loaded through JNI (A) as Dalvik bytecode, rendering all application and framework classes available for calling from policy rules (B). Rules take an **event|condition →action** form (inspired by [1]), where conditions distinguish between work/personal modes and actions prescribe execution resumption. All is captured in familiar Java/Android API syntax as per following 'Photo Capture' rule snippet:

```
wifi.ruleset.add(new Rule("Photo_capture"){
    public boolean condition(){
        if(wifi.ruleset_work_WIFI || wifi.ruleset_work_location) return true; else return false; }
    public void action() {
        wifi_ruleset.continue_exec = false; ShowToast("Access Denied"); } });
```

Experimentation. BYOD-RV was implemented on Android 4.4 using the DDI toolkit.[1] The following policy rules have been successfully experimented with. Conditions: identification of the workplace wifi; workplace geolocation; and executing corporate apps. Application access-control actions: blocking photo captures and video/voice recording at the workplace. Application modification actions: restrict Internet access in work mode to a URL white-list; append a corporate signature at the end of all outgoing messages in work mode. The device events experimented with so far are the low battery and incoming call events, resulting in the termination of non-work applications for the

---

[1] https://github.com/crmulliner/ddi

© Springer International Publishing Switzerland 2015
M. Conti et al. (Eds.): TRUST 2015, LNCS 9229, pp. 315–316, 2015.
DOI: 10.1007/978-3-319-22846-4

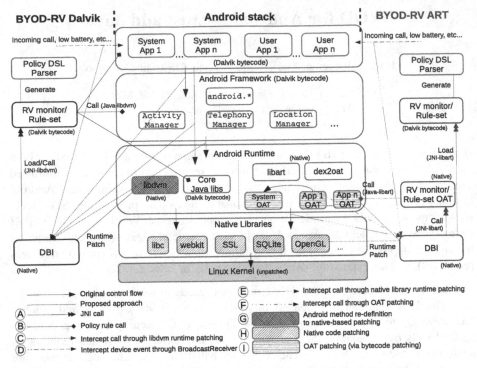

Fig. 1. BYOD-RV. Dalvik -left- and Android Runtime (ART) -right- versions.

prior and terminating calls in case of an ongoing video conference for the latter. Due to ahead-of-time compilation by **dex2oat** of all Dalvik bytecode to OAT files, porting to ART (**libart**) requires hooking Android methods at alternate locations (Fig. 1 - right). Patching native libraries (H) to intercept native library calls (E) made by the system OAT (compiled Android framework and core Java libraries) is one option, which however introduces a semantic gap challenge. Patching OAT files through pre-compilation bytecode patching (I) avoids this issue by intercepting Android method calls made by application OATs (F), but requires disabling OAT integrity checks. BYOD configuration is to be further simplified with a Domain-Specific Language (DSL).

References

[1] Colombo, C., Francalanza, A., Mizzi, R., Pace, G.J.: polyLarva: Runtime verification with configurable resource-aware monitoring boundaries. In: Eleftherakis, G., Hinchey, M., Holcombe, M. (eds.) SEFM 2012. LNCS, vol. 7504, pp. 218–232. Springer, Heidelberg (2012)

[2] Falcone, Y., Currea, S., Jaber, M.: Runtime verification and enforcement for android applications with RV-Droid. In: Qadeer, S., Tasiran, S. (eds.) RV 2012. LNCS, vol. 7687, pp. 88–95. Springer, Heidelberg (2013)

[3] Russello, G., Conti, M., Crispo, B., Fernandes, E.: MOSES: supporting operation modes on smartphones. In: SACMAT. pp. 3–12. ACM (2012)

Script Fuzzing with an Attacker's Mind-Set

John Galea[✉] and Mark Vella

PEST Research Lab, University of Malta, Msida, Malta
{john.galea.10,mark.vella}@um.edu.mt

Attackers primarily target memory corruption vulnerabilities inside script engine-hosting application, e.g. web browsers or most PDF viewers. Such applications are widely popular, and the discovery of vulnerabilities made by attackers ahead of security researchers diminishes the trustworthiness of their deployment. Typically, fuzzers are employed to generate unexpected inputs, with the aim of crashing applications and exposing errors. State-of-the-art fuzzers produce random byte sequences that comply with file/protocol formats. In the case of script fuzzers, random inputs need to constitute strings that are parse-able statements with respect to the scripting language used [1]. However, focusing solely on syntax-based randomness does not reflect the attacker's mind-set, as generated inputs are not optimized for narrowing in on vulnerabilities. A demand exists for smarter fuzzers in order to accelerate the process of finding exploitable errors.

The attacker's mind-set: Fundamentally, script engine-hosting applications embody two levels of abstraction, namely, the *script-level* which defines the interaction with host components as script statements, and the \emph{native-level} which parses and executes scripts. An example of this is when JavaScript statements access HTML DOM nodes in a web browser, where scripts are interpreted by an engine coded in C/C++, and in turn invokes other native routines.

When working at script-level, programmers are relieved from the concern of memory management, enabling them to focus on the task at hand such as web design. In contrast, attackers define script statements with the intention of triggering specific native-level behaviour to carry out exploitation. These differing mind-sets are depicted in Fig. 1. A web designer uses `createElement()` to alter the current web page. However, for an attacker, it is a method to force memory allocations whilst being confined at the script-level, where memory management is not available directly. This is due to the implementation of `createElement()`, as it involves a call to a memory allocation function, e.g. `malloc()`. Such a script statement is referred to as a *primitive* [2], which serves as an exploit building block to break through to the lower level. In particular, `createElement()` is one possible memory allocation primitive. Other types exist, including memory deallocation and access primitives.

Reaching the native-level through primitives is essential since it is in this level where memory vulnerabilities reside. Moreover, in the presence of such vulnerabilities, attackers gain access to the crucial primitive types that are required to complete the exploit. Examples include those with the ability to overwrite memory at key locations

---

J. Galea—The work disclosed is partially funded by the Master it! Scholarship Scheme (Malta).

M. Conti et al. (Eds.): TRUST 2015, LNCS 9229, pp. 317–318, 2015.
DOI: 10.1007/978-3-319-22846-4

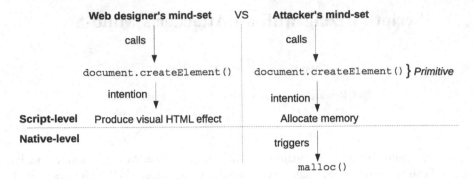

Fig. 1. The attacker's mind-set in comparison to that of a web designer.

defined by attackers, so that process-layout information may be leaked and allow the bypassing of ASLR and DEP [3]. Overall, a script exploit consists of a combination of primitives, which defines its generic exploit pattern.

Method and ongoing work: Our novel fuzzer is based on exploit patterns, that mirrors the attacker's mind-set. The key idea is that inputs are generated by randomly selecting primitives according to defined exploit patterns. The focus on primitives is due to their use as building blocks in triggering bugs, whilst exploit patterns describe their arrangement for test case generation. This technique is a step forward from the current syntax-centric approach in favour of a semantically-richer one. The three stages of the script fuzzer are: (1) Defining exploit patterns derived from existing exploits; (2) Identifying primitives from source scripts in relation to host application components; and (3) Generating inputs through the random selection of primitives for each type in the pattern.

A prototype was developed which uses the Apache Velocity Engine for expressing exploit patterns as HTML templates. In order to validate the approach, patterns were derived from two exploits that target Internet Explorer. Interestingly, the prototype generated multiple exploits that managed to crash the web browser and successfully expose the vulnerabilities. This result shows that a single pattern is capable of generating mutations from the original exploitation that is still fully capable of achieving its objective. The potential here lies in the generation of new exploits that exercise other possibly unknown vulnerabilities. The next research step will undertake the large-scale mining for patterns from exploit repositories.

References

[1] Guo, T., Zhang, P., Wang, X., Wei, Q.: Gramfuzz: fuzzing testing of web browsers based on grammar analysis and structural mutation. In: 2013 Second International Conference on Informatics and Applications (ICIA), pp. 212–215. IEEE (2013)
[2] Serna, F.J.: The info leak era on software exploitation. Black Hat USA (2012)
[3] Snow, K.Z., Monrose, F., Davi, L., Dmitrienko, A., Liebchen, C., Sadeghi, A.R.: Just-in-time code reuse: On the effectiveness of fine-grained address space layout randomization. In: 2013 IEEE Symposium on Security and Privacy, SP 2013, pp. 574–588 (2013)

Trust and Trustworthiness Maintenance: From Architecture to Evaluation

Mohamed Bishr[1(✉)], Christian Heinz[1], Torsten Bandyszak[1],
Micha Moffie[2], Abigail Goldsteen[2], Willis Chen[3], Thorsten Weyer[1],
Sotiris Ioannidis[4], and Costas Kalogiros[5]

[1] Paluno – The Ruhr Institute for Software Technology,
University of Duisburg-Essen, Essen, Germany
{Mohamed.Bishr,Christian.Heinz,Torsten.Bandyszak,
Thorsten.Weyer}@paluno.uni-due.de
[2] IBM Research Haifa, Haifa, Israel
{moffie,abigailt}@il.ibm.com
[3] IT Innovation Centre, Southampton, UK
wxc@it-innovation.soton.ac.uk
[4] FORTH, Heraklion, Greece
sotiris@ics.forth.gr
[5] AUEB, Athens Greece
ckalog@aueb.gr

1 The OPTET Approach for Maintaining User Trust and System Trustworthiness

Designing systems to be trustworthy is the first phase of OPTET. However, when such systems are deployed in real world scenarios they face externalities which are diverse and unpredictable. These externalities pose threats to trust and trustworthiness of these systems and require a technical solution for the maintenance of trust and trustworthiness throughout the lifetime and operation of the systems. During runtime of the system this maintenance requires continuous monitoring to detect potentially disruptive events, analysis of these events to identify threats to trust and trustworthi-ness followed by mitigation of these threats.

In this work, we build upon our previous work [1] and present an overview of the trust and trustworthiness maintenance architecture (as depicted in Fig. 1) followed by an overview of the evaluation scenarios.

The *Monitor Component* requires detection of data points of the monitored system, referred to as system behaviours, for example CPU load. The raw behaviours are risk-neutral and are not forwarded for management. System wide behaviours are fed into a *Complex Event Processing* engine (CEP) to identify irregularities during run-time. The CEP then juxtaposes multiple behaviours with different contexts and applies a set of detection patterns to identify "misbehaviours". User specific behaviours are fed to the *Trust Metric Estimator* to estimate the user's perception of the system behavior, and to the *User Behaviour Estimator* to estimate the user's overall trust in the system. Both of these also trigger "misbehaviours" in case of anomalous trust values. All misbehaviours are forwarded to the Management engine for deeper analysis.

© Springer International Publishing Switzerland 2015
M. Conti et al. (Eds.): TRUST 2015, LNCS 9229, pp. 319–320, 2015.
DOI: 10.1007/978-3-319-22846-4

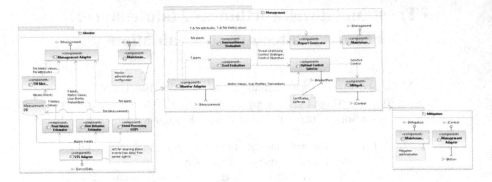

Fig. 1. Trust and Trustworthiness Maintenance Tool Architecture

The *Management Component* includes several components able to process the misbehaviour alerts reported by the Monitor. The processing of misbehaviours then translates to threats to trust and trustworthiness. This is achieved through the *Trustworthiness Evaluator* and *Trust Evaluator,* that analyze the current likelihood of active threats through complex processing enabled by a knowledge base of threats and controls, in addition to the Optimal Control Selector that identifies the optimal threat mitigation controls.

2   Evaluation Scenarios

To evaluate the trust and trustworthiness maintenance tool, we use a Secure Web Chat (SWC) use case with client/server architecture. It aims to support experts in managing a cyber-crisis, and it has to meet strict user trust and system trustworthiness requirements.

- In the *Trustworthiness Scenario* we will demonstrate the effectiveness of the OPTET approach in restoring system trustworthiness through performance and reliability as critical trustworthiness attributes in the Secure Web Chat.
- In the *Trust Scenario* we will monitor user behaviour in order to identify a user with low trust and propose a Trust related mitigation action.
- In the *Optimal Control Selector Scenario* we will demonstrate the selection of the most cost-effective control in order to meet customer expectations related to system response time.

Reference

1. Goldsteen, A., Moffie, M., Bandyszak, T., Gol Mohammadi, N., Chen, X., Meichanetzoglou, S., Ioannidis, S., Chatzidiam, P.: A tool for monitoring and maintaining system trustworthiness at runtime. In: Proceedings of the 1st International Workshop on Requirements Engineering for Self-Adaptive and Cyber Physical Systems (RESACS), CEUR Workshop Proceedings (2015)

Increasing the Trustworthiness of Embedded Applications

Elias Athanasopoulos[1], Martin Boehner[2], Cristiano Giuffrida[3],
Dmitry Pidan[4], Vassilis Prevelakis[5(✉)], Ioannis Sourdis[6],
Christos Strydis[7], and John Thomson[8]

[1] Foundation for Research and Technology – Hellas, Hellas, Greece
[2] Elektrobit Automotive GMBH, Erlangen, Germany
[3] Vrije Universiteit Amsterdam, Amsterdam, The Netherlands
[4] IBM – Science and Technology LTD, Haifa, Israel
[5] Technische Universität Braunschweig, Braunschweig, Germany
prevelakis@ida.ing.tu-bs.de
[6] Chalmers Tekniska Högskola, Göteborg, Sweeden
[7] Neurasmus BV, Rotterdam, The Netherlands
[8] OnApp Limited, Cambridge, UK

Abstract. Embedded systems, by their nature, often run unattended with opportunistic rather then scheduled software upgrades and, perhaps most significantly, have long operational lifetimes, and, hence, provide excellent targets for massive and remote exploitation. Thus, such systems mandate higher assurances of trust and cyber-security compared to those presently available in State-of-the-Art ICT systems. In this poster we present some techniques we utilize in the SHARCS project to ensure a higher level of security for embedded systems.

Keywords: Embedded systems · Security · Security-by-design · Instruction set randomization (ISR) · Control flow integrity · SHARCS

Through tremendous changes such as Medical IoT, Smart Cars, Smarter Grids etc., society as a whole and individual citizens rely more and more on critical applications that sense and control systems in the physical environment. Such embedded systems often run unattended with opportunistic rather then scheduled software upgrades and, most significantly, have long operational lifetimes. As the example with the hacked Internet-aware fridge amply demonstrates [1], when such devices get connected to the Internet, their security vulnerabilities can be massively and remotely exploited. Clearly, there is a need for a new way of attaining improved security in embedded platforms, and this can only be achieved by adopting a *security-by-design* approach. This is the objective of the SHARCS project (Secure Hardware-Software Architectures for Robust Computing Systems) and is based on the integration of software and hardware security techniques for achieving demonstrable improvements in security.

SHARCS utilizes techniques such as Instruction Set Randomization (ISR) [2], Control Flow Integrity (CFI) [3], Memory Protection, Dynamic Type Safety, and so on

---

This work was supported by the H2020 ICT-32-2014 project SHARCS under Grant Agreement No. 644571.

M. Conti et al. (Eds.): TRUST 2015, LNCS 9229, pp. 321–322, 2015.
DOI: 10.1007/978-3-319-22846-4

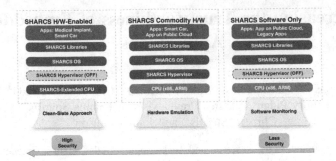

Fig. 1. Examples of different SHARCS framework operational models.

to allow the runtime environment to ensure the safe execution of applications. ISR encodes code regions in the address space of the executing process with different keys. The CPU has a special register where it stores the decryption key for the currently active code region. Thus, encrypted instructions from memory are correctly decoded by the key and then passed on to the CPU for execution. Injected code, or code that does not belong to the active region, will not be correctly decoded and will likely cause the program to crash. CFI carries the principle further by ensuring that changes in the control flow of the program comply with the call graph of that program. The last two techniques are concerned with memory violations whereby a program may attempt to access memory past the end of a buffer potentially overwriting other critical data, leading to security vulnerabilities. By encoding the length of the buffer in the pointer, or by creating a fine-grained memory protection architecture, we can detect such memory violations.

Where the selection of hardware architecture limits the native use of security techniques, SHARCS provides additional models of execution where execution speed is traded for security. In Fig. 1, the left hand model describes the hardware assisted mode of operation for the SHARCS architecture, while the other two depict the use of hardware emulation (middle) and software monitoring (right hand) models that allow the SHARCS techniques to work on commodity hardware architectures.

The SHARCS project will use the Leon processor as the basis for the hardware modifications and will demonstrate the above techniques in three applications concerning implantable medical devices, vehicular ECUs, and cloud applications.

References

1. Economist Newspaper. Spam in the fridge: When the internet of things misbehaves, 23 Jan 2014
2. Kc, G.S., Keromytis, A.D., Prevelakis, V.: Countering code-injection attacks with instruction-set randomization. In: ACM Conference on Computer and Communications Security (CCS) (2003)
3. Zhang, C., Wei, T., Chen, Z., Duan, L., Szekeres, L., McCamant, S., Song, D., Zou, W.: Practical control flow integrity and randomization for binary executables. In: Security and Privacy Symposium, pp. 559–573 (2013)

Exploring Graph Centralities for Detecting Anomalous Behavior in Large Networks

Nidhi Rastogi$^{(\boxtimes)}$ and James Hendler

Tetherless World Constellation, Rensselaer Polytechnic Institute, Troy, NY, USA
raston@rpi.edu, hendler@cs.rpi.edu

Abstract. Large-scale information retrieval, while a boon to modern needs of data analysis, poses a huge challenge for noise removal and information extraction. Researchers have targeted this problem through approaches like machine learning of data, clustering those with similar properties and labeling them accordingly. This complemented with other existing techniques, promises to reduce the amount of data to be analyzed making anomaly detection a much faster process. The goal, however remains to minimize data collection without compromising quality. Approaches to this end, however, differ in means, application and kind of data to be analyzed - stored vs. real time. This research introduces a graph theoretic approach to analyze large networks for detecting anomalies that may lead to systemic threats on the cyber world. It works by identifying specific nodes, known as node centralities that can monitor anomalies effectively and rapidly.

Keywords: Security · Networks · Graphs · Centrality

1 Introduction

Modern day critical infrastructures, from transportation systems to healthcare, face increasing complexity and connectivity with their networks. Threats of intrusion and corruption of these systems via cyber attacks can lead to crippling effects on nations worldwide. Stuxnet [5], known as one of the most infamous attacks on the cyber-physical network, was highly sophisticated and custom-designed for stealth and blitzkrieg critical infrastructure-systems. Duqu, Flame, and others ensued by exploiting a combination of multiple zero-day vulnerabilities, stolen certificates, and social engineering. With enough monetary support, expertise, and incentive, hackers cannot be assumed to stay limited to just attacking the cyber-physical world. Its effect shall be seen on sectors like IT, energy, banking, communication, defense, emergency services, healthcare, and transportation. Our solution, although under progress, is based on sound principles of computer science that have been successfully used for other applications. Graph analytics [4] provides several tools that can be used to study systemic behavior of large complex networks and we continue to challenge it with this unique problem. A graph model of the aforementioned network can capture anomalous data from a limited set of crucial nodes [3], forming a sparse network, thus preventing

© Springer International Publishing Switzerland 2015
M. Conti et al. (Eds.): TRUST 2015, LNCS 9229, pp. 323–324, 2015.
DOI: 10.1007/978-3-319-22846-4

the need to digitally collect everything. Although many challenges lie in expanding these for large networks comprising billions of nodes [1], increasing computability and advanced algorithms are bringing it closer to reality.

2 Main Idea

A common assumption in the security domain is that each and every node (or endpoint) should contribute to the detection. Data collected regularly is then stored locally or remotely. This capability mostly exists, but its relevance is low as analyzing big data can be an overwhelming task for even the most computationally capable infrastructures. It may not even lead to desirable results in the required time frame. Graph centralities will enable us to shift our focus to those nodes that can provide relevant information applicable in a given context. Our preliminary analysis of various centrality measures led us to focus on information centrality (IC), as a promising proposition closely matching with our research needs. IC by definition calculates the value of a node as an average of a characteristic of all paths originating from that node. For our purpose, it calculates the average number of times a characteristic's presence in a node and in nodes that lie on its path (or trail or path). For example, consider a graph where nodes are identified by unique IP address, an edge is referred by at least 3 TCP packet exchanges, edge weight by total packets exchanged divided by 3, TCP packet sent (received) to (from) a node and the anomaly being the value of the characteristic w.r.t. a baseline number 'x'. Our next steps involve exploring other statistics that can be calculated for a given set of characteristics and identifying anomalies based on analysis. This is the first work of its kind where graph analytics is being used for anomaly detection in large networks.

References

1. Ineichen, Y., Bekas, C., Curioni, A.: Scalable large scale graph analytics. In: The Sixth SIAM Workshop on Combinatorial Scientific Computing (2014)
2. Yim, U.-S.: Communication method among a plurality of virtual LANs in an IP subnet. U.S. Patent Application 09/939,558
3. Estrada, E.: The structure of complex networks: theory and applications. Oxford University Press (2011)
4. The Stuxnet Dossier. www.symantec.com/content/en/us/enterprise/media/security_response/whitepapers/w32_stuxnet_dossier.pdf

Extending the Operational Envelope
of Applications

Vassilis Prevelakis[✉] and Mohammad Hamad

Technische Universität Braunschweig, Braunschweig, Germany
{prevelakis,hamad}@ida.ing.tu-bs.de

Abstract. Despite continuing reliability problems, complex systems are still being developed using ad-hoc development practices and unsafe languages. The response to excursions outside the nominal profile usually lead to the termination of the program. In many situations, however, such a course of action may not be satisfactory. For example, systems such as air traffic control, on-line auctions etc. cannot afford to shut down just because we suspect that the software has a problem. Here we present the concept of *Red Zone* whereby we tolerate off-nominal behavior by taking actions to contain the misbehaving process.

Keywords: Red Zone · Resilience · Policy violation · Execution envelope

Despite continuing reliability problems, complex systems are still being developed using ad-hoc development practices and unsafe languages. Being unable to trust that a program will behave as intended, numerous techniques have been developed with the aim of detecting when a program has deviated from its intended execution envelope. The response to such excursions outside the nominal profile usually lead to the termination of the program. In many situations, however, such a course of action may not be satisfactory. For example, systems such as air traffic control, on-line auctions etc. cannot afford to shut down just because we *suspect* that the software has a problem.

Using the least priviledge methodology we wish to restrict the execution envelope of a program to the minimum required for it to carry out its objectives. By doing this we place outside the nominal execution of the program actions that are of different severity in terms of security (e.g. we prevent the program from accessing /etc/passwd as well as a file in /tmp). Recognizing that not all violations are equal, we define an area outside of the operational envelope of an application, which we call the *Red Zone*, and we define it to contain unauthorized actions that are nor considered critical to the security of the system. If the program enters the *Red Zone*, we know that the behavior of the program is off-nominal, but we do not know the cause and the severity of the problem. Rather than terminating the program, we place the runtime environment into an increased state of readiness and allow the code to continue running, taking actions to limit the damage caused by the misbehaving program. Figure 1 shows the program's intended execution envelope (blue rectangle) which represents the set of conditions that are assumed to be valid during the execution of the program. A program's actual execution envelope (green blob) represents the set of conditions exercised by the program during runtime.

This work is part of the Deutsche Forschungsgemeinschaft (DFG) Research Unit *Controlling Concurrent Change*, funding number FOR 1800.

M. Conti et al. (Eds.): TRUST 2015, LNCS 9229, pp. 325–326, 2015.
DOI: 10.1007/978-3-319-22846-4

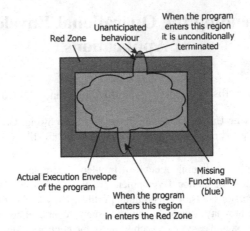

Fig. 1. Intended and actual program execution envelopes and *Red Zone* area.

Typically, the actual execution envelope does not cover exactly the intended execution envelope; the program may not exercise all its functionality, or unanticipated events (due to software faults or security attacks) may force the program to move outside the boundaries of the intended execution envelope. Typically, it is the role of software testing to ensure that the program has been exercised adequately (so that the entire envelope has been covered) before the software is released to its user community, but limitations in the testing regime in practically all cases allow both "bonus" (unintended) functionality as well as missing functionality in released software.

Beyond the intended execution envelope is the *Red Zone* area. Essentially, the *Red Zone* extends the operational envelope of the program. When a program violates its intended operational envelope, it may either enter or overflow the *Red Zone*. When the program enters the *Red Zone*, it continues with its execution, but the runtime system moves into a state of alert. When the program overflows the *Red Zone*, it is terminated by the runtime system. We implemented *Red Zone* processing in two prototypes. The first uses a custom memory allocator to provide overflow protection for buffers so that *Red Zone* processing allows a program, which overflowed a buffer, to continue operating by accessing the overflow area. The second prototype extends our existing library invocation protection system [1], and creates runtime policies consisting of allowed library calls. We have used this system to implement a dynamic honeypot whereby when a program makes an unauthorized library call, it enters its *Red Zone*. It is, then, placed in a sandbox and all further access to local files is simulated. We intend to use this to create a system that automatically tracks and keeps busy any detected attacker to the system.

Reference

1. Kim, J.W., Prevelakis, V.: Base line performance measurements of access controls for libraries and modules. In: Proceedings of the 2nd IEEE International Workshop on Security in Systems and Networks (SSN2006), Rhode Island, Greece, April 2006

Author Index

Printed in the United States
By Bookmasters